Normal Aging II

To the 773 panel members whose cooperation made these studies possible.

Normal Aging II

Reports from the Duke Longitudinal Studies, 1970–1973,
edited by Erdman Palmore
Duke University Press, Durham, N.C. 1974

612.67
P18N
90974
Dec. 1974

© 1974 by the Duke University Press
L.C.C. card no. 74–132028
I.S.B.N. 0–8223–0311–6
Printed in the United States of America
by Kingsport Press, Inc.

Foreword

Because the first NORMAL AGING volume found such widespread use, we decided to prepare a sequel which would update and extend the findings reported in the first volume. Assembling more than enough material for this sequel was not difficult because many findings had already been published, several reports were about to be published, and other reports were in the process of being written. Some of the reports were written especially for this volume because we wanted as comprehensive a summary of our findings as possible.

These volumes are more than a collection of reports on aging. From the inception of the Duke longitudinal studies of aging, we have made considerable effort to coordinate and integrate our research; to make it truly interdisciplinary, rather than just multidisciplinary, research. Throughout the academic year, two kinds of Monday evening meetings are scheduled to facilitate interdisciplinary exchange. Approximately twice a month, the investigators associated with the longitudinal studies meet together. The remaining Monday evenings are for all of the Center investigators. The purposes of the longitudinal study meetings are to share ideas, discuss findings, present preliminary reviews of papers to be presented or published, review current progress, and plan for the future. From the beginning we have been guided by the twin questions: what are the basic physical, mental, and social processes of normal aging? and what accounts for the variations in these processes? Furthermore, the editor, our project coordinator, has organized these reports into a logical sequence moving from physical aging, through mental and social aging, to factors associated with death or longevity. He has also provided an introductory chapter, introductory sections to each chapter, and a final summary which point up the significance of the main findings.

These longitudinal studies are only a part of the comprehensive program of research, training, and service at the Duke Center for the Study of Aging and Human Development.

They are considered a type of interdisciplinary or team research as contrasted with the multidisciplinary composition of the entire Center for the Study of Aging and Human Development. Interdisciplinary research is a team effort. A team is composed of two or more individuals representing distinct scientific disciplines who, because of their particular skills and interests, will accept certain responsibilities and will cooperate with other members of the team to achieve their goal. Multidisciplinary research is a type of group research involving several distinct scientific disciplines. The investigators are identified as a group because they are working in proximity and have interest in a common research topic. It is hoped and assumed that there is maximum communication between the investigators composing a group and that this increases the value of their work. The research program includes a number of other studies in biological, psychiatric, psychological, and sociological aspects of aging and human development. Training activities include a two-year program for pre- or post- Ph.D. or M.D. fellows who desire to pursue research training in some aspect of the behavioral sciences or psychophysiology related to aging and human development, and a two-year geropsychiatry training program for fellows with two or three years of psychiatric residency training. Service is combined with survey and experimental research in the Older Americans Resources and Services project. Further information on these and other programs of the Center may be obtained from:

> Dr. George L. Maddox, Director
> Center for the Study of Aging and Human Development
> Box 3003, Duke Medical Center
> Durham, North Carolina 27710

We hope this volume will serve several functions: to stimulate researchers in gerontology to modify or extend our findings to other populations, to inform government agencies and professionals working with older people about recent findings on normal aging, and to educate students and the public about this long neglected field of basic aging processes.

> Ewald W. Busse, M.D.
> J. P. Gibbons, Professor of Psychiatry
> Chairman, Duke University
> Council on Aging and
> Human Development

Contributors

Banks Anderson, Jr., M.D., Associate Professor of Ophthalmology, Duke University, Durham, North Carolina.

Kurt W. Back, Ph.D., Professor of Sociology, Duke University, Durham, North Carolina.

Linda M. Breytspraak, Ph.D., Postdoctoral Fellow, Department of Sociology, Duke University, Durham, North Carolina.

C. Edward Buckley III, M.D., Associate Professor of Medicine and Assistant Professor of Microbiology and Immunology, Director of Allergy-Immunology Laboratory, Duke University, Durham, North Carolina.

Ewald W. Busse, M.D., Sc.D., J.P. Gibbons Professor of Psychiatry and Chairman of the Department, Chairman of the Council on Aging and Human Development, Duke University, Durham, North Carolina.

Glenn C. Davis, M.D., Resident in Psychiatry, Duke University, Durham, North Carolina.

F. C. Dorsey, Ph.D., Assistant Professor of Community Health Sciences, Duke University, Durham, North Carolina.

Elizabeth B. Douglass, M.A., Research Assistant, Center for the Study of Aging and Human Development, Duke University, Durham, North Carolina.

Carl Eisdorfer, Ph.D., M.D., Chairman of the Department of Psychiatry, University of Washington, Seattle, Washington.

C. William Erwin, M.D., Associate Professor of Psychiatry, Duke University, Durham, North Carolina.

Daniel T. Gianturco, M.D., Associate Professor of Psychiatry, Duke University, Durham, North Carolina.

Stephen W. Harkins, A.B., Center for the Study of Aging and Human Development, Duke University, Durham, North Carolina.

Dorothy K. Heyman, M.S.W., Assistant Professor of Psychiatric Social Work and Executive Secretary of the Center for the Study of Aging and Human Development, Duke University, Durham, North Carolina.

Frances C. Jeffers, M.A., Research Associate in Psychiatry, Duke University, Durham, North Carolina.

Clark Luikart, M.A., Department of Education, University of North Carolina, Chapel Hill, North Carolina.

George L. Maddox, Ph.D., Professor of Medical Sociology, Director of the Center for the Study of Aging and Human Development, Duke University, Durham, North Carolina.

Joanna D. Morris, M.A., Research Assistant, Department of Sociology, Duke University, Durham, North Carolina.

John B. Nowlin, M.D., Assistant Professor of Community Health Sciences, Duke University, Durham, North Carolina.

Walter D. Obrist, Ph.D., Professor of Medical Psychology, Duke University, Durham, North Carolina.

Erdman Palmore, Ph.D., Professor of Sociology and of Medical Sociology, Duke University, Durham, North Carolina.

Eric Pfeiffer, M.D., Associate Professor of Psychiatry, Duke University, Durham, North Carolina.

Dietolf Ramm, Ph.D., Assistant Professor, Departments of Psychiatry and Community Science, Duke University, Durham, North Carolina.

Stephen Schroeder, Ph.D., Department of Psychology, University of North Carolina, Chapel Hill, North Carolina.

John P. Tindall, M.D., Associate Professor of Dermatology, Duke University, Durham, North Carolina.

Adriaan Verwoerdt, M.D., Professor of Psychiatry, Duke University, Durham, North Carolina.

H. Shan Wang, M.D., Associate Professor of Psychiatry, Duke University, Durham, North Carolina.

Alan D. Whanger, M.D., Assistant Professor of Psychiatry, Duke University, Durham, North Carolina.

Frances Wilkie, M.A., Research Associate in Medical Psychology, Duke University, Durham, North Carolina.

Contents

Figures

Tables

Normal Aging II

Chapter 1. Introduction

This volume is the sequel to *Normal Aging: Reports from the Duke Longitudinal Study, 1955–1969.* Its purpose is to bring together and summarize the main findings which build upon and extend those presented in the first volume. It contains all the reports from the Duke Longitudinal Studies published since 1969 as well as an almost equal number of papers presented at professional meetings or written especially for this volume. These reports present new findings on aging among the older longitudinal panel as well as the first findings on the middle-aged panel.

Both of these volumes deal with "normal aging" in two senses: healthy aging and typical aging. The aged and middle-aged persons studied were relatively healthy in that they were noninstitutionalized, ambulatory, community residents who were willing and able to come to the Duke Medical Center for one or two days of tests and examinations. Second, the more common or typical patterns and problems of aging are focused upon rather than the unusual abnormalities. This volume deals with the typical physical changes that accompany aging, typical health care patterns, typical patterns of mental aging, some common forms of mental illness among the aged, the normal social roles, self concepts, satisfactions, leisure and sexual behavior, and the overall factors related to longevity.

As pointed out in the first volume, investigations of normal aging are of crucial importance in advancing the science of gerontology and in helping aged persons develop and enjoy a richer and longer life. When we can distinguish normal and inevitable processes of aging from those which may accompany aging simply because of accident, stress, maladjustment, or disuse, we can better focus our attention and efforts on those factors which can be changed and corrected.

Both volumes also emphasize the theoretical and methodological advantages of the longitudinal and interdisciplinary methods used in these studies. Since aging is by definition a process of change over time, it would seem that the best way to study aging is longitudinally, by repeated observations over time. This is not meant to deny the value of cross-sectional studies, nor to deny the technical and methodological problems connected with longitudinal study, but it is meant to reassert the unique advantages of longitudinal studies such as the following: each panel member can be used as his own control, consistent trends can be distinguished from temporary fluctuations, errors due to retrospective distortion are minimized, early warning signs of disease or death can be studied, cohort differences can be distinguished from age changes, and the effects of one kind of change on another kind of change at a later time period can be studied.

The interdisciplinary nature of the study is useful because aging affects many interrelated types of behavior and functioning. When specialists from different disciplines work together, the mutual stimulation, correction, and combination of perspectives can result in more accurate, thorough, and comprehensive understanding of the aging process.

However, this sequel differs from the first volume in several respects. While most of the reports in the first volume were previously published elsewhere, this sequel contains fifteen original papers written especially for this volume or presented to professional meetings but not published elsewhere. Second, while the first volume was limited to reports from the first longitudinal study of aging (persons over 60 years of age), this sequel is about one-third devoted to reports from the Adaptation Study of middle-aged persons (46–70 years of age). Third, this sequel shows that the tempo of reports produced has increased, because it contains thirty-five reports produced in the past four years (about nine per year) compared to the fifty basic reports in the first volume which were produced during the preceeding fourteen years (about three and one-half per year).

The reader who is interested in detailed description and discussion of the first longitudinal study of aging is referred to chapter 1 of the first *Normal Aging* volume. Suffice it to say here that the first longitudinal study of aging began in 1955 with 271 persons 60–90 years of age. The subjects were not a strictly representative sample, but were selected from a pool of volunteers who lived in the community so that the overall sample reflected the age, sex, ethnic, and socioeconomic characteristics of the older population in Durham, N.C. Each panelist was brought in to the Medical Center for a two-day long series of medical, psychiatric, psychological, and social examinations. These examinations were repeated every three or four years until 1965, every two years until 1972, and since then the examinations are being repeated on an annual basis. In 1973, the eighth round of examinations on the survivors of this study was completed.

The second longitudinal study, or Adaptation Study, was begun in 1968 with 502 persons 46–70 years of age. These panelists were a random sample of the members of the local health insurance association stratified by age and sex. The sample and study was designed so that at the end of five years there would remain approximately 40 persons in each of ten five-year age-sex cohorts. This design makes possible various kinds of cross-sequential types of analyses in order to separate the effects of aging from cohort differences and from changes in the environment over time. Each subject was brought in for a one-day long series of physical, mental, and social examinations. The panelists are reexamined at two-year intervals and in 1973 the third round of examinations was completed. For more details and discussion of the adaptation study design, the reader is referred to Appendix A in this volume.

The articles which are reprinted by permission from various journals are presented with no deletions except for duplicate passages such as those that repeat the description of the panelists. Deletions of a sentence or more in these articles are indicated by ellipses, and minor changes have been made for uniformity. Since most of the reports are interdisciplinary, the placement of some reports in one chapter rather than another was somewhat arbitrary, but an attempt was made to group reports by the type of central variable under investigation. Each chapter first presents the reports from the first longitudinal study and then reports from the Adaptation Study. Brief summaries of the reports introduce the chapters, and the book closes with an overall summary of the main findings and themes. The reader may wish to start with these summaries in order to decide which reports to read in more detail.

We appreciate the cooperation of the many authors and journals or publishers for their permission to reprint their articles. Special thanks are due to Mrs. Elke Gordon and to Mrs. Celenzy Chavis for their help in preparing the manuscript. Most of this research was supported in part by the U.S. Public Health Service, National Institute of Child Health and Human Development, Grant HD–00668.

Chapter 2. Physical Aging

We begin with physical aging because it is basic to all the other aspects of aging. And most basic among the physical aspects are possible changes in cell function with age. The first report presents the age differences in one essential product of the body cells, immunoglobulins, which produce our various immunities. The major finding that the older persons (drawn from the older longitudinal study) had significantly lower average immunoglobulin concentration compared to younger persons suggests that lower immunity may partly account for the greater frequency of illness among the aged.

The next three reports present some of the first longitudinal data on dermatological, ophthalmological, and auditory changes among the normal aged. The report on dermatological changes also examines the relationship between certain skin problems and longevity. The report on ophthalmological changes also examines the relationship of certain vision defects with longevity and with indicators of activity and satisfaction. The report on auditory changes shows that while hearing acuity generally diminishes with increasing age, there are substantial differences between sex and racial groups.

Serum Immunoglobulin Concentrations *C. E. Buckley III and F. C. Dorsey*

The relationship between changes in serum immunoglobulin concentrations and immunologic diseases in adults is often obscure. Current difficulties in identifying alterations relevant to disease may result from several factors: the degree of departure from normal confidence intervals is usually small in comparison to dysimmunoglobulinemias occurring early in life; other sources of biologic variation, such as race (Rowe et al., 1968) and sex (Butterworth et al., 1967; Stoop et al., 1969) tend to obscure disease-related changes. Aging is another source of biologic variation only indirectly related to disease. Significant age-related changes occur prior to adult life (Buckley et al., 1968). Relatively little is known of the immunoglobulin content of the serum of humans late in life, a period associated with an increased frequency of disease. As a consequence observations of serum immunoglobulin concentra-

From *The Journal of Immunology* 105:4:964–972. Copyright 1970, The Williams & Wilkins Co. Reproduced by permission. This work was supported by grants from the United Public Health Service (AI–07499, 5–K3–AI–14797, HD–00668) and the American Medical Association (AMA–ERF).

tions in older patients are difficult to interpret. A systematic study of serum immunoglobulin concentrations throughout the life-span of man is a necessary requisite for the identification of disease-related changes.

The concentrations of IgG, IgA, and IgM were measured in the serum of 811 apparently healthy humans ranging in age from birth to 92 years. This work represents a part of continuing studies of the immunologic aspects of aging in man. Biometric analysis of these data suggests that valid contrasts of serum immunoglobulin concentrations between healthy and diseased adults are not possible without adequate control of biologic variation related to age.

Materials and Methods

Subjects

Sera were obtained from apparently healthy individuals who were free of complaints related to acute or chronic disease and exhibited no obvious abnormalities. The subjects included professional and paramedical hospital personnel, healthy family members and friends of patients who provided blood donations, and older individuals who are members of longitudinal study populations under periodic survey by the Duke University Center for the Study of Aging.

Preparation of Antigens and Antisera

Blood was collected by phlebotomy and serum separated within 1 hour. Sera were frozen at $-20°$ C until analyzed and retained at $4°$ C during the period of analysis.

Purified human immunoglobulins were used as antigens and primary reference standards. Each immunoglobulin was prepared from serum by a combination of gel filtration and ion exchange chromatography. Human IgG was prepared from Cohn fraction II human γ globulins and from sera or patients with heterogenous hyperglobulinemia and myeloma. Human IgA was prepared from the sera of patients with IgA multiple myeloma and from one patient with increased heterogenous IgA. Human IgM was prepared from the sera of two patients with monoclonal macroglobulinemia, a patient with cryomacroglobulin (Turkington et al., 1966) and a patient with heterogenous macroglobulinemia (Whitehouse et al., 1967).

Gel exclusion chromatography with G–200 Sephadex or P–300 Bio-Gel was performed on a 15 cm × 150 cm column as an initial enrichment step. Immunoglobulins in eluate peaks were initially identified by microimmuno-electrophoresis (Scheidegger, 1955) with a polyvalent antiserum to human serum proteins. More recently single radial diffusion (Mancini et al., 1965) against monospecific antisera has also been used in order to identify eluate fractions enriched with the desired human immunoglobulin. Chromatography was repeated on the same column after concentration of the desired eluate fraction by lyophilization. Solutions of each partially purified human immunoglobulin were chromatographed on a 5×100 cm DEAE Sephadex A–5 column. The resin bed and protein solution were equilibrated with a 0.01 M ionic strength, pH 8, Tris-propionate buffer, and elution was carried out with a continuous gradient developed by pH 7, 0.05 M ionic strength Tris-propionate buffer adjusted to a final ionic strength of 0.45 M with sodium chloride. Eluate fractions were monitored by measurement of the optical density, evaluated immunochemically and concentrated by lyophilization. Purified antigens were further characterized by analytical ultracentrifugation and further immunochemical analysis. Preparations having immunochemical or physicochemical evidence of impurities were rechromatographed under the same conditions, or alternately were chromatographed on CM-Sephadex A–50 after equilibration with a pH 5.0, 0.01 M ionic strength acetate buffer. Elution was accomplished with a continuous gradient developed by a pH 6, 0.5 M ionic strength acetate buffer.

The apparently immunochemically pure globulins obtained were adjusted to a pH of 5.5 and dialyzed into 0.01 M sodium chloride. Each solution of IgG and IgA was adjusted to a concentration range between 1 percent and 4 percent and each IgM solution to between 0.3 percent and 0.5 percent. Each preparation was sterilized by ultrafiltration prior to measurement of concentration by drying duplicate amounts to minimal weight at $107° \pm 0.2°$ C in a forced draft oven. All samples contained more than 20 mg protein and were weighed on an analytical balance having a precision of ± 0.0002 g. Weights obtained were corrected for the salt content of the initial solution and the concentration of each primary reference standard solution expressed in milligrams/milliliter of solution. The concentrations of some primary reference standard solutions were also evaluated in the analytical ultracentrifuge using Rayleigh interference optics ($\eta = 0.000465$ for 2.5 mg/ml, $\lambda = 546$ nm). Estimates of concentration by these two methods agree within ± 2 percent.

All antisera were prepared in goats. The quantity of primary reference standard used as antigen solution for each injection varied between 0.3 and 1.0 mg in a volume of 1 ml. Each antigen was homogenized with an equal volume of mixed complete Freund's adjuvant and injected intramuscularly in divided doses into each goat at weekly intervals for a period of six to eight weeks. Booster doses of antigen prepared as an alum toxoid (Kabat, 1961) were used twice monthly thereafter. Approximately 200-ml bleedings were obtained every two weeks after the development of precipitating antibodies, usually after the fourth week of immunization.

Each harvest of antiserum was evaluated for antibody to other human serum proteins by microimmunoelectrophoresis. Apparently monospecific antisera were evaluated against a panel of 12 or more κ and λ purified human L chains (Bence Jones proteins). Antibody activity to L chains or to other human serum proteins was removed by absorption with an appropriate antigen containing serum or partially purified antigen. After absorption each pool of goat antiserum was precipitated three times with ammonium sulfate (24 g/100 ml of serum or solution), dialyzed into physiologic saline, sterilized by ultrafiltration, and portions were sealed in 10-ml vials closed with a rubber bung and aluminum seal. Each antiserum globulin preparation was again evaluated for potency and specificity, dated and labeled, and retained at $-70°$ C until used. These goat antibody globulin preparations contained 90 percent or better 7S protein by ultracentrifugation and antibody activity was two- to fourfold greater than in neat serum.

Quantitation of Immunoglobulin Concentrations

The quantity of IgG, IgA, and IgM in serum was measured by a modification of the single radial diffusion method (Mancini et al., 1965; Fahey et al., 1965). Equal volumes (6 to 10 μl) of serum or antigen-standard were measured with a 50-μl syringe or micropipette into 3.6-mm wells cut in agar containing optimally diluted monospecific antisera to each human immunoglobulin. Each diffusion plate was allowed to incubate in a moist chamber at room temperature. Diffusion was allowed to progress for 4 hours for IgG and IgA and 12 hours for IgM. At the end of the diffusion the precipitate rings were photographed with the aid of an indirect light source. The photographed diameter of diffusion was measured with needle point calipers and a microcomparator. Initially, concentrations of each unknown immunoglobulin were estimated by interpolation of the diameter observed on a semilog graph of values obtained with a previously quantitated and diluted secondary reference standard (SRS) run on the same plate. More recently interpolated concentrations were calculated by a least squares regression of the $\log_e$ of the unknown SRS standards against observed diameters on a programmed calculating machine. These calculated regressions allow computation of known values and an estimate of minimal error. Replicate dilutions of the SRS, placed geometrically about each plate in such a way as to maximize error due to loading of wells and leveling the plate, were used to calculate the percentage standard error of the regression. Replicate determinations on each unknown serum on different days were done until the average estimates of concentration obtained agreed within the experimental limits of the method. The coefficient of variation of regression obtained by this technique currently averages 5.12 percent for IgG, 5.75 percent for IgA and 10.0 percent for IgM.

Analysis and Presentation of Data

Graphic plots of the cumulative frequency of serum concentrations observed in healthy individuals are curvilinear. The same frequency distribution plotted against logarithmically transformed serum concentrations is linear. Therefore, statistical evaluations of the serum immunoglobulin concentrations observed in healthy individuals were accomplished by multivariate analysis (Starmer et al., 1968) on the $\log_e$ of the value observed. Data were categorized as to the race, sex, and age of each individual. Age was initially treated as a variate. In the analysis presented in this report, age is treated as a linear covariate within each of the four age spans of human life in which similar age-related trends occur.

Results

The ranges of serum concentrations of IgG, IgA, and IgM observed throughout the life of man are presented in Figure 2–1. This figure shows the confidence interval derived from the antilog of the two standard deviation intervals about the means of sequential groups of healthy people from birth into the tenth decade of life. The magnitude of the variation observed differed considerably throughout life. However, the largest variance for equal sized groups was less than fourfold greater than the smallest variance observed. IgG reaches maximum variation and concentration between the second and fourth decades of life. IgA concentrations approximates the range of adult values by puberty, but continues to increase slowly through the third decade and shows increasing variation throughout life. IgM increases until the beginning of the second decade when it reaches maximum concentration and it reaches maximum variance by the fifth decade of life. Average IgG and IgM concentrations decrease toward neonate values beyond the fifth decade of life.

On the basis of the age-related trends pictured in Figure 2–1, data were divided into four age spans: 0 to 13 years, 14 to 27 years, 28 to 54 years, and 55 to 92 years. Multivariate analysis of the $\log_e$ of each value with the age of each apparently healthly individual as a different covariate for each age-race-sex group was accomplished in order to make use of age spans in which the transformed serum concentrations might approximate a linear function of age. The results of this analysis are presented in Table 2–1 as the age-adjusted mean and the standard error of the mean, and the slope and standard error of the slope within each of the 16 age-race-sex groups. All values presented in Table 2–1 are expressed as the $\log_e$ of units of W.H.O. reference standard 67/95. Mean values and slopes not statistically different from zero are identified. A graphic summary of these mean immunoglobulin concentrations and significant slopes is shown in Figure 2–2, which also presents an estimate of the variation between each race and sex in relation to the magnitude of change observed with aging. Age-race-sex groups having significant age-related changes within each age span are presented as a line. Group means without statistically significant within-group age effects are presented as single points at the mean age for the group. The general variation observed in group means and the time in life when race and sex differences are maximum are represented by the stippled areas in Figure 2–2.

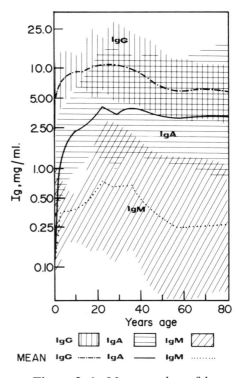

Figure 2–1. *Means and confidence intervals of serum immunoglobulin concentrations observed throughout the life of apparently healthy man. Note the logarithmic scale. The crosshatched areas represent the measured confidence intervals for each immunoglobulin. The mean IgG, mean IgA, and mean IgM show the relative magnitude of age-related trends and the basis for selection of age spans used for statistical analysis of these data.*

Generally, the magnitude of variation between different race and sex groups parallels the overall variation presented in Figure 2–1. Sex differences in whites were less than in blacks. Higher serum immunoglobulin concentrations were observed in blacks. Females have slightly higher serum IgM concentrations than males, but black females do not maintain this apparent difference into older age. The largest source of variation observed was related to age. In addition to the well documented increases in serum im-

Table 2-1. *Serum immunoglobulin concentrations of apparently healthy humans from birth to old age.*

Group	No.	Mean age ± S. D		IgG[a]	IgA[a]	IgM[a]
White males	47	6.2 ± 4.9	(1)[b]	4.1864 ± 0.0942	1.8567 ± 0.1936	3.9072 ± 0.1785
			(2)[c]	0.0557 ± 0.0118	0.2294 ± 0.0244	0.0384 ± 0.0225[d]
	55	20.0 ± 4.2	(1)	4.7487 ± 0.2619	4.1811 ± 0.5388	4.1447 ± 0.4963
			(2)	0.0060 ± 0.0049	0.0155 ± 0.0263[d]	0.0343 ± 0.0242[d]
	93	42.8 ± 3.3	(1)	5.5882 ± 0.2162	4.5415 ± 0.4445	6.1269 ± 0.4098
			(2)	−0.0253 ± 0.0049	0.0012 ± 0.0101[d]	−0.0390 ± 0.0093
	121	66.3 ± 8.8	(1)	3.8885 ± 0.2743	3.7506 ± 0.5638	4.4917 ± 0.5198
			(2)	0.0073 ± 0.0040[d]	0.0132 ± 0.0084[d]	−0.0053 ± 0.0077[d]
White females	43	4.6 ± 4.8	(1)	4.5342 ± 0.0084	0.7988 ± 0.1742	3.5007 ± 0.1606
			(2)	0.0192 ± 0.0127[d]	0.3365 ± 0.0261	0.1138 ± 0.0240
	63	19.7 ± 3.4	(1)	4.6726 ± 0.2925	3.5289 ± 0.6011	4.4382 ± 0.5543
			(2)	0.0096 ± 0.0145[d]	0.0464 ± 0.0299[d]	0.0293 ± 0.0275[d]
	66	43.3 ± 8.9	(1)	5.2746 ± 0.2438	4.4964 ± 0.5010	6.4197 ± 0.4620
			(2)	−0.0170 ± 0.0055	−0.0038 ± 0.0113[d]	−0.0388 ± 0.0104
	104	67.6 ± 9.3	(1)	3.2749 ± 0.2853	3.2344 ± 0.5864	3.3081 ± 0.5407
			(2)	0.0155 ± 0.0041	0.0150 ± 0.0085[d]	0.0113 ± 0.0079[d]
Black males	41	3.9 ± 4.3	(1)	4.1356 ± 0.0843	2.5512 ± 0.1733	3.9586 ± 0.1598
			(2)	0.0867 ± 0.0146	0.1866 ± 0.0300	0.0582 ± 0.0276
	19	20.7 ± 2.9	(1)	3.5219 ± 0.6586	1.1855 ± 1.3535[d]	2.9042 ± 1.2480[d]
			(2)	0.0874 ± 0.0313	0.1632 ± 0.0644	0.0891 ± 0.0594[d]
	29	40.6 ± 7.4	(1)	5.7566 ± 0.4174	4.3165 ± 0.8579	5.3767 ± 0.7910
			(2)	−0.0120 ± 0.0101[d]	0.0189 ± 0.0207[d]	−0.0100 ± 0.0191
	14	73.7 ± 10.5	(1)	6.8263 ± 0.7760	6.5533 ± 1.5948	5.6989 ± 1.4704
			(2)	−0.0254 ± 0.0104	−0.0224 ± 0.0214[d]	−0.0191 ± 0.0197[d]
Black females	32	3.7 ± 3.7	(1)	4.4689 ± 0.1009	1.7188 ± 0.2074	3.8320 ± 0.1912
			(2)	0.0623 ± 0.0191	0.3022 ± 0.0393	0.0816 ± 0.0362
	24	20.0 ± 4.8	(1)	5.2200 ± 0.3502	4.7301 ± 0.7198	3.7407 ± 0.6637
			(2)	−0.0047 ± 0.0170[d]	0.0017 ± 0.0349[d]	0.0702 ± 0.0322
	42	43.7 ± 7.2	(1)	4.7722 ± 0.3785	4.9701 ± 0.7779	5.3798 ± 0.7172
			(2)	−0.0011 ± 0.0085[d]	−0.0136 ± 0.0175[d]	−0.0447 ± 0.0161
	18	66.4 ± 9.9	(1)	3.7432 ± 0.6508	4.2112 ± 1.3376	1.7964 ± 1.2333[d]
			(2)	0.0130 ± 0.0096[d]	0.0042 ± 0.0199[d]	0.0317 ± 0.0183[d]

[a] All values expressed as $\log_e$ of units of W.H.O. reference standard 67/95.
[b] (1), age adjusted mean ± standard error of the mean.
[c] (2), slope ± standard error of the slope.
[d] Statistically not different from zero, $p < 0.05$.

munoglobulin during the first two decades of life, large age-related changes occur after maturity. IgM concentrations in older individuals decrease to values near those early in life. IgG decreases from the third through the sixth decade of life. Changes in IgG with age in blacks are less precipitous than in whites. Age-related changes of IgA in adults were small in comparison to changes in IgG and IgM.

Statistical comparisons of differences in serum immunoglobulin concentra-

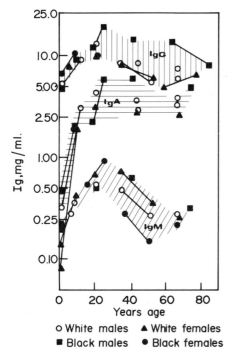

Figure 2–2. *Means of each race and sex group within each age span for each immunoglobulin shown as a function of age. Lines between two points within an age span represent statistically significant covariant effects within the particular age span; other group means in which the covariant effect of age was not significant are shown as a single point. Note the relative magnitude of age related variation in contrast to average differences related to race and sex.*

tions between age groups were made. These results are presented in Table 2–2, which lists probabilities that the differences observed could occur by chance alone. The probability that the mean difference or slope difference observed is not different from zero is presented for the adjusted mean and slope of each immunoglobulin for every possible contrast in the four selected age spans of life. Significant differences were found throughout life in all age spans for all immunoglobulins with but two exceptions: IgM in the interval from 0 to 27 years and IgA within the 28- to 92-year interval. Simultaneous

Table 2–2. *Significant age-related changes in human serum immuno-globulin concentrations.*

| Age range of grouped con-trasts (years) | Significance of the contrasts, $p <$ | | | | | |
| | IgG | | IgA | | IgM | |
	Mean	Slope	Mean	Slope	Mean	Slope
0–13 *vs* 14–27		0.0122	0.0001	0.0001		
0–13 *vs* 28–54	0.0001	0.0001	0.0001	0.0001	0.0001	0.0001
0–13 *vs* 55–92		0.0001	0.0001	0.0001		0.0001
14–27 *vs* 28–54	0.0029	0.0007	0.0301	0.0116	0.0001	0.0001
14–27 *vs* 55–92		0.0001	0.0001	0.0001		0.0001
28–54 *vs* 55–92	0.0043	0.0027			0.0008	0.0005
All age groups	0.0001	0.0001	0.0001	0.0001	0.0001	0.0001

contrasts between all age groups were highly significant for all immunoglobu-lins ($p < 0.0001$) with respect to both mean and slope differences. A similar simultaneous contrast of race and sex differences within all age groups (Table 2–3) suggests that only race differences in IgG are significant ($p < 0.0133$). These comparisons indicate that changes in serum immunoglobulin concentration occur throughout life, and that age-related differences are much more important than those related to race and sex.

Table 2–3. *Significant race, sex, and race-sex differences in human serum immuno-globulin concentrations.*

Age range (years)	Contrast	Significance of the contrasts, $p<$					
		IgG		IgA		IgM	
		Mean	Slope	Mean	Slope	Mean	Slope
0–13	Race		0.0124	0.0001			
	Sex	0.0004	0.0383	0.0001	0.0004		
	Race-sex inter-action						
14–27	Race						
	Sex		0.0277				
	Race-sex inter-action	0.0334	0.0177	0.0149	0.0202		
28–54	Race						
	Sex	0.0437					
	Race-sex inter-action						
55–92	Race	0.0022	0.0210				
	Sex	0.0011	0.0029			0.0132	0.0195
	Race-sex inter-action	0.0220	0.0466				
0–92	Race		0.0133				
	Sex						
	Race-sex inter-action						

Even though race and sex differences throughout life are minor in comparison to age-related trends, it was of interest to evaluate in which age range these differences are important. Table 2–3 presents the results of race, sex, and first-order interaction contrasts within each of the four age ranges studied. In the 0- to 13-year range mean IgG differences related to sex ($p < 0.0004$), and mean IgA differences related to race ($p < 0.0001$) and sex ($p < 0.0001$) could be detected. The covariate relationship of age on serum IgG was different in each race ($p < 0.0124$) and sex ($p < 0.0383$) and the age effect on serum IgA was different in each sex ($p < 0.0004$). In the next age span, 14 to 27 years, significant differences were restricted to the covariate effect of age on IgG in each sex ($p < 0.0277$) and mean and slope sex-age interaction effects for IgG and IgA. A difference in mean IgG related to sex was marginally significant in the 28- to 54-year age span ($p < 0.0437$). Late in life, in the 55- to 92-year age range, mean differences in IgG for race ($p < 0.0022$) and sex ($p < 0.0011$) and differences in the covariate effect of age on IgG with respect to race ($p < 0.0210$) and sex ($p < 0.0029$) were detected. Similar mean and slope differences related to sex exist for IgM ($p < 0.0132, 0.0195$). First-order interaction effects were also significant for IgG.

Discussion

Well documented changes in serum immunoglobulin concentrations occur during human development (Buckley et al., 1968). It has generally been assumed that changes beyond early adult life are small and of trivial consequence in comparison to those observed during the developmental years. Major emphasis in studies of healthy adults has been placed on differences related to race (Rowe et al., 1968) and sex (Butterworth et al., 1967; Stoop et al., 1969). Prior studies of the serum of older individuals have led to various conclusions. Studies of serum globulin concentrations by electrophoresis suggest that gamma migrating globulins increase with age (Karel, 1956; Das, 1961; Haferkamp et al., 1966). Other investigators have concluded on the basis of studies of a small number of subjects that IgG and IgM increase in older individuals (Haferkamp et al., 1966). Thus, the present data obtained by a quantitative immunochemical technique in a very large population of older healthy humans do not confirm earlier studies.

The information presented in this report identifies age-related changes as the major source of biologic variation in serum immunoglobulin concentrations. Although changes related to race and sex can be identified, these are small and can only be reliably identified early in life or in older age. It was of interest that blacks maintained relatively high serum IgG concentrations to a later point in adult life than whites. It is uncertain whether this difference is of genetic or environmental origin. However, a similar prolongation of increased IgM serum concentrations could not be demonstrated in blacks, suggesting that if this difference is of environmental origin, a similar ecologic effect does not involve IgM.

One of the most striking changes observed in these studies is the marked increase in variability of serum immunoglobulin concentrations with age. Only a small portion of this trend could be related to the expression of differences associated with race and sex later in life (Figure 2–2). Similar biologic variability as a function of aging has been identified in studies of other attributes of growth and development. For example, Tyler and Norris have observed a similar augmentation in variance in the weight of beagle dogs as a function of age (Tyler et al., 1968). This augmented variation tends to diminish the certainty with which other biologic effects can be identified and diminishes the usefulness of measurements in adults as a discriminator of health and disease.

Despite these reservations the fall in serum immunoglobulin concentrations with advancing age suggests an age-related abiotrophy of selected cells responsible for producing immunoglobulin molecules. The maintenance of concentrations of IgA suggests that this immunoglobulin may be of relatively greater importance with advancing age.

Comparable changes in immunity related to aging have been demonstrated in mice by Makinodan and Peterson, who measured the primary antibody-forming potential of fixed numbers of spleen cells from donors of varying age (Makinodan et al., 1964). These investigators found no age-related differences in the time of doubling of the antibody response of spleen cells passively transferred to irradiated and challenged recipients. Instead, a decrease in the number of responsive cells occurred with age. A similar decrease in the population of immunologically responsive cells could account for the age-related abiotrophy identified by these studies of human serum immunoglobulin concentrations. The relevance of this phenomenon to senescence and degenerative changes associated with aging and with diseases common in older humans remains to be explored. While the observed age-related changes in serum immunoglobulin concentration do not provide direct evidence of altered immunologic function in older individuals, they do provide the basis for the expectation of decreased complement fixing, precipitating, and perhaps agglutinating antibody activity in older individuals. Antibody activity decreases with age (Haferkamp et al., 1966). The extent to which this apparent decrement is made up by antibody activity within the IgA and other immunoglobulin classes having different modes of optimal serologic expression is important in diagnostic serologic studies in older individuals. The concentrations of immunoglobulin within each class may be important determinants of changes in humoral hypersensitivity reactions characteristic of disease states and their varied manifestations depending upon the age of the afflicted individual. Thus, the identification of age-related changes in immunoglobulin concentration throughout life provides additional evidence of the importance of resolution of disease-related changes in antibody activity in terms of the actual immunoglobulin classes involved.

The method of statistical analysis used to evaluate these data was adequate for the task, but is not necessarily optimal. The use of long age spans weakens the applications that can be made from the data in Table 2–1. We have made preliminary studies and categorized large patient populations and healthy controls into each of 27 possible categories evolved from the three possible alterations (high, normal, low) of three immunoglobulins. Each contrast was made with respect to the appropriate confidence interval for the individuals' age, race, and sex. The computed confidence intervals at the extremes of the age spans used in this report are very wide. When these wide confidence intervals are used to categorize individuals near the extremes of the selected age spans, the estimate of normality fails to discriminate sharply individuals who differ greatly from mean age for the selected age interval. Circumvention of this difficulty with smaller age spans and the identification of the frequency and kind of immunoglobulin alterations found in healthy individuals will be the subject of a separate report.

The magnitude and importance of the age effect are the major objects of this report. In preliminary analyses when age was evaluated as a variate, highly significant differences related to the race and sex of the individual could be readily identified. These differences were similar to those reported previously (Butterworth et al., 1967; Stoop et al., 1969). The ages of contrasted groups did not differ significantly. When the same data are analyzed with age as a covariate, many of these differences related to race and sex disappear leaving only those reported in Table 2–3. This observation suggests that some of the previously reported alterations related to race and sex are primarily a consequence of race-sex differences in the effect of aging. A second possible source of difference may be related to differences in the age distribution of the healthy subjects. The evidence presented in this report indicates the importance of either controlling age effects as a covariate, or alternately using age-matched controls (Buckley et al., 1970) in the evaluation of serum immunoglobulin alterations in disease states. Interpretations based on data in which age effects are not controlled are at risk.

References

Buckley, C. E., III, and Dorsey, F. C., *Ann. Int. Med.*, 72:37, 1970.
Buckley, R. H., Dees, S. C., and O'Fallon, W. M. *Pediatrics*, 41:600, 1968.
Butterworth, M., McClellan, B., and Allansmith, M. *Nature*, 214:1224, 1967.
Das, B. C. *Canad. J. Biochem. Physiol.*, 39:569, 1961.
Fahey, J. L. and McKelvey, E. M. *J. Immun.*, 94:84, 1965.
Haferkamp, O., Schlettwein-Gsell, D., Schwick, H. G., and Storiko, K. *Gerontologia*, 12:30, 1966.
Kabat, E. A. *Experimental Immunochemistry*, 2nd ed., Springfield, Ill.: Charles C. Thomas, 1961, p. 133.
Karel, J. L. *J. Amer. Geriat, Soc.*, 4:667, 1956.
Makinodan, T., and Peterson, W. J. *J. Immun.*, 93: 886, 1964.
Mancini, G., Carbonara, C. O., and Heremans, J. F. *Immunochemistry*, 2:235, 1965.
Rowe, D. S., McGregor, I. A., Smith, S. J., Hall, P., and Williams, K. *Clin. Exp. Immun.*, 3:63, 1968.
Scheidegger, J. J. *Int. Arch. Allerg.*, 7:103, 1955.
Starmer, C. F. and Grizzle, J. E. *A computer for analysis of data by general linear models*, Institute of Statistics Mimeo Series No. 560. Chapel Hill: University of North Carolina, 1968.
Stoop, J. W., Zegens, B. J. M., Sander, P. C., and Ballieux, R. E. *Clin. Exp. Immun.*, 4:101, 1969.
Turkington, R. W., and Buckley, C. E., III. *Amer. J. Med.*, 40:156, 1966.
Tyler, S. A., and Norris, W. P. *Growth*, 32:235, 1968.
Whitehouse, A. C., Buckley, C. E., III, and McCarter, J. *Amer. J. Med.*, 43:609, 1967.

Skin Conditions and Lesions in the Aged: A Longitudinal Study   *John P. Tindall and Erdman Palmore*

In any study of aging and aged persons, the largest organ of the body—the skin—deserves its portion of attention. This largest organ is also the principal one interacting with the environment and the gross changes with time in the integument require relatively little searching because of their obvious nature. The degree of the changes and how they are associated with longevity constitutes our present study.

An earlier report from the Duke Center for the Study of Aging (Tindall and Smith, 1970) described and evaluated data under two large headings: the incidence of skin lesions in a normal elderly, ambulatory population; and the relationships of these lesions to race, sex, and various cardiovascular conditions.

The present report is the first to view the surviving subjects longitudinally. A ten-year interval was chosen since it was anticipated that changes in the skin would occur slowly.

Materials and Methods

The original subjects in the longitudinal study were 271 community volunteers at least sixty years of age, selected in order to reflect the race, sex, and social status distribution among the aged in Durham, North Carolina. However, the initial group was somewhat above average, and the survivors in the second round of examinations, conducted between September 1959 and May 1961, were even more select.

One hundred sixty-three persons were seen for their first dermatologic examinations during this second round. A wide variety of skin lesions were carefully searched for over the entire body surface including oral mucous membranes. Seborrheic and actinic keratoses, vascular lesions including cherry angiomas, spider angiomas, venous lakes, common nevi, skin tags, comedones (blackheads), basal cell carcinomas, squamous cell carcinomas, sebaceous and epidermoid cysts, sebaceous adenomas, xanthelasma, lentigos, milia, dermatosis papulous nigra, purpura, neurogenous excoriations, cafe-au-lait spots and other "birthmarks," varicose veins, and venous bursts and oral leukokeratoses were noted in number and location. The presence and degree of other changes such as "lax" skin, asteatosis (xerosis—dry skin), dermatophytosis, actinic elastosis, seborrheic dermatitis, Schamberg's disease,

The authors wish to thank R. S. Rodgers III, M.D. and John R. Vydareny, M.D. for their contributions in making this paper possible.

rosacea, eczematous dermatitis, contact dermatitis, pruritus ani, stasis dermatitis, keratosis pilaris, rhinophyma, lichen sclerosis et atrophicas, and psoriasis were also noted.

Eye color and scalp hair distribution in both men and women, and degree of hair changes of the eyebrows, face, axillae, pubic area and legs were carefully estimated. A detailed dermatologic history for incidence of acne, chickenpox, herpes simplex, zoster, various skin tumors and dermatidities, allergies to medication, atopic conditions such as urticaria, hay fever, and venereal diseases were taken. In addition, detailed medical, social, and psychiatric evaluations together with laboratory studies were available for analysis for relationships with dermatologic variables. Much of the resulting data, including statistical evaluations have been reported (Tindall and Smith, 1970, Tindall, 1971).

Since the primary dermatologic survey conducted in 1960–1961, sixtynine persons survived and were reevaluated during 1970–1972. Most patients were seen by two observers at two different rounds of examinations, with any variations in the results being averaged to enhance accuracy. Some physical findings such as asteatosis would be expected to vary with time of year, temperature, and humidity. Others, however, such as cherry angiomas and seborrheic keratoses would not be expected to alter over short intervals.

The longevity quotient was also studied and is the observed years survived divided by the expected number of years to be survived based on actuarial tables by age, sex, and race. Thus, it is a standardized measure of longevity (see chapter 8).

Results

Most of the skin conditions examined are not considered to be abnormal except, perhaps, by degree. The most common finding, that of "lax" skin, denoting loss of subcutaneous fat and skin turgor, occurred in 94 percent of the original group of 163, and was slightly higher in the followup group. This finding, being practically universal, was difficult to further evaluate. Asteatosis, which had been observed in 77 percent in the primary study, proved a more useful variable because it was less universal. New growths which could actually be counted were also regarded as potentially meaningful and five types of lesions were particularly well suited. The incidence of these lesions in the primary study were: seborrheic keratoses 88 percent, cherry angiomas (ectasias) 75 percent, nevi (common moles) 63 percent, spider angiomas 29 percent, and scrotal angiomas (ectasias) 27 percent in men. Though three of the five lesions are vascular in nature, they were thought to be potentially dynamic and to warrant special notice.

Table 2–4 shows a breakdown of the differences of these six conditions in the primary study by ages. Whereas the percentages given above reflect the

Table 2-4. *Cross-sectional differences between age groups in dermatological conditions (primary study 1960–61).*

	Age group (%)			
	60–69 (N = 80)	70–79 (N = 67)	80+ (N = 11)	Total group (N = 158)
Spider angiomas (1 or more)	4	1	0	3
Asteatosis (moderate or severe)	13	16	27	15
Scrotal angiomas* (5 or more)	25	25	60	27
Seborrheic keratoses (10 or more)	46	60	46	52
Nevi (5 or more)	41	24	18	32
Cherry angiomas (10 or more)	41	36	55	40

* Men only

presence or absence of these variables, a better cross-section is evident when degree of asteatosis and higher numbers of the specific lesions are viewed. The exception is spider angiomas because of the relatively low overall incidence.

Although the number of subjects in the 80 and older age group is small, it would appear that the incidence of moderate and severe asteatosis increases with age, but that nevi decrease with age. Scrotal angiomas are more frequent among the men over 80. The other conditions show less variation by age groups.

This analysis does not consider variations in race and sex because of the relatively small numbers in each subgroup. It is noteworthy, however, that seborrheic keratoses (10 or more) were more frequent in both Negro men and women than their Caucasian counterparts; that nevi (5 or more) were more common on the men of both races than on the women, although the lesions were closely comparable between the races; and cherry angiomas (5 or more) were much more frequent in Caucasians, with an even greater difference occurring among men (Caucasian 77 percent and Negro 11 percent).

Table 2–5 compares the original percentages for the surviving subgroup with the percentages for these same individuals a decade later who had the skin conditions and lesions. There was a definite increase in the proportions with spider angiomas and asteatosis in the group, and a large increase in the proportion of men with scrotal angiomas. Seborrheic keratoses changed little

Table 2-5. *Longitudinal changes in findings (N = 69).*

	1960–62(%)	1970–72(%)	Change
Spider angiomas (1 or more)	4	27	+23
Asteatosis (moderate or severe)	12	30	+18
Scrotal angiomas* (5 or more)	6	19	+13
Seborrheic keratosis (10 or more)	45	48	+ 3
Nevi (10 or more)	15	7	− 8
Cherry angiomas (10 or more)	46	36	−10

* Men only

in numbers of lesions, but nevi and cherry angiomas decreased with the passage of time.

Thus, both the cross-sectional analysis by age and the longitudinal analysis show increases in asteatosis and scrotal angiomas, while showing decreases in nevi. We will see that these are the same three conditions linked to longevity.

Table 2–6 attempts to assess the data from a different viewpoint, that of longevity. Three variables were found to be significantly associated with longevity quotient; asteatosis, nevi, and scrotal angiomas. The other three variables included in this analysis were not significantly associated with longevity. The differences are particularly striking when no asteatosis is compared to moderate and severe asteatosis, no nevi to five or more nevi, and no

Table 2–6. *Conditions associated with longevity quotient.*

Condition	LQ	N
Asteatosis: None	1.44	37
Mild	1.24	99
Moderate or Severe	1.21	25
Nevi: None	1.34	61
1–4	1.31	49
5 or more	1.16	52
Scrotal angioma: None	1.32	56
(men only) 1–4	1.48	9
5 or more	1.07	12

Differences are statistically significant at .05 level.

scrotal angiomas to five or more scrotal angiomas. It should be noted that the longevity quotients for all groups are above average because those who survived and returned for the second round of examinations were generally above the average group.

Discussion

The skin is a very dynamic organ, working constantly to afford us protection from our environment while allowing us to interact with it. It is under the control of many endogenous forces while having a marvelous tolerance to external influences. This study is concerned with a series of essentially normal variations—normal in the sense that they are more important cosmetically than they are pathologically. Of the six conditions analyzed, only asteatosis is associated with any symptomatology, and only when it is severe may the individual perceive some pruritus.

The analysis by age groups and by longitudinal change tends to support previous impressions. The increase from 12 percent to 30 percent of individuals with moderate or severe asteatosis indicates that the aging skin tends to lose its ability to keep itself properly hydrated by retaining the proper fluid content in the epidermal cells. Increasing age apparently alters the functional capacity of the epidermis, particularly the "skin barrier" of the surface stratum corneum (Blank, 1952) so that it becomes more dry and brittle.

The tendency of different types of vascular lesions in the skin to be associated with each other was reported following the survey of the primary group (Tindall and Smith, 1970). Scrotal angiomas, cherry angiomas, and varicosities were all significantly related. Cherry angiomas and scrotal angiomas are uncommon in children, though spider angiomas occur much more frequently. Bean (1956) states that cherry angiomas are almost universal in individuals over seventy years of age.

Possible interrelationships among cutaneous and internal vascular lesions were also sought in the primary study. Arteriolarsclerotic retinopathy (grade II or greater), aortic calcification seen on chest X-ray, and coronary artery disease as evidenced by electrocardiographic change were utilized to reflect the changes associated with aging in different-sized internal blood vessels. Scrotal angiomas were related to arteriolarsclerotic retinopathy and to aortic calcification; coronary artery disease and varicosities were also related to each other.

Therefore, it appears reasonable that when viewed longitudinally, scrotal angiomas would become more numerous in an older population. That the proportion with many cherry angiomas did not increase seems to indicate less age relationship. Spider angiomas are known to be more dynamic and to reflect hormonal changes. An example would be the great increase in such lesions in pregnant women, with disappearance following childbirth. Though speculative, the longitudinal increase more likely reflects the hormonal system rather than aging as such. This separation is arbitrary and probably artificial.

True moles or nevocellular nevi, are interesting from a different viewpoint. These lesions begin to appear during the first two years of life and increase in number into adult life. With time, they disappear as mysteriously as they appear so that Caucasians over fifty years of age average about four such lesions (Stegmaier, 1959). In the primary study, 84 percent had fewer than ten nevi and only 3 percent had more than twenty nevi. The most frequently retained nevi were found about the scalp, face and neck and were only lightly pigmented or were flesh-colored. These observations are supported by the marked decrease seen in the longitudinal analysis, particularly in the percentage of subjects with ten or more nevi decreasing from 15 percent to only 7 percent.

Three of the six conditions studied were associated with reduced longevity —asteatosis, scrotal angiomas, and nevi. Loss of the ability of the skin to retain fluids resulting in the dry, parched appearance of advanced age seems to reflect the loss of competence of the epidermal cellular system most exposed to the environment and its many stimuli. In particular, the influence of external sources of hydration, or lack of it, is enhanced (Sams, 1951), resulting in the loss of suppleness and flexibility. Thus, severe asteatosis may be a sign of decline before death.

Weakness in the walls of the small blood vessels of the scrotum may have a basis in the individual's inheritance. This weakness appears to be emphasized with advanced age. Since vascular accidents, particularly in the cerebral areas, are a major cause of death in elderly persons, the observation of many scrotal angiomas could also be interpreted as a sign of approaching decline and death.

The association of many nevi with reduced longevity is more difficult to interpret. It may be merely a chance association or it may be an indication that the total immune competence of these individuals with many nevi has declined, which may be related to earlier death (see Buckley and Dorsey, pp. 6–17 in this volume).

Summary

Sixty-nine elderly subjects were completely examined dermatologically in 1960–1961 and again in 1970–1972. Incidences of lesions and degrees of conditions were carefully recorded to determine, if possible, any relationship with shortened or enhanced life span. Asteatosis, scrotal angiomas, and nevi appeared to be associated with a relatively shortened life expectancy. The first two findings increased with advancing age, while nevi decreased. It is possible that severe asteatosis, large numbers of scrotal angiomas, and retention of nevi are signs of decline and approaching death.

References

Bean, W. B. Changing incidence of certain vascular lesions of skin with aging. *Geriatrics,* 11:97, 1956.

Blank, I. H. Factors which influence the water content of the Stratum Corneum. *Journal of Investigative Dermatology,* 18:433, 1952.

Samoy, William, Sr. Humidity: Its relation to the problems in dermatology. *Southern Medical Journal,* 44:140, 1951.

Stegmaier, Otto C. Natural regression of the melanocytic nevus. *Journal of Investigative Dermatology,* 32:415, 1959.

Tindall, John P., Geriatric dermatology. In Austin B. Chin (Ed.), *Working with older people,* Vol. 4. Washington, D.C.: U.S. Government Printing Office, 1971.

Tindall, John P., and Smith, J. Graham, Jr. Skin lesions of the aged. In E. B. Palmore (Ed.), *Normal aging.* Durham, N.C.: Duke University Press, 1970. pp. 50–57.

Longitudinal Evaluation of Ocular Function   *Banks Anderson, Jr., and Erdman Palmore*

Introduction

It is common knowledge that many changes in visual function are age related. Those of you who read these lines through a bifocal lens or with reading glasses donned for the purpose are ill-equipped to dispute this assertion. Although few aging changes are so linear over so long a span as the loss of accommodation (Figure 2–3), cataract, glaucoma, and macular degeneration

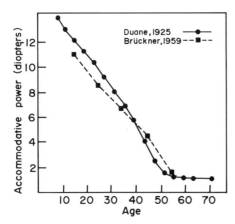

Figure 2–3. *Loss of accommodative power with age.*

all become more common with advancing age. As defined by legal blindness* visual incapacity increases strikingly after age 64 (Figure 2–4). Age has been correlated with loss of vision in several studies (National Society for the Prevention of Blindness, 1966; U.S. National Health Survey, 1968), but few data exist concerning the changes in a given population over time and there are almost no longitudinal data on aged populations. As a part of the Duke first longitudinal study, panelists received ocular examinations, and data concerning changes in vision and ocular status over time have been obtained. Because of the simultaneous collection of other longitudinal data, it has been possible to correlate these ocular findings with longevity and social and psychological parameters.

---

* Best corrected vision in the better eye 20/200 or worse or visual field limited to 20° in its greatest diameter.

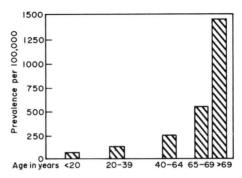

Figure 2–4. *Estimated prevalence of legal blindness by age, U.S., 1962. NSPB–1966.*

Methods

All ocular examinations were performed at the Duke University Medical Center. The panelists were escorted to the examining facility and seated in an examining chair. Visual acuity was obtained with and without the glasses worn by the patient testing each eye separately. Distance acuity was obtained from a Snellen chart projected at a distance of 20 feet. Reading vision was determined by allowing the patient to hold a graduated reading card under a 60-watt reflector lamp at the distance of his choice. Intraocular tensions were measured with the Goldmann applanation tonometer after corneal anesthesia with 0.5 percent proparacaine hydrochloride. The anterior segment of the eye was examined with a Zeiss slit lamp biomicroscope and the retina evaluated with a hand-held transformer-powered direct ophthalmoscope.

Although routine refractions were not performed, in cases of gross error, panelists were made aware of our findings and in some instances given prescriptions for new glasses. (In other cases cataracts were the cause of marked visual impairment and surgery was advised.) The data were recorded by circling numbers on the previously prepared examination form designed to allow computer storage and retrieval. This system of data recording was limiting in terms of possible descriptive alternatives: For example, visual acuities between 20/50 and 20/80 were recorded by circling the same number and could therefore not be discriminated. (Codes for the variables reported in this paper are summarized in an appendix at the end of the paper.)

Data concerning glaucoma, cataract, cornea guttata, and asteroid hyalitis are reported in this study. The patients were considered to have glaucoma if intraocular pressures of 26 or above were recorded or if they reported a previous diagnosis of glaucoma and were using glaucoma medication. Cataract was diagnosed if the patient had previously had cataract surgery or if an immature, mature, or hypermature cataract or marked nuclear sclerosis was present. Peripheral opacities, vacuoles, and incipient cataracts were not considered as "cataracts" for the purpose of this study.

Cornea guttata refers to the occurrence of drop-like deposits on Descemet's membrane in the posterior endothelial layer of the cornea. Sometimes called Henle's warts, these deposits are almost invariably seen in the periphery after age 60. The panelists were not considered to have cornea guttata for the purposes of this study if only a few peripheral endothelial guttata were noted. Central occurrence was listed as "moderate" and if it appeared that a function of the endothelial layer might be affected, the condition was called "marked." These determinations were made by slit lamp evaluation of the cornea and panelists were said to have cornea guttata if either moderate or marked guttata were noted.

Asteroid hyalitis refers to the occurrence of yellowish-white vitreous opacities which chemically seem to be deposits of calcium soaps. Sometimes called asteroid hyalosis, the condition is not inflammatory in origin and does seem to be more prevalent in aged populations. The mean age of a group studied by Jervey and Anderson (1965) was 65 while in a series of patients reported by Luxenberg and Sime (1969) the mean age was 71. The age range in the first group was 48 to 87 and in the second 42 to 96 years.

The longevity quotient is the number of years survived after the first examination, divided by the expected years remaining after the first examination based on actuarial tables of life expectancy by age, race, and sex. The longevity quotient thus standardizes for the known effects of age, race, and sex on longevity. (For more details, see "Predicting Longevity" in chapter 8.)

The three activity self-ratings in the areas of primary groups, leisure, and work were derived from questions in "Your Activities and Attitudes" (Burgess, 1949) and the scores ranged from 0 to 10. The score on primary group activities is based on questions dealing with living arrangements and frequency of contact with family and friends. The leisure activity score is based on number of leisure activities, time spent reading, and activity in organizations. The work activity score is based on the amount of current employment or housework and whether consumption had to be curtailed because of retirement or lowered income.

The five social worker ratings of primary group activities, secondary group activities, emotional security, status feelings, and happiness were 10-point scales ranging from 0 for the lowest activity or feeling to 9 for the highest.

Results

The panelists' corrected best distance vision in the better eye at their first examination is recorded in Table 2–7. These cross-sectional data illustrate the increased frequency of poor vision in panelists over 70. While

Table 2–7. *Corrected best distance vision in the better eye* (*initial examination*).

	Age group (%)			
	60–69	70–79	80+	Total N
20/20 or better	57	27	14	40
20/25	25	29	23	26
20/30–20/40	10	30	27	20
20/50 or worse	8	14	36	14
N	101	90	22	213

over half of those between 60 and 69 years had normal vision (20/20 or better), only one quarter of those between 70 and 79 and only 14 percent of those over 80 could read this line with the better eye. Although the age groupings in the 1960 to 1962 National Health Survey differ, these cross-sectional data are quite similar (Table 2–8). The corrected distance vision in the better eye was on the whole slightly lower in the National Health Survey for comparable ages. This may reflect a greater orientation toward health care in our volunteer panel and the fact that this panel was generally somewhat above average in most dimensions. A visual acuity of 20/50 or worse indicates a definite impairment. Newspaper print becomes difficult to read with vision at this level and most states begin to impose restrictions upon driving when vision is impaired to this degree. While only 8 percent of our panelists in the 60 to 69 group were in this category, 36 percent of those 80 and above were so impaired. In addition to visual acuity, the incidence of cataract, glaucoma, cornea guttata, and asteroid hyalitis at the time of this first examination is summarized in Table 2–9. Cataract was by far the most common finding and seemed to account for roughly one-half of the reduction in acuity to levels of 20/50 or below at every age level (as compared with the percent figure for those having the worse eye 20/50 or poorer).

In the National Health Survey from 1960 to 1962 a notation was made as to whether lens opacities were or were not present (U.S. National Health

Table 2–8. *Corrected best distance vision in the better eye* (*National Health Survey*).*

	Age group (%)		
	55–64	65–74	75–79
20/20 or better	39.8	26.1	10.1
20/30–20/40	51.4	55.6	58.9
20/50 or worse	8.8	18.2	30.8

* U.S. National Health Survey, April 1968.

Table 2–9. *Ocular findings at initial examination by age (percent).*

Finding	60–69	70–79	80+	Total	Sample N
Cataracts	9	18	36	16	260
Glaucoma	3	1	0	2	260
Cornea guttata	3	2	9	3	260
Asteroid hyalitis	3	4	3	3	260
Best eye 20/50 or worse	8	14	36	14	213
Worst eye 20/50 or worse	19	39	50	31	213

Survey, March 1968). A split lamp was not used and the pupils were not dilated. Presumably therefore, the subjects would have to have significant cataractous lens changes in order to be designated as having lens opacities. In spite of the differences in examination techniques, the data from this survey are quite comparable (Table 2–10).

Table 2–10. *Lens opacities found in National Health Survey, 1960–1962.**

Sex	Eye	Age (%) 55–64	65–74	75–79
Men	right	8.9	10.6	25.9
	left	10.3	11.0	22.7
Women	right	6.6	19.7	33.6
	left	7.0	20.4	37.0
Mean assuming all categories equal		8.2	15.4	29.8

* U.S. National Health Survey, March, 1968.

An incidence of glaucoma of 3 percent at age 60 to 69 and 1 percent at 70 to 79 was found initially. In a 1959 survey of 10,000 healthy workers and their relatives, Leydhecker found the incidence of glaucoma to be 2.3 percent in the population over 40 (Leydhecker, 1959). The age and sex relationships are shown in Table 2–11. In that population, glaucoma was twice as common in men at every age and was more common in older individuals. Although our cross-sectional data do not demonstrate an increased incidence in older individuals, the longitudinal data (see below) do show such a trend.

Table 2–11. *Occurrence of glaucoma by age group (Leydhecker, 1959).*

	20–29	30–39	40–49	50–59	60–69	Total after 40
Men	0.43	0.80	1.74	3.17	5.33	2.72
Women	0.20	0.40	0.75	1.75		1.07
Total	0.35	0.65	1.45	2.84	4.48	2.31

Cornea guttata was more prevalent after age 80, but there were no clear-cut changes in the incidence of asteroid hyalitis.

Longitudinal Data

The many advantages of the longitudinal approach to characterization of community samples such as ours have previously been discussed (chapter 1). One such advantage of particular importance in this study was the continued participation of many of our volunteers after chronic illness had intervened. Presumably many of these subjects might not have volunteered to come in for study save that they had been recruited years before when relatively healthy. These data, therefore, probably more accurately reflect the composition of an ambulatory aged community population than do the initial cross-sectional parameters discussed above.

The results of our longitudinal data cannot be compared with that of other populations since we have been unable to find any other such data. The number of panelists studied was smaller ($N = 93$) than in the cross-sectional group since the requirement for inclusion was a series of observations extending over a period of at least ten years.

Table 2–12 summarizes the ocular findings of the group observed longitudinally by age group. This table presents the differences between the percentage observed initially and the percentage observed in the same group ten years later, for two age groups. The first column presents the differences for those initially age 60–69 (who were age 70–79 ten years later), and the second column presents the differences for those initially age 70–80 (who were age 80–90 ten years later).

The most striking findings are the increases in glaucoma and cornea guttata and the marked decrement in visual acuity. The increases in cataracts and in asteroid hyalitis were relatively small. Comparing these longitudinal differences with the cross-sectional differences seems to indicate that glaucoma and cornea guttata increase more longitudinally in the normal aged who survive ten or more years than cross-sectional analysis would indicate. Con-

Table 2–12. *Change in ocular findings of group observed longitudinally by age.*

Finding	Age at initial observation	
	60–69	70–80
Cataracts	0	+ 3
Glaucoma	+ 9	+ 5
Cornea guttata	+ 7	+19
Asteroid hyalitis	0	+ 2
Best eye 20/50 or worse	+13	+32
Worst eye 20/50 or worse	+18	+58

versely, cataracts do not seem to increase longitudinally in such a relatively healthy group as much as cross-sectional age comparisons would indicate.

This led to an analysis to determine if vision was related to longevity and social variables such as participation in group activities, emotional security, and status feelings. Accordingly those individuals whose best distance vision was 20/50 or worse were compared with the other panelists with better vision. The results are outlined in Table 2–13. There was no significant difference in longevity quotient, self-rated primary group activities, or happiness. However, poorer vision was related to lower leisure activities, work activities, group activities, status feelings and to a lesser extent, emotional security.

Table 2–13. *Vision, longevity, social variables.*

Variable	Best distance 20/50 or worse (N = 29)	Others (N = 184)	Probability*
Longevity quotient	1.11	1.19	NS
Self-ratings			
Primary group activities	6.1	6.4	NS
Leisure activities	6.0	7.1	<.01
Work activities	4.4	6.3	<.01
Social worker ratings			
Primary group activities	5.1	7.3	<.01
Secondary group activities	3.6	4.5	<.01
Emotional security	3.9	4.6	<.05
Status feelings	4.6	5.4	<.02
Happiness	3.6	3.6	NS

* One-tailed t test.

The difference in primary group activity was more apparent when rated by the social worker whereas the individuals themselves seemed less aware of this difference.

Another subgroup, individuals with asteroid hyalitis, was compared to those without hyalitis. Although the group was small (N = 8) a similar analysis was performed (Table 2–14). The only parameter in which this group differed very significantly from the rest was in social worker rated primary group activity. Intuitively, one would assume that asteroid hyalitis would have no effect on longevity or social variables unless it were associated with marked visual decrement, which was seldom the case. Those with each of the other conditions studied (cataracts, glaucoma, and cornea guttata) were also compared with those not having the condition for each of the nine variables in Tables 2–13 and 2–14. These comparisons showed little or no significant difference. Thus, it appears that these conditions do not impair activity, attitudes or longevity unless they result in substantial visual loss in both eyes (as in Table 2–13). Even then, there seems to be no significant effect on longevity or over-all happiness.

Table 2-14. *Hyalitis, longevity, social variables.*

Variable	Persons with hyalitis (N = 8)	Others (N = 247)	Probability*
Longevity quotient	.96	1.14	NS
Self-ratings			
Primary group activities	5.3	6.3	<.10
Leisure activities	5.5	6.8	<.05
Work activities	5.1	5.9	NS
Social worker ratings			
Primary group activities	4.7	6.9	<.01
Secondary group activities	3.3	4.4	<.05
Emotional security	3.4	4.5	<.05
Status feelings	4.6	5.3	NS
Happiness	2.4	3.6	<.02

* One-tailed *t* test.

Summary

In this study, ocular function has been evaluated longitudinally and cross-sectionally as well as correlated with longevity and social variables. In the cross-sectional analysis a best corrected vision of 20/50 or worse occurred in 8 percent of those aged 60 to 69, 14 percent of those 70 to 79 and 36 percent of those over 80. The longitudinal analysis found increases in this percentage of 13 points for those initially 60–69 and increases of 32 points for those initially 70–80. This marked decrement in visual function has widespread implications in any discussion of habilitation of aged populations. The incidence of glaucoma increased longitudinally with age as did the incidence of cornea guttata. The incidence and increase in number of cataracts was less in the longitudinal analysis than in the cross-sectional. An explanation for this discrepancy may be the above average nature of those who returned ten years later and thus were available for longitudinal analysis. There was little association found between the specific conditions and the longevity and social variables but there were several significant relationships when corrected best eye vision was 20/50 or worse. Thus specific ocular conditions seem not generally related to impaired activity or attitudes unless they cause a substantial deterioration in the vision of both eyes.

Appendix

Corrected Visual Acuity Coding Alternatives

20/15	20/100–20/200
20/20	20/300–20/400

20/25	Counting fingers at 6 ft with good light projection
20/30–20/40	Counting fingers at 6 ft with faulty LP
20/50–20/60	Hand motions with good LP
20/70–20/80	Hand motions with poor LP

Intraocular Pressure Coding Alternatives (mm Hg)

10 or less	31–35
11–15	Greater than 35
16–20	Tactile tension normal
21–25	Tactile tension soft
26–30	Tactile tension elevated

Corneal Gutatta Coding Alternatives

Few or occasional endothelial gutatta
Moderate endothelial gutatta
Marked endothelial gutatta

References

Bruckner, R. Uber Methoden longitudinaler Alternsforschung am Auge. *Ophthalmo-logica*, 138:59–75, 1959.

Burgess, E., Cavan, R., Havighurst, R., and Goldhammer, H. *Your activities and attitudes*. Chicago: Science Research Associates, 1949.

Duane, A. Subnormal accommodation. *Archives of Ophthalmology*, 54:566–587, 1925.

Jervey, E. D., and Anderson, B., Jr. Asteroid hyalitis: A study of serum calcium levels in affected patients. *Southern Medical Journal*, 58:191–194, 1965.

Leydhecker, W. Zur Vervreitung des Glaucoma Simplex in der scheinbar gesunden augenarzlich nicht behandelten Bevolkerung. *Documenta Ophthalmologica*, 13:359–380, 1959.

Luxenberg, M., and Sime, D. Relationship of asteroid hyalosis to diabetes mellitus and plasma lipid levels. *American Journal of Ophthalmology*, 67:406–413, 1969.

National Society for the Prevention of Blindness. *Estimated statistics on blindness and vision problems*. New York: NSPB Inc., 1966.

U.S. National Health Survey. *Monocular-binocular visual acuity of adults*. PHS Pub. No. 100-Series 11-No. 30, U.S. 1960–1962. U.S. Department of HEW, April 1968.

U.S. National Health Survey. *History and examination findings related to visual acuity among adults*. PHS Pub. No. 100-Series 11-No. 28, U.S. 1960–1962. U.S. Department of HEW, March 1968.

Auditory Changes   *Carl Eisdorfer and Frances Wilkie*

Hearing loss is one of the major problems of the aged. Most studies of hearing patterns give the results of a cross-sectional study of populations.

Reprinted by permission from *Journal of American Geriatrics Society*, 20:377–382, 1972.

This report is essentially a follow-up study of changes in hearing thresholds among aged individuals.

Findings on hearing levels for audiometric pure-tones and for speech material are presented by age, sex, and race. The project was not designed specifically to investigate hearing levels among the aged, but rather each evaluation included a hearing test as well as physical, psychological, sociological, and various laboratory studies (Busse, 1965).

Method

Subjects

The subjects were 92 (out of 271) participants in a multidisciplinary, longitudinal study of ambulatory community volunteers at the Duke University Center for the Study of Aging and Human Development. The size of the present sample was determined by the number of subjects for whom measurements were available on two hearing tests separated by a seven-year period. . . .

Based upon their age at entering the program, in the present sample there were 56 subjects initially examined in their 60s and 36 subjects initially examined in their 70s, who completed the seven-year follow-up study. Among those subjects initially in their 60s, 38 were white (13 men and 25 women) and 18 were black (8 men and 10 women). Among those subjects initially in their 70s, 27 were white (14 men and 13 women) and 9 were black (6 men and 3 women).

Procedures

Hearing thresholds for the right and left ear were determined individually by using air-conduction THD-39 earphones with a standard pure-tone MAICO model H-1B audiometer at six frequencies—500, 1000, 2000, 3000, 4000, and 6000 cycles per second (cps.). The audiometer was factory calibrated and checked periodically in accordance with the 1951 American Standards Association (ASA) specifications. A one-way mirror allowed the examiner to view the subject in the testing chamber and a two-way voice communication system was provided. In this report, we define threshold as the lowest intensity of a pure-tone just audible to the examinee. During the pure-tone testing, the subject signalled having heard the tone by raising his hand.

Speech discrimination levels were based on the recorded list of spondee words, presented a 1000 cps. Each word had two syllables, each equally stressed (i.e., baseball and railroad). A carrier phrase introduced each word and instructed the subject to "say the word." An individual's threshold (of intelligibility) for speech was defined as the level at which the subject could repeat correctly 50 percent of the test material presented to him.

In accordance with previous work (Corso, 1963) combined mean thresholds for both ears are presented at each frequency from 500 to 6000 cps. with the realization that this is somewhat artificial; however, it serves as a useful comparison. In that regard, it should be noted that there were only minor differences (ranging from 0.1 to 3.3 db.) between the average thresholds for the right and left ears.

In addition to the thresholds for the spondee words, a pure-tone estimated hearing level for speech was obtained by averaging thresholds at 500, 1000, and 2000 cps., the frequencies generally considered most essential for speech reception (Committee on Medical Rating of Physical Impairment, 1961; Committee on Conservation of Hearing, 1959). Further, with findings limited to the "better" ear, the percent of impairment is reported in the pure-tone estimated hearing range for speech reception. The following classification (Special Committee on Aging, 1968) of converted ASA standards was used: "normal" hearing (i.e., thresholds less than 15 db.), "slight impairment" (i.e., thresholds between 15–35 db.), and "severe hearing impairment" (i.e., thresholds greater than 35 db.).

A series of analyses of variance and chi-square techniques was used to examine the age, sex, and racial differences in hearing levels.

Results

Figure 2–5 shows the age differences in pure-tone thresholds expressed as decibel deviations from audiometric zero at frequencies from 500 through 6000 cps. Group 1 includes those subjects initially in their 60s and group 2 those subjects initially in their 70s with the mean ages given at tests 1 and 3. Beginning at 1000 cps. and above, hearing acuity diminished significantly with increasing age in both groups, with the greatest loss found at the high frequencies. During the follow-up period, the magnitude of change in hearing levels was approximately the same for both groups. The average change over time was -2.5, -6.9, -8.4, -8.1, -7.2, and -10.5 db. at 500, 1000, 2000, 3000, 4000, and 6000 cps., respectively.

Figure 2–6 shows the threshold levels for the spondee words as well as the estimated speech thresholds based on the average thresholds for 500, 1000, and 2000 cps. For both groups, the initial estimated speech thresholds were 6 db. lower than the spondee word thresholds. Within both groups, the estimated levels for speech reception tended to decline over time between tests 1 and 3, while the hearing levels for the spondee words remained stable.

Figure 2–7 shows the data based on the thresholds limited to the "better" ear. It gives the percent of examinees at each testing with "normal" hearing, the percent with slight hearing impairment, and the percent with severe hearing impairment in the estimated pure-tone speech reception range. For our younger subjects, as age progressed from a mean of 67 to 74 years, the

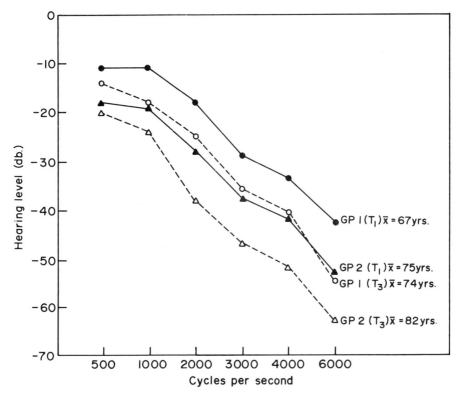

Figure 2–5. *Average hearing threshold levels for group 1 (subjects initially examined at age 60 to 69 years) and for group 2 (subjects initially examined at age 70 to 79 years) at tests 1 and 3.*

percentage with "normal" hearing declined by 17 percent (i.e., from 63 percent to 46). Slight impairments increased by 14 percent (i.e., from 33 percent to 47 percent) and severe impairments increased from 4 percent to 7 percent. For those subjects moving from a mean of 75 to 82 years, the percentage with "normal" hearing decreased by 11 percent (i.e., from 42 percent to 31 percent), the proportion with slight impairments remained stable at about 40 percent, while severe impairments increased by 12 percent (i.e., from 17 percent to 29 percent).

Figure 2–8 shows the difference in hearing levels between men and women, independent of age since the Sex-by-Age interaction was not significant. At both hearing tests, women tended to have poorer hearing than men at 500 and 1000 cps., while men had significantly worse hearing than women initially at 3000 and 4000 cps., and at the follow-up study at 4000 and 6000 cps. At the higher frequencies, hearing loss appears to occur at an earlier age among men than women by about 6 years. For both sexes, with increasing age there is a decrease in hearing sensitivity with women having a significantly

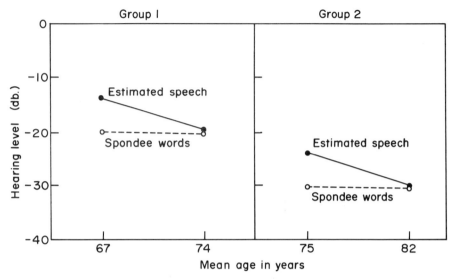

Figure 2–6. *The average estimated hearing threshold levels for speech (average of pure-tone levels at 500, 1000, and 2000 cycles per second) and the average hearing threshold levels for spondee words for age groups 1 and 2 at tests 1 and 3.*

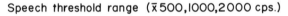

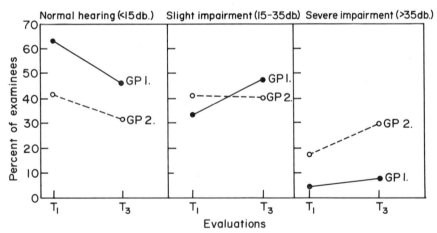

Figure 2–7. *The percent of examinees in group 1 (subjects initially examined at age 60 to 69 years) and in group 2 (subjects initially examined at age 70 to 79 years) who had "normal" hearing, slight, or severe hearing impairment in the "better" ear at the pure-tone estimated speech reception range at tests 1 and 3.*

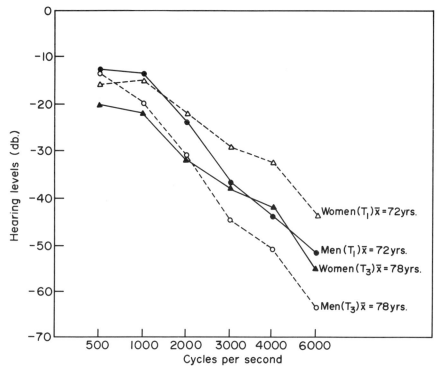

Figure 2–8. *The average hearing threshold levels for the total sample of men and women at tests 1 and 3.*

greater loss than men at only one of the six frequencies (i.e., 3000 cps.) and at 500, 1000, and 2000 cps. only when these frequencies were averaged to represent the estimated hearing level for speech.

Figure 2–9 gives the data for the proportion of hearing impairment for men and women for the "better" ear in the pure-tone estimated range for speech reception. Within our younger group, significant differences emerged between men and women at the follow-up study and were also found at both testings for the older group. It would appear that from about age 74 on, "normal" hearing was more prevalent among men than women. Particularly at the older age, slight impairments were more prevalent among women than men. In contrast, hearing levels for the spondee words did not yield significant sex differences, although across time women tended to have a greater loss than men.

Figure 2–10 shows the racial differences in hearing levels independent of age. At each evaluation, blacks had significantly better hearing than whites at all frequencies. Further, at the higher frequencies, whites appeared to develop worse hearing at an earlier age than blacks by about six years. Across the seven-year period, blacks had a significantly greater loss than whites only

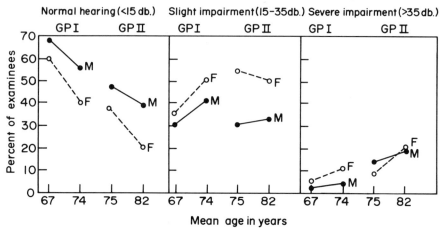

Figure 2–9. *The percent of men (M) and women (F) in age groups 1 and 2 who had "normal" hearing, slight, or severe hearing impairment in the "better" ear at the pure-tone estimated speech reception range at tests 1 and 3.*

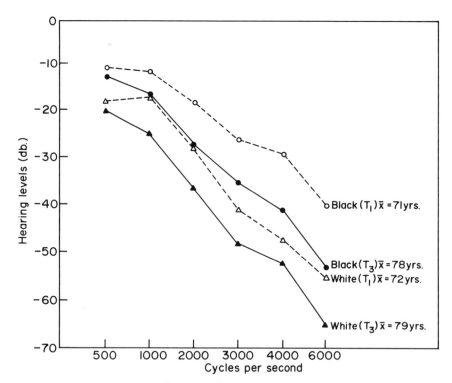

Figure 2–10. *The average hearing threshold levels for the total sample of white and black subjects at tests 1 and 3.*

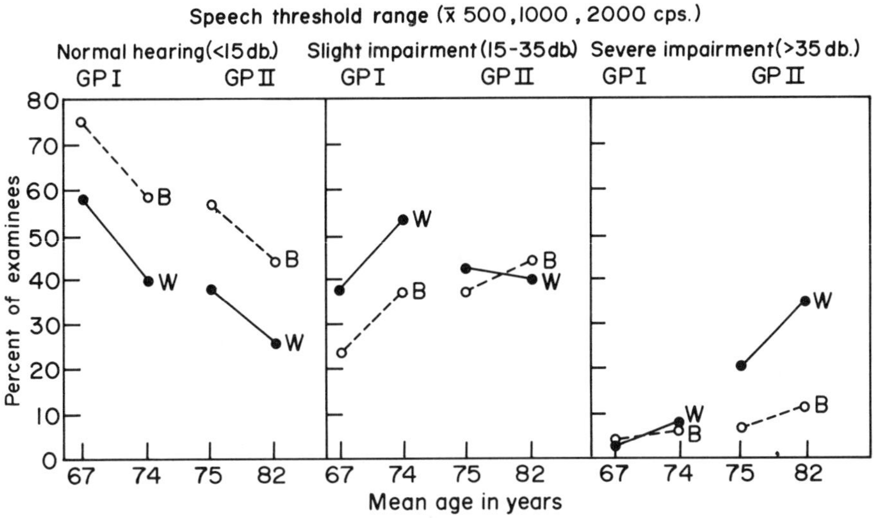

Speech threshold range (x̄ 500,1000, 2000 cps.)

Figure 2–11. *The percent of white (W) and black (B) subjects in age groups 1 and 2 who had "normal" hearing, slight, or severe hearing impairment in the "better" ear at the pure-tone estimated speech reception range at tests 1 and 3.*

at 4000 cps. It is important to note that black men within both the young and old age groups tended to have hearing levels similar to women of both races, with white men having the poorest hearing particularly at the higher frequencies.

Figure 2–11 shows the data on hearing deficits for the "better" ear in the pure-tone estimated speech reception range for blacks and whites. "Normal" hearing was significantly more prevalent among blacks than whites at both tests for both age groups. Slight impairments were more prevalent among whites at the younger age and severe impairments were more prevalent among whites at the older age than among blacks. At frequencies of 3000 cps. and higher, for the "better" ear hearing impairments were more prevalent among whites than blacks.

Further, at both evaluations, the blacks had better hearing for the actual speech material (i.e., spondee words) than did the whites.

Discussion

In contrast to most studies of hearing patterns which were based on cross-sectional samples, this report was a seven-year follow-up of changes in hearing levels among the same 92 individuals initially seen at ages 60 to 79 years.

As expected, hearing acuity diminishes with increasing age. It is of some interest to note that the increasing magnitude of the hearing loss across the seven-year period for our younger subjects, who advanced in average age from 67 to 74 years, was approximately the same as that for our older subjects aging from an average of 75 to 82 years. While previous findings (Pestalozza et al., 1955) suggested that hearing levels for easy speech material (i.e., spondee words) would be worse than expected from pure-tone audiograms among the aged, we found this to be true at the initial but not at the follow-up study. Further, while the estimated pure-tone hearing levels for speech (i.e., the average of 500, 1000, and 2000 cps.) became worse during the follow-up period, the hearing levels for the spondee words remained stable, suggesting that hearing levels for easy speech material may be influenced by practice effects since this test was given three times during the seven-year period.

Consistent with previous findings, we found women had better hearing than men at the higher frequencies. However, in contrast to the National Health Survey findings of 1960–62 (National Center for Health Statistics, 1965) we found sex differences in the estimated pure-tone hearing levels for speech for the "better" ear, with "normal" hearing more prevalent among men than women beginning at about age 74. During the follow-up period, women had a greater hearing loss than men only at 3000 cps. and in their pure-tone estimated hearing levels for speech.

Although the National Health Survey of 1960–1962 (National Center for Health Statistics, 1967) found that independent of age, blacks and particularly black men had better hearing than whites, when age was taken into account it appeared that past age 55 they found no racial differences at frequencies of 3000 cps. and higher for the "better" ear. In contrast, in this study we found at each evaluation that blacks and particularly black men had superior hearing to their white counterparts at the low as well as at the high frequencies with findings based on the average thresholds for both ears as well as for the "better" ear. Although these racial differences may be due to a variety of factors, we suspect that in large part it could be reflecting differences in the previous history of exposure to noise. The biases which may come from the rural history of many subjects in this sample and the limited number of aged black men should also be considered but the finding seems worthy of further exploration.

References

American Standards Association. *American standard specification for audiometers for general diagnostic purposes.* No. Z24.5–1951, New York: American Standards Association, 1951.

Busse, E. W. Physiological, psychological, and sociological study of aging. *J. Med. Educ.*, 40:832–839, 1965.

Committee on Conservation of Hearing. Guide for the evaluation of hearing impairment. *Tr. Am. Acad. Ophth.*, 63, 1959.

Committee on Medical Rating of Physical Impairment. Guides to the evaluation of permanent impairment—ear, nose, throat, and related structures. *J.A.M.A.*, 177: 489–501, 1961.

Corso, J. F., Age and sex differences in pure-tone thresholds. *Arch. Otolaryngol.*, 77:385–405, 1963.

Maddox, G. L., Selected methodological issues. *Proceedings of the Social Statistics of the American Statistical Association*, pp. 280–285, 1962.

National Center for Health Statistics. Hearing levels of adults by age and sex, United States, 1960–1962. *Vital and Health Statistics.* Public Health Service Publication No. 1000-Series 11-No. 11. Washington, D.C.: U.S. Government Printing Office, 1965.

National Center for Health Statistics. Hearing levels of adults by race, region, and area of residence, United States, 1960–1962. *Vital and Health Statistics.* Public Health Service Publication No. 1000-Series 11-No. 26. Washington D.C.: U.S. Government Printing Office, 1967.

Pestalozza, G., and Shore, I. Clinical evaluation of prebycusis on basis of different tests of auditory function. *Laryngoscope*, 65:1136–1163, 1955.

Special Committee on Aging. Hearing loss, hearing aids, and the elderly. *Hearing before the Subcommittee on Consumer Interests of the Elderly of the Special Committee on Aging, United States Senate, July, 1968*, Superintendent of Documents. Washington, D.C.: U.S. Government Printing Office, 1968.

Chapter 3. Health Care

This chapter deals with various aspects of health care which may affect health levels among the normal aged, which in turn may affect the process of aging itself. The first article reports that the advent of medicare had little effect on the overall rate of physicians' visits and hospitalization but did change the means of meeting medical expenses, especially among lower income groups.

The second article shows that the health practices of exercise, weight control, and avoiding cigarettes were followed by less illness and greater longevity. The third paper compares the panelists' own health assessment with that of physicians and reports a general congruence, although there are more who overestimate their health than there are who underestimate it. The next report finds that regardless of age and sex, there are significant relationships between obesity and various measures of cardiovascular disease risk.

The study of vitamin B_{12} levels among both normal aged and psychiatric patients found an increase with age. Furthermore, there appear to be substantial numbers of normal aged persons who have low levels of vitamin B_{12} without suffering any particular ill effects from it.

Finally, the study of anxiety was highest immediately before the examination and tended to subside during and after the examination. Women had higher initial anxiety, possibly because the physician was male.

Health Care Before and After Medicare *Erdman Palmore and Frances C. Jeffers*

The debate over Medicare (Health Insurance for the Aged) produced conflicting predictions about its effects. Opponents of the program warned that it would sharply increase medical care utilization and costs among the aged. Proponents of Medicare argued that it would increase over-all medical care among the aged by only small amounts but that it would ease the financial burden of health care for the aged, that it would improve the health care of low-income aged, and would improve the health of the aged in general (Fister, 1963; House Hearings, 1964, 1965; Mishell, 1962; *US News*, 1964).

It is already clear that the federal costs of Medicare are about double the estimated costs made in 1965 when Medicare was enacted. The federal costs

Reprinted by permission from *Journal of Gerontology*, 26:4:532–536, 1971.

of the Hospital Insurance Plan (Part A) have jumped from an original projection of $3.1 billion to a current estimate of $5.8 billion. The federal costs of the Medical Insurance Plan (Part B) will have increased from $623 million in fiscal year 1967 to an estimated $1,245 million in fiscal year 1971 (U.S. Senate Committee on Finance, 1970).

Similarly, total expenditures for personal health care among those 65 and over almost doubled from $7.8 billion in 1966 to $13.5 billion in 1969 (Cooper, 1970). However, most of this increased cost is not due to increased utilization. About half of the increased cost was caused by increased prices and about 10 percent was caused by the increased number of persons 65 and over. When both increased prices and increased population were controlled for, there remained a 36 percent increase in medical expenditures between 1966 and 1969, most of which presumably is attributable to increased utilization and higher levels of care (Cooper, 1970).

However, at the time of this writing, complete and comprehensive national data on the impact on utilization of Medicare are not yet available. The Social Security Administration plans to release such data based on two studies: the 1968 Survey of the Aged, which can be compared with the 1963 Survey of the Aged, and a study by the School of Public Health and Administrative Medicine of Columbia University.

In the meantime, the available scattered and somewhat conflicting evidence indicates that there have been either no increases or moderate increases in physician visits for the aged since Medicare, but that there were increases of between 11 percent to 20 percent in hospitalization. For example, the data from the Health Interview Survey indicated that there was a slight decrease in the average number of physician visits among persons 65 or over during the year after Medicare began (July 1966–June 1967) compared to earlier years (Ahmed, 1968). By contrast, the National Disease and Therapeutic Index estimates that visits by aged patients to physicians in the year ending June 30, 1968, were up by about 12 percent compared to the year before Medicare (Lea Associates, 1968).

As for hospital utilization, the Health Interview Survey shows an 11 percent increase during the year after Medicare in discharges from short-stay hospitals and a 20 percent increase in days of hospital care (Ahmed, 1968). This is supported by a study of 300 short-term general hospitals, which found an increase of 17 percent in admissions of the aged in 1967 compared to 1965 (Commission on Professional and Hospital Activities, 1968). Similarly, a continuing survey of 656 short-term general and special hospitals shows a 13 percent increase in admissions for those 65 or over in July 1968–June 1969 compared to admissions 2 years earlier (Hospital Indicators, 1968).

There are several difficulties with such statistics. Cross-sectional sample surveys do not include the same persons at two points in time. Thus, differences between surveys before and after Medicare may be partly due to chance variations in the samples surveyed (sampling error) and partly due to changes in the composition of the target population (some of the persons in the earlier population have died and new persons who have turned 65 have been added). Second, the statistics available so far do not allow examination of changes within subgroups, such as differences between the lower and higher socioeconomic groups. It might be expected, for example, that Medicare had a greater impact on the lower socioeconomic groups who could not otherwise have afforded as much medical care.

This paper reports changes in medical care in a small but intensive longitudinal study which allows comparisons of medical care before and after Medicare among the same individuals and permits examination of the medical care changes separately for manual and nonmanual occupational groups.

Methods

Subjects

The data for this report are derived from a longitudinal, interdisciplinary study of aging which began in 1954 with 271 community volunteers aged 60 and over at that time (Palmore, 1970). The 81 participants included in this report were those who had survived and who returned for the second series of examinations in 1959–1961 and who subsequently had survived to return for the fifth series of examinations in 1968. Thus, we have comparable data on the same individuals over the 8-year span before and after the advent of Medicare in July 1966. All the participants were over age 65 by 1966 and thus were included in the Hospital Insurance Plan of Medicare (Part A) and most were included also in the Medicare Insurance Plan (Part B).

By 1966 these subjects ranged in age from 69 to 89, with a mean age of 77. Thirty-eight of the participants were men and 43 were women. All were ambulatory, noninstitutionalized residents of the central North Carolina area. The initial panel did not constitute a random sample, but did approximate the sex, racial, and occupational distribution of this geographic area. However, analysis of selection and attrition factors indicates that the panelists who survived were actually a social, psychological, and physical elite among the aged (Maddox, 1962). Thus they may represent mainly the above-average aged in the area. However, since longitudinal analysis uses each person as his own control and examines changes in the same persons over time rather than using different samples at different times, the degree to which the sample represents the universe at each point in time is less critical than in cross-sectional studies. That is, the observed differences in health care before and after Medicare in this study cannot be due to chance variation in the samples surveyed, as may be the case in two different cross-section surveys.

Nevertheless, it should be recognized that since these 81 survivors are an above average group compared to the total aged population, these findings may not be representative of the total aged group. Nonsurvivors and other below average aged may well have used more medical care. On the other hand, they probably used more medical care before and after the advent of Medicare. We do not know whether their increase in medical care was greater than among the survivors. There are theoretical grounds for guessing either way. Perhaps the forthcoming Social Security data can answer this question. In the meantime, caution should be used in generalizing our findings.

Variables

There are basically five indicators of health and medical care changes used in this study. The first is a Physical Functioning Rating (PFR) given by the examining physician on the basis of the medical history, the physical and neurological examination, audiogram, chest X-ray, electroencephalogram, electrocardiogram, and laboratory studies of the blood and urine. The scores used in this analysis range from 0 for no pathology to 5 for total disability. The cutting point used for the percentage with moderate to severe disability was a rating of 3 or greater, which indicates a limitation in physical functioning of 21 percent or greater.

The number of physician's visits in the past 2 years was determined by responses to the question, "In the past 2 years have you seen a doctor? No, once, 2 to 5 times, 6 to 10 times, 10 to 20 times, more than 20 times?" This question was interpreted to include any contacts with physicians, either private, family, or company doctor, in the home, office, or clinic. The mean number of physician's visits was computed by assigning scores equal to the midpoint of the intervals and averaging these midpoints (eight persons were not included in the tabulations of number of physician's visits because of lack of information on this item in one or the other of the two studies).

The percentage hospitalized in the 12 months prior to examination was obtained from the medical history taken by the physician (six persons were not included in these tabulations because of incomplete information in one of the two studies).

The means of paying for medical expenses was taken from responses to the question, "How did you meet the expenses of your illnesses in the past 2 years?" Persons with no medical expenses during the past 2 years were omitted from these tabulations. Those paying for medical expenses with their own resources only were those who met these costs from their income or savings without assistance from health insurance, public assistance, other agencies, from relatives, friends, or by borrowing money. Those who paid by means of health insurance were those who paid part or all of their medical expenses through Medicare, commercial health insurance plans, or through company health insurance plans.

The manual-nonmanual dichotomy was an attempt to distinguish between those persons in the lower socioeconomic groups (manual) and those in the upper socioeconomic groups (nonmanual), based on the principal lifetime occupation of the head of the household. The manual group included skilled craftsmen, foremen, operatives, service workers, unskilled workers, and farm laborers. The nonmanual group included professionals, managers and proprietors, farmers who classify as proprietors or managers (owning or managing 100 or more acres), clerical or sales workers, and technicians.

Tests of significance

Even though the sample was not a random one, standard tests of statistical significance were applied to gain some information on the probability that the differences noted might be statistically significant. The tests used were non-parametric in order to avoid assumptions about the distribution of these characteristics in the larger universe of aged persons. The tests for significance of the differences between mean PFR and the differences between mean number of physician's visits was the standard t test for repeated observations on the same sample. The test for significance of changes in the percentage with PFR of moderate to severe disability, the percentage with 6+ visits to physicians, and the percentage hospitalized in the last year was the McNemar test for significance of changes based on the χ^2 test, with correction for continuity. The test for significance of changes in means of paying for medical expenses was simply the χ^2 test for independent samples. It was necessary to use this test rather than the McNemar test because the two bases for the percentage paying for medical care shifted, depending on whether the persons had illness or not during the past 2 years. This is a somewhat more conservative test than the McNemar test because it increases the variance involved. Thus any statistical significance found using this test would be greater if the bases for the two studies had been exactly the same persons at the two points in time.

Observations and Discussion

There were no significant changes in the subjects' Physical Functioning Rating in either the total group (Table 3–1) or in the manual and nonmanual breakdown (Table 3–2). There was a slight decrease in the proportion rated as having moderate to severe disability, reflected in the slight decrease in the mean PFR. This finding is contrary to the widely accepted belief that as older persons age, they usually decline in health and functioning ability. Previously reported research has indicated that there is often little or no decline in functioning ability over periods of several years in such longitudinal studies of normal aging (Palmore, 1970). It should be remembered that the sample in this longitudinal study was an above-average group of volunteers who survived and were healthy enough to return 8 years later for a 2-day long series of examinations. It seems unlikely that the small improvement in PFR could

Table 3-1. *Health and medical care, 1959–1961 compared to 1968 (N = 81).*

Variable (percentage)	1959–1961	1968
1a. % with PFR of moderate to severe disability	16%	13%
b. Mean PFR	1.6	1.5
2a. % with 6+ visits to physicians in 2 years	36%	41%
b. Mean # of physician visits in 2 years	7.7	6.2
3. % hospitalized in past year	17%	17%
4a. % of those with medical expenses who paid using own resources only	44%	20%*
b. % of those with medical expenses who paid using health insurance	51%	80%**

* Probability of this difference occurring by chance <0.05.
** Probability of this difference occurring by chance <0.01.

be attributed to the advent of Medicare, because the increase noted in physician visits and hospitalizations after Medicare appear to be minimal. Since the difference in PFR was not statistically significant, it was most likely due to chance fluctuations in the ratings assigned. It may be noted that the non-manual group had less disability than the manual group (Table 3–2), which is consistent with the general finding that the lower socioeconomic groups have poorer health and more disability than do the upper socioeconomic groups.

The proportions visiting physicians six or more times in the past 2 years shows an increase of 5 percentage points, although the mean number of physician visits shows a slight decrease (Table 3–1). This indicates that while there was some increase in those who visited physicians relatively often, the total number of visits had slightly decreased. Actually, neither of these changes is statistically significant; they are so small that they are most probably due to chance fluctuation.

Table 3-2. *Health and medical care, 1959–1961 compared to 1968 by manual and nonmanual groups.*

Variable	Manual (N = 28)		Nonmanual (N = 53)	
	1959–1961	1968	1959–1961	1968
1a. % with PFR of moderate to severe disability	28%	25%	9%	6%
b. Mean PFR	1.9	1.8	1.4	1.3
2a. % with 6± visits to physician in 2 years	28%	40%	40%	42%
b. Mean # of physician visits in 2 years	6.7	5.7	8.2	6.5
3. % hospitalized in past year	11%	14%	21%	19%
4a. % of those with medical expenses who paid using own resources only	46%	18%	44%	22%
b. % of those with medical expenses who paid using health insurance	46%	82%*	54%	78%

* Probability of this difference occurring by chance <0.05.

The percentage who were hospitalized in the 12 mo. prior to examination remained constant at 17 percent in each study for the total panel. However, in comparing the manual with the nonmanual group, it is clear that the manual had larger increases both in the proportion hospitalized and in the proportion visiting physicians frequently (Table 3–2). The proportion of the manual group seeing physicians frequently increased by almost a half (28 percent to 40 percent), while the proportion for the nonmanual group remained almost the same (40 percent compared to 42 percent). Similarly, the percentage hospitalized among the manual group increased from 11 percent to 14 percent, while the proportion hospitalized among the nonmanual showed a slight decrease. This supports the earlier expectation that Medicare would have more of an impact on the lower socioeconomic groups who had not been able to afford as much medical care prior to Medicare.

The largest change in the medical care pattern was shown in the means by which medical expenses were met. The overall proportion who paid for their medical expenses entirely from their own resources dropped from 44 percent to 20 percent, while the proportion who met part of their medical expenses through health insurance increased from 51 percent to 80 percent. Both of these differences are statistically and substantively significant. Again, as was expected, the manual group showed greater changes in these proportions, indicating that Medicare had a greater effect on the lower income group in relieving their financial burdens for medical care.

Summary

The predictions of the proponents of Medicare are generally supported by the findings of this longitudinal panel, which indicate little or no over-all increase in physicians' visits and hospitalization, but they do show a marked change in the means of meeting medical expenses. As expected, the lower income group appears to have benefited by Medicare more than the upper group. However, caution should be used in attempts to generalize from these findings to the total aged population.

References

Ahmed, P. Current estimates from the Health Interview Survey—U.S., July, 1966-June, 1967. *Vital & health statistics*, ser. 10, No. 43. Washington, D.C.: National Center for Health Statistics, 1968.

Commission on Professional and Hospital Activities. Patients 65 years or older: Days of care. *PAS Reporter*, 6:1–4, 1968.

Cooper, B. S. Medical care outlays for aged and non-aged persons, 1966–1969. *Social Security Bulletin*, July, 1970, 3–12.

Editors. Is socialized medicine on the way for U.S.? *U.S. News*, 57:40–44, 1964.

Fister, G. M. Speaking out against federalized medicine. *Saturday Evening Post,* 236:8ff, 1963.

Hospital Indicators. *Hospitals* (Mid-month issues), 1968.

House of Representative Hearings. *Medical care for the aged.* Washington, D.C.: U.S. Government Printing Office, 1964–1965.

Lea Associates, Inc. The impact of Medicare on current private medical practice. *National disease & therapeutic index.* Amber, Penn: The Associates, 1968.

Maddox, G. L. A longitudinal, multidisciplinary study of human aging. *Proceedings of the Social Statistics Section.* Washington, D.C.: American Statistical Association, 1962. Reprinted in E. Palmore (Ed.), *Normal aging.* Durham, N.C.: Duke University Press, 1970.

Mishell, R., Herzenberg, L.A., and Strauss, D. B. Medicare: Second round. *Nation,* 194:132–137, 1962.

Palmore, E. *Normal aging.* Durham, N.C.: Duke University Press, 1970.

U.S. Senate Committee on Finance. *Medicare and Medicaid.* Washington, D.C.: U.S. Government Printing Office, 1970.

Health Practices and Illness   *Erdman Palmore*

There is widespread agreement that inactivity, obesity, and cigarette smoking are usually associated with a higher incidence of various illnesses and higher mortality rates (Mayer, 1968; Metropolitan Life Insurance Co., 1960; Morris and Crawford, 1958; Society of Actuaries, 1959; U.S. Public Health Service, 1967). There is corresponding evidence that the health care practices of exercise, weight control, and avoiding cigarettes contribute to the lower incidence of several illnesses and to a lower mortality rate. Recently the question has been raised as to whether these health practices are associated with such lower rates of illness among the aged as to justify lower health insurance premiums for persons who exercise, have moderate weights, and avoid smoking. This paper presents the evidence from the Duke Longitudinal Study of Aging for the existence of such an association between health practices and lower rates of illness and mortality.

Methods

The data come from an ongoing longitudinal interdisciplinary study of 268 community volunteers, aged 60–94 at initial examination during 1955–1959 (Palmore, 1970). . . .

The health practices of exercise, keeping a moderate weight, and avoiding smoking, were recorded at the initial interview while the measures of illness are derived from interviews and examinations conducted three or four

Reprinted by permission from *The Gerontologist,* 10:4:313–316, 1970.

years later, except for the information on operations which was collected about ten years later. Since the health practices preceded the illnesses, there are better grounds for inferring a causal relationship than in cross-sectional studies when data on health practices and illness refer to the same point in time.

The measure of exercise was the number of locomotor activities recorded in response to the question "What do you do in your free time?" Locomotor activities were defined as involving physical mobility either in its performance or in getting to the place to do it. This was in contrast to sedentary activities such as listening to the radio or TV, writing letters, playing cards, reading, etc. This is not an ideal measure of the amount of exercise engaged in, because it does not indicate either the strenuousness of the exercise nor the amount of time spent in such exercise. It also does not ask about locomotor activities at work. However, this is the best measure available from the initial interviews. It is probably a safe assumption that most of those reporting more locomotor activities tend to get more exercise than those reporting less locomotor activities.

The measure of overweight and underweight was the ratio of weight to the square of height in inches. Careful statistical analysis of various indices of overweight show that this index is more closely related to the amount of excess fat than is the simple ratio of weight to height (Khosla and Lowe, 1967).

The indicator of tobacco use is a composite classification based on responses to two questions: "How often do you use tobacco?" and "In what form do you use tobacco?" The responses to the first question were coded into five categories: Never used; Not used in last year; Slight present use (cigarettes 1–4 a day, cigar and/or pipe 1–2 a day, occasional snuff or tobacco chewing); Moderate present use (cigarettes 5–10 a day, cigar and/or pipe 3–4 a day, frequent snuff or chewing tobacco); and Heavy present use (cigarettes 11 or more a day, cigar and/or pipe 5 or more a day, constant use of snuff or chewing tobacco). The responses to the second question were coded in five categories: Never used, Cigarettes, Cigar, Pipe, Snuff or chewing tobacco. Various ways of classifying subjects according to their responses to these questions were tried and the following three-way classification was found to give the clearest results: persons not using tobacco or using only slight amounts; persons using noncigarette tobacco in moderate or heavy amounts; and persons smoking cigarettes in moderate or heavy amounts. It was found that relatively few women (about 25 percent) used tobacco in moderate or heavy amounts and this use showed little relationship to illness. Therefore, the data on tobacco in this paper is for men only.

There were several measures of illness recorded in the second wave of examinations. The number of days during a year spent in bed was based on the subjects' response to the question "How many days did you spend in bed last year because of not feeling well?" The number of operations since the initial interview was also based on subjects' reports and physicians' examinations. There were so few operations reported in the first 3- or 4-year interval that we cumulated the operations reported over the approximately 10-year span between initial interview and fourth wave of the study. Sample attrition between the second and fourth waves reduced the numbers in the base by 46 percent for these tabulations. The hospitalization measure is also based on the physician interview with the subject in which he recorded all hospitalizations and operations since the initial examination. The number of physicians' visits per year is based on the subjects' response to the question "In the past two years have you seen a doctor? Once, 1–5 times, 6–10 times, 10–20 times, more than 20 times."

The longevity quotient is the observed number of years the subject lived after initial examination (or the estimated number of years for those still living) divided by the actuarily expected number of years remaining after examination based on the age, sex, and race of the subject (Palmore, 1969). Thus, an LQ of less than 1.0 would mean that a person lived less years than expected. The LQ has advantages of controlling precisely for the effects of age at initial examination and of providing a continuous variable indicator of longevity.

We also used two subjective indicators of illness based on responses to the question "Would you say your health has changed since you were here last time?" (the proportion saying their health had become worse was used in this analysis) and the question "How would you rate your health at the present time?" (the proportion saying very poor or poor was used in this analysis). It can be argued that these subjective self-evaluations of health may be even more closely related to actual functioning and use of medical care than the more objective physicians' ratings.

Observations

Of the three health practices examined, the amount of exercise was most closely related to more of the illness indicators than the other two health practices (Table 3–3). The proportion with two or more weeks in bed per

Table 3–3. *Locomotor activities are followed by less illness.*

Illness indicator (%)	Locomotor activities:			Kendall Tau C	*p*
	0–5	6–7	8 or More		
in bed 2+ weeks per year	26	11	10	.13	$p < 0.01$
with 3+ Dr's visits per year	44	31	33	.09	$p < 0.05$
hospitalized	32	31	24	.07	NS
with 1+ operations	30	20	19	.09	NS
rating health as worse	38	39	21	.16	$p < 0.01$
rating health as poor	18	6	4	.11	$p < 0.05$
with LQ of less than 1.00	54	28	33	.17	$p < 0.01$
Numbers in base	50	64	67		

year was two-and-a-half times greater among those with few locomotor activities than the others. The proportion with three or more physicians' visits per year was about one-and-a-half times as great among those with few locomotor activities as the others. The percentage hospitalized and the percentage with operations were substantially greater among those with a few locomotor activities, although these two relationships were not statistically significant at the .05 level. The proportions rating their health as becoming worse since the last examination was about half as large among those with the most locomotor activities as the others and the proportion rating their health as poor was more than four times as large among those with few locomotor activities as among those with many activities. Over half of those with few locomotor activities died sooner than actuarily expected compared to between a fourth and a third of those with more locomotor activities. Thus, even though some of the relationships were not statistically significant and

Table 3–4. *Overweight and underweight are followed by more illness.*

Illness indicator (%)	Weight/height^2			Kendall Tau C	p
	.031–.045	<.031	.046+		
in bed 2+ weeks per year	12	21	33	.09	$p < 0.05$
hospitalized	26	36	40	.07	NS
rating health as worse	32	21	53	.04	NS
rating health as poor	7	21	20	.08	NS
with LQ of less than 1.00	36	44	42	.05	NS
Numbers in base	145	14	15		

several of the relationships are not monotonic, regardless of which indicator is used, those who reported more locomotor activities at the initial interview had substantially less illness and lived longer than those with less locomotor activities.

Those overweight or underweight had more illness according to most of the indicators (Table 3–4). We found these relationships to be clearest when we used cutting points which separated out the tenth with the lowest weight/height^2 ratio (.030 or less), and the tenth with the highest weight/height^2 ratio (.046 or more). Using these cutting points, the underweight compared to the normal weight had almost twice as large a proportion who spent two or more weeks per year in bed and the overweight had almost three times as high a proportion compared to the normal. Similarly, the underweight had 10 percent more who had been hospitalized and the overweight had 14 percent more hospitalized compared to the normal. The underweight did not have a larger proportion rating their health as worse but the overweight had 21 percent more rating their health as worse. Both the underweight and the overweight had three times as large percentages rating their health as poor.

Table 3–5. *Cigarette smoking is followed by more illness among men.*

Illness indicator (%)	None or slight	Mod. or heavy non-cigarette	Mod. or heavy cigarette	Kendall Tau C	p
with 1+ operations	26	25	33	.04	NS
with 3+ Dr's visits per year	33	24	38	.01	NS
rating health as worse	23	29	29	.06	NS
with LQ of less than 1.00	39	38	67	.19	p < 0.01
Numbers in base (men)	48	21	21		

They also had substantially larger percentages who died earlier than actuarily expected. The other indicators of illness did not seem to be related to weight.

Cigarette smoking had relationships with fewer of the illness indicators than the other two health practices (Table 3–5). Only the proportion dying sooner than expected had a statistically significant relationship to cigarette smoking. Two-thirds of those who were moderate or heavy cigarette smokers died sooner than expected, compared to less than 40 percent of the others. The moderate or heavy cigarette smokers also had somewhat more with operations and more with three or more physicians' visits per year than the others. Those with no use or slight use of tobacco had somewhat less rating their health as having become worse compared to the moderate or heavy tobacco users. The other indicators of illness did not seem to be related to tobacco use.

When we combine the health practices, we see that there tends to be an additive effect on health (Table 3–6). Persons having all three health practices had about a third the percentage spending two or more weeks in bed per year compared to those with one or none of the health practices (there was only one person with none of the health practices). Similarly, those with all three health practices had substantially lower percentages seeing physicians frequently, hospitalized, having operations, rating their health as becoming worse, rating their health as poor, and living less years than actuarially ex-

Table 3–6. *More health practices are followed by less illness.*

Illness indicator (%)	Number of health practices			Kendall Tau C	p
	0–1	2	3		
in bed 2+ weeks per year	30	18	11	.12	p < 0.05
with 3+ Dr's visits per year	50	30	36	.02	NS
hospitalized	40	32	25	.10	p < 0.05
with 1+ operations	25	29	17	.10	NS
rating health as worse	45	32	33	.04	NS
rating health as poor	20	12	5	.10	p < 0.05
with LQ less than 1.00	59	42	29	.22	p < 0.01
Numbers in base	20	57	91		

pected. Four out of these seven relationships were statistically significant at the .05 level or below.

Discussion

Despite the small or moderate levels of these associations and the lack of statistical significance for about half the indicators, the consistent relationship of health practices to less illness which was found with most of the indicators supports the conclusion that health practices did contribute to better health among this group of elderly persons. The fact that these health practices were usually most strongly related to longer life indicates that they have a long-term effect on health that is greater than the short run effect on any of the illness indicators. We believe that the lack of statistical significance shown by several of the associations is due to the small numbers in some of the base groups and the gross nature of some of the measures.

When an association is found in a cross-sectional, one point in time study, there is the chicken-and-egg problem of which came first and which caused the other. In the present study this is less of a problem because it was longitudinal and the health practices were measured at the beginning of the study while the illness and mortality indicators were measured later. This does not eliminate the possibility that greater illness occurred both before and after the beginning of the study among those without the health practices and that these illnesses contributed to less locomotor activities, less weight control, and more cigarette smoking. There is also the possibility that both health practices and health are caused by some third set of uncontrolled variables such as greater education, higher intelligence, healthier environments, etc. It is difficult, if not impossible, to assess the importance of these possibilities without tightly controlled experiments. And of course, tightly controlled experiments in this area are very difficult and expensive. Lacking such experiments one has to rely on findings from other studies and generally accepted theories to interpret the meaning of these findings. We conclude that most other studies and theories of the relation of health practices to health support our interpretation that exercise, weight control, and avoiding cigarettes contribute to better health.

It would be interesting to know which of these practices had the strongest effect on health. Unfortunately, the complex multivariate analysis necessary to satisfactorily answer this question does not appear feasible due to the size of the sample and nature of the indicators used. However, the cross-tabulations do suggest that exercise may have the strongest effect, because it usually shows the highest level of association and statistical significance. Also it is important to note that regardless of relative importance, all three health practices tend to have an additive effect: each additional health practice tends to reduce the proportions with illness and early death.

References

Khosla, T., and Lowe, S. Indices of obesity derived from body weight and height. *British Journal of Preventive & Social Medicine*, 21:122–128, 1967.

Mayer, J. *Overweight: Causes, cost, and control.* Englewood Cliffs, N.J.: Prentice-Hall, 1968.

Metropolitan Life Insurance Co. *Overweight: Its prevention and significance.* 1960.

Morris, J., & Crawford, M. Coronary heart disease and physical activity of work. *British Medical Journal*, 1958, 2:1485.

Palmore, E. Predicting longevity. *Gerontologist*, 1969, 9:247–250.

Palmore, E. (Ed.). *Normal aging.* Durham, N.C.: Duke University Press, 1970.

Society of Actuaries: *Build and blood pressure study*, 1959.

U.S. Public Health Service. *The health consequences of smoking.* A Public Health Service Review, Public Health Publication No. 1696. Washington, D.C.: U.S. Government Printing Office, 1967.

Self-assessment of Health   *George L. Maddox and Elizabeth B. Douglass*

Health is a basic variable in the study of aging as a biosocial process. Informed research investigators thus uniformly make an effort to measure health in studies of human development or apologize for failing to do so. When research samples are small and in a laboratory setting, clinical assessments or reliance on medical records of subjects is at least feasible. Surveys of large populations outside laboratories, however, present a different problem. Objective assessment of health status is usually not possible and in such instances the substitution of self-reports of health for clinical assessment is considered. The legitimacy of this substitution has been the subject of extensive research in recent years.

A definitive review of the literature on the interchangeability of subjective and medical assessments of health by Paul Haberman (1969) argues conclusively against the use of self-reports of health in epidemiologic research. Respondents are demonstrably unreliable reporters of particular morbid conditions of interest to epidemiologists interested in determining prevalence rates. Furthermore, respondents are only modestly reliable reporters of their utilization of such health resources as physicians, clinics, and hospitals unless this use is recent or associated with a traumatic event.

This research is supported in part by grants M-668 and M-164 from the National Institute of Child Health and Human Development to the Duke Center for the Study of Aging and Human Development.
Reprinted by permission from the *Journal of Health and Social Behavior*, 14:87–93, 1973.

Although Haberman's conclusion is a proper warning to epidemiologists, there are several reasons to believe that self-assessment of health is an important, useful variable in research on human development, particularly in the later years of life. Illness is a social as well as physical phenomenon and the existence of a morbid condition does not predetermine a single pattern of response on the part of an individual. There is considerable variability, for instance, in the probability that a given morbid condition will result in the assumption of the sick role and the utilization of medical resources. The discrepancy between treated disease and the prevalence of disease is well known and consistently demonstrated even among well-educated populations with accessible, adequate health resources. Moreover, the demonstrated discrepancy in reporting specific diagnoses by physicians and laymen does not require one to conclude that gross judgments about health status by physicians and laymen are typically incongruous. Evidence suggests quite the contrary. In common sense terms good health generally implies the absence of debilitating illness which significantly interferes with personal and social functioning, not necessarily the absence of morbid conditions. This observation leads to a different formulation of the question discussed by Haberman. What is the probability of agreement between physicians and laymen regarding *general* health status? When an individual rates his health status as excellent or good (that is, essentially free from significant physical and social disability), what is the probability of concurrence by a physician? Similarly, what is the probability of concurrence when the physician's or layman's assessment of health status is that health is fair or poor?

We know that discrepancies in gross assessment of physicians and laymen exist. Discussions in the literature on denial of illness and on hypochondriasis are common. But no research investigator has ever suggested that inappropriate self-assessments of health status are the rule. On the contrary, the appropriate acceptance or rejection of the sick role, with its implied relief from social obligations, is a matter of considerable concern in all societies. Social surveillance response to illness is commonly observed, and, as a rule, one would be inclined to expect that individuals are more likely to be trained to deny illness than to exaggerate illness inappropriately. This issue is of special importance in this study of social aspects of human aging. For example, some investigators have speculated that older persons have a special temptation to assume the sick role inappropriately in the interest of evoking helping responses from others. Such speculation has persisted in the absence of adequate evidence.

There is at least one other reason for the continuing interest in self-assessment of health. The subjective belief that one is healthy or ill may be more important than actual medical status in predicting an individual's general emotional state and behavior. This paper presents some unique longitudinal data on self-assessment of health in the later years of life.

Development of Hypotheses

The most prevalent hypotheses about the correlates of self-estimates of health have been succinctly summarized by Friedsam and Martin (1963). They report that (1) self-health ratings are positively related to physicians' health ratings; (2) self-health ratings are more closely related to the attitudes of individuals than are physicians' ratings; (3) the health ratings by physicians are more closely related to the behavior of individuals than are self-health ratings; and (4) self-health ratings tend to overestimate the favorableness of individuals' health condition as indexed by physicians' ratings. Previous cross-sectional research, including that of the senior author of this paper (Maddox, 1969), has consistently supported the first and fourth of these hypotheses. This paper provides additional tests of these two hypotheses with longitudinal data. These data permit an assessment of (1) the relationship between the self- and physicians' health ratings; (2) the persistence of these over time; and (3) when ratings are incongruous, the probability of over and underestimations of health status in self ratings. In this brief paper we are only incidentally interested in the use of self and physicians' ratings to predict health related attitudes and behavior.

Our interest lies specifically in testing the following hypotheses:

1. A positive relationship persists over time between self and physicians' ratings of health.

2. When there is incongruence between self and physician ratings of health, the incongruence tends toward individual overestimating of health. A corollary of this hypothesis is suggested:

2.1 Changes from a congruent to an incongruent state tend toward over estimation (or positive) rather than underestimation (or negative) self-assessment of health.

Methodology

Subjects

Fifteen years after 271 noninstitutionalized persons 60 years of age and over were first studied in a comprehensive multidisciplinary longitudinal study of human aging, 83 panelists were available for a sixth series of observations. . . . We do not, however, consider sampling to be a critical issue in this paper since we are concerned about the relationship between two variables explored with appropriate controls; we are not interested in the distribution of congruent and incongruent health ratings among aging populations. Furthermore, we do not consider the selective dropout of subjects which produced the 83 subjects under investigation to be a crucial issue. Comparison of the surviving 83 panelists with all other panelists initially and at the third observation (seventh year) suggests minimal differences in demographic characteristics and in the probability of displaying congruent or incongruent health ratings. The nonsurvivors were more likely than survivors to have negative self- and physician ratings, even though the probability of congruence was similar among survivors and nonsurvivors. In longitudinal research, surviving panelists necessarily represent a physiological, psychological, and social elite. Most precisely, then, we are considering in this paper the dynamics of health ratings in an advantaged older population.

Measurement

Self-rating of health at each of 6 observations over a period of 15 years is based on responses to the question "How do you rate your health at the present time?" The basic response categories were excellent, good, fair, and poor. A subject could in fact qualify his response by selecting "excellent *for my age*," "good *for my age*," and so on. These modifications are infrequently chosen and analysis has not indicated that they contribute to our understanding of the self-rating process. A response of *excellent* (and excellent *for my age*) or *good* indicates for our purposes *subjectively good health.*

Objective health status was measured on a six-point scale of physical functioning following an extensive medical and psychiatric evaluation by a project physician. A panelist was considered in "objectively good health" if he had no symptoms of disease or, if symptoms were present, he experienced no more than minor impairment of normal daily living.

It is important to note that panelists were exposed repeatedly to information about their objective health status. Following each observation a letter summarizing the panelist's health status was written by the project physician to the personal physician designated by the panelist. Thus any incongruous subjective rating of health cannot readily be attributed to a panelist's ignorance about his objective health status.

Analysis

Contingency analysis provides a straightforward partial test of the basic hypotheses of the study. Additional insights into the dynamics of self and physicians' ratings of health are provided by lagged correlational analysis, the reconstruction of patterns of congruence or incongruence for individuals over time, analysis of variance tests on group means, and an intensive analysis of cases of extreme incongruence. Throughout the analysis of data, controls were introduced for sex and race. Except where specifically noted, these two variables had no significant effect on the relationship of the two principal variables —self and physicians' health rating.

Findings

The first hypothesis predicts that the congruence in self- and physicians' ratings of health would be the dominant pattern observed among panelists over time. In each of the six observations spanning 15 years, two of three panelists display congruous rating (Table 3–7). More than half (58 percent) of the panelists had congruent health ratings in at least four of the six observations.

Since the assignment of panelists as congruous or incongruous could be an artifact of a relatively crude measurement device, we investigated cases of extreme deviance; that is, a "no impairment" objective rating with a "poor"

Table 3–7. *Patterns of self (SR) and physicians' (PR) ratings of health over a 15-year period in a panel of elderly persons ($N = 83$).*

Observation	Congruous rating (%)		Incongruous rating (%)		
	Positive PR Positive SR	Negative PR Negative SR	Positive PR Negative SR	Negative PR Positive SR	
1	45	21	13	21	100
2	43	29	6	21	100
3	42	25	9	23	100
Average 1–3	43	25	9	22	
		68		31	
4	22	37	13	28	100
5	39	22	14	25	100
6	29	29	17	25	100
Average 4–6	30	29	15	26	
		59		41	
Average 1–6	37	27	12	24	100
		64		36	

subjective rating or a "significantly impaired" objective rating with a self-rating of "excellent health." Only 5 percent of the observations were found to be extremely deviant in this sense and only 24 percent of the panelists were observed in the category of extreme deviance in any of the 6 observations.

Self- and physician ratings of health are predominantly congruous. Among panelists with a positive self-health rating, on the average six out of ten also had a favorable report from the project physician. Among panelists with a negative self-assessment seven out of ten had an unfavorable report from the physician. Conversely, for those with a positive physician's rating, more than seven out of ten panelists presented a positive self-rating; more than half (53 percent) of the panelists rated by the physician to be in poor health rated their health to be poor.

At any observation, then, this panel of older persons tended to present congruous responses and the first hypothesis is supported. This conclusion, however, masks a considerable amount of shifting of individual panelists between categories in the six observations. Attention will be given to these changes subsequently.

Over a 15-year period some deterioration of physical health would be expected among this aged population. Comparing only observations one and six one finds that physicians' ratings did decline for 30 percent of the panelists while for half the panelists (52 percent) physicians' ratings remained constant; the remaining 18 percent experienced an improvement in objective health status. Comparing again only observations one and six one finds that self health ratings were more stable than physicians' ratings. Sixty-six percent of the self health assessments were stable; 23 percent declined; 11 percent improved.

When viewed separately, physician and self ratings over the six observations were each consistent from one round to the next about seven out of ten times on the average. Through the six observations, on the average, 44 percent of the panelists showed the same pattern of physician and self-ratings from one observation to the next.

Additional insight into the dynamic relationship between self and physicians' ratings of health is provided by a lagged correlational analysis (Rozelle and Campbell, 1969) over the six observations (Figure 3–1). The data previously presented would lead one to anticipate positive but only moderate correlations between the two ratings at any observation and between the same type of rating between observations. Self-ratings are not simply a function of objective health as indicated by physicians' ratings, although a positive relationship does appear at each observation as expected. Similarly, one would expect, as observed, a persistence of each rating between observations. The cross-lagged correlations nevertheless present an interesting pat-

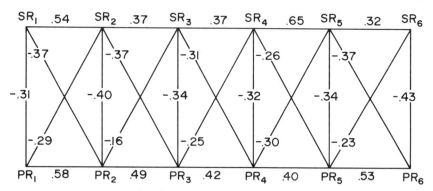

Figure 3–1. *Cross-lagged and other correlations between self (SR) and physicians' (PR) ratings of health in a panel of elderly persons (N = 83). All negative correlations in this figure are an artifact of scoring procedures. Hence, the substantive relationships among all the variables are positive.*

tern, a pattern which remains substantially unchanged when controls for sex and ethnicity are introduced. Consider, for example, the relationship between each type of rating between observations. A researchable hypothesis would be that physicians' ratings provide a substantive basis for predicting self-rating at the next observation; this would follow if one assumes that individuals are basically reality oriented in their self-ratings. In four of the five comparisons, however, self-ratings are better predictors of subsequent physician ratings than vice versa. There are at least two possible interpretations of this finding. A behavioral interpretation is that an individual's rating of his health modifies his reaction to physical disability; thus an overestimation of health reduces apparent impairment to disability and an underestimation exaggerates impairment; these responses to disability are then reflected in the subsequent rating of the physician. An alternative interpretation is that the individual's self evaluation is responsive to internal clues of organic changes which are subsequently noted by the physician.

The second hypothesis predicts that, when incongruity is observed, overestimation of health is more likely than underestimation. The data in Table 3–7 confirm this expectation also. Over the six rounds, overestimation of health (24 percent) was observed twice as often as underestimation (12 percent). In an analysis not shown, the same pattern is observed among nonsurviving panel members at each observation. On the average, 28 percent of the nonsurvivors overestimated their health while 13 percent underestimated their health.

A more powerful test of the relationship between self and physician ratings of health is the response of a panelist who at a point in time has a positive self-rating congruent with the physicians' positive rating but then experiences a decline or improvement in health as measured by the physician's rating. Over the six observations there were 56 such cases. Of these, 40 (71 percent) retain their positive self-rating, thus overestimating their health as predicted. Over the six observations, there were 64 instances in which a physician's rating improved; in this situation only 15 (23 percent) of the panelists displayed an incongruous self-rating, underestimating their health. Overestimation of health is clearly the rule when incongruity is observed.

While the number of incongruous health ratings observed in the panel is relatively small, even the observed number may be exaggerated as a consequence of our using relatively crude dichotomies of the two ratings. If the responses on each rating are trichotomized at natural breaking points, cases of extreme incongruity are indeed reduced below the 36 percent observed when a dichotomy is used. In the 498 assessments of congruity, only 5 percent of these observations were extremely incongruous when ratings were trichotomized. Extreme cases of underestimating of health (high PR/low SR) were rare (6/498); extreme overestimation (low PR/high SR) were more common (21/498). Persons strongly underestimating their health tended to be white females (3 out of 5 persons), while those strongly overestimating their health were white males (8 out of 15 persons). Overestimation of health by subjects might be explained by differences in objective health conditions masked by the crudeness of the objective health ratings. This, however, is apparently not the case. Overly optimistic persons in fact evidenced more pathology than overly pessimistic ones, when compared in terms of the presence or absence of seven chronic disease processes identified by clinical and laboratory examination: cardiovascular disease, arthritis, depression, pulmonary disease, right and left eye impairment, hearing loss. This finding is concurrent with an earlier observation by the senior author that, for among persons who display extremely incongruous assessments of their health, factors other than medical ones were important. In terms of health related behavior, overly pessimistic persons visited a physician more often and had more routine physical check-ups than did overly optimistic ones who, according to the physician's evaluation, were in poorer health. Health attitudes, as measured by two indices, were also more positive for overly optimistic persons than for the pessimistic ones.

Discussion and Conclusion

This paper has provided further demonstration of two hypotheses relating to self-health assessment of older persons. Using a unique set of data from an ongoing longitudinal study which thus far has spanned 15 years and involved six observations, we have demonstrated the following:

1. There is a persistent, positive congruence of self and physicians' ratings of health.

2. Whenever there is incongruity in the two types of ratings, the tendency is for the individual to overestimate, rather than underestimate, his health.

3. Substantial stability of both self- and physicians' ratings is observed through time, with the self-health rating showing slightly more stability.

4. An unexpected discovery was the tendency for the self-health rating to be a better predictor of future physicians' ratings than the reverse.

The data provided no clear pattern that would enable us to confirm or refute conclusively commonly reported findings regarding the relationship of these two types of health assessments to various health attitudes and health behavior. Self-health ratings are clearly measuring more than simple morale. In our analyses correlations between self-health ratings and various measures of morale or life satisfaction are consistently below + 0.50. Physicians' ratings were generally slightly less correlated with such attitudinal measures. When health related attitudes were investigated, we did observe a stronger relation between these attitude scores and self-health rating than between these scores and physicians' ratings. There was no indication that health-related behavior was more closely related to the physicians' than the subject's health rating, as had been suggested by Suchman, Phillips, and Streib (1958).

Self-rating of health cannot serve as a substitute for epidemiologic diagnoses. These ratings clearly measure something more—and something less—than objective medical ratings. However, our data demonstrate that self-assessment of health is not random but is persistently and positively related to objective evaluations of health status. Self-ratings of health clearly have some utility as a measure of health in research involving older persons when objective measurements of health are not feasible. Furthermore, these data confirm that, in regard to evaluation of health, older people have and maintain a strong reality orientation.

References

Friedsam, H., and Martin, H. A comparison of self and physicians' ratings in an older population. *Journal of Health and Social Behavior,* 4:179–183, 1963.

Haberman, P. The reliability of data. In *Poverty and health,* edited by Kosa, Antonovsky, and Zola. Cambridge, Mass.: Harvard University Press, 1969.

Maddox, G. Self assessment of health status. *Journal of Chronic Diseases,* 17:449–460, 1964.

Rozelle, R., and Campbell, D. More plausible rival hypotheses in the cross-lagged panel technique. *Psychological Bulletin,* 71:74–84, 1969.

Suchman, E., Phillips, B., and Streib, G. An analysis of the validity of health questionnaires. *Social Forces,* 36:223–232, 1958.

Vitamin B$_{12}$ Deficiency   *Alan D. Whanger and H. Shan Wang*

Introduction

In recent years there has been considerable interest in vitamin B$_{12}$ levels among the elderly. Although all of the functions of vitamin B$_{12}$ and its congeners in human metabolism and neurophysiology are not fully known, we do know this vitamin plays vital roles in many important reactions, such as propionic utilization, the conversion of glutamate, the conversion of ethylene glycol to acetaldehyde, and biosynthesis of methionine, the formation of deoxycytidylic acid in DNA synthesis, the catalyzation of oxidation of mercaptoethanol, and detoxification of cyanide (Smith, 1964; Baker et al., 1968; Searcy, 1969; Wokes et al., 1966; Matthews, 1971).

In the aged, several factors contribute to the difficulty in studying this vitamin deficiency. There is some uncertainty about what the ranges of normal vitamin B_{12} levels in the older person are. Some investigators have found a linear decrease over the life span, but others have not found this consistently. Some noted a sex-linked difference (Cape and Shinton, 1961; Kilpatrick and Withey, 1965). Most of these surveys and determinations have been done in Europe. Only six have been done in the United States (Boger et al., 1955; Chow et al., 1956; Davis et al., 1965; Gaffney et al., 1957; Halsted et al., 1959; Tauber et al., 1957). Davis found a decrement of serum vitamin B_{12} by age, and levels approaching the pernicious anemia range in 10 percent of domiciliary men.

A relationship between psychiatric symptoms and vitamin B_{12} deficiency has been known since 1849, when Addison wrote in his description of pernicious anemia of "languor and restlessness" and "indisposition to, or incapacity for, bodily or mental exertion." In severe hypovitaminosis, demyelination may occur not only in the spinal cord but also in the peripheral nerves and the brain.

A major question has been the possible effects of low, but not profoundly depressed, levels of B_{12} on the nervous system and the body, as B_{12} has been implicated in a wide variety of psychiatric disorders. The range of normal or nonpathogenic levels of B_{12} in aging persons has been open to some question. Numerous recent studies in European countries have reported widely varying incidences of hypovitaminosis B_{12} in elderly psychiatric patients. Dawson, (1966) in Scotland, for example, reported 20 percent low levels under age 75 and 39 percent low levels over age 75 as compared with Kallstrom (1969) from Norway, who reported only 2 percent low levels in a similar group.

Another major problem in this research are the varying methods used for determining vitamin B_{12} levels, which are measured in micromicrograms or picograms. All of the reported series have used either bacterial or protozoan microbiological techniques. There has been considerable disagreement about the specificity of these, as well as the vulnerability of the organisms to tranquilizers, antibiotics, and various inhibiting factors in serum.

Important in measuring the effects of treatment are finding objective parameters to follow. Davis (1965) again has studied serum lactic acid and LDH, but did not find these to change significantly with age or levels of B_{12}. Electroencephalogram changes occur in a high percentage of pernicious anemia, but the limited studies on those with borderline levels leave questions unanswered. Scheinberg (1951) measured cerebral blood flow and metabolism in pernicious anemia, using the nitrous oxide method. He found evidence that the mental symptoms were related to the decrease in cerebral metabolism associated directly with vitamin B_{12} deficiency and not the degree of anemia. This has not been followed up.

A preliminary survey among acutely admitted patients for moderate to marked glossitis, which may be an early sign of vitamin B_{12} deficiency, showed an incidence of about 28 percent.

Method

Three groupings of subjects were utilized, each major group being sub-divided into four groups of ten subjects each, matched on the basis of sex and age over or under 75. The general eliminating criterion was having received vitamin B$_{12}$ by injection within the past year.

The control subjects were from the geriatric longitudinal study groups at the Duke University Center for the Study of Aging and Human Development. These are volunteers living in the community and functioning fairly well mentally and physically. They were called in on a random basis.

The acute psychiatric patients were new admissions to a state hospital having a catchment area of one-fourth of the state of North Carolina. All new patients over age 65 were admitted to the geropsychiatry service, and they were studied on the basis of consecutive admission.

The chronically hospitalized patients were those who had been hospitalized for at least six months continuously, were ambulatory, and were able to feed themselves from the hospital diet of about 2500 calories a day including liver every other week, and had not lost over ten pounds weight in the past six months. They were otherwise selected randomly using an alphabetical basis.

A detailed psychiatric, medical, and social history was obtained to the extent possible, with attempts to ascertain the previous drug and vitamin use, as well as the adequacy of the diet in rather gross terms.

A battery of tests and examinations was carried out, including a serum sample for the vitamin B$_{12}$ determination, which was obtained within 24 hours of admission of the acute psychiatric patients before any supplemental vitamins were given. The blood was handled with all new vacuum equipment and serum promptly frozen and held at zero degrees for a maximum of four weeks until the accumulated specimens were sent frozen in dry ice to the processing laboratory. As controls on accuracy, specimens were split within the batch and also a pooled sample was submitted with each batch. Ten specimens were split and sent simultaneously to the primary processing laboratory and to another laboratory utilizing the same technique. The few folic acid specimens were handled in the same way, but were not stored frozen longer than a week.

The method used for the vitamin B$_{12}$ determination was the radioisotope dilution, charcoal absorption method of Lau and Herbert (1965). The laboratory found this equally as accurate as the Euglena microbiologic method and to be unaffected by various inhibiting agents. The laboratory range of presumed normals was found to be 150 through 900 picograms (pg) per ml with an overall mean of 386 pg. Their standard deviation of reproduceability at this level was plus and minus 39 pg. Lau and Herbert feel that this method is more accurate in the low range than the microbiologic techniques.

A sample survey for folic acid levels was made on the chronically hospitalized group who were known not to be on any drugs that would lower the serum folic acid nor potentially interfere with the *Lactobicillus casei* organism used in the assay. The range of normal for the laboratory is 4 to 16 nanograms (ng) per ml.

Results

Only a portion of the data will be presented herein, mainly that dealing with the composition of the groups and the prevalence of various vitamin B_{12} levels. During the period of gathering the acute psychiatric patients, 64 patients were admitted. Two of these had had pernicious anemia diagnosed previously, but had had parenteral vitamin B_{12}, and so were excluded from the study. The mean age for all 120 subjects in all groups was 75.7 years.

The racial composition of the three groups varied from 55 percent white in the control group to 60 percent white in the acute group to 75 percent white in the chronic group.

The percentage who were known to have had supplemental oral vitamin B_{12} in some form in the previous year was 22 percent of the controls, 12 percent of the acute, and 10 percent of the chronic patients.

There was a considerable amount of physical illness among all groups, but none with severe uremia, marked liver disease, or leukemia, all of which might abnormally elevate the serum vitamin B_{12}. There were none with gastric or intestinal surgery, which would tend to lower the B_{12} level. Those with doubtfully adequate or inadequate diets were 14 percent among the controls, 71 percent among the acute, and 5 percent among the chronically hospitalized.

Only 7 percent of the control group, about 55 percent of the acute patients, and about 60 percent of the chronic patients were on drugs such as the phenothiazines, barbiturates, antidepressants, antibiotics, or anticonvulsants which would potentially affect the ordinary microbiological determinations.

The results of the split and matched samples used as checks on the method showed generally fairly good agreement, with the correlation coefficient of $r = 0.987$.

The mean vitamin B_{12} levels by age and group are shown in Table 3–8, where the analysis of variance is also shown. The total older group had a higher mean B_{12} than the total younger group, but the difference was not significant. The mean B_{12} for the total group is very close to that of the normals for this laboratory.

The subjects are grouped by race and sex in Table 3–9. The differences between the sexes are not significant. The mean vitamin B_{12} levels of the total white group is highly significantly lower than that of the total nonwhite group (which was essentially black, as it included only one nonblack, an Indian).

Table 3–8. *Mean Vit B$_{12}$ levels,*[a] *by age and group.*[b]

Group	Control	Acute	Chronic	Total
Age 65–74	(20)[c]309	(20) 325	(20) 420	(60) 351
Age 75 +	(20) 307	(20) 353	(20) 486	(60) 382
Total	(40) 308	(40) 339	(40) 453	(120) 366

Analysis of variance		*t*	*p*
1. Control vs. acute		0.86	NS
2. Control vs. chronic		3.45	<.001
3. Acute vs. chronic		2.57	<.05
4. All 65–74 vs. 75 +		0.86	NS

[a] Vitamin B$_{12}$ = picograms (10^{-12} grams/ml).
[b] Mean normal for lab = 386 pg.
[c] Numbers in parentheses = N.

Table 3–10 shows the distribution of abnormal levels of vitamin B$_{12}$ according to the groupings of Lau (1965); namely, the "low" from 0 through 99 pg, the "questionably deficient" from 100 through 149 pg, the "indeterminate" between 150 and 199 pg, and the "high" over 900 pg. The subjects are divided variously by race, sex, group, and total number. Because of the varying numbers, percentages are listed. None of the subjects had a B$_{12}$ level below 100 pg, although one was found at that level. The percentage of questionably deficients and indeterminates is lowest in the chronics. Again a racial trend is observed, with the nonwhites having the lesser prevalence of the indeterminate values, and the only elevated ones. Some sex difference is also present, with the males having a greater risk of lower B$_{12}$ levels than the females.

In looking at the total subject pool of 164, which included all of those seen consecutively while getting enough subjects to fill the previously discussed matched groupings of the controls and acutes, we noted many differences between the groups, some of which are indicated in Table 3–11. These

Table 3–9. *Mean Vit B$_{12}$ levels*[a] *by race and sex.*

Group	White	Nonwhite	Total
Male (M)	(40)[b] 305	(20) 445	(60) 352
Female (F)	(36) 345	(24) 434	(60) 381
Total	(76) 324	(44) 439	(120) 366

Analysis of variance		*t*	*p*
1. White M vs. nonwhite M		2.51	<.05
2. White M vs. white F		1.26	NS
3. White F vs. nonwhite F		2.05	<.05
4. Nonwhite M vs. nonwhite F		0.15	NS
5. All M vs. all F		0.82	NS
6. All white vs. all nonwhite		3.17	<.005

[a] Vitamin B$_{12}$ in picograms.
[b] Numbers in parentheses = N.

Table 3–10. *Distribution of abnormal Vitamin B_{12} levels[a] by various groups in percentages[b]*

B_{12} group	Control (40)	Acute (40)	Chronic (40)	WM (40)	NWM (20)	WF (36)	NWF (24)	All M (60)	All F (60)	All W (76)	All NW (44)	Total (120)
0–99 Low (%)	0	0	0	0	0	0	0	0	0	0	0	0
100–149 Questionably deficient (%)	5	8	3	8	5	3	4	7	3	5	5	5
150–199 Indeterminate (%)	20	15	3	20	5	8	12	15	10	16	9	13
900+ High (%)	0	3	3	0	5	0	4	2	2	0	5	2

[a] Vitamin B_{12} in picograms.
[b] ( ) = N; M = male; F = female; W = white; NW = nonwhite.

Table 3–11. *Comparisons of the total subject pool.*

Group	N	Mean age	Serum B_{12} pg	SD of B_{12} pg	Oral vits (%)	Oral vits w/ B_{12} (%)	Inject B_{12} (%)	Hgb less 12 gm (%)	Physical malnourish (%)	No OBS (%)	Mean Syst. BP (mm Hg)
Control	65	77	340	150	42	33	2	5	3	77	164
Acute	56	73	370	180	20	13	14	16	39	13	140
Chronic	44	78	440	210	48	14	2	16	27	9	130

include the percentages of those who within the previous year had taken any type of oral vitamins, oral vitamins containing B_{12}, or B_{12} by injection; those with anemia with a hemoglobin below 12 gm; those who appeared mal-nourished on physical examination; those with no significant organic brain syndrome, and the mean systolic blood pressures. The total subject pool was grouped on the basis of five-year age increments only, and the mean vitamin B_{12} levels of each are listed in Table 3–12. It is to be noted that many of these are known to have taken B_{12}. Of the total group, 25 were known to have taken oral vitamins which did not contain vitamin B_{12} within the previous year, and their mean B_{12} level was 410 pg with a SD of 140 pg. Thirty-two were known to have taken supplemental vitamins containing B_{12}, and their mean B_{12} level was 420 pg, with a SD of 230 pg. Eight of the total

Table 3–12. *Mean Vitamin B_{12} levels of total subject group by age increments.*

Age range	N	Mean serum B_{12} (pg)	SD of B_{12} (pg)
65–69	27	372	193
70–74	43	345	133
75–79	42	377	163
80–84	31	374	175
85–89	10	397	208
90–94	9	402	143
95+	3	777	585

group had had at least one injection of vitamin B_{12} within the previous year, and their mean serum B_{12} was 500 pg, with a SD of 256 pg.

The folic acid determinations taken on the eleven chronically hospitalized psychiatric patients showed four of them had levels of three or less nanograms, meaning that over one-third of the patients sampled had subnormal folic acid levels.

Discussion

At first glance the results seem paradoxical if low B_{12} had anything to do with psychiatric problems, as the control group has the lowest mean B_{12} level, as well as a high number of subjects in the questionable deficient and indeterminate levels, while the chronically ill group has the highest mean B_{12} as well as the least number in the low level group. This illustrates the point that there are a number of elderly people around who have quite low levels of B_{12}, but who do not seem to be suffering particular ill effects from it, and others who do not seem to be improved by the administration of B_{12}.

There are several possible explanations of the difference in mean B_{12}

levels. One would be the adequacy of the diet which is more likely to be lacking in such things as milk and liver when the person has a choice at home than when it is presented to him in the hospital. It is likely that the increasing mean B$_{12}$ levels in the acute and chronic psychiatric patients reflects their more severe degree of physical illness, which may impair excretion or cause excessive release of stored liver B$_{12}$. Some illnesses may lead to excessive B$_{12}$ binding proteins in the serum.

Not only did we not find the previously mentioned tendency toward age regression of the B$_{12}$ levels, but rather found that in all three major groupings the mean B$_{12}$ level of the older contingent is equal to or greater than that of the younger. Actually in the age increment cohorts, there is a rise in B$_{12}$ levels with age, with the over-90 group having markedly increased levels. This lack of decrement with age may be because this is a relatively unselected group with a number of rather ill people in it, and a number of them had been taking vitamins.

Another factor we would wish to comment on as it may have implications for further B$_{12}$ research is the apparent increased level of serum B$_{12}$ in the nonwhite (or essentially black) group, along with the lesser likelihood of the indeterminate levels. It is uncertain as to whether a higher serum vitamin B$_{12}$ level provides any type of long-term advantage or protection to the individual, or whether this is a genetic or environmental factor. Of at least theoretical importance is the fact that the average lifespan of a black man or woman is about six to seven years shorter than that of whites, but that the remaining life expectancy of a black reaching age 70 is significantly longer than that of a white person (Riley and Foner, 1968).

We certainly have not answered the questions as to how vitamin B$_{12}$ levels are related to psychiatric illness, but this is an important issue which can only be elucidated by long-term studies of the relationship of low levels of B$_{12}$ to cerebral metabolism in relatively normal people, as well as the effect of B$_{12}$ administration on the psychiatrically ill. Results of our small sampling of folic acid levels indicate that this may be a much more important problem than the B$_{12}$ level. The EEG can be of help in following the course of B$_{12}$ related illness on cerebral metabolism, but this should be more accurate when combined with cerebral blood flow studies. The older methods are highly cumbersome, especially for older patients, but Dr. Shan Wang and Dr. Walter Obrist have developed a nontraumatic method for measuring cerebral blood flow by the inhalation of xenon gas, which should be of great value in this type of study.

It is of interest that the sampling of vitamin B$_{12}$ and folic acid levels among our subjects moderately approximates the incidence of these deficiencies which Leevy found in 1965 in a survey of 11 vitamins in a municipal hospital population, in which a deficiency of at least one vitamin was found in 88 percent of the patients, with folic acid being the most common at 45 percent and B$_{12}$ at 10 percent.

A further comment might be made on the use of the radioisotope dilution method of determining serum B_{12}. We did not attempt to run comparisons using the various microbiological assay methods, but this certainly should be done on a rather large number of psychiatric patients. It is important to see whether discrepancies between ours and other series might be related to noxious effects on the test organisms of the psychopharmacologic "soup" circulating in the systems of patients on six or eight different drugs.

The study of vitamin deficiencies is complicated, if you will, by the increasing use of vitamin preparations, even unwittingly, as evidenced by there being therapeutic doses of B_{12} in at least four different breakfast cereals. As reported by Howell and Loeb (1969), there are only occasionally single vitamin deficiencies in the elderly. In a substantial percentage of those using vitamin supplements, they were using ones which did not replace the vitamins in which they were deficient. There is some danger in using single or wrong supplements of further upsetting the metabolic imbalance when several vitamins are already deficient. Obviously the last word on the needs, role, and effect of vitamin B_{12} in both the elderly psychiatrically ill and the relatively normal older person is not yet in.

References

Baker, H., and Frank, O. Vitamin B_{12}. In *Clinical vitaminology*. New York: Interscience Publishers, 1968, pp. 116–152.

Boger, W. P., Wright, L. D., Strickland, S. C., Gylfe, J. S., and Ciminera, J. L. Vitamin B_{12}: Correlation of serum concentrations and age. *Proceedings of the Society for Experimental Biology and Medicine*, 89:375–378, 1955.

Cape, R. D. T., and Shinton, N. K. Serum vitamin B_{12} concentration in the elderly. *Gerontologia Clinica*, 3:163–172, 1961.

Chow, B. F., Wood, R., Horonick, A., and Akuda, K. Agewise variations of vitamin B_{12} serum levels. *Journal of Gerontology*, 11:142–146, 1956.

Davis, R. L., Lawton, A. H., Prouty, R., and Chow, B. F. The absorption of oral vitamin B_{12} in an aged population. *Journal of Gerontology*, 20:167–172, 1965.

Dawson, A. A., and Donald, D. The serum vitamin B_{12} in the elderly. *Gerontologia Clinica*, 8:220–225, 1966.

Gaffney, G. W., Horonick, A., Okuda, K., Meier, P., Chow, B. F., and Shock, N. W. Vitamin B_{12} serum concentrations in 528 apparently healthy human subjects of ages 12–94. *Journal of Gerontology*, 12:32–38, 1957.

Halsted, J. A., Carroll, J., and Rupert, S. Serum and tissue concentration of vitamin B_{12} in certain pathologic states. *New England Journal of Medicine*, 260:575–580, 1959.

Howell, S. C., and Loeb, M. B. Nutritional needs of the older adult. *Gerontologist*, 9:17–30, 1969.

Kallstrom, B., and Nylof, R. Vitamin B_{12} and folic acid in psychiatric disorders. *Acta Psychiatrica Scandinavica*, 45:137–152, 1969.

Kilpatrick, C. S., and Withey, J. L. The serum vitamin B_{12} concentration in the general population. *Scandinavian Journal of Haematology*, 2:220–229, 1965.

Lau, K., Gottlieb, C., Wasserman, L., and Herbert, V. Measurement of serum vitamin B_{12} level using radioisotope dilution and coated charcoal. *Blood*, 26:202–214, 1965.

Leevy, C. M., Cardi, L., Frank, O., Gellene, R., and Baker, H. Incidence and significance of hypovitaminemia in a randomly selected municipal hospital population. *American Journal of Clinical Nutrition*, 17:259–271, 1965.

Matthews, D. M., and Wilson, J. Cobalamins and cyanide metabolism in neurological diseases. In Arnstein, H. R. V., and Wrighton, R. J. (Eds.), *The cobalimins.* London: Churchill Livingston, 1971, pp. 115–135.

Riley, M. W., and Foner, A. The population: Longevity of individuals. In *Aging and society.* New York: Russell Sage Foundation, 1968, 1:28–31.

Scheinberg, P. Cerebral blood flow and metabolism in pernicious anemia. *Blood,* 6:213–227, 1951.

Searcy, R. L. Vitamin B₁₂. In *Diagnostic biochemistry,* New York: McGraw-Hill Book Company, 1969, pp. 573–582.

Smith, A. D. M. Cyanide encephalopathy in man. *Lancet,* Sept. 26, 1964, pp. 668–671.

Tauber, S. A., Goodhart, R. S., Hus, J. M., Blumberg, N., Kassab, J., and Chow, B. F. Vitamin B₁₂ deficiency in the aged. *Geriatrics,* 12:368–374, 1957.

Whanger, A. D., and Wang, H. S. Vitamin B₁₂ deficiency in aging psychiatric patients. *Gerontologist,* 10:31, no. 3, P. II, 1970.

Wokes, F., and Ellis, F. R. Plasma thiocyanate and vitamin B₁₂ in neurological disease. *Lancet,* July 2, 1966, pp. 49–50.

Obesity and Cardiovascular Function   *John B. Nowlin*

By common adage, the overweight individual runs an increased risk of falling prey to a number of health problems. In particular, the association between obesity and cardiovascular disease is often cited and had been frequently evaluated in large study populations (Kannel et al., 1967; Pell and D'Alonzo, 1961; Keys, 1954; Paul, 1963; Garn et al., 1951). The purpose of this paper is to reexamine the relationships between body stature and some of the widely accepted indicators of cardiovascular disease. Specifically, emphasis is placed on the individual's sex and age as potential influences upon any relationship which might exist between body stature and often-examined cardiovascular variables.

Methods

The population is that of the Adaptation Study at the Duke Center for the Study of Aging and Human Development. This study group is comprised of 502 white men and women from the Durham, North Carolina area; the age range is from 46 to 71 years of age. Information collected during the initial visit serves as the data base for this analysis.

Accurate measure of fatness or adiposity remains somewhat of a moot research issue. The profusion of methods to estimate this characteristic reflects the lack of resolution of this issue. Clearly, different weights and different body frames provide differing extents of adiposity. In this particular analysis, the basic, commonplace measures of height and weight were employed to estimate fatness. A number of arithmetical manipulations of height and weight values have been proposed to gauge fatness. This analysis uses the Quetelet index; that is, weight divided by the square of the height. It is of interest to see how the Quetelet ratio compares to body fat determined by more sophisticated methods. Bray (1970) reported the isotopic determinations of body water in a group of thirteen obese women. These determinations allow for a good estimate of total body fat. If the Quetelet ratio is calculated from their data and correlated with their values for total body fat, the resulting coefficient is 0.80. Thus, the Quetelet index offers at least a reasonable approximation of body fatness.

Employing Quetelet scores, the study population was divided into equal-sized low-score and high-score groups. The higher score group contains the individuals with more obesity while the lower-score group has little or no obesity. To control for sex and age, the population was also divided into four sex-age groups (using median age to divide older from younger participants).

Findings

Table 3–13 shows the cardiovascular function characteristics of the high-Quetelet-score groups. The first two characteristics show that the high-

Table 3-13. *Differences between body stature groups on cardiovascular variables.*

	Low Quetelet score (N = 247)	High Quetelet score (N = 251)	F or χ^2 ratio	Significance level
History of hypertension	6.9%	17.1%	13.3*	<.01
History of clinical coronary artery disease	6.1%	8.4	0.9*	ns
Systolic blood pressure	146	159	31.4	<.01
Diastolic blood pressure	85	91	33.3	<.01
Resting heart rate	68.0	69.5	2.7	ns
Functional cardiovascular impairment	0.50	0.71	4.9	<.05
Overall health rating	1.8	1.9	<1.0	ns
Serum cholesterol level	244	244	0.0	ns
Serum triglyceride level	134	154	5.8	<.05
ECG evidence of coronary artery disease	12.6%	18.1%	2.9*	<.10

* χ^2 values

Quetelet-score group reported histories of hypertension and clinical coronary artery disease more often than the low-score group (although the difference in coronary artery disease was not statistically significant). Additional analyses by age and sex showed no influence of these factors on the differences in hypertension or coronary artery disease reported by the low- and high-Quetelet-score groups.

A number of parameters based upon the medical examination were then considered in a three-factor analysis of variance based on age, sex, and Quetelet scores. Recumbent systolic blood pressure, as recorded at the beginning of the physical examination, proved far greater within the large body stature group. The initial diastolic pressure was likewise considerably higher in the group with the larger body stature. However, resting heart rate, as determined from a clinical cardiogram taken after the medical examination, did not differ significantly between the large and small body stature groups. There were no statistically significant sex or age influences upon the relationships between these three cardiovascular measures and body stature.

The examining physician also rated on a 0–9 scale the extent of functional impairment arising from cardiovascular disease. A score of 0 indicates no impairment while 9 reflected marked functional loss. Extent of functional impairment from cardiovascular disease, although minimal for this relatively healthy population, was more pronounced in the larger body stature group. Overall health-related loss of function, irrespective of etiology, was next evaluated in the three factor analysis of variance format. A scale of 1–9 was utilized with a score of 1 indicating no overall health impairment and 9 indicating marked impairment. No significant differences were apparent between the two body stature groups on the overall health rating. Moreover, there was no statistically significant age or sex interaction upon either the cardiovascular impairment or overall health rating scores.

Two serum lipids often associated with occurrence of cardiovascular disease were next examined in a three-way analysis of variance. Serum cholesterol level did not differ between the larger and smaller body stature groups. However, serum triglyceride levels were substantially higher among the larger body stature group. Again, sex and age did not interact significantly with body stature in influencing levels of these two serum lipids.

Finally, there was somewhat more electrocardiographic evidence of coronary artery disease among the large body group, although the difference was significant only at the 0.10 level. Coronary artery disease was considered present on the clinical electrocardiogram if there were evidence of ischemic T-wave changes, QRS complex defects associated with myocardial infarction or left bundle branch block. Further analysis by sex and age showed no significant interactions.

The variables examined in this report were also analyzed by product moment correlation coefficients for each variable with the Quetelet index (Table 3–14). Male and female groups were considered separately. (Age had

Table 3–14. *Correlations between the Quetelet Index and cardiovascular variables.**

	Men	Women
Systolic blood pressure	.30	.25
Diastolic blood pressure	.33	.35
Resting heart rate	.18	.09
Functional cardiovascular impairment	.19	.14
Overall health rating	.07	.15
Serum cholesterol	−.11	−.02
Serum triglyceride level	.07	.14

* A correlation of .13 or greater is significant at the .05 level.

almost no correlation with the Quetelet index.) The correlational data corroborate the findings provided by the analysis of variance. Both sex groups presented significant correlations between the Quetelet index and blood pressure values as well as the cardiovascular functional impairment score. These variables were then examined further in a multiple regression analysis. Only diastolic pressure emerged as presenting a statistically significant relationship with the Quetelet score in the multiple regression. This finding held true for both sexes.

Summary

In general, the data reported in this paper tend to support findings of other large-scale population studies. The tendency for the overweight individual to have an elevated blood pressure when compared to his thinner counterpart has been frequently noted.

In terms of serum lipids, triglyceride levels have generally been found more elevated among overweight groups. Serum cholesterol levels, on the other hand, less frequently differ between groups of overweight and normal weight individuals.

Most prior studies have shown little association between overweight and the incidence of cardiovascular disease. However, our data show significant relationships between the weight-height ratio and various measures of cardiovascular disease risk. Finally, our data imply that age and sex do not significantly influence these associations: they tend to exist in all the age-sex groups examined at about the same levels.

References

Kannel, William, LeBauer, E. Joseph, Dawber, Thomas R., McNamara, Patricia. Relation of body weight to development of coronary heart disease. *Circulation*, 35:334, 1967.

Pell, S., and D'Alonzo, C. Three year study of myocardial infarction in a large employed population. *J.A.M.A.* 175:463, 1961.

Keys, A. Obesity and degenerative heart disease. *Am. Jour. Pub. Health,* 44:864, 1954.

Paul, O., et al. Longitudinal study of coronary heart disease. *Circulation,* 28:864, 1963.

Garn, S. M., Gertler, M. M., Levine, S. A., and White, P. D. Body weight versus weight standards in coronary artery disease and a healthy group. *Ann. Intern. Med.* 34:1416, 1951.

Bray, G., Schwartz, M., Rozin, R., and Lister, J. Relationships between oxygen consumption and body composition of obese patients. *Metabolism,* 19:418, 1970.

Anxiety During A Medical Examination   *John B. Nowlin*

The prevalence of "anxiety" among individuals upon exposure to a general medical examination is so well known and widely accepted as to require little amplification. Consideration alone of the profusion of cartoons in popular magazines and the numerous word-of-mouth jokes about the medical examination setting provides strong circumstantial evidence for the lay person's sensitivity to this "anxiety." Moreover, the physician himself is not unaware of the anxiety arising during the course of his medical examination. Several general textbooks of medicine and physical diagnosis, at least in passing, make mention of feeling-states attendant to the medical examination. For the most part, terms such as *anxiety* or *fear* have been employed as descriptors of these feelings. McGehee et al. specifically mention fear in association with anticipation of a medical examination (Beeson et al., 1967). In the latest edition of Cecil and Loeb's *Textbook of Medicine,* the editors advise that "warmth and compassion break down the barriers of anxiety and fear that beset the patient coming as a stranger to the doctor" (Harvey, 1968). In his textbook of physical diagnosis, Leopold suggests that "most patients display variable amounts of anxiety, restlessness, or agitation during their initial examination" (Leopold, 1957).

This wide-spread recognition of anxiety in the medical examination setting, of course, rests largely on a speculative basis. There has been no precise characterization of the anxiety accompanying the medical examination. A more detailed appraisal of this feeling-state would seem to hold considerable merit since anxiety could conceivably influence not only the physician's examination findings, but, as well, the nature of subsequent physician-patient dealings. Based upon information collected by a carefully validated written self-report technique, this paper describes recognition of anxiety among a large population while involved in a standardized medical examination. Information collected from this study population permitted evaluation of three issues pertinent to the anxiety found in the medical examination setting: (1) The extent of change in anxiety self-report during the course of the medical examination; (2) the influence of the examinee's age and sex upon overall level and change of anxiety self-report; and (3) aspects of the physician-examinee interaction as influences upon examination anxiety self-report.

Materials and Methods

Study Population

Anxiety self-report during a general medical examination was evaluated within a subgroup (N = 279) of a larger subject population (N = 502) involved in a longitudinal study of aging sponsored by the Duke Center for the Study of Aging and Human Development. Examination anxiety self-report data was collected during the initial visit of this study population. The overall longitudinal study group was comprised of white residents of the immediate Durham, North Carolina area; their age range was 45–71.

Since time limitation prevented inclusion of all subjects in this evaluation of medical examination anxiety, a subgroup of the larger longitudinal population was selected for this purpose. Two study participants were usually seen during each working day of the project; the first individual to receive his medical examination was incorporated into the anxiety self-report subgroup. On days when only a single participant was scheduled, that individual was routinely included in the study subgroup. Frequency of subject distribution in terms of sex and five-year age category, as tested by the chi-square technique, did not significantly differ between the anxiety self-report subgroup and the group of individiuals excluded from this testing.

Medical Examination Format

The medical examination format to which all participants were exposed was tightly structured; a regular order of procedure was rigidly followed for each individual's examination. Moreover, effort was exerted to maintain the same examination atmosphere for each subject. (For example, even attempts at humor were consistent: e.g.—when telling the examinee that he was about to auscult for bowel sounds, the physician invariably said "Let me take a listen to the coffee we have been feeding you this morning." The same physician (JBN) performed all medical examinations.

The examination format consisted of three distinct periods of physician-examinee contact. Initially, the physician spent approximately ten minutes with each study participant, asking a set of standardized questions about possible organ system symptoms. The physician then left the examining room while the individual undressed in preparation for the examination. The second physician-examinee contact was the examination itself, which required approximately twenty minutes to perform. Included in the examination procedure was a rectal examination for men and a recto-pelvic examination for women participants. During his examination of women subjects, the physician was chaperoned by a nurse.

After the examinee had redressed, the physician spent ten to fifteen minutes with each person in a debriefing session. At that time, there was a careful explanation of the various examination procedures as well as a report of significant findings. The debriefing session was kept on a positive note, with the physician striving to convey the impression that the examinee was basically in good health. If necessary to alert the study participant about a health problem, the physician employed wording or phrasing designed to reassure the individual.

Anxiety Self-Report

The instrument used to assess self-report of anxiety in the medical examination setting was that of a mood adjective check list (MACL) designed by Nowlis (1956). This pencil-and-paper MACL is comprised of 38 words or phrases indicative of mood or feeling-state; clusters of these 38 items can be grouped to define broader statements of mood or affective state. Ten such general mood categories are accessible with the use of this MACL, including one indicative of "anxiety." (Other checklist affect categories include: "anger," "pleasantness-euphoria," "skepticism," "egotism," two "activation" scales, "depression," "de-activation," and "social affection." Since the primary focus of this paper is upon anxiety self-report, the influence of the examination procedure upon other MACL scales will not be described.)

In instructions for completion of the MACL form, subjects were told to indicate the extent to which each adjective conformed to his feeling-state at the precise moment that he was taking the test. For each word or phrase, there were four choices from which the individual could choose to indicate applicability to his momentary feeling-state: the item most definitely did apply (weighted with a score of 3), applied only slightly (weight score: 2), uncertain as to whether or not the item applied (weight score: 1), or that the item most definitely did not apply (weight score: 0).

Examinees self-rated the MACL items at three different times during the course of the examination procedure. The first MACL was completed just before the examinee was introduced to the examining physician. The second MACL was administered immediately after the examination procedure itself, although with the examinee still disrobed. A final MACL self-rating followed the debriefing session. While responding to the Nowlis MACL form, the examinees always remained alone.

Influence of Physician-Examinee Interaction on Self-Report

There are doubtless many aspects of the physician-examinee interaction which bear upon the level of the examinee's anxiety self-report during a medical examination. Reasonably, the medical examination would seem to pose, in particular, three large issues with which the examinee would have to contend: (1) the possibility that a previously unknown health defect might be found, (2) the requirement for bodily exposure characteristic of the examination setting, (3) the physician's manipulation of the examinee's body during the examination. In a short written questionnaire completed immediately after responding to the second Nowlis MACL form, examinees were requested to consider these three issues. Specifically, they were required to select, from among three possible explanations for discomfort in an examination setting, the one which best explained their own uneasiness. The options, as presented to the examinees, were: (1) "Embarrassment at having to undress," (2) "Discomfort at having someone push and press over your body," and (3) "Concern about what the doctor might find."

Results

Average scores for the Nowlis anxiety self-report scale at each of the three testings are presented in Figure 3–2; scores of men and women are graphed separately. Both sex groups presented a decrease in anxiety self-report over the three testings. However, women differed from men in reporting higher initial values; subsequently, on the final testing, they reported slightly less anxiety than did their male counterparts.

Using a repeated measures analysis of variance design for independent groups, differences in MACL anxiety scale response over the three testings was evaluated for statistical significance. The two factors defining the independent groups were age (based upon five-year age grouping) and sex of the study participant. The test-to-test change in anxiety self-report proved highly significant ($F = 58.8$, $df = 2/539$, $p < .01$); however, the between-

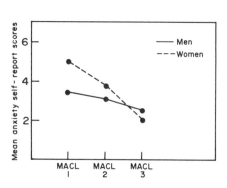

Figure 3–2. Influence of sex on examination anxiety self-report. Male population: 145; Female population: 134. Maximal anxiety self-report score: 24. MACL 1: Adjective check list anxiety self-report before introduction to examining physician. MACL 2: Adjective check list anxiety self-report with examination completed but examinee still disrobed. MACL 3: Adjective check list anxiety self-report following discussion of medical findings with examining physician.

sex difference in pattern of change likewise attained statistical significance ($F = 11.8$, $df = 2/539$, $p < .01$). Therefore, the significant trend for the entire group to present a test-by-test decrease in anxiety self-report level is, to a large extent, a reflection of the pattern of change among women. Age, based upon five-year age grouping, did not significantly influence either absolute level of anxiety self-report or pattern of change over the three MACL testings.

Selection frequency of the three examination discomfort options described earlier is shown in Figure 3–3. Approximately half of the study group designated "concern about what the doctor might find" (labelled "concern" in Figure 3–3) as their primary source of examination discomfort. The second

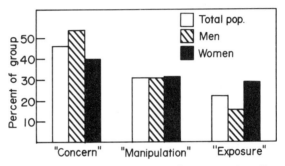

Figure 3–3. *Primary source of examination discomfort. "Concern"—Concern over what the physician might find. "Manipulation"—Discomfort at having someone push and press over your body. "Exposure"—Embarrassment at having to undress.*

most frequent selection was that of "discomfort at having someone push and press over your body" (labelled "manipulation" in Figure 3–3). The least frequently chosen option was that of "embarrassment at having to undress" (labelled "exposure" in Figure 3–3). Among the two sex groups, "concern" was the most commonly selected option; however, women reported more frequently than men that their examination discomfort arose from "exposure." The between-sex difference in selection frequency of each option proved statistically significant when this relationship was tested with the chi-square technique ($\chi^2 = 15.4$, $df = 2$, $p < .01$). When discomfort option frequency was considered on the basis of five-year age grouping, the distribution of option selection among the age groups did not differ in a statistically significant fashion. ($\chi^2 = 4.5$, $df = 8$, $p = $ ns).

Based upon their selection from among the three discomfort options, the study population was divided into three subgroups; then anxiety self-report for each of these subgroups was examined over the three MACL testings.

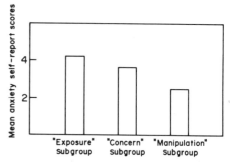

Figure 3–4. *Anxiety self-report as averaged over the three MACL testings. Subgroups were formed on the basis of selection among the three discomfort options.*

Primary source of medical examination discomfort, as it influenced anxiety self-report, is shown in Figures 3–4 and 3–5. A repeated measures analysis of variance for independent groups was again employed to assess statistical significance of differences in anxiety self-report among the three subgroups so formed. In this analysis, sex and selection of discomfort option constituted

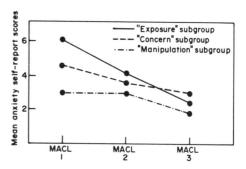

Figure 3–5. *Test-to-test level of anxiety self-report among discomfort subgroups. MACL 1: Adjective check list anxiety self-report before introduction to examining physician. MACL 2: Adjective check list anxiety self-report with examination completed but examinee still disrobed. MACL 3: Adjective check list anxiety self-report following discussion of medical findings with examining physician.*

the two independent factors. Since several study participants did not indicate a source of examination discomfort, the overall group size examined in this second analysis of variance was slightly smaller than that reported in the similar statistical analysis reported earlier. Anxiety self-report, as averaged of the three testings, differed among the three discomfort subgroups ($F = 6.0$, $df = 2/522$, $p < .01$). Group averages for anxiety self-report scores over the three MACL testing are shown in Figure 3–4. The "exposure" subgroup presented the highest average score while the "manipulation" subgroup presented the lowest, with the "concern" subgroup intermediate in level. Test-to-test change also differed in a statistically significant fashion between the three subgroups ($F = 6.6$, $df = 2/522$, $p < .01$). Responses for each subgroup are presented in Figure 3–5 where it is seen that anxiety self-reports within the three subgroups are more dispersed at the initial testing when compared to levels at the last two testings. Also, although all three subgroups presented a trend of test-to-test decrease in anxiety self-report levels, the most prominent change was evident among the "exposure" subgroup.

Within the three discomfort option subgroups, sex of the examinee did not significantly influence either anxiety self-report as averaged over the three MACL testings or trend of test-to-test change.

Discussions and Conclusions

Although the information collected in this study provides the basis for interesting speculation about the nature of anxiety associated with a general medical examination, there should be recognition of the limitations inherent to this set of data. First, the feeling state of "anxiety" itself is certainly not facilely quantitated. Even assuming that it were, many individuals might well be reticent to express or are, perhaps, even unaware of their "anxiety." Therefore, the scores of anxiety self-report described in this paper should be viewed, at best, as only tentative indicators of what might be called "real anxiety level." A second important qualification is posed by the medical examination setting in which these anxiety self-report scores were collected. In contrast to the usual physician-examinee interaction, initiated because of a patient's health concerns, this particular examination setting is made up of individuals actively solicited to receive medical attention. Entry into a medical setting on such a basis might be expected to introduce a bias into the reactions and responses of the individual. On the other hand, recruitment of this study population largely rested upon the enticement provided by a free, complete medical check-up. It seems reasonable to assume that such a catering to the individual's concerns about health mitigates, to some extent, the unusual nature of the commitment to this particular medical setting. Finally, use of a single medical examiner for the entire study population poses an additional problem in interpreting this survey of examination anxiety self-report.

In all probability, anxiety self-report was responsive to some degree to the physician as a person rather than exclusively to the procedural aspects of the medical examination. The use of more than a single examiner would have offered a clearer picture of the extent of this influence on examination anxiety self-report. However, the use of two or more examiners would have presented the countering disadvantage of diluting the consistency of the examination setting.

Anxiety self-report levels accompanying this medical examination, rather than being unitary, instead appear keyed to different, ongoing aspects of the examination format. Therefore, an appreciation of the events surrounding each administration of the mood adjective checklist becomes important in any interpretation of anxiety self-report change. The initial checklist testing, completed before the examinee's introduction to the examining physician, most likely reflects feeling-state prevalent in anticipation of the up-coming examination procedure. The second testing is presumably indicative of feeling-state found with the examination itself completed, but with the "trappings" of the examination setting maintained (e.g.—the examinee remains in the examination room, still disrobed). The final checklist testing would represent feeling-state extant, not only after the individual has the immediacy of the examination procedure behind him, but also after he has received reassurance about his state of health. Anxiety self-report at this third testing, therefore, serves as a convenient post hoc baseline with which earlier self-report scores can be compared. However, it is important to recognize that, although a convenient baseline, the final checklist testing might well reflect anxiety self-report suppressed somewhat below what could be termed "basal level" because of the optimistic nature of the just-preceding debriefing session. Such an interpretation of the final checklist scores as a baseline provides a rough schema to describe overall trends of anxiety self-report during this particular medical examination. Anticipation of the examination procedure appears associated with the highest level of anxiety self-report. The only partial dissipation of anxiety self-report level at the second MACL testing suggests that the examination milieu itself is an influence upon the level of anxiety reported during a medical examination.

Anxiety self-report in the medical examination setting is also influenced by the sex of the examinee. At the first two adjective checklist testings, women reported higher anxiety scores than did men. The most obvious explanation for this between-sex difference resides in the implication, for women, of interacting with a male examiner. Medical examination procedure, of course, is rendered acceptable by long-standing and ingrained attitudes about the physician-patient relationship. However, both the state of undress and the intimate physical contact characteristic of the examination situation, even though acceptable, might still contribute to the higher anxiety self-report among women in this study group as they dealt with a male examiner. A pair of findings offers support for this idea. First, once the examination procedure was completed and the examinees were again fully dressed (at the time of the third checklist testing), there was no sex difference in anxiety self-report level. Therefore, the between-sex difference in anxiety self-report cannot be explained on the simplistic basis that women, in general, reported more anxiety than did men. Instead, the sex disparity seems linked to the anticipation of and the actual involvement in the examination procedure; the most prominent difference in the examination setting at those points in time was the necessity for women to deal with a male physician. Also, among the three discomfort options, women more frequently than men selected the two choices most closely related to procedural aspects of the medical examination ("exposure" and "manipulation"). Their selection, in higher frequency, of these two options could also be interpreted as arising from concern at interacting with a male examiner.

Source of discomfort in his interaction with the physician proved to be a potent influence upon the examinee's examination anxiety self-report. Anxiety self-report, when averaged over the three MACL testings, differed significantly between the three discomfort option subgroups. Two of the discomfort option subgroups ("exposure" and "concern") were similar in averaged level of anxiety self-report, but together presented higher scores than did the third subgroup ("manipulation"). This between-group difference is best understood by a consideration of the issues underlying each of the three discomfort options. An indication that discomfort arises from either "exposure" or "concern" presumably reflects issues for the individual not entirely specific to the medical examination setting. "Embarrassment at having to undress" is a trait not necessarily exclusive to the medical setting. Likewise, "concern about what the doctor might find" implies antecedent doubts or worries about health. In contrast, "discomfort at having someone push and press over your body" is an experience largely limited to the medical examination itself. A source of discomfort in dealing with an examining physician which has implications beyond the confines of the medical examination setting would logically be accompanied by greater anxiety self-report than one peculiar to the examination format itself.

Moreover, a consideration of test-to-test response of anxiety self-report within each subgroup suggests that the issues of physician-examinee interaction reflected by the three discomfort options are most influential as the individual anticipates the medical examination. The divergence in level of anxiety self-report evident at the initial checklist testing is far less prominent at the last two testings. Apparently, once actively engaged with the physician in the examination setting, the examinee is less influenced by the issues underlying the three discomfort options in his reporting of anxiety.

References

Beeson, Paul B., and McDermott, Walsh (Ed.). *Cecil-Loeb textbook of medicine.* 12th ed. Philadelphia: W. B. Saunders Co., 1967.

Harvey, A. McGehee (Ed.). *The principles and practice of medicine*. 17th ed. New York: Appleton-Century-Crofts, 1968, p. 32.

Leopold, Simon S. (Ed.). *The principles and methods of physical diagnosis*. Philadelphia: W. B. Saunders Co., 1957.

Lindquist, E. F. *Design and analysis of experimentation in psychology and education*. Boston: Houghton Mifflin, 1953.

Nowlis, V. The descriptions and analysis of mood. *Annals of the New York Academy of Sciences*, 65:345–355, 1956.

Chapter 4. Mental Aging

This chapter contains a series of reports showing the relationship between various physical characteristics of the aged and their mental functioning. The first shows that aged persons with normal blood pressure have little change in mental ability over time. A group with borderline elevations of blood pressure have an increase in performance scores, and only those with high levels of blood pressure have significant intellectual loss. It concludes that cognitive decline is secondary to some pathologic process and not merely a normal aging process.

The second report shows that persons initially aged 60–69 who survived ten years had slight cognitive declines, but those initially 70–79 had larger declines. The study of terminal changes in intelligence found greatest change among those who sustained both acute and chronic illnesses during the study.

The study of neurophysiological correlates of intellectual functioning found that decline in intelligence scores was associated with slow EEG frequencies, focal abnormalities, and low cerebral blood flow. It suggested that most mental decline among the aged may be due to a depression of cerebral metabolism. The next report shows that there seems to be a general decline in EEG occipital rhythm, although this varies in different sex, socioeconomic, and age groups.

The final report in this chapter, from the Adaptation Study, found a small increase with age in reaction time, but no difference in percent correct detections within the middle-age groups.

When viewed as a group, these reports tend to refute the stereotype of general and inevitable decline in cognitive functioning with age. On the contrary, they suggest that when mental decline does occur among middle-age and older persons it is usually caused by specific cardiovascular or metabolic problems.

Intelligence and Blood Pressure   *Frances Wilkie and Carl Eisdorfer*

The incidence of hypertension increases with age and is frequently complicated by cardiovascular disease and strokes (Grover, 1948; Pickering, 1961;

Reprinted by permission from *Science*, 172:959–962, 1971. Copyright 1971 by the American Association for the Advancement of Science.

Harris, 1970; Masters et al., 1952).* Among the middle-aged and the aged, hypertension may also be related to psychomotor slowing (Birren et al., 1963; Birren et al., 1962; King, 1956; Spieth, 1962; Spieth, 1964), lowered flicker fusion threshold (Enzer et al., 1942), and organic brain impairment (Apter et al., 1951; Reitan, 1954). Despite these findings, however, relatively little attention has been paid to the long-term behavioral effects associated with hypertensive disorder.

This report examines the relation between blood pressure (BP) and intelligence, as measured by the Wechsler Adult Intelligence Scale (WAIS; Wechsler, 1955) in aged individuals over a ten-year period. It was hypothesized that intellectual decline over time would be related to heightened BP.

The results reported here stem from a longitudinal, multidisciplinary study at the Duke University Center for the Study of Aging and Human Development. The noninstitutionalized participants in this program were ambulatory volunteers, and although they do not represent a random sample, their sex, race, and socioeconomic characteristics approximate those in the Durham, N.C., area. The project was not designed specifically to investigate the relation between BP and intelligence, but rather the BP values were obtained during the programmed physical examination and the WAIS was one of several psychological tests administered. Each evaluation consisted of physical, psychiatric, psychological, and sociological examinations and various laboratory tests. Subjects for the study were examined for a two-day period about every two and one-half years (Heyman et al., 1964; Busse, 1970; Palmore, 1970).

In this report we focus on data obtained during the first and fourth examinations, separated by a ten-year period. The sample involved 202 individuals, initially aged 60 to 79 (mean age, 68.9), 87 of whom completed the follow-up study.

Because intellectual decline may be related to age, the subjects in both the returning and nonreturning groups were divided into a 60- to 69-year-old group (N = 106) and a 70- to 79-year-old group (N = 96) at the time of the first evaluation and further subdivided into categories based on the BP data obtained at the initial examination. The BP values in this report were obtained by standard auscultation technique with the person in a recumbent position. Diastolic rather than systolic pressure was used since the two measures were highly correlated ($p < .01$), and diastolic pressure is less sensitive to minor fluctuations. The physician rounded the BP values to the nearest 10 mm Hg. Approximating Masters, Garfield, and Walter's classification (Masters et al., 1952), the subjects were divided into a normal group with diastolic pressures between 66 and 95 mm Hg, a borderline elevated group with pressures between 96 and 105 mm Hg, and a high group with pressures

---

* Our use of "rounded" blood-pressure values has led to the inclusion of values in each category which are 4 mm Hg below Masters's levels.

of over 105 mm Hg. All the subjects with high BP who returned and 86 percent of their nonreturning counterparts had evidence of end-organ change (that is, a cardiac-thoracic ratio of more than 50 percent on the basis of actual measurements taken from X-ray photographs and clinical signs of eyeground changes of grade II or III at their last examination). In the group with mildly elevated BP, approximately 35 percent of the 60- to 79-year-olds, as well as approximately 10 percent of the normotensives, had eyeground changes of grade II, with heightened cardiac-thoracic ratio occurring significantly less often ($p < .02$) than in the high group. In terms of these indices of end-organ change, few differences were noted between the returning group and the nonreturning normotensive and borderline groups. Because of the nature of the study, antihypertensive drug usage could not be controlled. However, Spieth (1964) reported evidence that suggests that such drugs would tend to attenuate rather than exaggerate any differences in performance between our subjects.

Since the focus is upon normal BP and mild and heightened elevations of BP among older individuals with no clinical evidence of cerebrovascular disease, the data from 25 additional persons originally examined in the longitudinal study ($N < 5$ in each condition) were excluded here because of either missing data on intelligence tests, the presence of diagnosed cerebrovascular disease, hypotensive BP, or highly labile BP.

Among the returnees, there was no notable statistical difference between BP groups in terms of education, sex, race, or socioeconomic characteristics. Since the subjects were divided into two age groups at the time of the first examination and followed for ten years, the WAIS weighted scores uncorrected for age were used rather than intelligence quotients (IQ). The WAIS Full Scale Weighted Score is the sum of the Verbal and Performance Weighted Scores, which are based upon six and five subtest scores, respectively. Intellectual change (as delta scores) was obtained by subtracting the subjects' WAIS weighted scores on the first examination from those of the fourth examination.

Among the subjects initially examined at age 60 to 69, an analysis of variance indicates that there were significant ($p < .01$) differences between the BP groups on the full scale and performance delta scores ($df = 2/48$, $F = 6.5$ and 11.6, respectively) with the hypertensives having a greater loss in overall intellectual ability than the normotensive and borderline elevated groups ($df = 48$, $t = 2.9$, and 4.3, respectively), with these differences reflected in the performance scores ($t = 3.3$ and 5.9, respectively). Over the ten-year period, none of the BP groups at this age had a significant change in verbal ability; however, only the normals remained relatively stable in all areas. As depicted in Figure 4–1, the borderline elevated group had significantly higher scores in the performance area over time (related mean $t = 4.7$, $p < .01$, $df = 9$). In contrast, the hypertensive group had a significant decline in the performance area which was reflected as a loss in the full scale

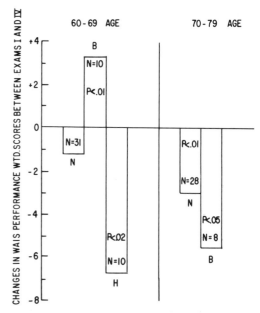

Figure 4–1. *Intellectual change (delta scores) over a 10-year period, as measured by the Wechsler Adult Intelligence Scale (WAIS) among individuals initially examined at ages 60 to 69 and 70 to 79 with either normal (N), borderline elevated (B), or heightened (H) diastolic blood pressure on the initial examination.*

score ($df = 9$, related $t = 3.1$, $p < .02$ and related $t = 2.4$, $p <.05$, respectively).

Figure 4–1 shows the performance weighted delta scores for the normal and borderline groups who were initially aged 70 to 79. There were no subjects with high BP at this age who completed the ten-year study. The normotensives had a significant decline in overall intellectual ability (related $t = 2.9$, $df = 27$, $p < .01$) which was reflected in the performance area ($t = 3.3$, $p < .01$), as did the borderline group ($df = 7$, $p <2.05$, $t = 2.5$ and 2.6, respectively). Although the borderline group tended to have a slightly greater loss in verbal ability than the normals, the two BP groups were not statistically different.

The data from individuals in each age group were pooled and a product moment correlation (see Table 4–1) was used to determine the relation between BP and intellectual change (delta scores) on the WAIS subtests and weighted scores. For the group initially aged 60 to 69 a heightened BP was significantly correlated with the loss on the Verbal, Performance, and Full

Table 4–1. *Product moment correlations between diastolic blood pressure (BP) and the Wechsler Adult Intelligence Scale (WAIS) scores. The "Initial examination" columns include all subjects initially examined and reflects the one test score. The "Longitudinal study" columns include those subjects completing the 10-year follow-up and relates initial BP with intellectual change over the 10-year period. Subjects were grouped according to their ages on the first examination. A negative correlation indicates an inverse relation between BP and performance.*

WAIS	Initial examination		Longitudinal study	
	Aged 60 to 69 (N = 106)	Aged 70 to 79 (N = 96)	Aged 60 to 69 (N = 51)	Aged 70 to 79* (N = 36)
Verbal weighted scores	−.10	−.27**	−.27***	−.36***
Information	−.10	−.26**	.04	−.25
Comprehension	−.10	−.25***	−.21	−.19
Arithmetic	−.13	−.27**	−.08	−.11
Similarities	−.06	−.25***	−.18	−.10
Digit span	−.01	−.22***	−.27***	−.29
Vocabulary	−.12	−.19	−.06	−.12
Performance weighted scores	−.09	−.32**	−.44**	−.23
Digit symbol	−.04	−.26**	−.40**	−.03
Picture completion	−.12	−.34**	.07	−.07
Block design	−.11	−.30**	−.35**	−.13
Picture arrangement	−.09	−.18	−.12	−.12
Object assembly	−.04	−.27**	−.39**	−.30
Full scale weighted scores	−.10	−.30**	−.42**	−.27

* In this age group, no individuals with heightened BP completed to 10-year study.
** $p < .01$.
*** $p < .05$.

Scale Weighted Scores. Among the subtests, the digit span, digit symbol, block design, and object assembly delta scores were also positively correlated with BP. Among those initially aged 70 to 79, a decline on the Verbal Weighted Score was positively related to BP. However, since there were no subjects at this older age with high BP who completed the follow-up study, this correlation was limited to the group with normal and mildly elevated BP.

On the first examination, the Verbal, Performance, and Full Scale WAIS Weighted Scores of the returnees were compared with those of their nonreturning counterparts in relation to BP. These Full Scale Weighted Scores are shown in Figure 4–2. In the 60- to 69-year-old group, a series of 2×3 analyses of variance indicated the returnees had significantly higher Verbal, Performance, and Full Scale Scores than the nonreturnees ($df = 1/100$, $p < .05$, $F = 5.3, 5.1$, and, 5.6, respectively). However, among the BP subgroups only the returning hypertensives had significantly higher Verbal, Performance, and Full Scale Scores than did their nonreturning counterparts ($df = 100$, $p < .05$, $t = 2.3$, and 2.4, respectively). Within the returning

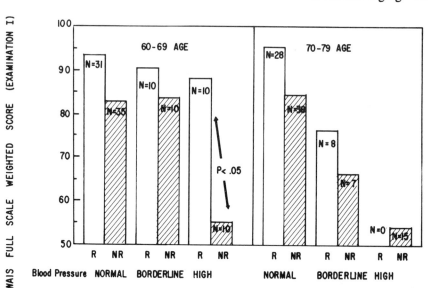

Figure 4–2. *The initial intelligence test scores (Wechsler Adult Intelligence Scale [WAIS]) of aged individuals with normal, borderline elevated, or heightened diastolic blood pressure who either returned (R) to complete a 10-year follow-up study or did not return (NR).*

group there were no significant differences between the BP subgroups. In contrast, within the nonreturning group, the hypertensives had lower Verbal, Performance, and Full Scale Scores than did the normals ($df = 100$, $p < .05$, $t = 2.4$, 2.5, and 2.1, respectively), as well as lower Performance Scores than the borderline subgroup ($t = 2.1$, $df = 100$, $p < .05$). Since the two subgroups with high BP were functioning at different levels, when data from all returning and nonreturning subjects were pooled, a product moment correlation (Table 4–1) indicated that on the first examination BP was not related to intelligence.

Figure 4–2 also shows the Full Scale Scores for the 70- to 79-year-olds on the first examination. There were no returning subjects with high BP and those who did return with normal and borderline pressure had WAIS scores similar to scores on the initial examination. In contrast, within the nonreturning group, the hypertensives had significantly lower Verbal, Performance, and Full Scale Scores than did the normals ($df = 51$, $p < .01$, independent $t = 3.1$, 3.1, and 3.2, respectively). When data for the returning and nonreturning subjects at this age were pooled, a product moment correlation (Table 4–1) indicated that heightened BP was associated ($p < .01$) with low Verbal Performance, and Full Scale Weighted Scores, and this was also true of all the subtests except for vocabulary and picture arrangement.

These results indicate that among individuals initially examined at ages

60 to 69, hypertensive levels of BP were associated with significant intellectual loss over a ten-year period. In contrast, their normotensive age peers remained relatively unchanged over time, while a group with borderline elevations of BP had higher performance scores. Since practice effects would be expected to slightly increase the scores across four testing sessions, the differences between the BP groups may reflect differential rates of decline in mental abilities rather than actual intellectual improvement among those with mildly elevated BP. Nevertheless, the increase in Performance Scores during this period for the group with borderline elevations of pressure tends to support Obrist's (1964) contention that mild elevations of BP may be necessary among the aged to maintain adequate cerebral circulation. Our failure to duplicate this pattern for the older subjects (those initially examined at ages 70 to 79) suggests that even in the face of mild elevations of BP other factors may be operating to compromise cerebral circulation. Perhaps the duration of cardiovascular disease, with consequent structural change or other interacting pathology relating to more advanced age, may intervene.

These results raise questions about adaptation to the effects of high BP. Since none of the older subjects with high BP completed the follow-up study and those of younger age who completed it were superior to their counterparts who were subsequently lost to the study, it might be appropriate to ask whether some individuals develop compensatory mechanisms to hypertension and therefore adjust to it with minimum difficulty for protracted periods, whereas others who do not develop adequate physiologic or anatomic compensations manifest central nervous system difficulties with cognitive deficits and progressively severe physical pathology.

An earlier cross-sectional study (Thompson et al., 1966), in which the same subjects were tested, suggested that socioeconomic status may be a contaminant in any investigation of cardiovascular disease difficulty, since the incidence of cardiovascular disease is high in the low socioeconomic group. In this context, it should be noted that in this ten-year longitudinal study, approximately 70 percent of the subjects within each BP group were of a nonmanual occupational background, and, furthermore, the amount of intellectual change over time was approximately the same for all subjects within each BP category regardless of whether the subjects were of a manual or nonmanual occupational background.

It is also of particular significance that in contrast to cross-sectional studies (Wechsler, 1958) which report a decline in intelligence across the later decade of life, longitudinal studies of intellectual ability (Blum et al., 1970) have raised some doubts as to the generality of such decline in relatively healthy aged at least through age 75. To this end, the presence of large numbers of aged with cardiovascular illness suggests that the basis for the cognitive decline associated with aging after maturity should be considered secondary to some pathologic processes and not merely as a "normal" aging process.

References

Apter, N. S., Halstead, W. C., Heimburger, R. F. Impaired cerebral functions in essential hypertension. *Amer. J. Psychiat.*, 107:808, 1951.

Birren, J. E., Butler, R. N., Greenhouse, S. W., Sokoloff, L., and Yarrow, M. R. Interdisciplinary relationships: Interrelations of physiological, psychological, and psychiatric findings in healthy men. In Birren, J. E., Butler, R. N., Greenhouse, S. W., Sokoloff, L., and Yarrow, M. R. (Eds.), *Human aging*. PHS Publ No. 986:283 Washington, D.C.: U.S. Government Printing Office, 1963.

Birren, J. E. and Spieth, W. Age, response, speed and cardiovascular functions. *J. Gerontol.*, 17:390, 1962.

Blum, J. E., Jarvik, L. F., and Clark, E. T. Rate of change on selective tests of intelligence: A twenty-year longitudinal study of aging. *J. Gerontol.*, 25:171, 1970.

Busse, E. W. A Physiological, psychological, and sociological study of aging. In Palmore, E. (Ed.), *Normal aging: Reports from the Duke Longitudinal Study, 1955–1969*, Durham, N.C.: Duke University Press, 1970, p. 3.

Enzer, N., Simonson, E., and Blakstein, S. S. Fatigue of patients with circulatory insufficiency, investigated by means of the fusion frequency of flicker. *Ann. Intern. Med.*, 16:701, 1942.

Grover, M. VIII. Variation of blood pressure and heart disease with age, and the correlation of blood pressure with height and weight. *Public Health Rep.* 63:1083, 1948.

Harris, R. *The Management of Geriatric Cardiovascular Disease*, Philadelphia: Lippincott, 1970.

Heyman, D. K. and Jeffers, F. C. Study of relative influences of race and socioeconomic status upon the activities and attitudes of a southern aged population. *J. Gerontol.*, 19:225, 1964.

King, H. E. Comparison of fine psychomotor by hypertensive and hypotensive subjects. *Percept. Mot. Skills*, 6:199, 1956.

Masters, A. M., Garfield, C. I., and Walters, M. B. *Normal blood pressure and hypertension*, Philadelphia: Lea & Febiger, 1952.

Obrist, W. D. Cerebral ischemia and the senescent electroencephalogram. In Simonson, E., and McGavack, T. H. (Eds.), *Cerebral ischemia*. Springfield, Ill.: Charles C Thomas, p. 71, 1964.

Pickering, F. *The nature of essential hypertension*. New York: Grune and Stratton, 1961.

Reitan, R. M. Intellectual and affective changes in essential hypertension. *Amer. J. Psychiat.*, 110:817, 1954.

Spieth, W. Abnormally slow perceptual motor task performance in individuals with stable mild to moderate heart disease. *Aerosp. Med.* 33:370, 1962.

Speith, W. Cardiovascular health status, age, and psychological performance. *J. Gerontol.*, 19:277, 1964.

Thompson, L. W., Eisdorfer, C., and Estes, E. H. Cardiovascular disease and behavioral changes in the elderly. In *Proceedings of the 7th International Congress of Gerontology*. Vienna: Wiener Medizinischen Akademie, 1966, p. 387.

Wechsler, D. *Manual for the Wechsler Adult Intelligence Scale*. New York: Psychological Cooperation, 1955.

Wechsler, D. *The measurement and appraisal of adult intelligence*. Baltimore: Williams & Wilkins, 1958, p. 96.

Intellectual Changes   *Carl Eisdorfer and Frances Wilkie*

The effect of advancing adult age on intellectual performance has been a topic of some interest in recent years. Numerous investigators (Bell and Zubek, 1960; Eisdorfer, Busse, and Cohen, 1959; Jarvik, Kallmann, and Falek, 1962; Kleemeier, 1961) have suggested that the data reported by Kaplan (1956) and Doppelt and Wallace (1955) on the standardization of the Wechsler Adult Intelligence Scale (WAIS) for the postmaturity years should be subject to further scrutiny. Also of major interest has been the discrepancy in results between the cross-sectional studies which show an age related decline (Doppelt and Wallace, 1955; Wechsler, 1958) and the longitudinal studies which have reported little age decrement in intellective abilities (Berkowitz and Green, 1963; Eisdorfer, 1963; Jarvik, Kallmann, and Falek, 1962; Jarvik, Kallmann, Falek, and Klaber, 1957; Kallmann and Jarvik, 1959; Kleemeier, 1961, 1962). Another relevant issue is whether the initial level of intelligence might affect the differential rates of intellectual decline among the aged (Bayley and Oden, 1955; Eisdorfer, 1963; Eisdorfer and Cohen, 1961; Owens, 1957).

The results reported here represent the most recent findings on intellectual functioning among a group of relatively healthy community volunteers who were participants in a longitudinal, interdisciplinary study at the Duke University Center for the Study of Aging and Human Development. . . .

Based upon data obtained during the early stages of the Duke Study, several reports were presented which questioned the generality of the WAIS norms for older individuals (Eisdorfer and Cohen, 1961; Eisdorfer, Busse, and Cohen, 1959). In addition, Eisdorfer (1963) reported on the initial three-year retest evaluation which demonstrated little overall decline with the subjects tending to show minor changes in test performance in the general direction of a regression toward the mean.

Method

The testing involved 224 subjects in the 60–79 age range, 98 of whom completed four examinations during the ten-year follow-up period. Employing a cross-sectional as well as a longitudinal strategy, the focus in this report is upon the intellectual changes among the survivors of the ten-year study as well as upon the intellectual performance of the subjects who were lost to the program prior to the fourth evaluation. In addition, differential rates of in-

Reprinted by permission from *Intellectual Functioning in Adults,* edited by Lissy F. Jarvik, Carl Eisdorfer, and June E. Blum. New York: Springer Publishing Co., 1973.

tellectual decline will be examined as a function of initial intellectual level.

The results have been tabulated into three separate analyses. In each analysis, the data for the 120 subjects who were initially examined in the 60–69 age range and the 104 subjects initially in the 70–79 age range were treated separately. The data to be reported upon in this paper consists of the Full Scale, Verbal, Performance and IQ scores.

The first analysis examines the Full Scale Scores from all subjects who had a given examination regardless of whether or not they returned for subsequent examinations. In addition, this sample was divided into a survivor's group which included subjects who had completed the ten-year follow-up study and a nonsurvivor's group which included subjects who were lost to the program following the first, second, or third examinations. In the second analysis, a cross-sectional strategy is employed to examine the intellectual changes for the total sample across the ten-year period as a function of initial intellectual level. The third analysis focuses upon those subjects who completed all (i.e., four) examinations during the ten-year period and employs a longitudinal strategy to examine the intellectual changes over time as a function of initial intellectual level.

Results

Analysis

The first analysis examines the Full Scale Scores using both a cross-sectional and a longitudinal paradigm. For the subjects initially examined in the 60–69 and 70–79 age range, Figure 4–3 presents the mean Full Scale Scores for the total sample, which includes the entire testing sample at each examination independent of whether the subjects returned for subsequent examinations. Figure 4–3 also shows the survivors and nonsurvivors, separately. The data for the nonsurvivors are presented in three categories according to the number of examinations they had: (1) only the initial test; (2) tests 1 and 2; (3) tests 1, 2, and 3. Since the scores are plotted according to the mean age of the subjects at each examination, it should be noted that the third and fourth examinations of the younger age group (initially examined at age 60–69) occurred at about the same age of the subjects as that of the first testing of the older group (initially examined at age 70–79). This results in the two curves overlapping between the ages of 72 and 74 years.

There was a positive linear relationship between the Full Scale Scores on the initial examination and the survivorship of the subjects during the ten-year period. This was true of both the young and old age groups ($r = .20$, $df = 118$, $p < .05$; and $r = .28$, $df = 102$, $p < .01$, respectively) with an identical relationship significantly ($p < .01$) seen in the verbal and performance areas. Thus, the survivors (subjects who had four examinations) had markedly higher Full Scale Scores than did their counterparts who did not

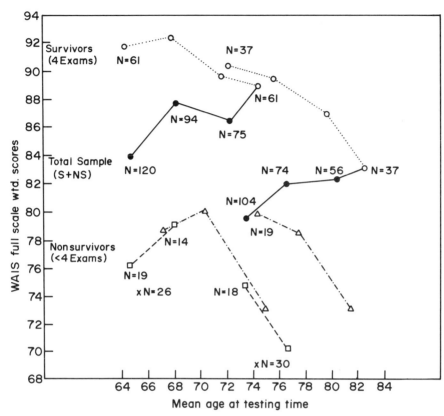

Figure 4–3. *The Wechsler Adult Intelligence Scale (WAIS) scores during a ten-year longitudinal study of individuals initially examined at ages 60–69 and 70–79. The total sample, represented by the solid line, includes all subjects at each testing, regardless of whether they returned for subsequent examinations. The survivors, represented by the dotted curve, includes only those subjects who had all four examinations during the ten-year period. The nonsurvivors, represented by the dashes, are grouped according to whether the subjects had only the initial test (represented by the X); tests 1 and 2 (represented by the squares); or tests 1, 2, and 3 (represented by the triangles).*

return for all four examinations. The scores for the total sample fell between the scores of the survivors and nonsurvivors. It should be noted that with repeated examinations the total sample becomes more identical with the survivor's sample so that they are identical by the fourth examination. In general, the survivors tended to be more stable across the first three examinations than were the nonsurvivors although both groups had changes in the same direction (i.e., increases or losses) between examinations.

Although the survivors were not as labile as were the nonsurvivors across the first three examinations, nevertheless by the fourth examination the survivors did show some loss from their initial level. Across the 10-year period, the survivors who were initially examined at age 60–69 had a significant loss of 2.6 points in Full Scale Score ($t = 2.1$, $df = 60$, $p < .05$) which was primarily attributed to a 2.0 loss in the performance area ($t = 2.8$, $p < .01$). Over the ten-year period, the survivors initially examined at ages 70–79 had significant ($p < .01$) decrements of 7.3 points in Full Scale Score ($t = 4.0$, $df = 36$) and a 3.7 and 3.6 point loss in the verbal and performance areas ($t = 3.1$ and 4.4, respectively). Over the ten-year period, the older group of survivors had a significantly greater decrement in Verbal and Total Scores ($t = 2.2$ and 2.2, respectively, $df = 96$, $p < .05$) than did their younger counterparts. It was interesting to note that the younger group of survivors had significant gains in Full Scale, Verbal, and Performance IQ Scores over time (mean increments = 8.4, 8.0, and 8.3, respectively) which were significant at the 0.01 level ($t = 10.2$; 9.1; and 8.2, respectively, $df = 60$). On the other hand, the older group of survivors remained relatively unchanged in IQ over time.

Analysis 2

The second analysis employs a cross-sectional paradigm. The entire sample was divided into a low-, middle-, or high-IQ group based upon the subject's Full Scale Score on the initial examination with each subject retained in that category through any subsequent examinations. For all subjects, the categorization was based upon the IQ equivalent of their Full Scale Score using Wechsler's conversion table (Wechsler, 1955) for the 55–64 age group. According to this categorization the low group had an IQ equivalent to 85; the middle group had an IQ range equivalent to 85–115; and the high group had an IQ equivalent to 116+. It is important to note that these numbers do not reflect the subjects' actual IQ scores at the time of the examination but rather enable us to evaluate all subjects against the same baseline categories.

Figure 4–4 shows the difference between the mean Full Scale Scores at the beginning and at the end of the ten-year period for those subjects in the low-, middle-, or high-IQ groups. In this analysis, the results of the entire sample tested at test one and test four were incorporated into the analytic schema. Thus, for the group initially examined at age 60–69 years, there were 120 subjects at test 1 and 61 subjects at test 4. For the group initially examined at age 70–79 years, there were 104 subjects at test 1 and 37 subjects at test 4. The intellectual difference scores for both the younger and older age groups were obtained by subtracting the initial examination scores of the total sample (which included all subjects independent of whether they returned for subsequent examinations) from the fourth examination scores of the subjects who returned to complete the fourth evaluation.

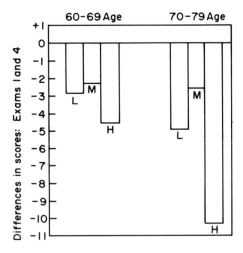

Figure 4–4. *Cross-sectional differences in Weschsler Adult Intelligence Scale (WAIS) full scale
weighted scores between the beginning and end of a ten-year period
among individuals initially examined
at ages 60–69 and 70–79, with
either low, middle, or high WAIS
scores on the initial examination.*

For both age groups, in this analysis all three IQ groups showed some
loss in the verbal and performance areas which was reflected in their Full
Scale Scores. At both ages, the middle IQ group remained relatively more
stable over time than did the remaining IQ groups with the high IQ group
having the greatest loss. A comparison of the young and old subjects at each
IQ level indicated little difference between the two age groups in the middle
IQ range, while the older groups (initially aged 70–79) in the low and high
IQ categories had losses of 1.9 and 5.9 points greater than that of their
younger (initially aged 60–69) counterparts, respectively.

Analysis 3

The longitudinal analysis included only the data from the survivors of the
ten-year study and examined intellectual change across time as a function of
initial test score level, using the three IQ categories described in the second
analysis (above). Intellectual change was determined by subtracting the
subject's score on the initial examination from their scores on the fourth
examination. At each age level, Figure 4–5 shows the mean Full Scale Score
changes between the initial and fourth examinations.

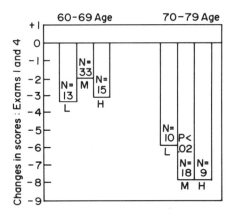

Figure 4–5. *Longitudinal change (delta scores) over a ten-year period as measured by the WAIS (full scale weighted scores) among individuals initially examined at ages 60–69 and 70–79, with either low, middle, or high WAIS scores on the initial examination.*

Based upon a series of one way analysis of variance, the results indicated that at each age level the low-, middle-, and high-IQ groups had approximately the same magnitude of intellectual change over time in Full Scale, Verbal, and Performance Scores. Although the initial level of intelligence was not related to the magnitude of intellectual loss over time, nevertheless at the younger age the middle-IQ group did have a significant loss in the performance area over time (related $t = 2.1$, $df = 32$, $p < .05$). At the older age, the middle IQ group also had a significant loss in the performance area ($t = 3.4$, $df = 17$, $p < .01$) as well as in the verbal ($t = 2.2$, $p < .05$) and over-all scores ($t = 2.8$, $p < .02$). In addition, at the older age the high IQ group had a significant loss in the performance area ($t = 2.6$, $df = 8$, $p < .05$). A comparison of the Full Scale Score changes between the younger and older subjects at each IQ level indicated that the middle IQ group at the older age had a loss almost three times as great as that experienced by their younger counterparts in the Full Scale Score ($t = 2.1$, $df = 49$, $p < .05$). The old and young subjects at the low and high IQ levels did not differ significantly in the magnitude of decline over time.

Conclusions

Our results replicate previous findings in that our sample of aged individuals who were able to complete a ten-year longitudinal study were functioning at a higher intellectual level than were their counterparts who were unable to complete this program. Viewed somewhat differently, the initial over-all intellectual level of our subjects was positively correlated with survivorship (i.e., continued participation in the study).

The total sample, which included the scores of the survivors and nonsurvivors pooled, showed an increase over time, in contrast to the decrement noted among the survivors and nonsurvivors separately. This appears to reflect a potential artifact in analyzing such data across time. The appropriate analysis of longitudinal data should involve using data only from the same subjects across time where subjects are lost secondary to death or drop out. The resultant analysis may in fact be that of a repeated measurement of cross-sectional samples (i.e., where the total N at each time slice is analyzed and the consequent slices compared across time). In this instance the survivors were more stable and at a higher level than the nonsurvivors. Thus, repeated analyses of the total sample were increasingly limited to and affected by the superior performance of the survivors. During the ten-year study there was a substantial loss of subjects with the lowest IQ group having a loss of 72 percent, the middle IQ group 51.4 percent, and the high IQ group sustaining a loss of only 36.8 percent of their subjects. Thus, in the final stages of this study, the data are biased to the extent that a smaller percentage of the initially less able were available for subsequent retesting than were the initially more able.

The survivors of the ten-year study who were initially examined at ages 60–69 had a significant decrement over time in the performance area which was reflected in a slight but reliable 2.6 mean drop in their over-all scores. The survivors first examined at ages 70–79 had a significant loss in all areas.

The literature offers somewhat contradictory findings with respect to the relationship between initial levels of ability and the subsequent rate and magnitude of decline. At the more advanced ages there is little data available on people with superior or subnormal abilities. However, previous findings have suggested that through the mid-fifties, the initially more able remain relatively stable or show some gains particularly in verbal abilities (Bayley and Oden, 1955; Gilbert, 1935; Nisbet, 1957). The data on people of subnormal abilities have been inconsistent (Bell and Zubek, 1960; Foulds and Raven, 1948; Kaplan, 1943; Thompson, 1951). The slight decline noted among aged individuals of average abilities has been somewhat less in longitudinal studies than that observed in cross-sectional studies (Doppelt and Wallace, 1955; Eisdorfer, 1963; Kallmann and Jarvik, 1959; Kleemeier, 1961; Jarvik, Kallmann, and Falek, 1962; Jarvik, Kallmann, Falek, and Klaber, 1957; Miles, 1934). When examined longitudinally, our results support Birren and Morrison's (1961) findings in that individuals at different initial levels of intellectual functioning (i.e., low-, middle-, or high-IQ) subsequently maintain relatively similar patterns of intellectual change over time. In spite of this finding, some of our IQ subgroups did have significant losses over time from their initial level. Thus, our subjects in the middle IQ range who were initially tested at ages 60–69 years had a slight but significant decline in the performance area while their older counterparts (initially tested at ages 70–79) had a decrement in all areas. Our older group of initially more able individuals (high IQ) had a loss over time in the performance area. In contrast, our people with low IQ at both age levels had a slight but nonsignificant loss over time. Thus, the decline noted in the performance area among the entire sample (independent of initial IQ level) of survivors first examined at ages

60–69 years could be primarily attributed to those subjects in the middle IQ range at this age. Further, the significant losses in all areas observed among the entire sample of survivors initially tested at age 70–79 could be primarily attributed to those subjects in the middle IQ range, with the high IQ individuals also accounting for some of the decline noted in the performance area.

Summary

In a ten-year longitudinal study, intellectual functioning as measured by the Wechsler Adult Intelligence Scale (WAIS) was examined in 224 community volunteers in the 60–79 age range, 98 of whom returned to complete all four examinations during the ten-year period.

Longitudinal analysis demonstrated that persons with initially higher WAIS scores appear to show a better prospect for survivorship, have more stable ability levels (at least on repeated WAIS testing), and certain IQ subgroups showed a slight, albeit significant, drop in intellectual functioning. This intellectual decline over the 10 year period appeared to be primarily among our older individuals who were initially of average and superior intellectual functioning (mean age at initial testing was 72 years and at the fourth examination was 82 years) and among the middle ability range of the younger subjects who were 64 years old at the initial testing and 74 years old at the fourth examination. The role of initial level of ability in survivorship and its relation to a possible methodologic error of repeated cross-sectional analyses over time is highlighted by these data.

References

Bayley, Nancy, and Oden, Melita H. The maintenance of intellectual ability in gifted adults. *Journal of Gerontology*, 10:91–107, 1955.

Bell, Anne, and Zubek, J. P. The effect of age on the intellectual performance of mental defectives. *Journal of Gerontology*, 15:285–295, 1960.

Berkowitz, B., and Green, R. F. Changes in intellect with age: I. Longitudinal study of Wechsler-Bellevue sources. *Journal of Genetic Psychology*, 103:3–21, 1963.

Birren, J. E., and Morrison, D. F. Analysis of the WAIS subtests in relation to age and education. *Journal of Gerontology*, 16:363–369, 1961.

Doppelt, J. E., and Wallace, W. L. Standardization of the Wechsler Adult Intelligence Scale for older persons. *Journal of Abnormal and Social Psychology*, 51:312–330, 1955.

Eisdorfer, C. The WAIS performance of the aged: A retest evaluation. *Journal of Gerontology*, 18:169–172, 1963.

Eisdorfer, C., Busse, E. W., and Cohen, L. D. The WAIS performance of an aged sample: The relationship between verbal and performance I. Q.s. *Journal of Gerontology*, 14:197–201, 1959.

Eisdorfer, C., and Cohen, L. D. The generality of the WAIS standardization for the aged: A regional comparison. *Journal of Abnormal and Social Psychology*, 62:520–527, 1961.

Foulds, G. A., and Raven, J. C. Normal changes in the mental abilities of adults as age advances. *Journal of Mental Science*, 94:133–142, 1948.

Gilbert, J. G. Mental efficiency in senescence. *Archives of Psychology*, 27 (whole no. 188), 1935.

Jarvik, Lissy F., Kallmann, F. J., and Falek, A. Intellectual changes in aged twins. *Journal of Gerontology*, 17:289–294, 1962.

Jarvik, Lissy F., Kallman, F. J., Falek, A., and Klaber, M. M. Changing intellectual functions in senescent twins. *Acta Genetica Et Statistica Medica*, 7:421–430, 1957.

Kallmann, F. J., and Jarvik, Lissy F. Individual differences in constitution and genetic background. In J. E. Birren (Ed.), *Handbook of aging and the individual: Psychological and biological aspects*, Chicago: University of Chicago Press, 1959.

Kaplan, O. J. Mental decline in older morons. *American Journal of Mental Deficiency*, 47:277–285, 1943.

Kaplan, O. J. *Mental disorders in later life*. Stanford, Calif.: Stanford University Press, 1956.

Kleemeier, R. W. Intellectual changes in the senium, or death and the I. Q. Presidential address, Division of Maturity and Old Age, American Psychological Association, September 1, 1961.

Kleemeier, R. W. Intellectual change in the senium. *Proceedings of the Statistics Section of the American Statistical Association*, 1962, pp. 290–295.

Maddox, G. L. Selected methodological issues. *Proceedings of the Social Statistics Section of the American Statistical Association*, 1962, pp. 280–285.

Miles, Catherine C. The influence of speed and age on intelligence scores of adults. *Journal of General Psychology*, 10:208–210, 1934.

Nisbet, J. D. Intelligence and age: Retesting with twenty four years interval. *British Journal of Educational Psychology*, 27:190–198, 1957.

Owens, W. A., Jr. Is age kinder to the initially more able? *Proceedings of the Fourth Congress of the International Association of Gerontology*, Florence, Italy: Tipographia Tito Mattiolo, 4:151–157, 1957.

Thompson, C. W. Decline in limit of performance among adult morons. *American Journal of Psychology*, 64:203–215, 1951.

Wechsler, D. *Manual for the Wechsler Adult Intelligence Scale*. New York: Psychological Corporation, 1955.

Wechsler, D. *The Measurement and appraisal of adult intelligence*, 4th ed. Baltimore: Williams and Wilkins, 1958.

Terminal Changes in Intelligence   *Frances Wilkie and Carl Eisdorfer*

During the past decade increased attention has been focused upon identifying some of the physiological, psychological, and sociological predictors of longevity, or conversely, of impending death among the aged. As discussed by Granick (1971) in a review of the cognitive aspects of longevity, health status and various social or demographic factors appeared to be the predominant predictors of longevity although there was strong evidence to indi-

This paper was presented at the 25th annual meeting of the Gerontological Society on Dec. 22, 1972 in San Juan, Puerto Rico.

cate that cognitive functioning may also be a good psychological predictor of survival. There is, in fact, evidence that a marked decrement in intellectual performance is associated with death within one to five years (Berkowitz, 1965; Goldfarb, 1969; J. Jarvik and Blum, 1971; L. F. Jarvik and Falek, 1963; Kleemeier, 1962, 1961; Lieberman, 1965; K. F. Riegel, 1971; K. F. Riegel, R. M. Riegel, and Meyer, 1967; Sanderson, 1961). Despite this evidence, however, relatively little is known about the relationship to other factors that appear to be associated with cognitive functioning in the aged. Recent reviews by Botwinick (1970), Granick (1971), Palmore (1971a, 1971b), and Rose (1971) suggest that the intellectual changes before death may be a function of such factors as initial intellectual level, physical health, or the distance from death at the time of testing.

This report, with findings from a 15-year follow-up study of aged individuals, tests the hypothesis that intellectual changes are related to nearness to death. In addition, however, such changes if found will be examined in relationship to initial level of intellectual performance and physical health.

Method

The subjects were 37 nonsurviving and 66 surviving participants in an interdisciplinary, longitudinal study of ambulatory, community volunteers at the Duke University Center for the Study of Aging and Human Development. The subjects do not represent a random sample, although the sex, race, and socioeconomic characteristics of the original panel of 256 subjects approximated those in the central North Carolina area (Maddox, 1962). In this ongoing study, there were six evaluations over a 15-year period. Each evaluation consisted of physical, psychiatric, psychological, and sociological examinations and various laboratory tests (Busse, 1965). The study sample is limited to those who were seen for at least three evaluations.

Because cognitive changes may occur a number of years prior to death, the focus among our nonsurvivors is upon intellectual changes on three evaluations over approximately a six-year period prior to the death of each subject. The sample was also limited to those who died from natural causes within a three-year period after their final test. Their mean ages on the first, second, and third tests focused upon in this report were 74, 77, and 80 years, respectively, and their mean age at death was approximately 82 years. Based upon the time interval between the final test and death, the 37 nonsurviving subjects were divided into three subgroups which included 13 subjects who died within 0 to 12 months after their final test, 16 subjects who died within 13 to 24 months, and 8 subjects who died within 25 to 32 months after their final test.

The sample of 66 survivors included only those subjects who have survived for more than four years since the last of the three tests focused upon in this report when their mean ages were 74, 77, and 79 years respectively.

Intellectual performance was measured by the Wechsler Adult Intelligence Scale (WAIS) (Wechsler, 1955). Our focus is upon the Full Scale, Verbal, and Performance Weighted (Wtd.) Scores on three tests as well as upon the change in these scores (as delta scores) between evaluations.

Results and Discussions

On the issue of a decline before death

The results indicated that the survivors and nonsurvivors did not differ significantly in age, with subjects initially ranging in age between the late 60s to the early 80s. Further, within the surviving and nonsurviving groups there were no significant age effects on the actual WAIS scores or on the magnitude of change in these scores between evaluations.

Figure 4–6 shows the mean Full Scale, Verbal, and Performance Weighted Scores for the survivors and the three nonsurviving subgroups on the three tests. Analyses of variance indicated that there were no significant differences between the survivors and the three nonsurviving subgroups in the actual WAIS scores. Even when the nonsurvivors were pooled independently of distance from death, their actual scores were not statistically different from those of the survivors. Among the nonsurvivors those nearest to death tended to have the lowest scores, however, nonsignificant product moment correlations ranging from .090 to .224 indicated that there was no significant relationship between the actual scores and nearness to death.

Although the survivors and nonsurvivors did not differ in the actual scores

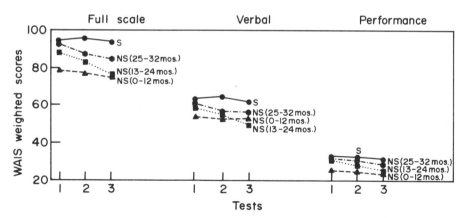

Figure 4–6. *The intelligence test scores [Wechsler Adult Intelligence Scale (WAIS)] on three evaluations of aged individuals who either have survived (S) for more than four years after the third test or died (NS) within 0–12 mos., 13–24 mos., or 25–32 mos. after the third test.*

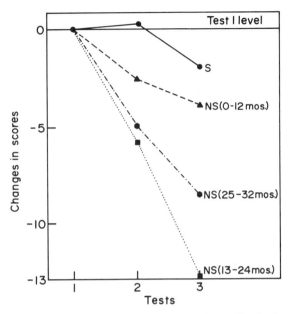

Figure 4–7. *Changes in WAIS Full Scale Weighted Scores from the test 1 level for the survivors (S) and the nonsurvivors (NS) whose deaths occurred within 0–12 mos., 13–24 mos., or 25–32 mos. after the third test.*

they did differ significantly in the magnitude of change in scores between evaluations. Figure 4–7 shows the mean changes in the Full Scale Weighted Scores from the test 1 level for the survivors and the three nonsurviving sub-groups. Analyses of variance indicated that only the nonsurviving 13–24 month and 25–32 month subgroups had significantly greater losses than the survivors which occurred between tests 1 and 2 and were reflected in their overall changes between tests 1 and 3 ($df = 3/102$, $F = 3.30$, $p < .05$; and $F = 6.94$, $p < .01$, respectively). Differences between tests 2 and 3 were not significant with the survivors as well as the nonsurvivors experiencing some decline.

Figure 4–8 shows the mean changes in the Verbal Weighted Scores from the test 1 level for the survivors and the three nonsurviving subgroups. Significant between-group differences were found between each evaluation. Thus, between tests 1 and 2, the nonsurviving 25–32 month and 13–24 month subgroups had significantly greater losses than the survivors, with the 13–24 month group also experiencing a greater loss between tests 2 and 3 which for this latter group was reflected in a greater loss over the three tests ($df = 3/102$, $F = 2.93$ and 3.06, $p < .05$; and $F = 5.82$, $p < .01$, respectively).

Figure 4–9 shows the mean changes in the Performance Weighted Scores

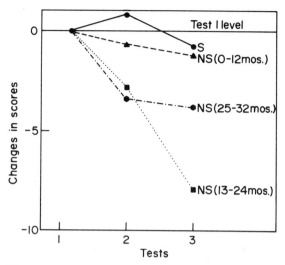

Figure 4–8. *Changes in WAIS Verbal Weighted Scores from the test 1 level for the survivors (S) and the nonsurvivors (NS) whose deaths occurred within 0–12 mos., 13–24 mos., or 25–32 mos. after the third test.*

from the test 1 level for the survivors and the nonsurviving subgroups. All groups had some loss, however, only the nonsurviving 13–24 month and 25–32 month subgroups had significantly greater losses than the survivors occurring only between tests 1 and 3 ($df = 3/102$, $F = 4.15$, $p < .01$).

These results in part support previous findings of a terminal drop in in-

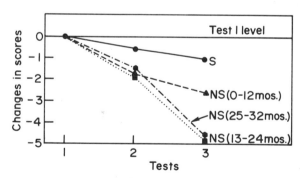

Figure 4–9. *Changes in WAIS Performance Weighted Scores from the test 1 level for the survivors (S) and the nonsurvivors (NS) whose deaths occurred within 0–12 mos., 13–24 mos., or 25–32 mos. after the third test.*

tellectual performance. Thus, the groups that died within 13 to 32 months after testing had greater losses than did the survivors and the major portion of observed loss occurred approximately 7 to 10 years before death. In contrast, the group that died within one year after the final test had intellectual changes that were not markedly different from those of the survivors. We also examined the earlier performance of the subjects whose deaths occurred within one year after the final testing. Although only 8 out of the 13 subjects in this group could be followed back for 12 to 15 years, no significant decline was noted.

In contrast to Berkowitz's (1965) and Lieberman's (1965) findings, these results suggest that psychological changes do not always increase with increasing nearness to death. In fact, among our nonsurvivors nonsignificant product moment correlations ranging from $-.06$ to $-.18$ indicated that the magnitude of observed intellectual changes was not related to distance from death. Further, our findings do suggest that some but not all individuals experience a marked intellectual loss before death. Thus, independent of distance from death, 24 percent of the nonsurvivors had no change or even gains of up to 3 points in the Full Scale Weighted Scores over the three tests, with an additional 22 percent having losses of less than 6 points. The remaining nonsurvivors had losses ranging up to 44 points.

Why do some subjects decline?

There is then the question of why do some individuals have dramatic intellectual loss and others have little change before death? In an attempt to provide some answers to this complex problem we examined intellectual changes before death in relationship to initial level of performance as well as in relationship to physical health.

Initial intellectual level as a variable. As indicated in the reviews by Botwinick (1967, 1970) and Granick (1971) the initially less able intellectually tend to die sooner than the initially more able. It might also be assumed that differential rates of intellectual decline may be associated with differential initial levels of performance. In order to examine the effect of initial performance level upon subsequent intellectual changes before death, the survivors and the total sample of nonsurvivors (i.e., independent of distance from death) were divided into low-, middle-, or high-IQ groups based upon the subject's Full Scale Weighted Score on the first test focused upon in this report with each individual retained in that category through subsequent examinations. For all subjects, the categorization was based upon the IQ equivalent of their Full Scale Weighted Scores using Wechsler's conversion table (1955) for the 55–64 age group. According to this categorization, the low group had an IQ equivalent to less than 85; the middle group had an IQ range equivalent to 85–115; and the high group had an IQ equivalent to 116 or more. It is important to note that these numbers do not reflect the subjects' actual IQ scores at the time of the examination; rather they enable us to evaluate all subjects against the same baseline categories.

Figure 4–10 shows the mean changes in the Full Scale scores between tests 1 and 3 for the survivors and nonsurvivors in the low, middle, and high IQ groups. When compared to the survivors, only the middle and high IQ nonsurvivors showed significant losses ($t = 2.77$ and 3.09, $p < .01$, $df = 55$ and 21, respectively). Further, the high IQ nonsurvivors had a significantly greater loss than their surviving counterparts in the verbal ($p < .05$) as well as in the performance areas ($p < .01$) while the nonsurviving middle IQ group had a significantly greater loss than their surviving counterpart only in the verbal area ($p < .01$). The nonsurviving low IQ group did not differ significantly from their surviving counterpart. In view of

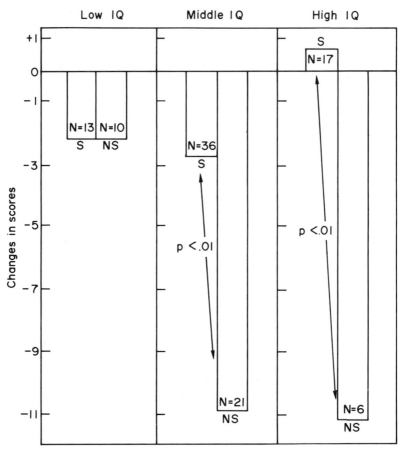

Figure 4–10. *Changes in WAIS Full Scale Weighted Scores between tests 1 and 3 for the survivors (S) and nonsurvivors (NS) with either low, middle, or high WAIS scores on test 1.*

our finding that the group within one year from death at the final testing had less intellectual change than did their counterparts who were 13–32 months away from death, it should be noted that the nonsurvivors did not differ significantly with respect to the proportion of subjects in the low-, middle-, or high-IQ categories.

Physical health as a variable. In a further attempt to identify some of the underlying factors associated with intellectual changes before death, the physical health status of each subject was examined over the period focused upon in this report. As suggested by Granick (1971) poor physical health may be the basic factor related to a short life span as well as to the low level of cognitive functioning observed among these individuals. However, the relationship between cognitive functioning and physical health appears to be a complex one. Estes (1969) in discussing the health experience of the elderly, suggests that the aged person once he has put aside the anxiety about the significance of various symptoms, for which little may be done in a curative sense, may actually accept these symptoms as a part of growing old. Thus, he suggested that chronic diseases among the aged may frequently result in only mild physical limitation. On the other hand, the aged have a special problem in that a given illness is frequently superimposed upon a variety of preexisting chronic diseases and upon an organ system which may have lost much of its reserve capacity. In such cases the older person's health may be in such a delicate state of balance that even a "minor" or acute illness (i.e., respiratory infections, injuries, etc.) may lead to major consequences resulting in prolonged physical disability. Relatively little attention has been focused upon examining the relationship between chronic diseases and cognitive functioning, with even less attention directed towards the effects of an acute illness upon performance.

This raises the issue of whether differential rates of intellectual change among the aged may in part be related to acute illnesses superimposed upon chronic diseases. Our first analysis focused upon cardiovascular disease because it is a major health problem of the aged (Estes, 1969; Grover, 1948; Harris, 1970; Masters, Garfield, and Walters, 1952) and has been related to low levels of cognitive functioning (Apter, Halstead, and Heimburger, 1951; Birren, Butler, Greenhouse, Sokoloff, and Yarrow, 1963; Birren and Spieth, 1962; Eisdorfer, 1967; Enzer, Simonson, and Blakstein, 1942; King, 1956; Reitan, 1954; Spieth, 1964, 1962; Wilkie and Eisdorfer, 1971, 1972, 1973). The second analysis is focused upon intellectual changes in relationship to the presence or absence of acute illnesses (i.e., infections, injuries, surgery, etc.) superimposed upon chronic diseases (i.e., heart disease, emphysema, etc.).

The first analysis examined the association between change in intellectual functioning and cardiovascular disease among the survivors and nonsurvivors independent of distance from death. For each subject an internist made an overall assessment of cardiovascular disease (CVD) on the basis of physical findings, electrocardiographic interpretation, estimates of heart size on the basis of actual measurements from X-ray photographs, aortic calcification, hypertension, and cardiac decompensation by history. Subjects were rated on a 9-point scale on which 0 represented no heart disease and 9 represented definite heart disease with severe symptoms and signs despite rest in bed (preterminal state). Based upon each subject's CVD rating on his third evaluation reported here, subjects with CVD were divided into two categories: those with mild and those with moderately severe disease. The *mild* category included those with ratings of 2 or 3 (definite heart disease, no limiting symptoms, no therapy for failure, or definite heart disease with no limiting symptoms controlled by drugs). The *moderate* category included the subjects with ratings of 4 or 5 (definite heart disease and mild to moderate limitation of activity). The *NCVD* category included subjects with no symptoms or evidence of heart disease.

Figure 4–11 shows the mean changes in Full Scale Weighted Scores between tests 1 and 3 for the survivors and nonsurvivors in the NCVD, Mild and Moderate CVD groups. Although 59 percent of the survivors and 62 percent of the nonsurvivors had CVD, only 6 percent of the survivors compared to 32 percent of the nonsurvivors had moderately severe CVD. Among the survivors, there was relatively little intellectual change independent of the pres-

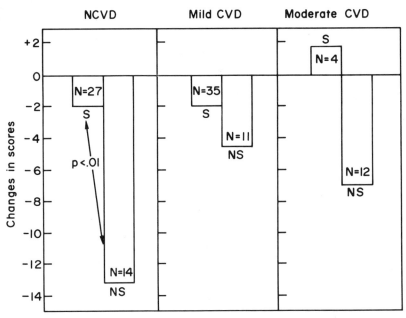

Figure 4–11. *Changes in WAIS Full Scale Weighted Scores between tests 1 and 3 for the survivors (S) and nonsurvivors (NS) with either no cardiovascular disease (NCVD), mild or moderately severe CVD.*

ence or absence of CVD. In contrast, among the nonsurvivors intellectual loss tended to increase with increasing severity of CVD, however, it should be noted that the NCVD group tended to have the greatest loss. When compared to their surviving counterpart, the nonsurviving NCVD group had a significantly greater loss ($t = 2.95$, $p < .01$, $df = 39$). In contrast, no statistical difference was found between the surviving and nonsurviving groups with mild CVD. Because there were only four survivors with moderately severe CVD, no statistical comparison was done with their nonsurviving counterpart, however, it should be noted that the survivors had a gain of 1.5 points while the nonsurvivors had a mean loss of about 7 points.

The finding that nonsurvivors with no cardiovascular disease not only had a significantly greater intellectual loss than survivors but also tended to have a greater loss than the nonsurvivors with cardiovascular disease pointed to the need to examine the effects of all chronic diseases as well as the effects of acute illnesses upon intellectual changes among the aged. For purposes of this analysis, each subject's medical record was reviewed for the period focused upon in this report. The chronic disease category included subjects with cardiovascular disease, emphysema, arthritis, diabetes, epilepsy, etc. None of the subjects in the chronic disease category had experienced an acute illness during the period focused upon in this report. The second category included subjects with acute illnesses or with acute illnesses along with a chronic disease. Acute illnesses were defined as any infections, injuries, or other minor illnesses requiring medical care. Subjects undergoing surgery were also included in this group. The presence of such events at any time during the period under examination led to the subjects being considered in this second category.

The results indicated that the survivors appeared to be relatively free of chronic diseases other than cardiovascular disease with only about 17 percent of the group having experienced an acute illness. In contrast, all (i.e., 100 percent) of the nonsurvivors had chronic diseases (i.e., mild to moderate CVD, emphysema, long history of diabetes, epilepsy, etc.) with 46 percent of the group also presenting symptoms or a history of recent acute illnesses including pulmonary and urinary tract infections, serious injuries, and/or major surgery, the latter sometimes occurring only a few months before the subject was tested in our laboratory.

Because only a small number of survivors had experienced acute illnesses and these did not appear to be accompanied by intellectual decline, our focus in this case was limited to the nonsurvivors. Figure 4–12 shows the mean changes in Full Scale Weighted Scores between tests 1 and 3 for the nonsurvivors in the chronic disease category as well as those in the acute illness plus chronic disease category. Among the nonsurvivors, the combination of an acute illness and chronic disease was associated with about a 13-point loss which was significantly greater than that observed among those with a chronic disease alone who showed about a 5-point loss ($t = 2.20$, $p < .05$, $df = 35$). This finding appeared to be independent of cardiovascular disease. Thus, both

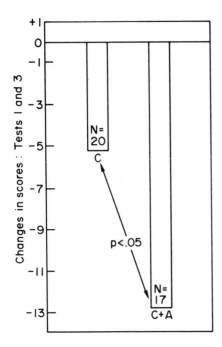

Figure 4–12. *Changes in WAIS Full Scale Weighted Scores between tests 1 and 3 for the nonsurvivors who had either chronic diseases but no acute illnesses (C) or the combination of chronic diseases along with acute illnesses (C + A).*

groups had mean CVD ratings of about 2.3 (i.e., mild CVD). Further, 9 out of the 20 subjects (45 percent) in the chronic disease group had moderately severe CVD (i.e., ratings of 3 or 4) compared to 7 out of the 17 subjects (41 percent) in the acute illness plus a chronic disease group. In regard to the other factors that were examined in this report in relationship to intellectual changes before death, it should be noted that the presence or absence of an acute illness with a chronic disease was significantly related to distance from death among our nonsurvivors. It was unclear from our findings why the group that was within one year away from death at the final testing had relatively little intellectual change and did not differ from the survivors. We can only speculate that despite their poor health they may have adapted to the symptoms or the nature of the condition was such that there was less disability resulting in their being able to come into the medical center for two days of extensive testing even though they were at a mean age of 82 years and were near death.

Comments

These findings suggest that there may be a number of factors interacting in a complex manner to account for the intellectual changes observed among the aged. Initial level of performance, ongoing physical health and acute illness are factors that should be considered in examining terminal changes in intellectual functioning. Particularly noteworthy was the finding that the nonsurvivors who sustained both acute and chronic illnesses had a greater intellectual loss than their counterparts with chronic disease but no serious acute illnesses during the time frame of this study. As noted by Estes (1969) the majority of acute illnesses among the aged can be detected and respond well to treatment. However, many physicians are overly cautious in their approach to treatment of the elderly. In view of our findings, however, it would appear that the aged might experience less intellectual loss if their acute illnesses could be vigorously treated.

References

Apter, N. S., Halstead, W. C., Heimburger, R. F. Impaired cerebral functions in essential hypertension. *Am. J. Psychiatry*, 107:803–813, 1951.

Berkowitz, B. Changes in intellect with age: IV. Changes in achievement and survival in older people. *J. Genet. Psychol.*, 107:3–14, 1965.

Birren, J. E., Butler, R. N., Greenhouse, S. W., Sokoloff, L., Yarrow, M. R., (Eds.). *Human aging*. PHS Publ. No 986. Washington, D.C.: U.S. Government Printing Office, 1963.

Birren, J. E., Spieth, S. Age response speed and cardiovascular functions. *J. Geront.*, 10:390–391, 1962.

Botwinick, J. *Cognitive processes in maturity and old age*. New York: Springer, 1967.

Botwinick, J. Geropsychology. *Annual review of psychology*, 21. Palo Alto, Calif.: Annual Reviews, 1970.

Busse, E. W. A physiological, psychological, and sociological study of aging. *J. Med. Educ.*, 40:832–839, 1965.

Eisdorfer, C. Psychologic reaction to cardiovascular change in the aged. *Mayo Clinic Proceedings*, 42:620–636, 1967.

Enzer, N., Simonson, E., Blakstein, S. S. Fatigue of patients with circulatory insufficiency, investigated by means of the fusion frequency of flicker. *Ann. Intern. Med.*, 16:701–707, 1942.

Estes, E. Health experience in the elderly. In E. W. Busse and E. Pfieffer (Eds.), *Behavior and adaptation in late life*. Boston: Little, Brown, 1969, pp. 115–128.

Goldfarb, A. I. Predicting mortality in the institutionalized aged. *Arch. Gen. Psychiatry*, 21:172–176, 1969.

Granick, S. Cognitive aspects of longevity. In E. Palmore and F. Jeffers (Eds.), *Prediction of life span*. Lexington, Mass.: D. C. Heath, 1971, pp. 109–122.

Grover, M. VIII. Variation of blood pressure and heart disease with age, and the correlation of blood pressure with height and weight. *Public Health Rep.*, 63:1083–1101, 1948.

Harris, R. *The management of geriatric Cardiovascular Disease*. Philadelphia: J. B. Lippincott, 1970.

Jarvik, J., and Blum, J. E. Cognitive declines as predictors of mortality in twin pairs: A twenty-year longitudinal study of aging. In Palmore and Jeffers (Eds.), *Prediction of life span*. 1971, pp. 199–211.

Jarvik, L. F., and Falek, A. Intellectual stability and survival in the aged. *J. Geront.* 18:173–176, 1963.

King, H. E. Comparison of fine psychomotor movement by hypertensive and hypotensive subjects. *Percept. Mot. Skills*, 6:199–204, 1956.

Kleemeier, R. W. Intellectual change in the senium. *Proceedings of the Social Statistics Section of the American Statistical Association*, 1962, pp. 290–295.

Kleemeier, R. W. Intellectual change in the senium or death and the I.Q. Presidential Address, American Psychological Association, Div. 20, 1961. (Mimeograph)

Lieberman, M. A. Psychological correlates of impending death: Some preliminary observations. *J. Geront.*, 20:182–190, 1965.

Maddox, G. L. Selected methodological issues. *Proceedings of the Social Section of the American Statistical Association*, 1962, pp. 280–285.

Masters, A. M., Garfield, C. I., Walters, M. B., *Normal blood pressure and hypertension.* Philadelphia: Lea & Febiger, 1952.

Palmore, E., The promise and problems of longevity studies. In Palmore and Jeffers (Eds.). *Prediction of life span.* 1971a, pp. 3–10.

Palmore, E., Summary and the future. In Palmore and Jeffers (Eds.), *Prediction of Life Span.* 1971b, pp. 283–288.

Reitan, R. M., Intellectual and affective changes in essential hypertension. *Am. J. Psychiatry*, 110:817–824, 1954.

Riegel, K. F., The prediction of death and longevity in longitudinal research. In Palmore and Jeffers (Eds.), *Prediction of life span.* 1971, pp. 139–152.

Riegel, K. F., Riegel, R. M., Meyer, G., A study of the dropout rates in longitudinal research on aging and the prediction of death. *J. Personality & Soc. Psychol.*, 5:342–348, 1967.

Rose, C. L., Critique of longevity studies. In Palmore and Jeffers (Eds.), *Prediction of life span.* 1971, pp. 13–29.

Sanderson, R. E., Inglis, J., Learning and mortality in elderly psychiatric patients. *J. Geront.*, 16:375–376, 1961.

Spieth, W., Abnormally slow perceptual motor task performance in individuals with stable mild to moderate heart disease. *Aerosp. Med.*, 33:370, 1962.

Spieth, W., Cardiovascular health status, age, and psychological performance. *J. Geront.*, 19:277–284, 1964.

Wechsler, D. *Manual for the Wechsler Adult Intelligence Scale.* New York: Psychological Corporation, 1955.

Wilkie, F. and Eisdorfer, C., Blood pressure and behavioral correlates. Paper read at the 9th International Congress of Gerontology, Kiev, USSR, July 1972.

Wilkie, F. and Eisdorfer, C., Intelligence and blood pressure in the aged. *Science*, 172:959–962, 1971.

Wilkie, F. and Eisdorfer, C., Systemic disease and behavioral correlates. In L. F. Jarvik, C. Eisdorfer, and J. E. Blum (Eds.), *Intellectual functioning in adults.* New York: Springer, 1973, pp. 83–93.

Neurophysiological Correlates of the Intellectual Function

H. Shan Wang, Walter D. Obrist, and Ewald W. Busse

The effect of age on intellectual function is well documented. Most of the measurable intellectual abilities seem to reach a peak in early adulthood and thenceforth decline progressively (Wechsler, 1958). As a rule, the decline in performance in nonverbal abilities is appreciably more rapid than that in verbal abilities (Botwinick, 1967). Consequently, there is a better correlation between age and performance than between age and verbal abilities.

Reprinted by permission from the *American Journal of Psychiatry*, 126:1205–1212, 1970. Copyright 1970, the American Psychiatric Association.

These generalizations concerning intellectual changes in senescence are derived mainly from cross-sectional studies. Data from several longitudinal studies have just recently become available. In follow-up studies made one year after the initial tests, Jarvik and associates (Jarvik et al., 1962) could not demonstrate any significant decline of intellectual function; there was, in fact, some evidence of improved performance on the second series of tests, which Jarvik and her coworkers attributed to "test wiseness." The minor changes observed by Eisdorfer (Eisdorfer, 1963) in two sets of studies done three years apart on a group of elderly subjects tended to regress toward the mean—a finding commonly associated with repeated measurements.

In studies with longer follow-up periods (eight and five years respectively), Jarvik and associates (Jarvik et al., 1962) and Birren (Birren, 1968) found clear evidence of decline in intellectual function, although in Jarvik's subjects this was noted only on a limited number of subtests. In the group of 29 elderly subjects retested by Birren after an interval of five years, the mean Full Scale Score on the Wechsler Adult Intelligence Scale (WAIS) was 9.6 points lower than the initial one; five out of these 29 subjects, however, showed a gain or no change at all on the second series of tests.

The findings from these longitudinal studies clearly indicate that intellectual changes in a given age group are subject to considerable individual variation. They also cast some doubt on the validity of many stereotyped views on intellectual function in senescence that have been derived mainly from cross-sectional studies. Eisdorfer (Eisdorfer, 1963) suggested that the normative data for intelligence, collected by cross-sectional sampling, may exaggerate the pattern of decline in old age, at least for a relatively short period. Birren (Birren, 1968) concluded from his observations that both stability of mental functioning and dramatic decline can be found in persons over the age of 70, and that mental decline in the later years does not occur in everyone to the same extent, but rather is irregularly distributed in the population. He suggested that expectations of mental performance must be based upon the elderly person's characteristics rather than on his age.

Many factors are known to be capable of affecting or modifying intellectual function and its assessment (Botwinick, 1967). Among sociocultural factors, for example, the important ones are education, socioeconomic status, sex, and race; among psychological factors, motivation, anxiety, cooperation, personality, and psychosis are most important. Nonetheless, the principal determinant of intellectual function and its change, particularly in senescence, is the status of the brain. Mental abilities are the expression of brain activities, which will inevitably be altered sooner or later in old age.

Much has been written about the relationship between these two parameters—the brain and intellectual function. A review of some of the pertinent literature (Wang, 1968) indicates that there is generally a good correlation between the degree of intellectual deterioration and the structural status of the brain, as indicated by histopathological findings or by radiological evidence of cortical atrophy or ventricular dilatation. The information in this regard, however, is limited to patients with obvious neuropsychiatric disorders or severe mental deterioration. All methods currently available for evaluating the structural status of the brain in vivo involve so much risk and trauma that they have to be reserved for highly selected cases.

Electroencephalography (EEG) and the measurement of cerebral oxygen consumption or cerebral blood flow are the methods most frequently employed for evaluating the functional status of the brain. Because of its established reliability and sensitivity as an indicator of brain function and because it carries no trauma or risk, EEG study is probably the most practical method for routine evaluation of the brain. The EEG tends to show considerable changes during senescence; even among elderly subjects having excellent health, EEG abnormalities are quite common (Obrist, 1963; Wang et al.). The characteristic abnormalities in the EEGs of senescent subjects are slowing of the dominant frequency and the presence of focal disturbances, predominantly over the left anterior temporal region.

A relationship between EEG abnormalities and intellectual deterioration has been repeatedly observed in patients with various neuropsychiatric disorders (Bankier, 1967; Bauer et al., 1966; Hoagland, 1954; Ingram, 1966; Jenkins, 1962; Silverman et al., 1953) and in residents of homes for the aged (Ermentini, et al., 1960; Justiss, 1962; Obrist, et al., 1962). With one exception (Thaler, 1956), a similar relationship could not be demonstrated among elderly community subjects (Birren et al., 1963; Busse et al., 1956; Obrist, et al., 1962). The lack of consistency or agreement in these studies may result in part from variations in sampling, techniques, or criteria employed. For example, some studies considered focal disturbance and diffuse slowing separately; others considered them together. In very few studies was there any control of the health status, education, and socioeconomic status of the subjects; yet all these factors are known to be capable of affecting the intellectual function and its assessment.

It is well known that insults to the brain from any cause usually result in a loss of neurons and a reduction in neuronal functioning, both of which lead to a reduction in metabolic activity of the brain. This activity can be represented by the rate at which the brain consumes oxygen or by the cerebral flow, which under normal conditions is regulated to some degree by the metabolic needs of the brain tissue. Both cerebral oxygen consumption and cerebral blood flow tend to decline in old age (Sokoloff, 1959), most likely as a result of pathological processes such as cerebral atherosclerosis or senile dementia.

In neuropsychiatric patients, these declines correlate well with the clinical manifestation of brain syndromes or intellectual impairments (Hedlund et al., 1964; Klee, 1964; Lassen et al., 1957). Very few data are available concerning the degree of correlation in community subjects. Dastur and his coworkers (Dastur et al., 1963) showed that the cerebral oxygen consumption and blood flow declined slightly, if at all, in elderly persons with optimal health.

In these subjects, neither of these measures correlated well with the results of psychological testing (Birren et al., 1963); in subjects with "senile qualities," however, cerebral oxygen consumption was significantly lower than in those without such findings (Butler et al., 1965).

The lack of data on the cerebral oxygen consumption and cerebral blood flow of healthy old persons in the community can be attributed to the fact that all quantitative measurements of these variables have required puncture of an artery or of the internal jugular vein. Recently, however, Obrist and his co-workers (Obrist et al., 1967) developed an inhalation method using 133-xenon, an inert gas, for the estimation of the grey-matter and white-matter blood flow cf a region of the brain. This method, which is completely free of risk and trauma, gives results quite comparable to those obtained by methods requiring carotid injection (Obrist et al., 1967).

The present study was undertaken in an effort to determine the degree of correlation between tests of intellectual function and neurophysiological measures of cerebral function (EEG findings and estimation of the cerebral blood flow by the xenon-inhalation method) in elderly community volunteers.

Subjects

Between 1955 and 1959, 260 community volunteers above the age of 60 were recruited to participate in a longitudinal project at the Duke University Center for the Study of Aging and Human Development. Each subject who entered the study was initially given a thorough clinical and laboratory examination by a multidisciplinary team; this study was then repeated at intervals of three or four years. Out of these subjects two samples were drawn.

1. EEG sample. The 32 subjects in this group were selected because they were free from any clinical evidence of cardiopulmonary and neurological disease on the first two examinations (study 1 and 2), which were made 3.5 years apart. The mean age of these 32 subjects was 69.8 years (SD = 5.1); 63 percent were male; and 88 percent were Caucasian. On the basis of occupation, income, etc., the socioeconomic status was classified as high for 81 percent of the group (Wang et al.). All these subjects had had 12 or more years of schooling, the mean being 15.9 years (SD = 2.3).

2. Cerebral blood flow (CBF) sample. The 24 subjects in this group were selected at random from those subjects returning for their fifth examination, about 12 years after the initial one. The majority of these subjects were also included in the EEG sample, but during the interval many of them had begun to show evidence of cardiopulmonary or neurological disease. The mean age of subjects in the CBF sample was 79.4 years (SD = 4.2) and the mean educational level, 10.0 years (SD = 6.2). Men and women were equally represented in this sample; 79 percent of the subjects were Caucasian, and only 50 percent were classified as having a high socioeconomic status.

Methods

WAIS and EEG studies were made routinely as part of the initial and follow-up examinations. The methods used for these studies have already been described (Busse et al., 1965; Eisdorfer, 1963; Obrist et al., 1962; Wang et al.). For the present study, only the waking EEG was used. The mean frequency of the occipital dominant rhythm was measured manually. Focal disturbances, if present, were evaluated with respect to their prevalence and type, as well as the location and laterality of their maximum appearance.

The cerebral blood flow was studied with the xenon-inhalation method described by Obrist and his coworkers (Obrist et al., 1967). In this method, the subject inhales for one minute a mixture of air and 133-xenon. Thereafter, the radioactivity of the left parietal region and that of expired air are monitored continuously by sodium iodide crystal scintillation detectors. The rate at which radioactivity disappears from the left parietal region is used to calculate the cortical blood flow in milliliters per 100 grams of brain tissue per minute. The expired air curve is used to correct the recirculation factor inherent in this inhalation method.

Results

1. EEG sample. At the time of the initial examination, the 32 subjects in the EEG sample obtained a mean Verbal Score of 74.2 (SD = 13.8) and a mean Performance Score of 39.4 (SD = 9.0) on the WAIS test. At the time of the second examination, 3.5 years later, the Verbal Score had declined by a mean of 0.9 (SD = 6.2); the Performance Score, by 1.7 (SD = 5.1). Neither of these changes is statistically significant. The changes were not related to the initial WAIS scores ($r = -.16$ for Verbal; $-.07$ for Performance), and they showed considerable individual variation (Figure 4–13). The verbal changes

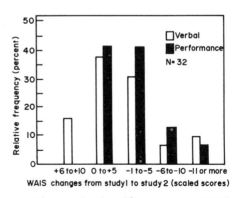

Figure 4–13. *Changes in WAIS Scores from study 1 to study 2.*

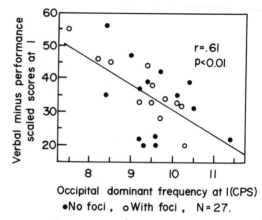

Figure 4–14. *Correlation between WAIS Verbal-Performance discrepancy and EEG dominant frequency.*

ranged from an increase of ten to a decrease of 15 points; the performance changes from an increase of five to a decrease of 16 points.

For the 27 subjects who had measurable occipital rhythms as well as WAIS data at both studies, the mean occipital frequency at study 1 was 9.5 cycles per second (SD = 0.8). There was no relationship between occipital frequencies and initial Verbal or Performance Scores on the WAIS study ($r = -0.35$ and $+0.12$ respectively). There was, however, a significant association between slow frequencies and verbal-performance discrepancy (Figure 4–14). Slow frequencies at study 1 were also associated with a greater decline in both Performance and Verbal Scores at study 2 (Figures 4–15); for the Performance Scores, this association was significant ($p < 0.05$). Between study

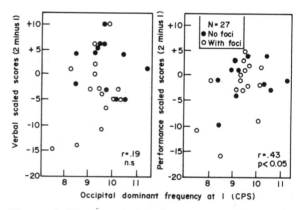

Figure 4–15. *Correlation between WAIS change and initial EEG dominant frequency.*

1 and study 2, the mean occipital frequency declined by 0.2 cps. (SD = 0.4); there was no relationship between the changes in frequency and the WAIS scores.

The EEGs of 26 subjects were divided into two groups—those having focal abnormalities (foci) at both studies (ten subjects) and those having no foci or foci at only one study (16 subjects). The six subjects in whom the dominant background activity at study 1 was fast activity or very slow rhythm (less than 8.5 cps.) were excluded from the classification. The "foci" and "nonfoci" groups were quite similar in sex, race, socioeconomic status, age, education, occipital dominant frequency, and initial verbal performance WAIS scores (Table 4–2). The decline in both verbal and performance ability

Table 4–2. *Comparison of subjects with and without EEG focal abnormalities.*

	Without	With
Number of subjects	16	10
Male:female	9:7	5:5
Caucasian:Negro	15:1	8:2
Socioeconomic status high:low	12:4	8:2
Age at study 1	70.3 ± 5.8	68.7 ± 4.7
Education (years)	15.8 ± 2.4	16.1 ± 2.5
Mean occipital frequency at study 1 (cps.)	9.6 ± 0.8	9.6 ± 0.6
Interval between study 1 and 2 (months)	44.8 ± 8.6	40.2 ± 11.0
WAIS (scaled scores)		
At study 1:		
Verbal	72.6 ± 15.3	72.5 ± 12.8
Performance	39.1 ± 7.2	38.7 ± 10.6
Verbal—Performance discrepancy	33.4 ± 10.4	33.8 ± 7.4
Changes from study 1 to 2:		
Verbal	+1.3* ± 5.9	−4.3* ± 5.6
Performance	−0.3 ± 3.8	−2.6 ± 6.0

* $t = 2.43$. $p < 0.025$.

between study 1 and study 2 was greater in the foci group than in the nonfoci group: the difference in Verbal Scores was significant at the 0.025 level.

2. Cerebral blood flow sample. In the 24 subjects whose regional cerebral blood flow was studied with the xenon-inhalation method, the cortical (or grey-matter) blood flow of the left parietal region ranged from 33 to 72 ml/100 gm/min, the mean being 52.4 ml (SD = 11.11). With 55 ml as the median, these subjects were divided into two groups of 12 each: those having high blood flow and those having low blood flow (table 4–3). These two groups were quite similar in sex, race, socioeconomic status, age, and education.

The WAIS findings in these two groups are also shown in Table 4–3. At the time of the blood flow study, WAIS scores, both Verbal and Performance, were consistently lower in the low blood flow group than in the high blood flow group. The former also showed a greater decline in both scores during

Table 4–3. *Comparison of subjects with high and low cortical flow (left parietal region; median 55 ml).*

	High	Low
Number of subjects	12	12
Male:female	6:6	6:6
Caucasian:Negro	10:2	9:3
Socioeconomic status, high:low	5:7	7:5
Age at blood flow study	78.8 ± 3.7	80.1 ± 4.4
Education (years)	10.5 ± 5.2	9.7 ± 6.8
Cortical blood flow (ml./100 gm./min.)		
Range	55.1 − 72.0	32.5 − 54.5
Mean	61.1 ± 5.0	43.7 ± 6.3
WAIS (scaled scores) at blood flow study:		
Verbal	57.3 ± 18.3	54.0 ± 22.8
Performance	28.3 ± 10.3	22.2 ± 13.4
Verbal—Performance discrepancy	29.0 ± 15.1	31.8 ± 12.6
Changes prior to blood flow study (12 years):		
Verbal	−1.1 ± 3.3	−5.8 ± 14.4
Performance	−0.6 ± 3.7	−6.6 ± 9.4

the 12 years prior to the blood flow study. Statistically, none of these differences was significant beyond the 0.01 level by *t* test.

Figure 4–16 shows the relationship between blood flow and WAIS scores separately for ten subjects having a high socioeconomic status and more than 11 years of schooling, and for ten subjects whose socioeconomic and educa-

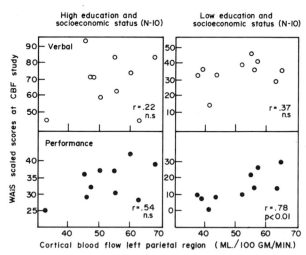

Figure 4–16. *Correlation between cerebral blood flow and WAIS scores (Verbal and Performance), with socioeconomic and educational factors controlled.*

tional levels were both low. In both groups the correlation between blood flow and performance scores was greater than that between blood flow and verbal scores. In the group with low educational socioeconomic status, the relationship between blood flow and performance was highly significant.

A correlation was also demonstrated between cortical blood flow and changes in the WAIS scores during the 12 years prior to the blood flow study (Figure 4–16). Low blood flow was associated with a greater decline in Performance Scores than in Verbal Scores. The only statistically significant correlation, however, was that between blood flow and performance change in the group with high educational and socioeconomic status.

Discussion

As a group, the 32 healthy elderly subjects in our EEG study showed no significant change on the WAIS in a study made 3.5 years after the initial examination. The finding of considerable individual variation supports Birren's view (1968) that mental stability is found in old age and that mental decline is irregularly distributed among the aging population. The stability of the WAIS scores, however, does not necessarily indicate a complete absence of intellectual changes. As Jarvik and her associates (1962) suggested, a slight decline in intellectual ability may be counterbalanced by "test wiseness" that develops with repeated measurements.

The diffuse slowing of the dominant EEG frequency is very common among aged persons having various neuropsychiatric disorders or brain syndromes, as well as among those having good health (Busse et al., 1965; Obrist, et al., 1965). Such slowing is probably related to the depression of cerebral metabolism, a common feature of many brain disorders in old age. This theory is supported by the good correlation that usually exists between EEG frequency and cerebral oxygen consumption or cerebral blood flow (Ingvar et al., 1965; Obrist et al., 1963); both, under normal circumstances, are measures of cerebral metabolism.

The significance of focal disturbances in senescent EEGs is still unclear. The foci may begin to appear in middle age, increasing in incidence with advancing age (Busse et al., 1965). It has been speculated that these foci may originate either from a deep-lying lesion, possibly in the hippocampal region, or from remote areas outside the temporal lobe. Geschwind (Geschwind et al., 1968) has shown that marked anatomic asymmetries exist between the upper surfaces of the left and right temporal lobe in the human brain; the left temporal plane is usually larger and longer than the right one. There is also evidence to suggest that the temporal lobes, particularly the left one, are susceptible to vascular insufficiency (Busse et al., 1965; Busse et al., 1965; Obrist et al., 1965). The EEG foci observed in our study involved predominantly the left temporal region and were significantly associated with a decline in verbal, but not in performance, ability. These findings suggest the presence of a disorder of the left temporal lobe, the integrity of which is known to be essential for verbal comprehension and retention (Milner, 1958).

Although the mean cerebral blood flow in our elderly subjects (52 ml) was significantly lower than that obtained by the same method in healthy young adults (75 ml) (Obrist et al., 1967), there was considerable overlapping between these two groups. The range in blood flow was 33 to 73 ml for the elderly subjects and 57 to 92 ml for the young adults. The decline in cerebral blood flow may result from a depression of cerebral metabolism secondary to functional or structural impairment of the brain or from cerebrovascular insufficiency. It is therefore not specific for any particular pathological process but only indicates the presence of brain impairment.

If the alteration in the EEG and cerebral blood flow can be taken as indicative of cerebral changes, the findings from our study suggest that the intellectual changes in aged persons having relatively good health and living in the community do not necessarily follow a set pattern and that they depend, to a great extent, on the severity as well as the extent of the cerebral changes. Decline in performance abilities was associated chiefly with diffuse slowing in the occipital rhythm or with a reduction of blood flow in the left parietal cortex; decline in verbal abilities, with focal disturbances in the left anterior temporal EEG tracings. The neurophysiological variables in our study tended to correlate better with intellectual changes over time than with the absolute level of intellectual abilities—an observation that confirms the value of longitudinal studies and suggests that EEG studies and measurements of cerebral blood flow may be useful in predicting the intellectual changes that may occur in healthy persons during senescence. Factors that helped to demonstrate the relationship between neurophysiological and intellectual variables in our elderly community subjects included: (1) controlling the sociocultural background of the subjects; (2) assessing verbal and performance abilities separately; and (3) employing relatively specific methods to evaluate a particular region of the brain.

Summary

From a panel of subjects who volunteered to participate in a longitudinal study on aging, two groups of elderly persons having relatively good health and leading active lives in the community were selected for EEG studies and measurements of cerebral blood flow by the xenon-inhalation method. The intellectual abilities of these subjects were measured by the WAIS test at intervals of approximately 3.5 years. Verbal and Performance Scores obtained at the time of the neurophysiological studies, as well as the changes observed between periods of testing, were correlated with the EEG findings and measurements of cortical blood flow. The implications of our findings have been discussed.

The results of this study emphasize the value of longitudinal studies on senescent individuals and the importance of (1) controlling various factors that may affect the cognitive or neurophysiological variables and (2) employing more specific methods for assessing these variables.

References

Bankier, R. G. A correlative study of psychological and EEG findings in normal, physically ill and mentally ill seniles. *Electroenceph. Clin. Neurophysiol.,* 22:189–190, 1967.

Bauer, H. G., Apfeldorf, M., and Hoch, H. Relationship Between Alpha Frequency, Age, Disease and Intelligence. In *Proceedings of the 7th International Congress of Gerontology,* Vienna: Wien Medizinische Akademie, 1966, 2:341–349.

Birren, J. E. Increments and decrements in the intellectual status of the aged. In Simon, A., and Epstein, L. J. (Eds.), *Aging in modern society,* Psychiatric Research Report 23. Washington, D.C.: American Psychiatric Association, 1968, pp. 207–214.

Birren, J. E., Butler, R. N., Greenhouse, S. W., Sokoloff, L., and Yarrow, M. R. Interdisciplinary relationships: Interrelations of physiological, psychological, and psychiatric findings in healthy elderly men. In Birren, J. E., Butler, R. N., Greenhouse, S. W., Sokoloff, L., and Yarrow, M. R. (eds.), *Human aging: A biological and behavioral study,* Washington, D.C.: U.S. Government Printing Office, 1963, pp. 283–305.

Botwinick, J. *Cognitive processes in maturity and old age.* New York: Springer Publishing Co., 1967.

Busse, E. W., Barnes, R. H., Friedman, E. I., and Kelty, E. J. Psychological functioning of aged individuals with normal and abnormal electroencephalograms. *J. Nerv. Ment. Dis.,* 124:135–141, 1956.

Busse, E. W., and Obrist, W. D. Pre-senescent electroencephalographic changes in normal subjects. *J. Geront.* 20:315–320, 1965.

Busse, E. W., and Wang, H. S. The value of electroencephalography in geriatrics. *Geriatrics,* 20:906–924, 1965.

Butler, R. N., Dastur, D. K., and Perlin S. Relationships of senile manifestations and chronic brain syndromes to cerebral circulation and metabolism. *J. Psychiat. Res.,* 3:229–238, 1965.

Dastur, D. K., Lane, M. H., Hansen, D. B., Kety, S. S., Perlin, S., Butler, R. N., and Sokoloff, L. Effects of aging on cerebral circulation and metabolism in man, in Birren, et al. (Eds.), *Human aging.* 1963, pp. 59–76.

Eisdorfer, C. The WAIS performance of the aged: A retest evaluation. *J. Geront.,* 18:169–172, 1963.

Ermentini, A., and Marinato, G. Correlazioni Tra Attivita Bioeletrica Cerebrale Ed Efficienza Intellecttiva In Up Gruppo Di Anzian, G, *G. Geront.,* 8:1179–1189, 1960.

Geschwind, N., and Levitsky, W. Human brain: Left-right asymmetries in temporal speech region. *Science,* 161:186–187, 1968.

Hedlund, S., Kohler, V., Nylin, G., Olsson, R., Regenstrom, O., Rothstrom E., and Astrom, K. E. Cerebral blood circulation in dementia, *Acta Psychiat. Scand.,* 40:77–160, 1964.

Hoagland, H. Studies of Brain Metabolism and Electrical Activity in Relation to Adrenocortical Physiology. In Pincus, G. (Ed.), *Recent progress in hormone research.* New York: Academic Press, 1954, pp. 29–63.

Ingram, I. M. EEG slowing and intellectual deterioration in the elderly, in *Proceedings of the 7th International Congress of Gerontology,* Vienna: Wien Medizinische Akademie, 1966, 1:347–350.

Ingvar, D. H., Baldy-Mouliner, M., Sulg, I., and Horman S. Regional cerebral blood flow related to EEG. *Acta. Neurol. Scand. Suppl.,* 14:179–182, 1965.

Jarvik, L. F., Kallman, F. J., and Falek, A. Intellectual changes in aged twins. *J. Geront.*, 17:289–294, 1962.

Jenkins, C. D. The relation of EEG slowing to selected indices of intellective impairment. *J. Nerv. Ment. Dis.*, 135:162–170, 1962.

Justiss, W. A. The electroencephalogram of the frontal lobes and abstract behavior in old age. In Blumenthal, H. T. (Ed.), *Medical and clinical aspects of aging.* New York: Columbia University Press, 1962, pp. 566–574.

Klee, A. The relationship between clinical evaluation of mental deterioration, psychological test results, and the cerebral metabolic rate of oxygen. *Acta Neurol. Scand.*, 40:337–345, 1964.

Lassen, N. A., Munck, O., and Tottey, E. R. Mental function and cerebral oxygen consumption of organic dementia. *Arch. Neurol. Psychiat.*, 77:126–133, 1957.

Milner, B. Psychological Defects Produced by Temporal Lobe Excision. In Solomon, H. C., Cobb, S., and Penfield, W. (Eds.), *The brain and human behavior.* Baltimore: Williams and Wilkins Co., 1958, pp. 244–257.

Obrist, W. D. The electroencephalogram of healthy aged males. In Birren et al. (Eds.), *Human aging.* 1963, pp. 79–93.

Obrist, W. D., and Busse, E. W. The electroencephalogram in old age. In Wilson, W. P. (Ed.) *Applications of electroencephalography in psychiatry.* Durham, N.C.: Duke University Press, 1965, pp. 185–205.

Obrist, W. D., Busse, E. W., Eisdorfer, C., and Kleemeier, R. W. Relation of the electroencephalogram to intellectual function in senescence. *J. Geront.*, 17:197–206, 1962.

Obrist, W. D., Sokoloff, L., Lassen, N. A., Lane, M. H., Butler, R. N., and Feinberg, I. Relation of EEG to Cerebral Blood Flow and Metabolism in Old Age. *Electroenceph. Clin. Neurophysiol.*, 15:610–619, 1963.

Obrist, W. D., Thompson, H. K., Jr., King, C. H., and Wang, H. S. Determination of Regional Cerebral Blood Flow by Inhalation by 133-xenon. *Circ. Res.*, 20:124–135, 1967.

Silverman, A. J., Busse, E. W., Barnes, R. H., Frost, L. L., and Thaler, M. B. Studies on the process of aging: 4. Physiological influences on psychic functioning in elderly people. *Geriatrics*, 8:370–376, 1953.

Sokoloff, L. Circulation and Metabolism of Brain in Relation to the Process of Aging. In Birren, J. E., Imus, H. A., and Windle, W. F., (Eds.), *The process of aging in the nervous system.* Springfield, Ill.: Charles C. Thomas, 1959, 113–126.

Thaler, M. Relationships among Wechsler, Weigl, Rorschach, EEG findings, and abstract-concrete behavior in a group of normal aged subjects. *J. Geront.*, 11:404–409, 1956.

Wang, H. S. The brain and intellectual function in senescence. Paper read at the annual meeting of the American Psychological Association, San Francisco, Calif., September 1, 1968.

Wang, H. S., and Busse, E. W. EEG of healthy old persons, pp. 126–140 in this volume.

Wechsler, D. *The measurement and appraisal of adult intelligence.* 4th ed. Baltimore: Williams and Wilkins Co., 1958.

EEG of Healthy Old Persons   *H. Shan Wang and Ewald W. Busse*

Electroencephalography (EEG) has long been employed to evaluate the status of the senescent brain which is expected to undergo, sooner or later,

Reprinted by permission from the *Journal of Gerontology*, 24:4:419–426, 1969.

considerable changes with advancing age. Among the many EEG changes that have been observed from aged persons, the most common one is an alteration of the dominant background activity (Busse and Wang, 1965; Obrist and Busse, 1965). The alpha rhythm of aged persons, as a rule, has a mean frequency about 1 c/s slower than that of young adults. In some elderly persons, it also shows a reduction in amplitude or percent-time. Another characteristic of the EEG in senescence, observed in as many as 50 percent of elderly subjects, is the presence of fast (beta) activity.

Whether these EEG changes are related primarily to chronological age or to pathological processes in the senile brain is still uncertain. Most studies in the past were performed on patients hospitalized with various psychiatric or neurological disorders. Among the few studies that have been done on aged persons in relatively good health and with little evidence of mental deterioration (Table 1), variation in sampling has been considerable. Some studies recruited volunteers from a community or a social club; others obtained subjects from a home for the aged, a geriatric hospital, or the outpatient clinic of a general hospital. Not infrequently, the subjects in a single study were obtained from several different sources. Subjects coming from such diverse sources can be expected to vary considerably in health. Because many diseases that are common among old persons—disorders of the heart, lungs, and central nervous system (CNS), for example—are known to affect the EEG (Busse and Wang, 1965), interpretation and comparison of these various studies is often difficult. In Table 1, several studies included subjects with diseases involving the CNS or the cardio-vascular system (Mengoli, 1952; Mundy-Castle, 1962; Obrist, 1954), or subjects with physical illnesses who showed no evidence of any mental or neurological disorder (Busse, Barnes, Friedman, and Kelty, 1956; Mundy-Castle, 1951; Mundy-Castle, Hurst, Beerstecher, and Prinsloo, 1954; Silverman, Busse, and Barnes, 1955). In other studies it was emphasized that the subjects were active in community life or were independent of any sustained medical help (Andermann and Stoller, 1961; Maggs and Turton, 1956); but in only a few investigations was the health status of the subjects clearly defined by thorough physical and laboratory examinations (Obrist, 1963; Otomo, 1966).

Interpreting the results of these various studies is made more difficult by the fact that very few of them describe the *demographic characteristic* of their samples. It has been demonstrated that there is a higher alpha frequency and a greater incidence of fast (beta) activity in females than in males. This sex difference has been observed in young adults (Mundy-Castle, 1951) as well as in middle-aged and elderly subjects (Busse and Obrist, 1965; Mundy-Castle, 1962). It is possible that racial differences also affect the EEG. Mundy-Castle (1951) noted that the Europeans in his series had significantly more fast activity than the Africans, although this difference could not be demonstrated between American Caucasians and American Negroes (Obrist and Busse, 1965). Silverman et al. (1955) noted fewer EEG abnormalities of all types among subjects whose socioeconomic level was high than among those from lower socioeconomic levels. This finding, however, could not be confirmed by Obrist and Busse (1965).

The present report, based on the EEG findings in a group of healthy "senior citizens" who are community residents, is concerned with the dominant background activity and occipital rhythms, their relationships to age, sex, race, and socioeconomic factors, and their change over time. Focal alterations in the EEG's of these subjects will be the subject of another report.

Materials and Methods

Subjects

Two hundred and sixty volunteers above the age of 59 were recruited from the nearby community to participate in a longitudinal project at the Duke University Center for the Study of Aging and Human Development. All subjects initially went through two full days of examination by a multidisciplinary team (study 1). Among 182 subjects who subsequently returned and went through the same battery of examinations 3 to 4 years later (study 2), 55 were selected for the present study on the basis of health. These 55 subjects were considered to be free from any clinical evidence of cardiac, pulmonary, or CNS disease on both examinations, according to the following criteria:

1. No significant symptoms of heart disease such as chest pain, dyspnea, or fluid retention; no signs suggestive of heart disease on physical examination and chest X-ray; normal electrocardiogram.

2. No significant symptoms of pulmonary disease and no signs of emphysema, chronic bronchitis, or asthma on physical examination and chest X-ray.

3. No significant history of cerebrovascular insufficiency, stroke, or seizure; no signs of CNS disorder on neurological examination.

These 55 subjects were predominantly Caucasian (80 percent), male (58 percent), and had attended school for a mean of 12.3 years. Their ages ranged from 59 to 85 years; the mean was 69.7 (SD ± 5.6). On the basis of occupation, source of income, house type, dwelling area, and education the socioeconomic status of 29 subjects was classified following Warner's "Index of Status Characteristics" (Warner, Meeker, and Eells, 1957) as above average or "high," that of the remaining 26 as below average or "low." The mean interval between study 1 and study 2 in these 55 subjects was 42.5 months. (SD ± 9.6).

EEG Recording and Evaluation

All EEG's were recorded with an 8-channel Grass Electroencephalograph, using both monopolar and bipolar techniques, from placements that are com-

Table 4-4. *Summary of reported EEG studies on elderly subjects in relatively good health with little mental deterioration.*

	Source, health status, and age	Sex	Race	Sociocultural background
Andermann & Stoller, 1961	50 volunteers from social club; mean age, 69.8	Female	—	—
Busse et al., 1956	223 community volunteers without known psychiatric or neurological illness; mean age, 72.2	53% Female	—	—
Maggs & Turton, 1956	82 elderly leading normal home existence and independent of any sustained medical help; age, over 60	78% Female	—	From all social strata
Mengoli, 1952	34 healthy subjects mixed with 71 patients with CNS disease; age range, 55–93	Mixed	—	—
Mundy-Castle, 1951;	50 mentally normal volunteers with or without physical disease; mean age, 75.1	Mixed?	60% Negro	—
Mundy-Castle et al., 1954	81 mentally normal residents of old-age home, 12% with CNS disorders; age range, 59–96	48% Female	Caucasian?	—
Mundy-Castle, 1962				
Obrist, 1954	150 residents of old-age home, 10% with cardiac disease, 5% with CVA; mean age, 78.3	Male	Caucasian	Mean IQ, 100.3
Obrist, 1963	44 community volunteers and 3 from home for aged, 27 with optimal health and 20 with subclinical disease; mean age, 71.5	Male	Caucasian	Detailed description of education, income, occupation, cultural background, and retirement status
Otomo, 1966	354 elderly with good health and 329 with physical disease but neurologically normal; age, over 60	—	Mongoloid?	—
Silverman et al., 1955	145 community volunteers without known psychiatric or neurological illness; mean age, 72	—	—	90 indigent; 30 retired, finances adequate; 25 active and working

parable to the frontal, central, parietal, occipital, and posterior temporal leads of the 10–20 system. In addition, an anterior temporal electrode was employed; it was more anterior than any lead used in the latter system, being placed one third of the distance from the auditory meatus to the external canthus of the eye at the level of the superior orbital ridge (Busse and Obrist, 1965; Obrist, Busse, Eisdorfer, and Kleemeier, 1962).

All EEG records were rated with respect to dominant background activity and focal disturbances. Care was taken to select only waking sections of record for evaluation. The dominant activity was classified in one of the following categories:

1. Alpha Activity (A): between 8.5 and 12.5 c/s, with an amplitude greater than 15μV.
2. Low-voltage fast activity (LVF): observable activity predominantly fast and less than 15μV in amplitude, with little or no alpha activity.
3. Diffuse fast activity (DF): between 13.0 and 30.0 c/s and greater than 20 μV in amplitude.
4. Diffuse slow activity (DS): 8.0 c/s or slower, with an amplitude greater than 20 μV.

It has been suggested that, in senescence, waves slightly slower than 8.5 c/s may be a slow variant of the alpha waves. To avoid confusion, the term *occipital rhythm* was used in the present study to include all rhythmic waves from the occipital tracing that were in a sequence of three or more and had a frequency between 7.0 and 12.5 c/s and an amplitude of 15 μV or greater. It thus included all waves within the alpha range and those slightly below it. From each record, samples of the occipital rhythm, totaling 20 sec. or more, were measured manually. The sum of waves in these samples divided by the sum of sampling time in seconds was the *occipital frequency*.

The relative abundance of the occipital rhythm—that is, the percent-time of its appearance in the EEG record—was rated on a four-point scale: dominant (>75 percent), subdominant (50–75 percent), mixed (25–50 percent), and rare (<25 percent). There were three categories of amplitude: high, medium, and low. An amplitude between 25 and 49 μV was considered as medium; amplitudes above or below this range were classified, respectively, as high or low.

Results

Dominant Background Activity

In study 1, the most common dominant background activity was A and the least common one was DS (I in Figure 4–17). These two were observed, respectively, in 61 percent and 7 percent of the EEGs; LVF and DF accounted almost equally for the remaining 31 percent. The various dominant

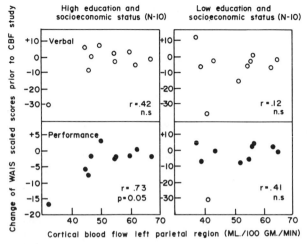

Figure 4–17. *Correlation between cerebral blood flow and changes in WAIS scores (Verbal and Performance) over a 12-year period, with socioeconomic and educational factors controlled.*

activities were associated with widely varying amounts of focal disturbances. Foci were present in 75 percent of the DS, 38 percent of the A, and 25 percent of the DF, but in none of the LVF ($\chi^2 = 8.28$, $p < 0.05$).

The incidence of various dominant activities was almost identical in Caucasians and Negroes and did not differ significantly in males and females, although in the low socioeconomic group females showed a tendency to have less alpha and more fast activity than males (Table 4–5). The only statistically significant difference was associated with socioeconomic status ($\chi^2 = 10.87$, $p < 0.025$). DF was completely absent in the high socioeconomic group, which had more A and DS than the low socioeconomic group. This discrepancy was not related to age, which was almost identical in these two

Table 4–5. *Incidence of dominant background activities in relation to sex and socioeconomic status in study 1.*

		N	Mean age	Dominant Activity (Relative incidence in %)			
				A	LVF	DF	DS
Low socioeconomic status	Female	15	68.2	40.0	20.0	33.3	6.7
	Male	11	70.4	63.6	9.1	27.3	0.0
	Subtotal	26	69.2	50.0	15.4	30.8	3.8
High socioeconomic status	Female	8	68.9	87.5	12.5	0.0	0.0
	Male	21	70.9	66.7	19.1	0.0	14.3
	Subtotal	29	70.3	72.4	17.2	0.0	10.3
	Total	55	69.7	61.8	16.4	14.5	7.3

groups; nor to sex, although the high socioeconomic group had significantly more males than the low one.

Figure 4–18 shows the age distribution of these dominant activities. Subjects under the age of 70 accounted for 75 percent of the DF but were not represented in the DS group. The mean age of subjects in the former group was 66.7 years (SD ± 3.5); in the latter, it was 77.7 years (SD ± 5.3). Subjects with A and LVF were about equally divided between those over 70 and those under that age. The mean ages of the subjects in these two groups were 69.7 (SD ± 5.3) and 68.7 years (SD ± 6.0), respectively.

In study 2, 15 subjects (27.3 percent) showed a change in dominant activity of their EEGs. The incidence of changes observed in those originally

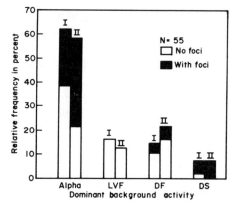

Figure 4–18. *Relative incidence of various dominant background activities in studies 1 and 2.*

classified as LVF was 55.6 percent—greater than that in the other three groups which was only 21.7 percent. Although there was a slight increase in the number of subjects with predominantly DF and a slight decrease in those classified as A and LVF, the distribution of dominant activities in study 2 followed closely that noted in study 1 (Figure 1). During this interval, the incidence of foci increased from 38 percent to 63 percent in the A group and was almost unchanged in the other classifications.

Occipital Rhythm

In study 1, measurable amounts of occipital rhythm were present in 46 EEGs: 34 with alpha waves as the dominant activity, 8 with alpha waves present but not dominant, and 4 with slower waves (7.0–8.0 c/s) as the dominant rhythm.

The mean occipital frequency for these 46 EEGs was 9.50 c/s (SD ± 0.83). The mean frequency was related to sex and age but not to race, socio-

Table 4–6. Occipital frequency in relation to sex and age in study 1.

	≤69 Years		≥70 Years		Total	
	N	Mean frequency (c/s)	N	Mean frequency (c/s)	N	Mean frequency (c/s)
Female	12	10.04	7	9.44	19	9.82
Male	10	9.61	17	9.08	27	9.27
Total	22	9.85	24	9.18	46	9.50

Between sexes $F = 5.78; p < 0.05$.
Between ages $F = 8.72; p < 0.01$.

economic status, or focal disturbances. Females had a faster frequency than males, and this difference was not age-dependent (Table 4–6). Figure 4–19 shows the inverse relationship between frequency and age (that is, as age advanced, frequency declined). The product-moment correlation coefficient between these two variables was -0.56 ($p < 0.01$) and was not significantly affected by sex, race, socioeconomic status, or focal disturbances.

The occipital rhythm was rated as dominant in 41 percent of these 46 EEGs, subdominant in 28 percent, mixed in 22 percent, and rare in 9 percent. The percent-time of occipital rhythm in the EEG record was independent of the occipital frequency or the demographic characteristics of these subjects.

Occipital frequencies of 9.4 c/s or slower tended to be associated with medium amplitude, while faster frequencies tended to have either high or low

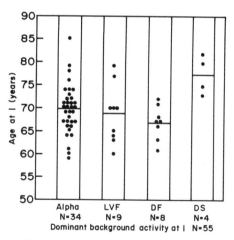

Figure 4–19. *Age distribution of various dominant background activities in study 1 (horizontal line = mean age).*

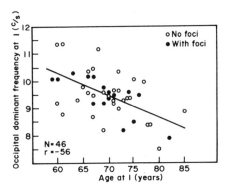

Figure 4–20. *Relationship between occipital frequency and age in study 1 (Regression line: Occipital frequency = 15.09 − 0.08 × Age).*

amplitude (Table 4–7). Amplitude was also significantly related to sex (Table 4–7), but not to race, socioeconomic status, or age. High amplitudes were more common in females; low amplitudes, in males.

In study 2, no significant change was observed in the amplitude or the percent-time of occipital rhythm. Changes in occipital *frequency*, however—ranging from a decrease of 1.0 c/s to an increase of 0.9 c/s—were observed in 43 of the 46 subjects who originally had measurable occipital rhythms. The frequency became slower in 32, faster in 11. The mean frequency for this group in study 2 was 9.28 c/s—0.22 c/s (SD ± 0.44) slower than that in Study I. Although this mean decline was small, the possibility of its occurring by chance was less than 0.005 ($t = 3.34$). In spite of these changes in frequency, there was a good correlation between the frequencies recorded at the two examinations ($r = 0.86$, $p < 0.01$).

For these 46 subjects, the changes in frequency were not directly related to age or to the initial frequency in study 1, but they were significantly affected by the interaction of these two variables (Table 4–8). Among subjects in their sixties, those whose original frequency was 9.4 c/s or less showed a mean increase of 0.29 c/s; subjects in the same age range with a faster frequency at study 1 showed a mean decrease of 0.40 c/s—a difference which is significant at the 0.001 level ($t = 3.92$). However, the correlation coefficient between initial frequency and subsequent change in these younger subjects was only -0.36 ($p < 0.1$).

Table 4–7. *Amplitude of occipital rhythm (%) in relation to occipital frequency and sex in study 1.*

	N	Low	Medium	High	
Occipital frequency					
≤9.4 c/s	21	4.8	72.4	23.8	$\chi^2 = 9.02$
≥9.5 c/s	25	36.0	32.0	32.0	$p < 0.025$
Sex					
Female	19	5.3	52.5	42.3	$\chi^2 = 6.16$
Male	27	33.3	48.1	18.5	$p < 0.05$
Total	46	21.7	50.0	28.3	

Table 4–8. *Change of occipital frequency in relation to age and initial frequency in study 1.*

Age	$\leq$9.4 c/s N	Mean change (c/s)	$\geq$9.5 c/s N	Mean change (c/s)	Total N	Mean change (c/s)
$\leq$69	7	+0.29	15	−0.40	22	−0.18
$\geq$70	14	−0.28	10	−0.20	24	−0.25
Total	21	−0.09	25	−0.32	46	−0.22

Between ages $F = 0.32$.'s
Between frequencies $F = 3.99$.'s
Interaction (age $\times$ frequency) $F = 11.29, p < 0.01$.'s

The changes in frequency did not differ significantly between races. They were also not directly related to sex. A significant difference between socioeconomic groups *was* present (Table 4–9), but the greatest effect on frequency change was produced by the interaction of sex and socioeconomic status. Females of low socioeconomic status showed the greatest decline in frequency, while females of high status showed an increase instead of a decrease.

Table 4–9. *Change of occipital frequency in relation to sex and socioeconomic status.*

	High N	Mean change (c/s)	Low N	Mean change (c/s)	Total N	Mean change (c/s)
Female	6	+0.27	13	−0.45	19	−0.22
Male	17	−0.22	10	−0.20	27	−0.21
Total	23	−0.09	23	−0.34	46	−0.22

Between sexes $F = 0.01$.
Between socioeconomic status $F = 4.53; p < 0.05$.
Interaction (Sex $\times$ Socioeconomic status) $F = 8.91; p < 0.01$.

Discussion

The subjects we studied had several characteristics in common. They all were volunteers and all remained active in the community. Although their health was by no means perfect (a few had relatively elevated blood pressures or minor illnesses such as arthritis or mild peripheral arteriosclerosis), careful screening by extensive clinical and laboratory examinations showed no evidence of cardiac, pulmonary, or CNS disease. No similar group can be found in the literature. The most comparable one is group 1 of the NIMH study reported by Obrist (1963), which closely resembles our group in mean age, type of subject, and health status. The health of their subjects, in fact, met somewhat stricter standards than ours, but it was not evaluated longitudinally. Our subjects were healthy not only at the first examination but also at the second one, 3 to 4 years later. Their health can be considered better than that of most elderly people in the community. The results presented here may therefore be viewed as characteristic of sustained good health.

Our findings generally agree with those of the NIMH study. The incidence of LVF was quite similar. Although the NIMH study did not include the DF classification, it did mention that 6 percent of their EEGs showed persistent fast activity of more than 20 μV—the same criterion applied to our DF. In a study on residents of a home for the aged reported by Obrist (1954), the incidences of LVF and DF in inmates between 65 and 79 years were 9 percent and 12 percent, respectively. These percentages are lower than ours. The incidence of DS in our group at both examinations was 7 percent—a figure identical to the incidence reported in the NIMH study. It should be noted, however, that the latter study employed 8.0 c/s, rather than 8.5 c/s, as the cutoff point of alpha frequency. The incidence of DS in our group is much lower than the incidence of 15 to 25 percent usually reported in the literature (Busse et al., 1956; Gibbs and Gibbs, 1950; Maggs and Turton, 1956; Mengoli, 1952; Mundy-Castle, 1951; Obrist, 1954; Silverman et al., 1955). Our findings thus support the belief that good health in senescence is associated with more fast activity and less slow activity.

From study 1 to 2, the EEG classification of A, DF, DS appeared to be quite consistent, while that of LVF tended to change. Although the significance of these changes is still unclear, they do suggest that either LVF tracings are unstable or the reliability of their classification is questionable.In this connection, it should be noted that the overall ratings of dominant EEG activity are consistent among investigators, showing an inter-judge agreement of 88 percent (Busse and Obrist, 1965).

All EEG variables, except the percent-time of occipital rhythm, were related either to age, sex, or socioeconomic factors (Table 4–10). The previously reported tendency for occipital frequency to decline with advanced age (Mengoli, 1952; Mundy-Castle, 1962; Mundy-Castle et al., 1954; Obrist, 1954; Obrist, 1963; Obrist and Busse, 1965; Obrist, Henry, and Justiss, 1966; Otomo, 1966) was confirmed in our longitudinal as well as our cross-sectional observations. In view of the fact that this relationship between occipital frequency and age was highly significant and was only slightly affected by concurrent focal disturbances in the EEG or by any demographic characteristic of the subjects, it is hypothesized that the occipital frequency in healthy old people is closely related to "physiological aging," and that the relationship between these two variables may be altered by the presence of various pathological conditions affecting the central nervous system.

Comparison of the males and females in our study showed that occipital

Table 4–10. *Summary of the relation between EEG findings and other variables in healthy old people.*

Variables	Dominant background activity	Occipital rhythm			
		Frequency	%-Time	Amplitude	Frequency change between I and II
Age	+	++	−	−	−
Sex	−	+	−	+	−
Socioeconomic status	+	−	−	−	+
Race	−	−	−	−	−
EEG foci	+	−	−	−	−
Occipital frequency			−	+	−
Interaction of occipital frequency and age					++
Interaction of socio- economic status and sex					++

− No significant relationship
+ Significant at 0.05 level
++ Significant at 0.01 level

rhythms had somewhat faster frequencies and higher amplitudes in the females. Our study did not confirm the sex difference in beta activity previously reported (Busse and Obrist, 1965; Mundy-Castle, 1951; Mundy-Castle, 1962), but showed instead a close association between fast activity and low socioeconomic status. Since the other two studies made no clear reference to the socioeconomic backgrounds of their subjects, it is possible that the sex difference they observed was in fact related to socioeconomic factors. Mundy-Castle (1951) noted that fast activity was more common in Europeans than in Africans and speculated that this discrepancy might be related to cultural factors, which apparently were quite different between the Africans and the Europeans. Our study failed to demonstrate that race had any significant effect on fast activity or on other EEG variables. This failure may be due in part to the fact that the Negroes in our study comprised only 20 percent of the sample and closely resembled the Caucasians in socioeconomic background. The association of fast activity with low socioeconomic status in our study is clearly in contrast to Mundy-Castle's observation. It should be noted that our study was concerned only with fast activity that was the dominant rhythm of the EEG record, while Mundy-Castle's included all fast activity, whether dominant or not.

Changes in occipital frequency, although independent of age, were related in a rather complex way to several other characteristics of the subjects. Females of high socioeconomic status differed significantly from all other subjects in that their occipital frequency either increased or showed very little decline during the interval between examinations. Only in the younger subjects (those in the seventh decade) did there appear to be an inverse relationship between initial frequency and subsequent change.

From the statistical point of view, it is unlikely that the changes in frequency can be attributed to chance. A systematic error associated with repeated measurements cannot be ruled out, since most changes were quite small (only a fraction of one cycle) and there seemed to be a tendency for them to regress toward the mean. On the other hand, measurement error alone can hardly explain why a significant difference was present between age or socioeconomic groups. Furthermore, the rate of decline observed in the longitudinal study (0.22 cycles in 3.5 years) compares well with the cross-sectional observation that the frequency decreased with advancing age at a rate of 0.08 cycles per year.

If these frequency changes are indeed not artifacts, our findings indicate that socioeconomic status has a greater effect on the EEGs of aged females than on those of aged males. They also suggest that these frequency changes —and possibly other EEG changes as well—are associated with two different aspects of the senile brain. Changes occurring in early senescence are more likely to be related to the functional or metabolic status of the brain; those in late senescence, to the structural status of the brain. The former condition would be expected to be more susceptible to many extraneous factors (environmental, psychological, physiological) and, therefore, to be more unstable or fluctuating than the latter.

In conclusion, our study shows that, even in old people whose good health is maintained for several years, the EEG undergoes considerable change over a period of 3 to 4 years. The discrepancies between our observations and those of other investigators could result in part from differences in sampling, methodology, and criteria used.

The relationship of these EEG changes to intellectual function and to other physiological variables such as blood pressure, serum cholesterol, and peripheral arteriosclerosis will be presented and discussed in a future report. Thus, the primary conclusion that can be drawn from the data so far reported is that the EEG changes in senescence are not simple monotonic ones. Some may be closely related to aging, while others are affected by many other demographic factors as well—particularly the socioeconomic background and the sex of the subject. This report thus emphasizes the importance of controlling these demographic variables, as well as the age and health of the subjects, in any study of the senescent EEG and, probably, in any clinical study of the senile brain.

Summary

Separate EEG studies were made, at an interval of 3 to 4 years, in 55 elderly volunteers who were leading an active life in the community and were free from any clinical evidence of cardiac, pulmonary, or CNS disease during this time. The present report deals with the dominant background activity and occipital rhythm of these EEGs, particularly with regard to the changes observed over this period and their relationship to age, sex, race, and socioeconomic factors.

Our observations that fast activity was more common in early than in late senescence and that there was a negative correlation between age and the frequency of occipital rhythm were consistent with previous reports.

Several of the EEG variables were related to the demographic characteristics of the subjects. Occipital rhythm in females tended to have a faster frequency and a higher amplitude than that in males. Subjects of low socioeconomic status had much more beta activity than those of high status.

In some instances, the interaction of two factors had a greater effect on the EEG variables than either factor alone. Females of low socioeconomic status showed a greater decline in occipital frequency during the interval between examinations than females of high status; a similar difference was not demonstrated in males. In the younger subjects (those in the seventh decade) a fast occipital rhythm had a greater tendency to decline than a slow one; this statement is not true of the older subjects.

In the present study, no EEG variable was significantly related to race. The percent-time of occipital rhythm was independent of age, sex, race, or socioeconomic factors.

Although the clinical implications of our findings are still unclear, our study emphasizes the need to control the demographic characteristics as well as the health status of the subjects in any investigation of the senescent EEG or the senile brain.

References

Andermann, K., and Stoller, A. EEG patterns in hospitalized and non-hospitalized aged. *Electroencephalography & Clinical Neurophysiology,* 13:319, 1961.

Busse, E. W., Barnes, R. H., Friedman, E. I., and Kelty, E. J. Psychological functioning of aged individuals with normal and abnormal electroencephalograms. I. A study of non-hospitalized community volunteers. *Journal of Nervous & Mental Disease,* 124:135–141, 1956.

Busse, E. W., and Obrist, W. D. Pre-senescent electroencephalographic changes in normal subjects. *Journal of Gerontology,* 20:315–320, 1965.

Busse, E. W., and Wang, H. S. The value of electroencephalography in geriatrics. *Geriatrics,* 20:906–924, 1965.

Gibbs, F. A., and Gibbs, E. L. *Atlas of electroencephalography,* Vol. 1. Cambridge, Mass.: Addison-Wesley Press, 1950.

Maggs, R., and Turton, E. C. Some EEG findings in old age and their relationship to affective disorder. *Journal of Mental Science,* 102:812–818, 1956.

Mengoli, G. The EEG in old age. *Electroencephalography & Clinical Neurophysiology,* 4:232–233, 1952.

Mundy-Castle, A. C. Theta and beta rhythm in the electroencephalograms of normal adults. *Electroencephalography & Clinical Neurophysiology,* 3:477–486, 1951.

Mundy-Castle, A. C. Central excitability in the aged. In H. T. Blumenthal (Ed.), *Medical and clinical aspects of aging*. New York: Columbia University Press, 1962.

Mundy-Castle, A. C., Hurst, L. A., Beerstecher, D. M., and Prinsloo, T. The electroencephalogram in the senile psychoses. *Eelectroencephalography & Clinical Neurophysiology*, 6:245–252, 1954.

Obrist, W. D. The electroencephalogram of normal aged adults. *Electroencephalography & Clinical Neurophysiology*, 6:235–244, 1954.

Obrist, W. D. The electroencephalogram of healthy aged males. In J. E. Birren, R. N. Butler, S. W. Greenhouse, L. Sokoloff, and M. R. Yarrow (Eds.), *Human aging: A biological and behavioral study*. Washington: U.S. Government Printing Office, 1963.

Obrist, W. D., and Busse, E. W. The electroencephalogram in old age. In W. P. Wilson (Ed.), *Applications of electroencephalography in psychiatry*. Durham, N.C.: Duke University Press, 1965.

Obrist, W. D., Busse, E. W., Eisdorfer, C., and Kleemeier, R. W. Relation of the electroencephalogram to intellectual function in senescence. *Journal of Gerontology*, 17:197–206, 1962.

Obrist, W. D., Henry, C. E., and Justiss, W. A. Longitudinal changes in the senescent EEG: A 15-year study. In *Proceedings of the 7th International Congress of Gerontology*. Vienna: Wiener Medizinischen Akademie, 1966.

Otomo, E. Electroencephalography in old age: Dominant alpha pattern. *Electroencephalography & Clinical Neurophysiology*, 21:489–491, 1966.

Silverman, A. J., Busse, E. W., and Barnes, R. H. Studies in the processes of aging: Electroencephalographic findings in 400 elderly subjects. *Electroencephalography & Clinical Neurophysiology*, 7:67–74, 1955.

Warner, W. L., Meeker, M., and Eells, K. *Social class in America*. Gloucester, Mass.: Peter Smith, 1957.

Effects of Age, Sex, and Time-on-watch on a Brief Continuous Performance Task
Stephen W. Harkins, John B. Nowlin, Dietolf Ramm, and Stephen Schroeder

Recent reviews of paced and unpaced inspection tasks and vigilance tasks (Mostofsky, 1970; Sanders, 1970; Mackworth, 1969 and 1970; Evans and Mulholland, 1969) show that little attention has been paid to the effect of age and sex upon performance in these tasks. The few studies concerned with age effects on vigilance performance and, to a lesser extent, paced and unpaced inspection tasks, have been summarized by Davies and Tune (1969), Davies and Griew (1965), and Davies (1968). The present study deals with an analysis of age and sex differences on a paced inspection task.

Paced inspection tasks involve presentations of transient signals or stimulus events to subjects instructed to report the occurrence of such signal events. The signals presented are transient in the sense that they are presented to the subject for a discrete time interval. Unpaced tasks involve presentation of signals which remain until the subject responds appropriately. These tasks, which may be as short as 5 minutes or as long as 45 minutes in length, involve the subject in a situation which demands the maintenance of an attentive state if he is to perform efficiently and accurately. In the unpaced task, performance is usually assessed in terms of response time or the interval between the presentation of a signal event and the subject's response to that event. Paced tasks, because of the transient nature of the signal event, allow assessment not only of response time but also frequency of correct detections. Further, if nonsignal events or background stimuli are presented, commission errors or false positive responses may also be assessed.

Paced inspection tasks differ from vigilance tasks in the frequency of occurrence of the signal event. In vigilance tasks, where the dependent measure of performance is usually the number of correctly detected signal events, the stimuli are generally faint and infrequent. In paced inspection tasks the signal events are usually well above sensory threshold and occur more frequently than in vigilance tasks. Thus, vigilance tasks involve subjects in a situation which might be characterized as resulting in "underload," requiring less than 1 response a minute, while paced inspection tasks involve continuously changing signals requiring up to 12 responses or more per minute and thereby providing a potential "overload."

Using brief, paced inspection tasks with rapid stimulus presentation rates (1 per second), Thompson, Opton and Cohen (1963), Davies (1968), Talland (1966), and Canestrari (1961) found that detection performance of old men was poorer than that of young men. Similar results were reported by Davies and Griew (experiment 1, 1962), and Kirchner (1958) on longer paced inspection tasks. Generally, paced inspection tasks have failed to show age differences in performance as a function of time-on-watch. Surwillo and Quilter (1964), using a visual vigilance task, found that old subjects did tend to show a greater performance decrement as a function of time-on-watch than young subjects. This effect, however, was apparent only after 45 minutes of task performance.

The question of frequency of occurrence of false positive responses is important in assessing the overall accuracy of performance. As Davies (1968) has pointed out, if only correct detections are taken into account, old subjects, who make fewer correct responses, may be considered to be disengaging from the situation. However, if old subjects have a significantly larger number of false positive responses than young subjects, then their lower correct response rates do not support a disengagement position. In fact, Tune (1966), who used a forced choice task, found that old subjects did make more false positive responses than younger subjects. Canestrari (1961), using a task in which responses could be withheld, reported that old men made more false positive responses than young men, but in a second study failed to reproduce this age difference.

The present study was undertaken to characterize the performance of young, middle-aged and elderly subjects on a brief paced inspection task evaluating not only correct detection performance, false positive responses and response times for correct detections, but also changes in these measures of performance as a function of time-on-watch. Since there is clear evidence that sensory and perceptual efficiency tend to decrease with age (Welford, 1959), and performance differences become more evident at faster stimulus presentation rates (Thompson et al., 1963), a more "overloading" paced inspection task was chosen rather than a vigilance task or unpaced inspection task. Both men and women were used to allow evaluation of sex differences in the performance of a task demanding maintenance of an attentive state.

Method

Subjects

The middle-aged and elderly individuals (165 men and 161 women; age range 46 to 72) who took part in the present study are involved in a longitudinal study of aging sponsored by the Duke Center for the Study of Aging and Human Development. A paid group of 18- to 25-year-old (21 men and 20 women) university students provided the young group. All subjects were caucasian and in good health at the time of the study. The middle-aged and elderly subjects were divided into three groups on the basis of age. Table 4–11 presents the age and sex breakdown for all subjects.

Table 4–11. *Number of subjects, age, and standard deviation of age for each age and sex group.*

| | Young Subjects | | Middle-Aged and Elderly Subjects | | | | | |
| | Group 1 | | Group 2 | | Group 3 | | Group 4 | |
	Women	Men	Women	Men	Women	Men	Women	Men
N	20	21	56	56	55	56	50	55
Mean age	21.0	21.5	51.5	51.7	59.4	59.4	67.5	67.8
SD	2.2	1.9	2.7	3.0	2.0	2.0	2.6	2.7

Materials

The paced inspection task (or odd-even numbers task) consisted of presentation of single digit numbers (1–9) at a rate of one per second. Stimulus duration was 1 second. The numbers were presented in a pseudorandom order such that pairs of odd and even numbers occurred irregularly with a mean frequency of one per six numbers (SD = 1.99). Successive stimulus events (pairs of odd and even numbers) did not overlap. The task lasted for ten minutes and twelve seconds. An Industrial Electronics Engineers Inc. (IEE) rear-projected digital read-out was used to display the single digit numbers. Digits were approximately 7.3 by 3.2 cm. in size. The sequence of numbers was punched on paper-tape and controlled by a BRS tape reader system (BRS-3) and precision clock (MR-4).

A Grass Model 7 polygraph was used to record the occurrence of odd and even number pairs, the response of the subject and physiological measures. Subjects' response consisted of a press of a key which closed a microswitch, making an appropriate mark on the polygraph. All data were recorded on magnetic tape and reduced using a Redcor analog-to-digital converter interfaced with an IBM 1130 computer. Response times for each correct detection were accurate to within 2.5 msec.

Procedure

Subjects were seated in a comfortable chair, 3.5 feet in front of the IEE digital display. Electrodes were placed on the subject at this time in order to monitor the physiological variables. All sessions were conducted in a sound attenuated, electrically shielded chamber at the same time of day.

Subjects were instructed to press the key with the index finger of their dominant hand as quickly as possible after they observed two consecutive odd or two consecutive even numbers. Subjects were told that speed and accuracy were important. Following instructions, the subjects were practiced to an asymptotic performance level. After practice trials, there was a five minute rest period during which baseline physiological measures were recorded. Instructions were then reiterated and subjects exposed to the paced inspection task.

Data reduction

Correct detections (hits), false positive responses (commission errors), and response times for correct detections were computed for each subject for each third of the task and for the entire task. Percent correct detections was computed for each subject by dividing the number of stimulus events (odd or even number pairs) reported by the number of pairs presented.

Results

This preliminary report is concerned only with detection performance and response time during the continuous performance task. Multivariate and univariate analyses of variance were used to test the effects of age, sex, and their interactions on overall performance. Multivariate analysis of variance for repeated measures (Starmer and Grizzle, 1968; Jones, 1966) was used to assess time-on-watch changes in performance across thirds of the task.

Average performance for the total session.

Age. When average percent correct detections, false positive responses, and response times for correct detections were considered simultaneously, the multivariate analysis of variance was significant for the effect of age ($F = 9.54$; $df = 9$, 871.4; $p < .001$) but not for the age by sex interaction ($F = 1.45$; $df = 9$, 871.4; $p > .1$). Univariate analysis of variance was therefore performed to assess the contributions of each of the dependent measures to the significant multivariate statistic. Further, since little is known about false positive responses in paced inspection tasks, this measure was assessed for possible Age by Sex interactions using univariate analysis of variance.

Inspection of the univariate analyses for the age effect showed that percent correct detections decreased significantly as a function of age ($F = 21.00$; $df = 3$, 360; $p < .001$), that false positive responses increased ($F = 6.26$; $df = 3$, 360; $p < .001$) and that response times increased across age groups ($F = 4.30$; $df = 3$, 360; $p < .005$). Figure 4–21 shows percent correct detections for each age and sex group and illustrates the fact that young sub-

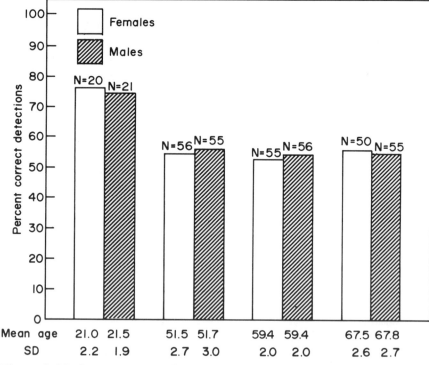

Figure 4–21. *Percent correct detections for each age and sex group for the entire task.*

jects performed more efficiently than middle-aged or elderly subjects. This figure also suggests that although there was a large decrease in detection efficiency between the ages of 21 and 51, there was no apparent progressive deterioration in detection performance between 51 and 67 years of age.

Figure 4–22 shows false positive responses for each age and sex group and illustrates the significant increase in false positive responses across the age groups. The univariate analysis of variance was significant for the test of the Age by Sex interaction for false positive responses ($F = 3.58$; $df = 3, 360$; $p < .01$); however, as Figure 4–22 illustrates, the younger subjects made markedly fewer false positive responses, irregardless of sex, while the oldest group of women made the largest number of false positive responses. Inspection of the variance within each age-sex group suggests that the large number of false positive responses made by the older women was not a function of a few older women in this group committing a very large number of such errors.

With respect to response time, the significant age groups effect is illustrated in Figure 4–23. As this figure shows, there is a monotonic increase in response time across the four age groups.

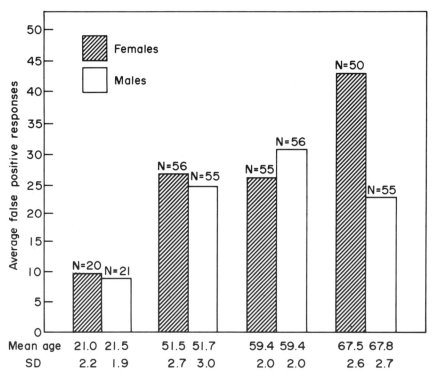

Figure 4–22. *False positive responses (commission errors) for each age and sex group for the entire task.*

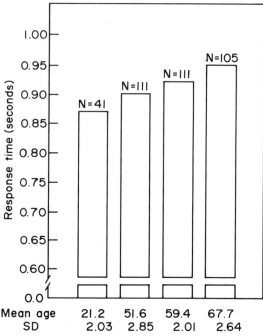

Figure 4–23. *Response time for each age group.*

Sex. When the three dependent measures of performance were considered simultaneously, the multivariate analysis of variance was significant for the effect of sex $(F = 4.23; df = 5, 358; p < .005)$. Univariate analysis of variance was therefore performed to assess how each of the dependent measures contributed to the significant multivariate sex effect. Inspection of the univariate analyses for the sex effect showed that percent correct detections did not differ as a function of sex $(F = 0.17; df = 1, 360; p > .6)$. Figure 4–21 shows that across the various age groups there was no difference in percent correct detections for men and women. The univariate test of sex effect for false positive responses was also not significant $(F = 2.80; df = 1, 360; p > .09)$. This was true even though the older women made the largest number of false positive responses (see Figure 4–21). Men were significantly faster than women $(F = 12.51; df = 1, 360; p < .001)$ in the detection of signal events (mean response times for men = 893 msec; mean response times for women = 941 msec).

Performance change within the session

Changes in performance as a function of time-on-watch were assessed using multivariate analysis of variance for repeated measures. The per-

Table 4–12. *Percent correct detections (%CD), false positive responses (FP), and response latency (RL) in seconds across each time segment of the continuous performance task (all subjects pooled).*

	%CD	FP	RL
First time period	63.34	12.60	.883
Second time period	58.87	7.93	.919
Third time period	56.88	6.96	.929

formance change with all subjects pooled was highly significant across segments of the session. Percent correct detections and false positive responses both decreased as a function of time-on-watch ($F = 31.73$; $df = 2$, 358; $p < .0001$ and $F = 12.05$; $df = 2$, 358; $p < .0001$, respectively). Response latency increased significantly across time segments of the task ($F = 13.29$; $df = 2$, 358; $p < .0001$). Mean performance for each of the dependent measures of performance for the three time periods is given in Table 4–12. There was a significant interaction of age and time-on-watch for percent correct detections. As shown in Figure 4–24, the young group showed an initial high level of performance followed by a decrement of approximately seven percent correct detections. This was followed by a very slight increase in percent correct detections from the second to the third time periods of the task. The middle-aged and elderly subjects, besides having a lower initial

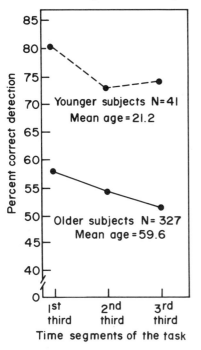

Figure 4–24. *Effect of time-on-watch on percent correct detection for younger and older subjects.*

level of performance, showed a continual decline in percent correct detections from the first through the third time periods of the continuous performance task. Thus, the younger subjects showed a performance plateau while the older subjects showed a monotonic decline. There was no significant interaction of age and time-on-watch for false positive responses or response latency. Neither the interaction of sex and time-on-watch, nor of age, sex, and time-on-watch was significant for any of the dependent measures.

Discussion

The most consistent age-related difference in paced inspection tasks has been that old subjects make more errors of omission (fewer correct detections) than younger subjects (Griew and Davies, experiment 1, 1962; Thompson et al., 1963; Davies, 1968; Talland, 1966). In unpaced tasks older subjects may be as accurate as young subjects but work at a slower rate (Botwinick and Shock, 1952). The age effect, in paced tasks, appears to be a rate limited phenomenon in that age differences appear only at relatively fast (1 per second) stimulus presentation rates. At slower rates, old and young subjects perform equally well with respect to omission errors (Thompson et al., 1963; Davies, 1968). The results of the present study show that young subjects perform more accurately and efficiently than middle-aged and elderly subjects. This was true not only for correct detections but also false positive responses and response times for correct detections. Further, the present study extends this general finding to include women. Middle-aged and elderly women performed much less accurately than young women. There was no significant sex difference in correct detections as Figure 4–21 shows.

The importance of assessing errors of commission or false positive responses in performance on paced inspection tasks is evidenced in the fact that false positive responses increased across age groups even though correct detections decreased. This suggests that the middle-aged and elderly subjects are not withdrawing from the experimental situation. Rather, it would appear that the middle-aged and elderly subjects are less efficient in distinguishing the occurrence of signal events from background stimuli and have a less strict criterion for responding than the young subjects.

The lack of a significant age by sex multivariate statistic for the three dependent measures of performance taken simultaneously would normally preclude the univariate age by sex analysis of any one of these measures. However, since little is known about changes in false positive responses in paced inspection tasks in relation to age and sex, these response errors were analyzed separately in a univariate design. The significant univariate age by sex interaction for false positive responses illustrated in Figure 4–22 is apparently a function of the increase in these response errors on the part of the oldest group of women. This group made a disproportionately large number of false positive responses when contrasted either with men of comparable age or with women 7 to 16 years younger. This suggests that, for paced inspection tasks of the type used in this study, women in the older age range respond more to nonsignal stimuli and may be maintaining their overall detection performance by relaxing their criterion for responding. Further investigation of this phenomenon is necessary to establish it as reliable.

Detection performance clearly decreased as a function of time-on-watch. The decrease in correct detections and false positive responses with the concomitant increase in response times for correct detections (Table 4–12) suggests that there is a decrease in ability to sustain directed attention to rapidly changing signal events. This decrease in efficiency parallels the well-documented decrement in performance on longer vigilance tasks (Mackworth, 1969 and 1970). It would appear that in the present task, changes in ability to sustain attention occur early-on. Table 4–12 shows that the performance decrement between the first and second time periods of the task is greater than between the second and third time periods.

The significant age by time-on-watch interaction is a result of the fact that the young subjects are able to maintain detection efficiency between the second and third time periods while the middle-aged and elderly continue to evidence a decrement. Prolonging the duration of the paced inspection task would be of interest to find if the middle-aged and elderly subjects continue to show a monotonic decrease in efficiency or if their performance plateaus.

In summary, the present study characterized the response patterns of young, middle-aged and elderly men and women on a brief, paced inspection task. Young subjects were found to make fewer errors of omission and commission than middle-aged and elderly subjects. A monotonic increase in response times for correctly detected signal events was observed across age groups. The results suggest that a major performance decrement may occur between the ages of 21 and 46 and stress the need for further investigation of the performance of individuals in this age range on paced inspection tasks. The interaction of age and sex for false positive responses is taken here as suggestive rather than conclusive. Parametric manipulation of task variables is necessary to clearly establish this preliminary finding before generalization may be made.

References

Botwinick, Jack, and Shock, N. W. Age differences in performance decrement with continuous work. *Journal of Gerontology*, 7:41–46, 1952.

Canestrari, R. E. The relationship of vigilance to paced and self-paced learning in young and elderly adults. Ph.D. dissertation, Duke University, 1961

Davies, D. R. Age differences in paced inspection tasks. In G. A. Talland (Ed.), *Human aging and behavior: Recent Advances in Research & Theory*. New York: Academic Press, 1968, pp 217–238.

Davies, D. R., and Griew, S. Age and vigilance. In A. T. Welford and J. E. Birren (Eds.), *Behavior, aging and the nervous system.* Springfield, Ill.: Charles A. Thomas, 1965.

Davies, D. R., and Griew, S. A further note on the effect of aging on auditory vigilance performance: The effect of low signal frequency. *Journal of Gerontology,* 18:370–371, 1963.

Davies, D. R., and Tune, G. S. *Human vigilance performance.* New York: American Elsevier, 1969.

Doppelt, J. E., and Wallace, W. L. Standardization of the Wechsler Adult Intelligence Scale for older persons. *Journal of Abnormal and Social Psychology,* 51:312–330, 1955.

Eisdorfer, C., and Cohen, L. D. The generality of the WAIS standardization for the aged: A regional comparison. *Journal of Abnormal and Social Psychology,* 62:520–527, 1961.

Evans, C. R., and Mulholland, T. B. *Attention in neurophysiology.* New York: Appleton-Century-Crofts, 1969.

Griew, S., and Davies, D. R. The effect of aging on auditory vigilance performance. *Journal of Gerontology,* 17:88–90, 1962.

Jones, L. V. Analysis of variance in its multivariate developments. In R. C. Cattell (Ed.), *Handbook of multivariate experimental psychology.* Chicago: Rand McNally, 1966.

Kirchner, W. K. Age differences in short-term retention of rapidly changing information. *Journal of Experimental Psychology,* 55:352–358, 1958.

Mackworth, J. F. *Vigilance and habituation.* Middlesex, England: Penguin Books, Ltd., 1969.

Mackworth, J. F. *Vigilance and attention.* Middlesex, England: Penguin Books, Ltd., 1970.

Mostofsky, D. I. (Ed.). *Attention: Contemporary theory and analysis.* New York: Appleton-Century-Crofts, 1970.

Sanders, A. F. *Attention and performance, III.* Amsterdam: North-Holland, 1970.

Starmer, C. F., and Grizzle, J. E. A computer program for analysis of data by general linear models. The Institute of Statistics Mimeo Series, No. 560. Chapel Hill, N.C.: Institute of Statistics, February 1968.

Surwillo, W. W., and Quilter, R. E. Vigilance, age, and response-time. *American Journal of Psychology,* 63:105–115, 1966.

Thompson, L. W., Opton, E. and Cohen, L. D. Effects of age, presentation speed, and sensory modality on performance of a "vigilance" task. *Journal of Gerontology,* 18:366–369, 1963.

Chapter 5. Mental Illness

Although most of the participants in our longitudinal studies were relatively healthy, both physically and mentally, there were enough subjects with various degrees of mental impairment to study what factors are associated and which may explain mental illness among the relatively normal aged. The first report found that brain impairment was more common among those with decompensated heart disease, those with lower socioeconomic status, and those with fewer activities. It also suggests that a mild elevation of blood pressure may help to preserve the brain in some aged persons. The second report uses somewhat different methods of analysis, but comes to essentially the same conclusions.

The report on depression and health found a prominent and persisting association between depression and subjective as well as objective measures of poor health. The report concludes that poor health may lead to depression or visa versa, but it appears probable that each tends to lead to the other.

The Multiple Factors Contributing to Dementia in Old Age
Ewald W. Busse and H. Shan Wang

Although dementia in the elderly is a common clinical syndrome and has been the subject of numerous studies, we do not yet know why some elderly individuals are more demented than others. Since intellectual processes are dependent on brain activities, one would naturally expect impairment of brain tissue to be the most critical determinant of dementia. Such impairment may result both from degenerative changes involving the brain primarily and from physical illnesses which secondarily affect the aging brain. In many elderly persons, therefore, dementia can be at least partially attributed to their poor physical health.

The relationship between dementia and brain impairment that can be measured by physical or physiological measures is by no means consistent (Wang, 1971). Although most studies have demonstrated more brain impairment in elderly individuals with dementia than in nondemented old people, the correlation between the severity of dementia and that of brain impairment has only been a gross one. Discrepancies between these variables were observed in more than a fourth of the cases (Corsellis, 1962; Obrist,

Reprinted by permission from the *Proceedings of the Fifth World Congress of Psychiatry*, Mexico City, Mexico, 1971.

Busse, Eisdorfer, and Kleemeier, 1962; Blessed, Tomlinson, and Roth, 1968; Wang, Obrist, and Busse, 1970). Some elderly persons with severe dementia had little brain impairment; others who had severe brain impairments showed only mild dementia. The poor correlation may be due in part to the methodological difficulties encountered in the study of brain impairment and dementia.

Data from the literature suggest that social and psychological factors may also play a role in the development or outcome of dementia. The factors that have been repeatedly mentioned are preexisting personality patterns, social isolation, environmental stress, and emotional disorders such as depression and anxiety.

In the past, almost all extensive studies on dementia have been carried out in elderly patients living in neuropsychiatric institutions or nursing homes. Lesser degrees of dementia are also very common among aged persons who are maintaining an active life in the community. It was our belief that a careful study of these active old people might provide a better understanding of the role of various factors in the early development of dementia, and thus might lead eventually to more effective preventive or therapeutic measures. On the basis of this belief, we are reporting this review of some findings from a longitudinal study made of such subjects at the Duke University Center for the Study of Aging and Human Development. The subjects were 265 volunteers, at least 60 years of age, who were recruited from the community in 1956 to participate in a longitudinal study.

Findings

On the basis of the medical history and findings from physical and laboratory examinations, the 265 subjects were divided into six groups according to their lung and heart conditions at study 1 (Table 5–1). About half the subjects showed no evidence of pulmonary or cardiac disease (group 1). The remaining subjects were divided almost equally among those having only compensated heart disease (group 2), those having only decompensated heart disease (group 3), and those having lung disease, with or without concomitant heart disease (groups 4, 5 and 6).

The prevalence of brain impairment and the level of intellectual functioning in these groups are also illustrated in Table 5–1. The three findings taken to indicate brain impairment were evidence of central nervous system disorder on the neurological examination and, in the EEG, the presence of excessive slow waves in background activity ("diffuse slow" in Gibbs's classification), and the slowing of the occipital dominant frequency. Intellectual functioning was judged on the basis of the Verbal and Performance Scaled Scores and the deterioration quotient from the Wechsler Adult Intelligence Scale (WAIS).

Table 5–1 shows two interesting findings: (1) Brain impairments are clearly more common in subjects having decompensated heart disease (group 3 and 6) and in those having only lung disease (group 4) than in healthy subjects (group 1) or in subjects having compensated heart disease (group 2 and 5); (2) the level of intellectual functioning did not consistently parallel the indications of brain impairment. The intellectual functioning tended to be below the level expected on the basis of the brain condition. In groups 2 and 5, Verbal and Performance Scores on the WAIS were lower than those of the healthy subjects, in spite of the absence of any significant difference in brain impairment.

Table 5–1. *Brain impairment and intellectual functioning in groups with and without heart and lung disease.*

Group	1	2	3	4	5	6
Heart disease	−	+	++	−	+	++
Lung disease	−	−	−	+	+	+
N	132	47	48	19	6	13
% all subjects	49.8	17.7	18.1	7.2	2.3	4.9
EEG examination						
Percent classified as "diffuse slow" (Gibbs)	11.4	6.4	27.1	31.6	16.7	46.2
Mean occipital dominant frequency (c/s)	9.40	9.69	9.17	9.12	9.58	8.85
Neurological examination						
Percent with CNS disorder	9.1	2.6	27.1	21.1	0	53.8
Psychometric evaluation (WAIS)						
Verbal Scaled Scores	59.8	51.2	49.0	45.8	56.2	39.8
Performance Scaled Scores	30.6	25.1	20.4	22.0	26.7	14.9
Deterioration quotient	.189	.172	.208	.256	.199	.285

− = absent
+ = present (without decompensation, in the case of heart disease)
++ = present with decompensation

In searching for factors that might account for these two observations, we found that the subjects in groups 2–6 (those with heart and/or lung disease) were slightly older and less well educated than the healthy subjects. These groups also contained more blacks, more males, and more persons who had done manual labor. We found that these demographic and socioeconomic factors were responsible in part, but not entirely, for the intellectual differences. When race, age, and education were carefully matched, the intellectual differences between the healthy and the diseased groups were still present but became less apparent.

No differences were found among the groups in regard to their contact with family, relatives or friends, their living arrangements, or their depressive symptoms. The two groups of subjects with decompensated heart disease, however, did contain more separated or widowed persons than the remaining four groups.

By far the most conspicuous differences among these six groups were related to blood pressure and daily activities. The mean arterial blood pressure (MABP), which is the sum of diastolic pressure and one-third of the pulse pressure, was clearly much higher in the four groups with heart disease than in the two without such disease. The group means for the former were all above 120 mm Hg; those for the latter were 102 and 104 mm Hg.

Figure 5–1 illustrates the relationship between blood pressure and the EEG occipital dominant frequency. In the three groups that had no lung

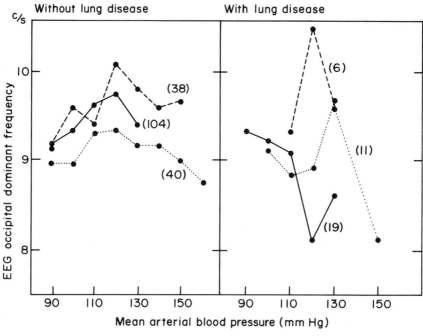

Figure 5–1. *The relationship between EEG occipital dominant frequency (cycles per second) and the mean arterial pressure (mm Hg) in subjects with or without heart and lung disease at study 1. The number of subjects in each group is shown in parentheses next to the curve.*

disease, increases in MABP up to 120 mm Hg were associated with an increase of EEG frequency. As the blood pressure in these groups rose above 120 mm Hg, EEG frequency decreased in the group having no heart disease and in the one having decompensated heart disease, but not in the group having compensated heart disease. A similar finding was not apparent in the three groups that had lung disease.

The other conspicuous difference observed was in the amount of daily activities engaged in by these subjects (Figure 5–2). In the healthy group, 61 percent had seven to nine and 33 percent had four to six locomotor activities. In the same group, 17 percent had seven to nine and 58 percent had four to six sedentary activities. The subjects in all five diseased groups clearly had fewer locomotor or sedentary activities than those in the healthy group.

On the basis of these observations, we formed two hypotheses: (1) The elevation of blood pressure may help to maintain cerebral functioning in some elderly subjects; (2) inactivity, which in many cases is due to physical

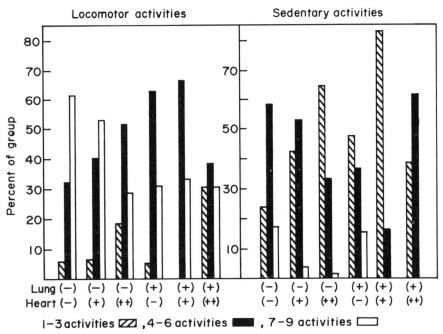

Figure 5–2. *Locomotor and sedentary activities in subjects with or without heart and lung disease at study 1, expressed in percentage of subjects having 1–3, 4–6, and 7–9 activities.*

illness, may play an important role in the intellectual deterioration of some elderly persons and may account to some degree for the discrepancies observed between brain impairment and dementia.

In an effort to test these hypotheses, we have analyzed the data from the first three studies of the subjects in the healthy group. Figure 5–3 shows the relationship between the average MABP and the average EEG occipital dominant frequency found on these three examinations, which covered a span of about seven years. Blood pressures below 95 or above 115 mm Hg were associated with slower average EEG frequencies than blood pressures between these two limits. High blood pressure was associated with an increased incidence of heart disease. During this seven-year interval, definite evidence of

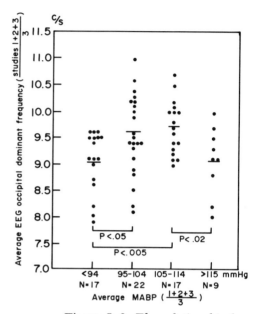

Figure 5–3. *The relationship between the average EEG occipital dominant frequency (cycles per second) and average mean arterial blood pressure (mm Hg) in the first three examinations (studies 1, 2, and 3), which spanned a period of about seven years. The statistical probabilities indicate the significance of the difference between groupings.*

heart disease developed in only 6 percent of subjects with blood pressures below 95 mm Hg. For subjects with an average MABP between 95 and 104, the corresponding figure was 14 percent; with pressures between 105 and 114, 36 percent and with pressure over 114, 44 percent.

The originally healthy subjects can be divided into three groups according to the activities they reported at the time of the first study:

Group A (28 subjects): Those with many activities, both locomotor and sedentary.

Group B (29 subjects): Those reporting many locomotor but few sedentary activities.

Group C (25 subjects): Those with few activities of either type. One subject who had many sedentary but few locomotor activities was excluded.

Figure 5–4 shows the changes of the intellectual indicators in these

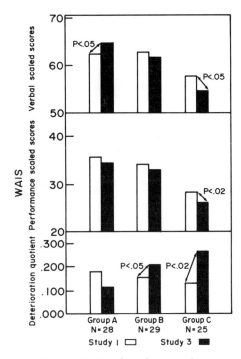

Figure 5–4. *The changes between study 1 and study 3 in Verbal and Performance Scaled Scores and in the deterioration quotient on the Wechsler Adult Intelligence Scale. At study 1, the subjects in group A had many locomotor and sedentary activities; those in group B engaged in only locomotor activities, and those in group C were inactive. The statistical probabilities indicate the significance of the changes.*

three groups between study 1 and study 3. The WAIS Verbal Scores increased in Group A but decreased in groups B and C. The Performance Scores decreased in all three groups. The deterioration quotient, on the other hand, decreased in group A but increased in groups B and C.

Some of the differences found among these three groups were statistically significant (Table 5–2). The lack of sedentary activities—that is, the difference between groups A and B—was associated with significantly different changes between studies 1 and 3 in Verbal Scores and in deterioration quotients but not in the Performance Scores. The changes occurring in group B (high in locomotor activity) did not differ significantly from those in the

Table 5–2. *Statistical significance of WAIS differences between groups.*

	A vs. B	B vs. C	A vs. C
Verbal Scaled Scores			
Study 1	NS	NS	NS
Study 3	NS	NS	p < .05
Changes (3–1)	p < .02	NS	p < .005
Performance Scaled Scores			
Study 1	NS	NS	NS
Study 3	NS	p < .05	p < .02
Changes (3–1)	NS	NS	NS
Deterioration quotient			
Study 1	NS	NS	NS
Study 3	p < .02	NS	p < .005
Changes (3–1)	p < .01	NS	p < .005

NS = not significant

inactive subjects (group C). The greatest differences were found between groups A and C—the most active and the most inactive groups.

Comment

Our study on a group of elderly community volunteers indicates that many factors are related to dementia in old age, although the interpretation of some of our findings doubtless needs to be cautious. Our study, like all similar studies, was limited by methodological difficulties, foremost of which is probably the reliability and validity of measures for brain impairment and intellectual functioning. In general, the three brain variables employed in our study agree better than the three intellectual indicators, which are more dependent on the demographic and socioeconomic characteristics of the subjects.

Our findings are not unexpected. The association between illness and socioeconomic status and that between brain impairment and cardiopulmonary disease, as well as the discrepancy between brain impairment and dementia, are well known. Of greatest interest, especially from the clinical point of view, are probably the findings of a relationship between blood pressure and brain impairment and between activities (primarily sedentary activities) and intellectual functioning.

While our study confirms the well-established observation of an association between *severe* hypertension and cerebral complications, it also indicates that a mild elevation of blood pressure, instead of being detrimental to the brain, may help to preserve the brain in some aged persons. We hypothesize that these elderly probably have significant cerebral atherosclerosis and require a relatively high blood pressure to maintain a sufficient blood supply to the brain and hence the cerebral functioning. This hypothesis is consistent with Hedlund's finding (1964) that cerebral blood flow in atherosclerotic patients tends to increase in proportion to the systolic blood pressure.

Our findings are not reported with the idea of suggesting that high blood pressure is good for elderly persons, because we also found that high blood pressure tends to result in heart disease. It is not clear why, in some individuals, the brain is protected at the expense of the heart, and in other individuals the heart is protected at the expense of the brain. Nevertheless, our findings do raise the question as to the effect on the aging brain of many widely used drugs, such as tranquilizers and antidepressants, that tend to lower the blood pressure.

Although there is generally believed to be a close relationship between mental illness in general and social variables such as isolation, data regarding the role played by these social variables in the dementia of old age are rather sparse. While Kay and his coworkers (1964) reported that poverty and isolation played a contributory role in mental deterioration, this finding was not confirmed by the San Francisco project. On the basis of the latter study, Lowenthal (1965) concluded that isolation may well be a consequence rather than a cause of many psychogenic and most organic mental illnesses that develop in old age.

Our study suggests that dementia in the elderly is related to the type and amount of activities rather than to social contacts. Inactivity is one common characteristic of old age. It may be dependent on the preexisting personality or on the socioeconomic or educational background of the individual, or it may be secondary to physical illness, emotional disorder, or institutionalization. The last two factors—emotional disorders and institutionalization—are probably of the greatest clinical significance, since they are often amenable to treatment or prevention.

Conclusion

Among the many factors that contribute to dementia, some affect the brain directly, while others affect mainly the intellectual functioning or the behavior. Although the dementia of old age is primarily the result of brain impairment, its severity is frequently determined by the interaction of many physical, social and psychological factors. It should therefore be viewed as a sociopsychosomatic disorder which warrants more aggressive preventive and therapeutic measures.

References

Blessed, G., Tomlinson, B. E., and Roth, M. The association between quantitative measures of dementia and of senile change in the cerebral grey matter of elderly subjects. *British Journal of Psychiatry*, 114:797, 1968.

Corsellis, J. A. N. *Mental illness and the aging brain.* London: Oxford University Press, 1962.

Hedlund, S., Kohler, V., Nylin, G., Olsson, R., Regenstrom, O., Rothstrom, E., and Astrom, K. E. Cerebral blood circulation in dementia. *Acta Psychiatrica Scandinavica*, 40:77, 1964.

Kay, D. W. K., Beamish, P., and Roth, M. Old age and mental disorders in Newcastle upon Tyne. Part II. A study of possible social and medical causes. *British Journal of Psychiatry*, 110:668, 1964.

Lowenthal, M. F. Antecedents of isolation and mental illness in old age. *Archives of General Psychiatry*, 12:245, 1965.

Obrist, W. D., Busse, E. W., Eisdorfer, C., and Kleemeier, R. W. Relation of the electroencephalogram to intellectual function in senescence. *Journal of Gerontology*, 17:197, 1962.

Wang, H. S., Obrist, W. D., and Busse, E. W. Neurophysiological correlations of the intellectual function of elderly persons living in the community. *American Journal of Psychiatry*, 126:1205, 1970.

Wang, H. S. Cerebral correlations of intellectual function in senescence. In Jarvik, L., Eisdorfer, C. and Blum, J. E. (Eds.), *Intellectual changes from childhood through maturity: Some psychological and biological aspects.* New York: Springer, 1971.

Heart Disease and Brain Impairment Among Aged Persons
H. Shan Wang and Ewald W. Busse

Heart disease is one of the most common causes of death in old age. According to the vital statistics published by the U.S. Public Health Service (1969), the mortality rate from heart disease in the age group from 65 to 74 is about 1,700 per 100,000. For the age group 75 to 84, this rate is more than doubled; and among persons aged 85 and above, it is almost six times this high. Almost all of these deaths (about 90 percent) were attributed to either arteriosclerotic or hypertensive heart disease.

Heart disease is also one of the most prevalent clinical problems in old age. Of the elderly subjects studied in Evans County, Georgia (McDonough, Hames, Stulb, and Garrison, 1965), 5.5 percent had coronary heart disease. Using somewhat broader criteria, the Tecumseh study (Epstein, Ostrander, Johnson, Payne, Hayner, Keller and Francis, 1965) disclosed a much greater prevalence of heart disease among its elderly subjects: about 17 percent had coronary heart disease; 7 percent hypertensive heart disease; and 8 percent, either rheumatic heart disease or congestive heart failure.

It is a common belief that brain impairment or intellectual deterioration in many elderly persons is closely related to heart disease. This belief is

The authors would like to thank Dr. Carl Eisdorfer for the psychological data collected in his laboratory and Dr. Walter Obrist for his contribution in the collection of EEG data.

based to a great extent on the many studies carried out on patients with congenital and rheumatic heart disease, and on patients undergoing cardiac surgery—all of these conditions being consistently associated with high incidence of cognitive impairment and of neuropsychiatric or electroencephalographic abnormalities (Eisdorfer, 1967; Ewalt and Ruskin, 1944). Very few studies, however, have been concerned specifically with arteriosclerotic and hypertensive heart disease in old age. A postmortem study by Vost and his group (Vost, Wolochow, and Howell, 1964) showed histopathological evidence of cerebral infarction in more than half the patients with old myocardial infarction or pure hypertensive heart disease, but in only 12 percent of those with normal hearts. An association between arteriosclerotic heart disease and cerebral dysfunctioning is also indicated by the finding that patients with such heart disease had an abnormally low flicker-fusion frequency (Enzer, Simonson, and Blakstein, 1942) and were slow and poor on a number of psychological tests (Spieth, 1964). In an EEG study of elderly patients with heart disease (predominantly arteriosclerotic), Obrist and Bissell (1955) observed that occipital alpha frequency was significantly slower and the incidence of delta waves greater in such patients than in healthy subjects. They also found an inverse relationship between heart size and mean alpha frequency.

Findings in 227 Elderly Volunteers

A group of elderly citizens living in the community have volunteered to participate in a longitudinal study being conducted at the Duke University Center for the Study of Aging and Human Development. At intervals of three to four years, each of these subjects is given physical, neurological, and psychiatric examinations, together with many laboratory and psychological tests. Some of the data bearing on the relationship between cognitive functioning and cardiovascular disease have previously been reported (Thompson, Eisdorfer, and Estes, 1966). The present report is a further evaluation of the relationship between brain impairment and varying degrees of heart disease in 227 subjects—all those included in the longitudinal project except patients with apparent pulmonary disease.

The brain status was evaluated on the basis of the neurological and EEG examinations and the Verbal and Performance Scaled Scores of Wechsler Adult Intelligence Scale (WAIS). The medical history, physical examination, electrocardiogram, and chest X-ray were used as criteria for dividing the subjects into four groups, as follows:

Group 0: no heart disease (105 subjects).
Group 1: questionable heart disease (27 subjects).
Group 2: definite and compensated heart disease (47 subjects).
Group 3: definite and decompensated heart disease (48 subjects).

Table 5–3. *Characteristics of groups with varying degrees of heart disease.*

	Group 0 No heart disease	Group 1 Questionable heart disease	Group 2 Compensated heart disease	Group 3 Decompensated heart disease
Number of subjects	105	27	47	48
Mean age (years)	69.5	72.2[a]	70.2	73.6[c]
% white	72.4	77.7	53.2[b]	52.0[b]
% male	46.7	48.1	36.2	41.7
% with nonmanual occupation	50.5	59.3	40.4	29.2[b]
Mean education (years)	11.3	10.6	9.3[a]	9.2[b]

Significance of differences as compared with group 0: [a] $p < 0.10$; [b] $p < 0.05$; [c] $p < 0.01$.
* In all the tables and figures, the symbols *a*, *b*, and *c* are used to indicate findings differing from group 0: *a* means that $p < 0.10$; *b*, that $p < 0.05$; *c*, that $p < 0.01$.

The characteristics of these four groups at the time of the initial examination are summarized in Table 5–3.* Except for being slightly older, the subjects in group 1 were almost identical to those in group 0. Group 2 contained significantly fewer white subjects and had a slightly lower level of education; in group 3 there were significant differences in age, race, occupation, and

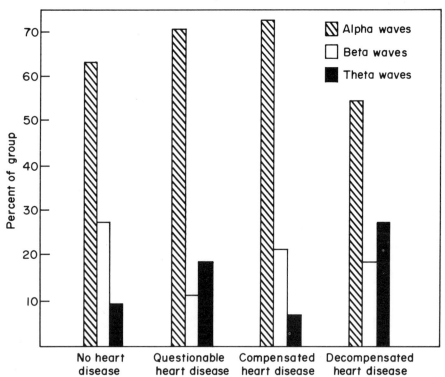

Figure 5–5. *EEG dominant background activities.*

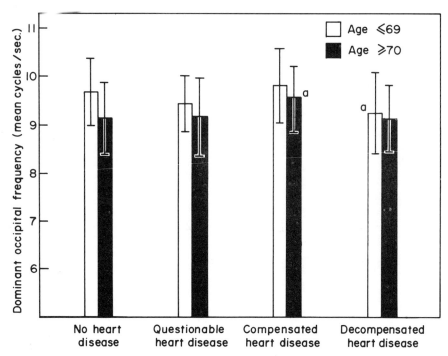

Figure 5–6. *Mean alpha frequency from occipital tracings.*

education. The subjects in this group were on the average four years older and had two years less education than those in group 0, and the group contained more nonwhite subjects and more manual laborers.

The neurological examination disclosed evidence of brain disorder in 27 percent of the subjects in group 3 and only 9.5 percent in those in group 0; this difference is significant at the .05 level. The incidence of brain disorder was only 7.4 percent in group 1 and 2.1 percent in group 2.

EEG background dominant activities in each group were classified as predominately alpha, beta, or theta (Figure 5–5). The significant difference found was between group 0 and group 3: theta waves were dominant in 27 percent of the subjects in group 3 and in only 10 percent of those in group 0.

Figure 5–6 shows the mean alpha frequency from occipital tracings. Subjects in group 3 under 70 years of age had a slightly slower mean frequency and sujects in group 2 above 69 years had a slightly faster mean frequency than those of comparable ages in group 0.

The mean WAIS Verbal and Performance Scaled Scores are shown in Figure 5–7. Verbal and Performance Scores were significantly higher in group 0 than in group 2 and 3. This difference was due in part to the demographic differences among these groups. As reported above, groups 2 and 3 were older and had a relatively large number of subjects who were nonwhite and had manual occupations and little education. When the subjects were matched by

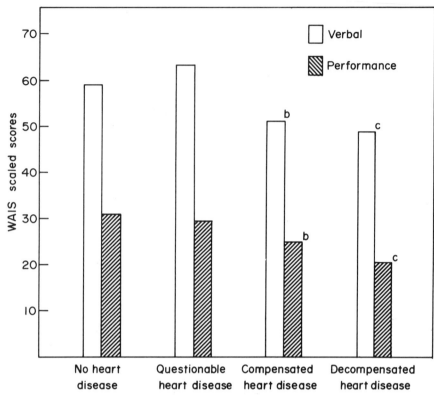

Figure 5–7. *Mean WAIS Verbal and Performance Scaled Scores.*

age, race, and education, however, the WAIS scores, particularly on performance tests, were still slightly lower in groups 2 and 3 than in group 0.

Figure 5–8 shows the mean systolic and diastolic blood pressure (supine) in these four groups. Both means were significantly higher in groups 2 and 3 than in group 0.

Figure 5–9 shows the number of activities engaged in by the subjects in each group. Those in group 2 had significantly fewer sedentary activities (such as writing letters, reading, playing cards) than those in group 0, but about the same number of locomotor activities (working in the garden, fishing, etc.); the subjects in group 3 were significantly less active in both categories.

The amount of social contact in these four groups is summarized in Table 5–4. There were significantly more widowed individuals in group 3 than in group 0, and subjects in the former group reported less contact with friends and young persons than those in the latter. The subjects in group 2, though having the same amount of contact with family, relatives, and friends, appeared to have somewhat less contact with young persons than those in group 0.

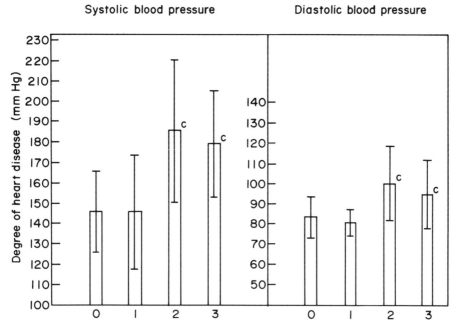

Figure 5–8. *Mean systolic and diastolic blood pressure.*

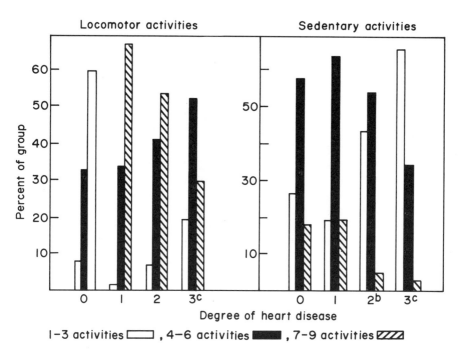

Figure 5–9. *Number of activities engaged in by subjects in each group.*

Table 5-4. *Social contacts of groups with varying degrees of heart disease.*

Percent of subjects	Group 0 No heart disease (N = 105)	Group 1 Questionable heart disease (N = 27)	Group 2 Compensated heart disease (N = 47)	Group 3 Decompensated heart disease (N = 48)
Widowed	22.9	33.3	29.8	45.9[c]
Not living with spouse and/or children	24.8	26.0	23.4	33.4
Having little contact with family or close relatives	6.7	7.4	10.6	8.3
Having little contact with distant relatives	41.9	37.0	40.4	50.0
Having little contact with friends	46.7	48.2	44.7	68.8[b]
Having little contact with family, friends, close and distant relatives	4.8	7.4	10.6	10.4
Having little contact with children and young friends	19.0	29.6	34.0[a]	33.3[a]

Significance of differences as compared with group 0: [a] $p < 0.10$; [b] $p < 0.05$; [c] $p < 0.01$.

Mild to moderate depression was evident in 29 percent of the subjects in group 3 and 21 percent of those in group 0, but this difference is not statistically significant.

Discussion

From the standpoint of the electroencephalographic and neurological findings, the evidence of CNS disorder was significantly greater in subjects with decompensated heart disease but slightly less in those with compensated heart disease than in those without heart disease. This finding suggested that brain impairment in old age is related to heart failure but not to heart disease per se. The brain impairment seen in patients with heart failure is probably due to a profound reduction of cerebral blood flow, which has been shown to be proportional to the reduction in cardiac output (Scheinberg, 1950; Novack, 1953; Eisenberg, Madison, and Sensebach, 1960; Porje, 1967).

The lack of brain impairment in subjects with compensated heart disease is probably attributable to the relatively high blood pressure in this group. It is well known that severe hypertension is associated with a high incidence of cerebral complications. Our findings, however, suggest that mild hypertension in some elderly patients may help to maintain the blood flow to the brain and hence to preserve the status of the brain, but at the expense of the heart. Thus the possibility is raised that the elevation of blood pressure in some elderly patients is a compensatory response to cerebral ischemia secondary to cerebral arteriosclerosis. This view is consistent with Dickinson's theory of neurogenic hypertension (Dickinson, 1965).

The WAIS scores in patients with either compensated or decompensated heart disease were lower than one would expect on the basis of the EEG and neurological findings. It is postulated that the poor performance on psychological testing in these cardiac subjects may be related in part to brain impairment and in part to decreased use of the remaining intellectual faculties. The latter part of this hypothesis is supported by the reported lack of sedentary activities such as reading and playing bridge, and by the lack of contact with young people.

References

Dickinson, C. J. Neurogenic hypertension. Oxford: Blackwell Scientific Publications, 1965.

Eisdorfer, C. Reaction to cardiovascular change. *Mayo Clinic Proceedings,* 42:620–636, 1967.

Eisenberg, S., Madison, L., and Sensebach, W. Cerebral hemodynamic and metabolic studies in patients with congestive heart failure. II. observations in confused failure. *Circulation,* 21:704–709, 1960.

Enzer, N., Simonson, E., and Blakstein, S. S. Fatigue of patients with circulatory insufficiency, investigated by means of the fusion frequency of flicker. *Annals of Internal Medicine,* 16:701–707, 1942.

Epstein, F. H., Ostrander, L. D., Johnson, B. C., Payne, M. W., Hayner, N. S., Keller, J. B., and Francis, T. F., Jr. Epidemiological studies of cardiovascular disease in a total community—Tecumseh, Michigan. *Annals of Internal Medicine,* 62:1170–1187, 1965.

Ewalt, J. R. and Ruskin, A. The EEG in patients with heart disease. *Texas Rep. Biol & Med.,* 2:164–174, 1944.

McDonough, J. R., Hames, C. G., Stulb, S. C., and Garrison, G. E. Coronary heart disease among negroes and whites in Evans County, Georgia. *J. Chron. Dis.,* 18:443–468, 1965.

Novack, P., Go, B., Bortin, L., Soffe, A., and Shenkin, H. A. Studies of the cerebral circulation and metabolism in congestive heart failure. *Circulation,* 7:724–731, 1953.

Obrist, W. D., and Bissell, L. F. The electroencephalogram of aged patients with cardiac and cerebral vascular disease. *J. Gerontol.,* 10:315–330, 1955.

Porje, I. G. The systemic circulation and the development of cerebral infarction. In Enger, A., and Larsson, T. (Eds.), *Stroke.* Stockholm: Nordiska Bokhandelns Forlag, 1967, pp. 145–151.

Scheinberg, P. Cerebral Circulation in heart failure. *Am. J. Med.,* 8:148–152, 1950.

Thompson, L. W., Eisdorfer, C., and Estes, E. H. Cardiovascular disease and behavioral changes in the elderly. Proceedings of the 7th International Congress of Gerontology, 1966.

Spieth, W. Cardiovascular health status, age and psychological performance. *J. Geront.,* 19:277–284, 1964.

U.S. Public Health Service. *Vital statistics of the United States,* 1967. Vol. *Mortality,* Part A. 1–22–1–28. Washington, D.C.: U.S. Government Printing Office, 1969.

Vost, A., Wolochow, D. A., and Howell, D. A. Incidence of infarcts of the brain in heart disease. *J. Path. Bact.,* 88:463–470, 1964.

Depression and Health   *John B. Nowlin*

Among all age groups, symptoms of depression have long been linked with poor health. Moreover, the feeling-state of depression is often said to be accompanied by the tendency for an individual to view his own health less positively. For the older person, the relationship between depression and decrement in the sense of physical well-being would seem particularly poignant. The older years are often a life epoch characterized by social and psychologic readjustment as well as being a time of increasing loss of physical vigor. A further important issue is the extent to which the association between depression and health is altered by the passage of time. If the feeling-state of depression appears to have strong association with health outlook and objective health status during short time spans, its effect over longer periods of time is less clear.

To examine these potential relationships, an older population carefully followed over the 1960–1970 decade served as a data source. These ambulatory community volunteers in Durham, N.C. numbered 157 in 1960 with an average age of 72.3 years; all were participants in a longitudinal study of aging conducted by the Duke Center for the Study of Aging and Human Development. In the initial selection of this volunteer population, care was taken to insure that the make-up of the study group approximated that of the local community in terms of racial composition and socioeconomic status. During the course of the subsequent decade, this study group was seen on four occasions. The interval between each visit was approximately two years; as the decade progressed, visits were scheduled less further apart because of an increasing attrition rate within the study group. At each two-day visit to the Aging Center, study participants received a thorough medical examination, blood testing, appraisal of current level of social activity, and standardized assessments of psychologic state.

As part of the two-day evaluation procedure, each study participant spent 45 minutes to an hour involved in a psychiatric interview. On the basis of this interview, each person was rated for severity of depressive symptoms on a 0 through 5 graduated scale. From the 1960 ratings of depression, two subject groups were defined: first, a "depression group" comprised of individuals found to exhibit depressive symptoms. This group numbered 52 individuals. Study volunteers, free of depressive symptomatology in 1960, formed the "no depression group" and numbered 105 persons. Comparison of these groups, in terms of 1960 data, revealed no difference in age, socioeconomic status, or in sex or racial composition. Health attitudes and objective health

Presented at the 9th International Congress of Gerontology, Kiev, U.S.S.R., July, 1972.

status among these two longitudinal population subgroups were then contrasted for the 1960 study and over the following ten years.

Table 5–5 contrasts selected health characteristics of the two groups from 1960 to 1970. Beneath the approximate revisit dates of this population to the Aging Center, the total number of individuals at each revisit is listed in parentheses. Moreover, the number of individuals in the "depression" and "no depression" groups are provided for each visit across the decade. As is evident, there is a moderate fall-off in group size, either from death or physical infirmity. Each individual variable reported in the table was tested for statistical significance in a two-factor analysis of variance format. One factor, of course, was the subject grouping on the basis of the presence or absence of depression in 1960. The alternate factor was a division of this volunteer elderly population based upon sex of the study participant.

The first variable is that of average depression score during the five visits of the decade. As mentioned earlier, the range of this scale was from 0 to 5. Zero indicated no evidence of depression while 5 implied severe depression. A significant difference exists at each testing period, with the group originally depressed in 1960 maintaining its higher "depression score" throughout the decade. This finding suggests that depression among an older population is not easily dissipated. The next variable is average subject age at each longitudinal visit. As is evident, the age differences of the returning subjects over the decade did not differ when depression and no depression groups are compared. This could be interpreted to indicate that presence or absence of depression is not a strictly age-related phenomenon. However, depression scores did tend to increase over the decade, especially for those starting out with no depression in 1960.

The next three variables in the table are those reflecting subject definition of and attitudes about health. At each visit, the study population members were requested to rate their own health on a 0 through 5 scale, with 5 indicating excellent health and 0 implying very poor health. The depression group consistently rated itself to be in less robust health than did the no depression group. A somewhat related issue is this population's concern about their health. Again, a 0 through 5 continuum scale was employed for the rating of health concern. In this instance, 0 connoted no concern, while a value of 5 reflected a high degree of concern. At each visit, the depression group indicated higher level of concern about their health than did the no depression group. Finally, this study population was asked to indicate the extent to which they perceived their health as interfering in their daily activities. Use was made again of a 0 through 5 scale with the zero value reflecting no health compromise of daily activity, and 5, reflecting a large extent of activity compromise. As shown in the table, the depression group perceived more compromise of activity than did the no depression group.

Next, more objective measures of health status were examined. These data are based upon a physician's findings during the medical examination provided

Table 5-5. *Characteristics of depressed and nondepressed older persons.*

	1960 (157)		1963 (111)		1966 (92)		1968 (81)		1970 (77)	
	D (52)	ND (105)	D (38)	ND (73)	D (34)	ND (58)	D (26)	ND (55)	D (23)	ND (54)
Depression score (range: 0–5)	1.8	0.0*	1.3	0.5*	2.1	1.0*	2.3	1.7*	2.2	1.6*
Age	73.7	72.2	76.8	75.5	79.1	77.6	80.1	78.7	81.2	79.2
Self-health rating (range: 0–5)	3.3	4.1*	3.4	4.0*	3.3	3.9*	3.2	3.8*	3.5	3.8*
Concern about health (range: 0–4)	1.2	0.7*	1.1	0.7*	1.0	0.7*	1.2	0.8*	1.1	0.7*
Activity compromise by health (range: 0–4)	0.9	0.6*	1.1	0.5*	1.0	0.7*	1.2	0.8*	1.4	1.0*
Systolic blood pressure	162	152*	175	161*	158	151	170	165	170	162
Diastolic blood pressure	85	80	82	76	85	82	87	85	88	84
% Subjects with electrocardiographic abnormality	53	47	56	49	58	42	59	41	55	45
Cardiovascular rating (range: 0–8)	1.4	1.0*	1.9	0.9*	1.3	1.0	1.2	0.9	1.4	0.8*
Overall health rating (range: 0–5)	2.4	2.0	1.9	1.3*	1.9	1.7	2.0	1.3*	2.1	1.6

D = Depressed group; ND = Nondepressed group.
* Significant at p < .05 level or lower.

at each visit. First, cuff readings of recumbent systolic pressure attained statistical significance at the 1960 and 1963 visits. Also, diastolic pressure was consistently slightly more elevated among the depression group.

Prevalence of electrocardiographic abnormality was next examined. For analysis purposes, cardiographic presentation of left ventricular hypertrophy, bundle branch block, or evidence of coronary artery disease were considered "abnormal." A higher percentage of cardiographic abnormality was consistently seen among the depression group.

Physician ratings of cardiovascular disease were also compared between the two study groups. A 0 through 8 graduated scale was employed. In the formulation of this score, consideration was given to the subject's history, his physical findings, and his electrocardiogram. A value of 0 described the subject without any evidence of cardiovascular disease; 8 reflected severe cardiovascular disease. Throughout the decade, degree of cardiovascular was more pronounced within the depression group. During the first two visits of the decade, these between-group differences proved to be statistically significant.

Finally, at the conclusion of his interaction with the longitudinal volunteer, the examining physician rated each subject in terms of overall health. The physician assigned values on a 0 through 5 scale, with lower scores denoting better health. This overall health rating score has proven to be relatively independent of the more specific cardiovascular rating just described. The physician's health rating averaged "higher," that is, poorer, among the depression group of subjects. On two revisits during the decade, these differences were statistically significant. Although serum cholesterol also proved to average higher among the depression group, between-group differences in this parameter were not statistically significant.

An even more precise health end-point to gauge is that of death. Among the depression group as constituted in 1960, 33 percent subsequently died over the course of the decade, compared to 34 percent of the no depression group. This difference is obviously not significant, but if the nonsurvivor groups are examined separately, a rather prominent between-group distinction is evident. Those in depression group, as defined in 1960, who subsequently died during the decade, lived an average of 43.4 months beyond their 1960 visit. In comparison, their no depression counterparts survived 72.5 months. Thus, the no depression members who died, did survive much longer than their depression counterparts.

As mentioned earlier, sex of the study participant was employed as the alternate factor in the analysis of variance. With one exception, sex of the individual did not significantly influence the relationships just described. However, women on the average were rated as more depressed throughout the decade than were men.

To summarize: The findings of this study indicate a prominent association between depressive feeling-states and the older individual's subjective and objective health status. Equally important, this relationship does not appear transient in nature; in this population, the association persists over the course of a decade. Admittedly, some qualification is necessary before broadly generalizing from the findings offered by this study. It should be emphasized that the study population under consideration was a volunteer rather than a randomly selected group of individuals. A population composed exclusively of volunteers may be biased in terms of the information which it provides. Moreover, the data collected from this population do not clarify, in any way, the issue of "cause and effect." Although a relationship exists between depression and health in this population, the nature and direction of the relationship can only be described as unclear. Two obvious interpretations present themselves. First, depression could be viewed as providing, in itself, a substrate for physiologic derangement leading to ill health. Conversely, it might well be that poor health, with its attendant discomfort and limitations, evokes the feeling-state of depression. Formidable logic could be brought to bear in support of either contention.

Chapter 6. Social Roles and Self-Concepts

This chapter turns to the more social-psychological aspects of aging and analyzes relationship between social roles, self-concepts and life satisfaction. The first report finds that older persons who are able to continue driving cars are in relatively good physical condition, have a realistic appreciation of their limitations, restrict their driving accordingly, and are able to maintain more activities and life satisfaction. It was found in the second study that widowhood produced surprisingly little change in activities, attitudes, adjustment, and health. The authors conclude that most normal aged utilize supportive social structures, reduced pressures, and psychological preparation to reduce the strains of bereavement.

Moving to the Adaptation Study, the third report finds that self-rated health is the predominant variable associated with life satisfaction in middle age, but organizational activity, internal control, performance status, and productivity all make additional contributions to satisfactions in middle age.

The fact that attitudes toward time and death varied by sex and age is discussed in the next study. Those over 55 see time as speeding faster than those under 55. Men see death more as an opponent while women are more accepting of it, more realistic, and more accepting of the passage of time.

Discrepancies in the self-image, as the next report shows, tend to increase with age, and separation from children affects women more than men; retirement or nonworking affects both sexes, but men have a greater problem with this discrepancy than women. Another analysis of self-image finds that change in job status is more important than change in relationship to one's children. Males seem to be more disturbed by changes associated with aging than women.

Self-concepts, the last report finds, can largely be accounted for by differences in aspirations and in the amount of resources to fulfill these aspirations. These factors may explain many of the inconsistencies found when activity or disengagement theories of aging are applied to actual persons.

The Elderly Driver and Ex-driver   *Daniel T. Gianturco, Dietolf Ramm, and C. William Erwin*

Since over 12 percent of the drivers on the road are over age 60, the topic of the elderly driver is a relevant one. In addition, the movement to the suburbs of friends, goods, and services usually makes transportation essential to a good life. The elderly and infirm who cannot drive have great transportation problems. In our society there is a definite lack of transit systems that are accessible, safe, and inexpensive for the elderly person. The mobility, status, and independence which results from driving makes our senior citizens very reluctant to give up their driving privileges.

Our current generation of elderly really grew to adulthood before cars became readily available. Yet a great proportion learned to drive and to value it. It seemed desirable therefore to study the driving habits of these elderly citizens. What is their physical condition? Do they, in fact, stop driving when physical infirmities make it hazardous? If they continue to drive do they have a realistic appreciation of their limitations? What effect, if any, has giving up driving had on their leisure, and social life?

Methodology

This report is based on data obtained from a panel of elderly participants in the Duke Longitudinal Study of Aging. Mortality and attrition reduced the panel to approximately one hundred survivors by 1970.

During the sixth series of observations each panelist, as part of the social worker's interview, was asked (1) whether he ever learned to drive; (2) whether he was continuing to drive; (3) what limitations or restrictions were placed on his driving, voluntary and otherwise; and (4) if he had stopped driving, why?

Data about activities and attitudes were obtained by the social worker during the social history interview with the older subjects using the Havinghurst scale (1953). The activity inventory consists of twenty questions dealing with five areas of activities; (1) health, (2) leisure, (3) security, (4) family and friends, and (5) religious activity. A total activity score is obtained by adding the scores in these five categories. Each subscore could range from 0 to 10. Life satisfaction was measured by 56 agree-disagree items about the subject's satisfaction with eight areas of his life, including friends, family, work, religion, health, economic status, general state of happiness, and feeling of usefulness.

The Physical Function Rating (PFR) is based on the extensive medical examination given each subject by the examining physician, including medical history, physical and visual testing, audiology examinations, and laboratory studies. The subjects were rated by him on a scale from 0 to 5 on the presence of disease and degree of function limitation. One hundred elderly subjects, ages 75 to 99, 62 women and 38 men, were evaluated; the average age of the subjects was 81.

Results

Prevalence and Characteristics

A quarter of the subjects never drive (more of the women than men), almost half have stopped driving, but almost one-third continue to drive (Table 6–1). The largest percentage of drivers were from the white collar

Table 6–1. *Prevalence of drivers by sex (percent).*

Subjects	Men (N = 38)	Women (N = 62)	Total (N = 100)
Nondrivers	8	37	26
Ex-drivers	53	39	44
Current drivers	39	24	30
Total	100	100	100

occupations. Their driving average age was 78 years and their average physical function rating was 1.2. This indicated that despite their advanced age, there was little limitation of function.

Perception

Fourteen of our 30 drivers had "glasses" restriction. Their corrected visual acuity was generally good. None was worse than 20/50 in either eye. Average corrected acuity was 20/30 to 20/40. Twelve drivers still had no cortical lenticular opacities; eleven had incipient cataracts characterized by lameliar separations and vacuoles; two had cuneiform peripheral opacities, and two had already had cataract surgery. (Corrected vision in each of these was good: 20/20 and 20/40). All these elderly people showed mild to moderate nuclear lenticular changes.

Hearing

Hearing level was determined by auditory thresholds to pure tones (ASA standard). A pure tone estimated hearing level for speech was obtained by averaging thresholds at 500, 1000, and 2000 cps. A formula which gives greater weight to the better ear is then computed to give an estimated hearing level for speech to both ears. The AMA standard classification was used: "Normal" hearing (i.e., thresholds less than 15 db), "slight impairment" (i.e., thresholds between 15–35 db), and "severe hearing impairment" (i.e., thresholds greater than 35 db). Twelve drivers had normal hearing; 12 had slight impairment, and only 4 had severe impairment.

Reaction Time

Reaction time data for our group of elderly drivers were compared with younger people as well as with other study subjects of comparable age. The subject responds to a signal light stimulus by first lifting his finger off a start key, then quickly pressing the response key (Wilkie, 1972). Only the total reaction times will be discussed.

The first part of the experiment utilizes first the preferred hand, for 10 trials and then the other hand for 10 trials. The mean time in mscs. and standard deviation for each group of subjects are presented in Table 6–2. The next experiment consisted of a mixed trial and the subject was required to make a differential response with either the right or left hand depending on the stimulus (Table 6–3). This slowed all the subject groups slightly, but it added roughly the same number of msc. to each group.

Table 6–2. *Reaction time hand predesignated (20 trials).*

	Mean (msec.)	Standard deviation
Young subjects	443	97
Elderly drivers	739	155
Elderly nondrivers	879	313

Table 6–3. *Reaction time, mixed (20 trials).*

	Mean (msec.)	Standard deviation
Young subjects	502	99
Elderly drivers	805	155
Elderly nondrivers	957	289

While the mean reaction time for the elderly drivers was substantially longer than for young subjects, many of the elderly drivers still had reaction times comparable to young subjects. Also the slower reactions of the elderly drivers did not result in a higher rate of vehicular accidents. Our elderly drivers' reactions, though slower than the young, are fast enough for ordinary driving.

Attitudes toward Driving

Virtually all the elderly drivers preferred to continue driving as long as possible. Most had already restricted their driving to "necessary trips" in the neighborhood and city. Many deliberately chose circuitous routes to avoid highways. Night driving was avoided whenever possible for two major reasons. Early cataracts, which many of the elderly already had, caused excessive glare problems from oncoming headlights. Cataracts are opacities in the lens of the eye which scatter incoming light in much the same way as a dirty windshield produces glare (Anderson, 1971). In addition, many of the elderly fear returning to an empty house at night. Most of the elderly described their driving as cautious.

The Ex-Drivers

Forty-four subjects had already stopped driving. Their average age was 80 years (roughly two years older than drivers). Their average physical function rating was 2.1 which indicates a twenty percent loss of function.

Table 6–4 categorizes the reasons the elderly persons gave for stopping

Table 6–4. *Reasons for stopping driving.*

	Men	Women	Total
Physical infirmities	11	8	19
Psychological	3	5	8
Economic		4	4
Other	2	2	4
None given	4	5	9
Total	20	24	44

driving. Vision problems were by far the most common physical infirmity listed (twelve persons); four more considered themselves no longer physically able to drive after they had been involved in minor accidents. Only two stopped on the advice of doctors, and one stopped because the licensing bureau refused to renew his license at age 85. The psychological reasons were mostly intense fears of accidents on their part or on their families' part. In addition, four of the five women in this category pointed out that they had never driven very much at any time in their lives. The expense of maintaining an automobile, including insurance, repairs, and gas and oil costs were cited by only four of the elderly persons. The "other reasons" were mostly situations in which the elderly person felt that it was inconvenient or not necessary to maintain a car.

Activities and Life Satisfaction

Total activities and life satisfaction were markedly higher in the drivers as compared to the ex-drivers (Table 6–5). When men and women were analyzed separately, the male drivers compared to ex-drivers had greater differences in activities (29.3 versus 21.6, $p < .001$) than did the women. The differences in satisfaction were similar for men and women.

Table 6–5. *Health, activities, and life satisfaction in drivers and ex-drivers.*

	Drivers	Ex-drivers
Physical function	1.2	2.1
Activities	29.9	24.2 $p < .001$
Life satisfaction	36.5	31.9 $p < .001$

Since age, PFR difference, and sex could account for some of these observed differences in activities and life satisfaction, drivers and ex-drivers were matched for PFR, age and sex, and then activities and life satisfaction scores were compared. Thirteen pairs were matched (Table 6–6). The drivers still had higher activity and life satisfaction scores, although the difference in activity scores became statistically not significant.

Table 6–6. *Activities and life satisfaction in subjects matched for age, sex, and PFR.*

	Drivers (13)	Ex-drivers (13)
Activities	29.0	27.5 n.s.
Life satisfaction	37.4	34.3 $p < .03$

Discussion

Many states now require senior citizens to have examinations upon reaching a certain age in order to renew their operator's license. Senior drivers do have special traffic problems. However, a decision on whether a person should be allowed to drive a car should not be based on age alone. Physical and mental condition, knowledge of laws, actual driving techniques, and the individual's previous driving record should be taken into consideration (*Traffic Digest*, 1965).

Older drivers do have accidents at a higher rate than younger adults. Their accident frequency experience (per miles driven) resembles that of adolescent drivers. However, because of their cautiousness and self-imposed driving restrictions, their actual liability (that is, their percentage of all accidents as compared to the percentage of drivers in their age group) is relatively low (Planck, 1972). This is accounted for by their avoidance of high-risk driving situations and the usually fewer miles driven per year. Usually their driving accidents are caused by errors of omission rather than commission, e.g., incorrect turning or failing to keep a proper lookout, rather than speeding or tailgating. A high percentage of their accidents occur at relatively low speeds (Planck, 1972). There are some data to indicate that very few of the elderly drink while driving (Baker et al., 1970). Also most elderly drivers are survivors of forty or more years of driving. Perhaps only cautious drivers survive and continue to drive in old age.

Our drivers were definitely happier and more satisfied than ex-drivers. Their physical condition was good. Age had thus far been kind to them. Yet many of them probably would not continue to drive if easy and accessible transportation were available to them. However, these drivers live in an area in which the style of living is shaped largely by the motor vehicle. Shopping facilities, friends and doctors are usually beyond walking distance, making transportation essential to obtain the goods and services conducive to a happy life. We need to improve bus services, particularly in the inner cities, and we need to develop cars that are easy and safe for old people to drive (Gianturco, 1971).

The loss of mobility, status, and increased dependence on others makes it particularly difficult for elderly males to give up driving or even their cars. For example, "A 74 year old man had several minor accidents. He was no longer a safe driver. He reluctantly agreed to stop road driving but absolutely refused to sell his car. For the next several years until his death he kept it in his garage. Every Saturday he would pull it out, run the engine for a while and then give the car a thorough cleaning inside and out." In this example the symbolic equation of car and manhood was not hard to find.

Summary

Old drivers in this study are in good physical condition. They do have a realistic appreciation of their limitations and restrict their driving accordingly. They do, in fact, give up driving when their condition warrants it. However, becoming an ex-driver is associated with lower activities and life satisfaction.

References

Anderson, Banks, Jr. The aging eye. *Postgraduate Medicine,* 50, No. 3, 1971.
Baker, S. P., and Spitz, W. U. Age effects and autopsy evidence of disease in fatally injured drivers. *Journal of the American Medical Association,* 214, No. 6, 1970.
Gianturco, D. T., and Ramm, D. Use of the computer in caring for the elderly. *Postgraduate Medicine,* 50, No. 2, 1971.
Planck, T. W. The aging driver in today's traffic: A critical review. *Proceedings of the North Carolina Symposium on Highway Safety,* Chapel Hill, 1972.
Traffic Digest and Review, March 1965.
Wilkie, F. L., and Eisdorfer, C. Components of reaction time change in old age. Paper presented at the American Psychological Society Meeting, Honolulu, Hawaii, September 1972.

Long-Term Adaptation by the Elderly to Bereavement
Dorothy K. Heyman and Daniel T. Gianturco

While widowhood is an inevitable event in the life of most adults, little research interest has been focused on the effects of this occurrence on the lives of elderly persons. The plight of younger women trying to cope with widowhood has been reported by Parkes (1964) and Maddison and Viola (1968) who describe the difficulties which arise from sudden loss of income, and the continuing demands to educate and care for young children in the face of serious personal and social problems. Many of these problems are identical for young widowers. In contrast, the elderly person who loses a spouse usually enters widowhood with grown independent children, often has relative financial stability and undoubtedly has had opportunities for rehearsal of the widowed role.

The period of widowhood is often a lengthy one with women more apt to face an even longer period of widowhood than men, as life expectancy for women at age 65 is 16.3 years while life expectancy of men at age 65 is only 12.8 years (*Statistical Bulletin*, Metropolitan Life Insurance Company, 1971).

Observations by the authors of elderly persons over a period of years during the course of the longitudinal study at the Duke University Center for the Study of Aging and Human Development have suggested that the elderly adapt to the death of the spouse in a fashion which is characterized by (1) emotional stability supported by deep religious faith, (2) a stable social network of family and friends, and (3) relatively few life changes made following the death of the spouse. This report describes the pilot study which tested the validity of these impressions. Specifically, this research examined the activities, attitudes, psychiatric and physical health of a group of older people before and after bereavement.

Method

A panel of 256 elderly volunteers (60–94 years of age, median age 72) has been followed at two year intervals at the Duke University Center for the Study of Aging and Human Development since 1955. . . . The criteria for inclusion in the present study are: (*a*) the subjects be married at the time of the initial study (1955) and living with spouse until widowhood and (*b*) comparable data be collected before and after the death of the spouse. Data are available on a rather small number of only fourteen males and twenty-seven

Reprinted by permission from the *Journal of Gerontology*, 28:3:359–362, 1973.

females, of whom 9 were black and 32 were white. Eighteen women and 7 men were classified as nonmanual in occupational status; and 9 women and 7 men, in manual occupational status. The mean for education was 9.8 years for women and 9.7 years for men. Home ownership was high, with 21 women and 11 men in this category.

The time interval between bereavement and interview varied, with a mean lapse of 21 months. No subject was interviewed less than 3 months following bereavement. Seven persons were seen within 3 to 9 months; 9 within 9 to 18 months; 14 within 18 to 27 months; 6 within 27 to 36 months; and 5, 36 months or later. The mean lapse of time between the "before" and "after" examinations was 36 months. The mean age of widowhood was 74.8 years for the men and 73.1 years for the women. The student's *t* was used to test the significance of differences between status before and after bereavement.

This paper reports on the results obtained using four measurements:

1. *Activities and Attitudes.* Data about activities and attitudes were obtained by the social worker during hour long social history interviews with the older subjects, using the Havighurst (1953) scale. The activity inventory consists of 20 questions dealing with five areas of activities: (*a*) health; (*b*) leisure; (*c*) security; (*d*) family and friends and (*e*) religious activity. A total activity score is obtained by totaling the scores in these five categories. Each subscore could range from 0 to 10.

The attitude inventory consists of 56 agree-disagree items about the subject's satisfaction with eight areas of his life, including friends, family, work, religion, health, economic status, general state of happiness and feeling of usefulness. The score in each area could range from 0 to 6. The total attitude score is the sum of the scores in these eight areas.

2. *The Cavan Adjustment Rating Scale* (Havighurst and Albrecht, 1953) was used by the social workers to independently evaluate the subjects on their activities and attitudes.

3. *Psychiatric evaluations* were made by psychiatrists and consisted of checklist ratings of neurotic signs, including affect, anxiety and hypochondriasis. (For a more thorough discussion of the psychiatric evaluation see Busse, Dovenmuehle, and Brown, 1960.)

4. *The Physical Function Rating* (PFR) is based on the extensive medical examination given each subject by the examining physician including medical history, physical and neurologic examinations and laboratory studies. The subjects were rated by him on a scale from 0 (no pathology or limitation) to 5 (limitation over 80 percent).

Results

Table 6–7 compares the PFR of all widowed subjects "before" and "after" widowhood.

Table 6–7. *Mean physical function ratings before and after widowhood.*

	Before	After
Male	1.4	1.7
Female	2.0	2.2

Using a multivariate analysis of variance, the results were: (1) there were no significant differences in the overall health level when men and women were compared to each other, and (2) there was no significant difference in health status before and after widowhood for the entire group.

Table 6–8. *Mean activity scores before and after widowhood.*

N = 41	Before	After
Health	2.8	3.0
Family and friends	5.4	5.1
Leisure	5.3	4.8
Economic	6.6	7.3
Religious	6.4	6.3
Total	26.5	26.5

Table 6–8 shows no significant changes in activities. Despite widowhood these subjects continue to have relatively high activity levels. These scores reflect the fact that our subjects remain considerably involved with their friends, family, neighbors, and church. Although the differential levels of activity among the areas were not evaluated, it is of interest to note that religious activity was one of those remaining highest after bereavement, thus reinforcing our impression that traditional religious beliefs and church related activities are central to the lives of many (Jeffers et al., 1961).

Table 6–9. *Mean attitude scores before and after widowhood.*

N = 41	Before	After
Health	3.9	3.7
Family and friends	4.7	4.4
Work	3.8	3.2 $p < .01$
Economic security	3.8	4.0
Religion	5.5	5.6
Usefulness	4.7	4.1 $p < .01$
Family	5.0	5.0
Happiness	4.3	3.5
Total	35.7	33.6 $p < .01$

While the changes observed in attitude scores following bereavement are small (Table 6–9), there does seem to be a significant decline in the Work, Usefulness, and Total attitude scores. Inspection of the scores of men and women reveals some suggestion of greater decline for men in Work attitudes and for women in Usefulness. Since an average of 21 months has passed between T_1 and T_2 some of the changes observed may be due to aging.

These ratings point to a persistence of life style among the widowed elderly indicating a relatively high and satisfactory level of interaction with the environment. Widowhood does not appear to alter patterns of living.

The social workers' ratings of happiness and adjustment (Table 6–10) also showed no significant changes. Evaluations by psychiatrists were available on 23 women and 10 men. Of the 20 women rated "not depressed" prior to widowhood, 4 women become "depressed" after widowhood. Three women

Table 6–10. *Mean Cavan adjustment ratings (by social worker) before and after widowhood.*

	Before	After
Men (N = 14)		
Happiness and contentment	4.2	4.1
Adjustment	4.6	3.9
Women (N = 27)		
Happiness and contentment	4.1	3.8
Adjustment	5.1	4.7

rated "depressed" before widowhood did not change following the death of the husband. This trend in the direction of increased depressive feelings for women was absent in widowed men. The 8 men rated "not depressed" prior to widowhood continued "not depressed" after widowhood. Interestingly, the two men rated "depressed" prior to widowhood reverted back to nondepressed ratings after widowhood. There were no significant changes in the ratings for anxiety or hypochondriasis before or after widowhood for both men and women.

Thus it can be seen that the "before" and "after" psychiatric ratings showed only a mild increase in depressive feelings for some women after widowhood. This agrees with both the social workers' impressions and self-reports that some women are less happy and feel less useful after the event of widowhood. Generally, the changes observed appear to be minimal.

Discussion

The data confirm our impression that most of our subjects adapt reasonably well to their loss. There are a number of factors which appear to account for this. We suspect that the relatively advanced age at which our subjects were widowed plays an important role. (All 41 were over sixty-five years of age; 33 were seventy years old or older.) In these late decades, there is an apparent placidity which settles over their lives as the role of worker has been concluded and career goals (including those of the family) have either been reached or put aside. Family responsibilities have become minimal and the settled social role has already been established for many years.

Indeed, the quality of stable, orderly lives seems characteristic of all our subjects. Of the total subject group (181) on whom such data are available, only 8 were not living in their own homes and benefiting from the continuity and familiarity of location and neighborhood ties made possible by long-time occupancy. There were only two instances of widows moving in with children, although in one case a sister moved in with her widowed brother. Life style changes in the elderly may more often result from the cumulative effects of chronic illnesses and limitations in physical functioning than from bereavement.

No longer dependent upon contacts at work, but relying upon kin and friends among church groups and neighbors, the social networks of our subject group did not appear to be disrupted by the death of the spouse. The consistency of activities "before" and "after" widowhood reported by the widows in our study may be explained by the kinds of activities engaged in. Typically these relationships are with kin, neighbors, long-time friends, memberships in garden, bridge, women's clubs or civic clubs for men and similar activities which did not involve the presence of the spouse. The importance of continuing long-time associations is illustrated by many of the older persons in our panel who maintain memberships in organizations but attend only infrequently or not at all.

According to the self-reports and the ratings by the social workers and the examining psychiatrists, female subjects tended to be less happy than male subjects after widowhood, with women reporting an increase in depressive feelings in spite of remaining slightly more active than the men. The mild depression could probably be accounted for by the loss of a role central in the self-esteem and gratification necessary to these homemakers and the lack of the familiar person to engage in the intimate interchanges which occur all day long between two people who compose a household.

Two male subjects are reported in this paper as changing from a "depressed" state before the death of the wife to "not depressed" after the loss. Other subjects, not notably depressed, were reported as having some improvement in morale following the death of the spouse. Our interviews indicate that the relief felt in these situations was due to several factors: relief experienced at having survived a long dreaded event, a feeling that nothing more could be expected from the survivor, a sense of peace that the suffering of the spouse was ended and finally, a lessening of the sheer physical exhaustion which nursing care had required of the aged survivor.

The stability of the health activity rating for our elderly women contrasts with the health activities of younger widows who consulted their practitioners because of psychosomatic symptoms more than three times as often during the six months following the bereavement. (Parkes, 1972). Elderly women, again, appear to tolerate the stress of loss of spouse well.

Summary

A pilot project to test reactions to widowhood in elderly men and women indicates that the years following bereavement of those over 65, are not characterized by social disintegration. These older subjects have little or no health deterioration. There appears to be a small, though significant decline in work, usefulness and total attitude scores, with an apparent greater decline for men in work attitudes and for women, in feelings of usefulness. The subjects utilize such supportive social structures as networks of relatives, friends and neighbors and long-time home ownership and occupancy. With advancing age and retirement there is an easing of social and economic pressures. They are psychologically prepared to accept the death of the spouse through mechanisms which permit gradual identification with the role of widowhood before the actual event. Religious supports appear to be particularly important sources of strength.

References

Busse, E. W., Dovenmuehle, R. H., and Brown, R. C. Psychoneurotic reactions of the aged. *Geriatrics*, 15:97–105, 1960.
Havighurst, R. J., and Albrecht, R. *Older people*. New York: Longmans, Green, 1953.
Jeffers, F. C., Nichols, C. R., and Eisdorfer, C. Attitudes of older persons toward death: A preliminary study. *Journal of Gerontology*, 16:53–56, 1961.
Maddison, D., and Viola, A. The health of widows in the year following bereavement. *Journal of Psychosomatic Research*, 12:297–306, 1968.
Parkes, C. M. Effects of bereavement on physical and mental health: A study of the medical records of widows. *British Medical Journal*, 2:274–279, 1964.
Parkes, C. M. *Bereavement studies of grief in adult life*. New York: International Universities Press, Inc., 1972.
Statistical bulletin, Metropolitan Life Insurance Company, July, 1971.

Health and Social Factors Related to Life Satisfaction
Erdman Palmore and Clark Luikart

Most researchers and professionals seem to agree with laymen that life satisfaction should be a major component of any comprehensive conception of "adjustment" or "mental health" (Sells, 1969). Because of this consensus

Reprinted by permission from the *Journal of Health and Social Behavior*, 13:68–80, 1972.

there has been considerable research and writing on life satisfaction in old age (see review by Riley, 1968) and in earlier years (Cantril, 1965; Bradburn and Caplovitz, 1965; Soddy, 1967; Berkman, 1971). This research has generally found substantial relationships between life satisfaction and health, activity, socioeconomic status, and to some extent with age. That is, the more satisfied tend to be healthier, more socially active, tend to have more income and education, and tend to be younger. There are, of course, good theoretical and common sense reasons for these associations.

However, almost none of this research attempts to assess the *relative* importance of these several variables for life satisfaction or to assess the independent effects of each of these variables when the others are controlled. Thus, we do not know whether health is more important for satisfaction than income or education or activity or age, etc. Nor do we know whether there is any independent effect of each of these variables when the others are controlled. Thus, it has been asserted that health is the only important factor and that all others pale into insignificance by comparison. Or that "money can (or can't) buy happiness." Or that if a person will just keep active and socially involved he will be assured life satisfaction.

This paper reports an attempt to evaluate such assertions through multiple regression analysis of the relative influence of health, activity, social-psychological, and socioeconomic variables upon life satisfaction in early and late middle-age. It also analyzes the interrelations between these variables, particularly the correlates of self-rated health, organizational activity, and internal control orientation. We believe middle age is an important time in which to analyze life satisfaction because it is supposed to be a period with relatively high rewards and yet it usually contains many potential stresses such as physical decline, menopause, approaching retirement, etc.

Methods

Sample

The data for this analysis come from the Duke Adaptation Study, an interdisciplinary longitudinal study of 502 persons aged 45–69 at the beginning of the study in 1968.

Measures

A. Dependent variable. Life satisfaction was measured by the "Cantril Ladder" (Cantril, 1965). The respondent was first asked to describe his "wishes and hopes for your future" and then to describe "what would be the most unhappy life for you." He was then presented with a picture of a ladder numbered from zero on the bottom rung to nine on the top rung. The respondent was asked to suppose "that the top of the ladder represents the best possible life for you and the bottom represents the worst possible life for you. Where on the ladder do you feel you stand at the present time?" Advantages of this technique is that it is "self-anchoring" and results in a continuous and theoretically equal-interval measure. It is self-anchoring in the sense that it is relative to each person's own conception of maximum and minimum life satisfaction. Other methods of measuring happiness or life satisfaction were used in this study, but the satisfaction ladder is used in this analysis because it ap-

Table 6–11. *Ranges, means, standard deviations and zero-order correlations of 18 variables with life satisfaction (N = 502).*

Variable	Actual range	Mean	Standard deviation	Correlation with life satisfaction
Life satisfaction				
	0–9	7.0	1.5	. . .
Health				
1. Self-rated health	1–9	6.8	1.5	.43
2. Performance status	4–10	9.2	0.8	.11
Activity				
3. Organizational activity	0–18	5.2	3.7	.18
4. Social activity hours	0–34	9.9	6.3	.09
5. Productive hours	0–87	41.3	18.5	.12
6. Social contacts	1–306	101.4	59.9	.01
7. Employment	0–1	0.7	0.5	.06
Social-psychological				
8. Internal control	0–4	2.4	1.0	.16
9. Career anchorage	0–6	2.0	1.2	.03
10. Confidant	0–1	0.6	0.5	.04
11. Marital status	0–1	0.9	0.4	.05
12. Sexual enjoyment	0–3	1.4	1.1	.14
13. Moves	0–7	0.5	1.0	−.05
14. Intelligence	10–60	36.1	9.0	.05
Socioeconomic				
15. Income	0–15	8.1	4.4	.10
16. Education	0–27	11.8	4.0	.03
17. Age (at interviews)	46–71	58.9	7.2	−.04
18. Sex	0–1	0.5	0.5	−.02

pears to be the most stable and global assessment of life satisfaction in general. The other measures refer specifically to affect in the past week, or to "anomia," or to psychosomatic symptoms of stress. Table 6–11 presents the actual range, the mean score, and the standard deviation for life satisfaction and the other measures used in this analysis.

B. Health variables. The self-rated health measure also used a similar ladder with the bottom of the ladder (0) representing the most serious illness and the top of the ladder (9) representing perfect health. The performance status was a rating given by the examining physician based on his examination, the medical history, and results of laboratory tests. The ratings had a theoretical range of one for "moribund; fatal processes progressing rapidly" to ten for "normal; no complaints; no evidence of disease." Actually, most of the participants in this study were given high health ratings (Table 6–11).

C. *Activity variables.* Organizational activity was measured by the sum of the number of religious services and meetings of other groups such as clubs, unions, or associations which the respondent reported usually attending each month. There was a maximum of nine religious services and maximum of nine other meetings coded, giving a possible range of 0 through 18.

Social activity hours was measured by summing the number of hours spent during the last typical week "attending a sports event such as baseball or football game; attending church or other meetings, lectures, or concerts; doing volunteer work for church, other organizations, or relatives; visiting, telephoning, or writing friends or relatives; parties, eating out, or entertaining." Work and housework were not included because we did not know how much social contact occurred during these hours.

Productive hours were measured by summing the number of hours spent during the last typical week working or doing housework; doing volunteer work for church, other organizations or relatives; yard care, gardening, repairing, building, mending, sewing, and other such activities. The total number of social contacts per month was measured by summing the number of reported visits or telephone conversations with children, close relatives, close friends, neighbors; and number of religious services or other meetings. Work contacts were not included because these are not "voluntary" types of contacts. The employment variable was simply scored one if the respondent had a job or business and zero if he did not.

D. *Social-psychological variables.* Internal control orientation was measured by the first-person items in the Jessor scale known as the "Internal-External Control of Reinforcement Scale" (Jessor, 1968). For this analysis we used four pairs of statements and asked the respondent to decide which one of each pair is more true for him. An example is "Some of the good and some of the bad things in my life have happened by chance (external control). What's happened to me has been my own doing (internal control)." In this analysis, external items were scored zero and internal items were scored one, making a higher score indicate greater belief in internal control. We used only the first-person items in this analysis because some research has shown higher associations of other variables with the first-person items than with the 12-item scale (Gurin, 1969), and because we also found that the first-person items had a somewhat higher correlation with life satisfaction than did the total of 11 items included in our interview.

The career-anchorage scale (Tausky and Dubin, 1965) is a measure of whether a person tends to evaluate success in terms of how far a person has come (downward anchorage) or in terms of how far a person has to go before he reaches the top of his career (upward anchorage). It too is based on forced choices between six pairs of statements such as, "Which man do you feel is giving his son the best advice? A. When you start your career (trade), don't be satisfied until you reach the top (upward anchorage). B. When you start your career (trade), don't be satisfied until you have gone just as far as you can (downward anchorage)." In this analysis, the downward orientation response was scored zero and the upward orientation response was scored one, so that higher scores indicate more upward orientation.

The "confidant" measure was based on responses to the question, "Is there one person in particular you confide in or talk to about yourself or your problems?" A "no" response was coded zero and a "yes" response was coded one. Marital status was coded one for married persons living with their spouse and zero for all others. The measure of sexual enjoyment was based on responses to the following question: "How much pleasure or enjoyment do you have during sex relations at the present time? None, mild pleasure and enjoyment, moderate pleasure and enjoyment, very much pleasure and enjoyment." The coded responses range from 0 for "none" up to 3 for "very much pleasure and enjoyment." Most nonmarried persons responded "none."

The measure of moves is simply the number of times a person moved his residence in the past ten years. Intelligence was measured by four subtests of the Wechsler Adult Intelligence Scale (Wechsler, 1955): information, vocabulary, digit symbol, and picture arrangement. Scaled scores rather than raw scores were used in order to give each subtest equal weight.

E. Socioeconomic variables. Income was based on responses to the question, "About how much was your (and your spouse's) total income from all sources during the last twelve months?" Responses were coded, by $1,000 intervals, from 0 for under $1,000 through 6 for $6,000 to $6,999, 7 for $7,000 to $9,999, 10 for $10,000 to $14,999 and 15 for $15,000 and over. Education was simply the highest grade of regular school or college ever attended by the respondent.

Age was the actual age at the time of interview rather than at the time of sampling. One might question whether those over 60 should be called "middle-aged." The chronological age at which middle-age ends is of course arbitrary and opinions vary widely. In our sample, a majority (52 percent) of those 61–65 defined themselves as middle-aged, and 40 percent of those over 65 still defined themselves as middle-aged. Persons age 60–70 were included in this study in order to examine the adaptation process in this critical "late middle-aged" period.

Sex was coded as zero for men and one for women.

Analysis

The measures in this analysis were designed to meet the requirements of true metric scales, in order to make correlation and regression analysis possible. That is, they have a true zero point representing a complete absence of the variable being measured and each point on the scale is designed to represent an equal interval. However, there is one variable which does not quite meet these requirements in the usual sense. Sexual enjoyment, while having a zero point representing no sexual enjoyment, may not have equal intervals because we cannot be sure that "mild pleasure and enjoyment" is exactly half as much "moderate pleasure and enjoyment," etc. Also there are several "dummy variables" with only zero and one scores: employment, confidant, marital status, and sex. Even though such "dummy variables" are not true metrics in the usual sense, their characteristics are close enough to be widely used in regression analysis. Furthermore, several statisticians argue that variables which do not completely meet all the assumptions supposedly required for true metrics, can be used in regression analysis without introducing substantial error in the results (Labovitz, 1967; Blalock, 1961).

The primary methods of analysis for this report are linear correlations and step-wise multiple regression. The reader should be aware that this type of analysis ideally requires linear relationships, normal distributions, and equal variances among the variables. These ideals are not fully met by some of the variables and relationships. We do not yet know what the effects of these departures from the ideal are on our data, but we are pursuing other types of analysis such as curvilinear and nonparametric methods to answer this question. So far, the other types of analysis confirm the general relationships presented here.

Seventeen percent of the interviews did not have a usable score on one or two of the variables. In order to save these cases for the multiple regression analysis, we used the mean value of the missing variable as an estimate of the missing score. This procedure did not substantially affect the results, except that it prevented an unnecessary loss in the number of cases used in the analysis.

We will examine both the zero-order correlations of each variable with life satisfaction for the total sample (Table 6–11), and the results of step-wise multiple regression analysis for the total group and for separate age and sex groups, in order to get a more precise picture of the relative influence of each variable when the others are statistically controlled (Table 6–12). In the step-wise multiple regression procedure used in this analysis, the computer determines which one variable explains the largest proportion of the variance. This variable is listed first along with its multiple correlation, beta or slope value, F value, etc. The computer then lists the second variable which explains the largest amount of the remaining variance after the first variable has been taken into account. This procedure is repeated until no variable adds a statistically significant amount of explained variance (.05 level). The multiple regression Tables 2–5 present in the second column the zero-order correlations (the separate associations of each independent variable with dependent variable), the multiple correlation in the third column (the total association of the independent variables listed at that point), the cumulative variance explained by those variables (the square of the multiple regression) in the fourth column, and the beta value (unstandardized) or slope in the fifth column (how

Table 6–12. *Multiple regressions of strongest* variables related to life satisfaction, by sex and age groups.*

Variable	Zero-order correlation	Multiple correlation	Cumulative variance	Beta (slope)
Total group (N = 502)				
Self-rated health	.43	.431	.186	.445
Organizational activity	.18	.456	.208	.065
Internal control	.16	.470	.221	.155
Performance status	.11	.480	.230	.252
Productive hours	.12	.486	.236	.001
Men (N = 261)				
Self-rated health	.44	.439	.193	.458
Organizational activity	.18	.461	.213	.043
Confidant	.15	.478	.228	.328
Performance status	.09	.492	.242	.278
Employment	.10	.499	.249	.366
Social activity	.17	.507	.257	.030
Women (N = 241)				
Self-rated health	.42	.421	.177	.401
Organizational activity	.19	.452	.204	.062
Internal control	.20	.473	.224	.204
Ages 46–59 (N = 268)				
Self-rated health	.47	.465	.216	.485
Organizational activity	.26	.509	.259	.080
Performance status	.09	.529	.280	.333
Income	.14	.536	.287	.060
Education	.01	.553	.306	−.062
Ages 60–71 (N = 234)				
Self-rated health	.40	.398	.158	.398
Internal control	.21	.436	.190	.277
Organizational activity	.10	.446	.199	.042

* All variables significant at .05 level.

much a change of one point in the independent variable affects the value of the dependent variable).

Findings and Discussion

Correlates of Life Satisfaction

It is clear that self-rated health is by far the strongest variable related to life satisfaction, both in the total group and in each of the subgroups analyzed (Table 6–12). The zero-order correlations of self-rated health with life satisfaction is more than twice that of any other variable, and it accounts for two-thirds or more of the explained variance in all the groups analyzed. This association of health with satisfaction is similar to the findings of other studies of life satisfaction in old age (Maddox and Eisdorfer, 1962; Streib, 1956; Kutner, 1956; Suchman, 1958). However, the other studies have not clearly shown that health is the preponderant variable influencing life satisfaction. The present analysis shows not only that health is the strongest variable, but that it alone accounts for the large majority of the explained variance in life satisfaction. All the other variables put together are of secondary importance. The beta value of .445 shows that for each point difference in self-health rating, there is almost a half point difference in life satisfaction.

Furthermore, the person's own conception of his health (as shown by the self-rated health) is more important than the physician's rating of his health (as shown by the performance status rating). Indeed, the performance status rating had a lower correlation with life satisfaction than several of the other variables (Table 6–11). This greater importance of self assessment compared to medical assessment is also similar to the findings of several studies of life satisfaction among the aged (Maddox, 1962; Suchman, 1958). Apparently, it is less the objective status of a person's health (as assessed by a physician) that influences his life satisfaction, than the persons own evaluation of his health. This implies that a person with poor objective health may still have high life satisfaction if he believes his health is relatively good, and similarly a person with good objective health may have low life satisfaction if he is convinced his health is relatively poor.

This is not to say that life satisfaction is unaffected by his objective health. Indeed, physician's rating of performance was the third strongest variable in the total group after the self-rated health was controlled. The fact that the performance status added a significant increase in the explained variance after the other variables had been statistically controlled, indicates that it does have an important independent effect on life satisfaction.

One caution should be borne in mind in evaluating this strong association of self-rated health with life satisfaction. Part of this association may be due to the fact that both life satisfaction and self-rated health were measured by the same device: a ladder ranging from 0 through 9. There may be some generalized tendency for persons to pick similar numbers on such a ladder despite its use to represent different dimensions. In order to estimate the possible effect of such a tendency, we also correlated life satisfaction with another estimate of self-health: responses to the question, "In general, how is your health right now: excellent, good, fair, or poor?" When this was coded on a four point scale, it had a correlation of .26 with satisfaction. This correlation is considerably less than the .44 of the ladder rating, but it is still substantially higher than any other correlations with satisfaction. Thus, we conclude that self-rated health would be the strongest variable related to life satisfaction, regardless of how it is measured.

The second strongest variable related to life satisfaction was organizational activity, a simple sum of the number of church and other meetings attended per month. This was also the second strongest factor for persons over 60. This association of organizational activity and life satisfaction is in accordance with the findings of most studies of activity and life satisfaction among the aged (Palmore, 1968; Havighurst and Albrecht, 1953; Tobin and Neugarten, 1961; Kutner, 1956; Morrison and Kristjanson, 1958). There is probably a two-way effect which explains this strong association: persons who are more active in organizations usually derive substantial life satisfaction from such activities; and depressed persons with low life satisfaction may tend to withdraw from organizational activities. Furthermore, both organizational activity and life satisfaction are related to better health, but organizational activity still appears to have an independent effect on life satisfaction after self-rated health is statistically controlled. We will discuss further the determinants of organizational activity in the next section.

However, there is a striking contrast between the strong association of organizational activity with satisfaction, and the relatively weak associations of the other activity measures with satisfaction (Table 6–11). The number of hours spent in social activity has a correlation with satisfaction that is less than half that of the organizational activity correlation; productive hours is barely significant in the total group; employment is significantly related only among the men; and the total number of social contacts has almost no relation to life satisfaction. This finding is in contrast to much of the literature which has stressed the importance to life satisfaction of remaining productive, socially involved, and generally active. Our results suggest that the most important activity determinant of life satisfaction in middle age is organizational involvement and that other forms of activity are of secondary importance at best. As might be expected, employment is significantly related to satisfaction among the men (.10), but has almost no relation to satisfaction among the women (.02).

The third strongest variable in the total group (and the second variable for persons over 60) was the internal control orientation (Table 6–12). Apparently the middle-aged (and especially the females and older middle-aged) who believe that they tend to control their life have greater life satisfaction than those who believe that their life tends to be controlled by luck, fate, destiny, or powerful others. The reasons for this relationship are somewhat unclear at this point. Part of the answer may be that internal control is associated with such concepts as autonomy (Erikson, 1959; Havighurst, 1963), competence (White, 1969; Neugarten, 1963), and achievement motivation (Atkinson and Feather, 1966; McClelland et al., 1963), all of which probably contribute to life satisfaction; and internal control is negatively related to alienation, hopelessness, and powerlessness (Seeman, 1959), which would reduce life satisfaction.

Having a confidant in whom one confides or talks to about himself and his problems is moderately related to life satisfaction among men (third strongest variable, $r = .15$, Table 6–12), but is somewhat negatively related to satisfaction among women ($-.07$). Lowenthal found in a study of aged in San Francisco, that having a confidant was related to higher morale and served as a buffer against depression resulting from decreases in social interaction (1968). However, her article reports no sex difference in this relationship between confidant and morale. It is theoretically clear why having a confidant would increase life satisfaction by providing an intimate, sympathetic, and supported relationship (as among the men); but it is puzzling why having a confidant is negatively related to satisfaction among the women. We hope to explore this question with further analysis in the future.

It is noteworthy that, while all the other social psychological variables had low correlations with satisfaction, none were strong enough to add a significant increase in the variance explained for any of the groups analyzed.

Turning now to the socioeconomic variables, income has an over-all moderately positive relationship to satisfaction, as might be expected (.10, Table 6–11). Among persons age 46–59, this relationship increases to .14 and becomes the fourth strongest variable related to satisfaction (Table 6–12). Among persons with incomes under $7,000, this relationship increases to .16, while among those with $7,000 or more, the correlation drops to .10. Thus it appears that while it may be true that "money can't buy happiness," adequate income may provide more of the basic necessities related to life satisfaction such as adequate food, housing, security, recreation, and social status. This is especially true among those with lower than average incomes, indicating that increased income above the average level provides diminishing returns. It is also more true of the younger middle age, indicating that income is less related to satisfaction among the older middle age.

Education has surprisingly little relationship to life satisfaction in the total group ($r = .03$, Table 6–11). However, we again found differences between those with above average and those with below average incomes: those with incomes below $7,000 had a low positive correlation between education and satisfaction (.06), while those with incomes of $7,000 or above have a low negative correlation between these two variables ($-.04$). This is similar to the findings of Bradburn and Caplovitz (1965) that those with incomes under $7,000 had a strong positive relationship between education and happiness, while those with over $7,000 had a negative relationship between those two variables. There seems to be no clear explanation for this finding at present, but one might speculate that among those with comfortable incomes, greater education is associated with a greater discrepancy between ideal and actual levels of achievements, or more unrealistic expectations, or more cynicism, etc.

There was also a low negative correlation between age and satisfaction ($-.04$, Table 6–11), indicating that the older middle-aged tend to be slightly less satisfied than the younger middle-aged. However, this is such a weak relationship that it does not contribute any significant increase in the multiple regression for any of the groups analyzed. This weak relationship is in contrast to the strong relationships found in other studies including the middle-aged (Bradburn and Caplovitz, 1965, Gurin, 1960; Kutner, 1956). Cantril (1965), the originator of the satisfaction ladder, found a small increase (7 percent) in the proportion of persons aged 50 and over who had high satisfaction compared to those aged 30–49. He concluded that the older middle-aged "appear somewhat more resigned to their status in life" (p. 258). Since we found only one-tenth of a point difference in the mean satifaction scores between those under and those over age 60, we conclude that there is probably little or no difference between the younger and the older middle-aged in their life satisfaction *relative to their life expectations.*

Finally, sex was the variable least related to satisfaction ($r = -.02$, Table 6–11). This lack of difference between men and women agrees with the findings of both Bradburn and Cantril, but contradicts Kutner's findings of higher morale among men over age 60 (1956).

The main differences between men and women were that, after self-rated health and organizational activity had been accounted for, internal control was the only other significant variable for women, while having a confidant, high performance status, amount of employment, and social activity were significant for men (Table 6–12). It appears that men's life satisfaction is more dependent on a variety of active roles.

Correlates of Self-Rated Health

Since self-rated health is the strongest variable related to life satisfaction, we will analyze next the variables that might explain or are related to self-rated health. It has been suggested that a person's perception of his health is mainly a function of his overall optimistic or pessimistic view of life. This would explain its high association with life satisfaction. While there is probably some effect of the overall view on self-rated health, there is also evidence that about three-fourths of respondents' ratings of their own health are in fairly close agreement with the ratings of physicians (Maddox, 1964; Suchman, 1958). Furthermore, good health is one of the most frequent reasons given for happiness in this study and in others (Gurin, 1960). Therefore, we believe that the major direction of causality is from health to life satisfaction, rather than the other way around.

This is further supported by the strong and predominant association of the physician's rating of performance status with self-rated health in this study (Table 6–13). The performance status rating explains over 80 percent of the explainable variance for the total group and it is also the dominant factor for men and women considered separately. Thus, the major explanation of how these respondents perceived their health appears to be their objective health as rated by the physician.

Intelligence (or education among men) is the second strongest variable, which seems to indicate that healthier people are also intellectually superior and able to perform better mentally as well as physically. This may in turn be related to better nutrition, health care, and the generally more favorable environment of the upper socioeconomic levels.

For the total group, there were smaller associations of self-rated health with more productive hours, younger age, and more sexual enjoyment. These associations are in the expected directions, but add little to the explained vari-

Table 6–13. *Multiple regression of strongest* variables related to self-rated health, by sex.*

Variable	Zero-order correlation	Multiple correlation	Cumulative variance	Beta (slope)
Total group (N = 502)				
Performance status	.43	.430	.185	.79
Intelligence	.20	.452	.204	.02
Productive hours	.18	.458	.210	.01
Age	−.06	.469	.220	.03
Sexual enjoyment	.16	.476	.227	.12
Men (N = 261)				
Performance status	.45	.452	.204	.88
Education	.17	.466	.217	.04
Women (N = 241)				
Performance status	.41	.406	.165	.81
Intelligence	.27	.461	.213	.04

* All variables significant at .05 level.

ance and were not significant variables for men and women considered separately.

Correlates of Organization Activity

Organizational activity was the second strongest variable related to life satisfaction and we now turn to an analysis of what variables may influence the amount of organizational activity (Table 6–14). The variables of social activity hours and productive hours were omitted from this analysis because of the overlap between these measures and organizational activity.

Table 6–14. *Multiple regression of strongest* variables related to organizational activity, by sex.*

Variable	Zero-order correlation	Multiple correlation	Cumulative variance	Beta (slope)
Total Group (N = 502)				
Employment	−.12	.120	.014	−1.24
Performance status	.11	.177	.031	0.55
Intelligence	.11	.201	.040	0.04
Internal control	.08	.222	.049	0.35
Men (N = 261)				
Intelligence	.13	.129	.017	0.05
Internal control	.12	.183	.033	0.47
Women (N = 241)				
Employment	−.18	.175	.031	−1.61
Performance status	.14	.242	.059	0.80
Sexual enjoyment	.11	.267	.071	0.44

* All variables significant at .05 level.

Employment was the variable most closely related (negatively) to organizational activity in the total group, but this was entirely due to its strong negative relationship to organizational activity among women ($r = -.18$). There was no such relationship among the men. Apparently, employed women had less time and interests for organizational activities than non-employed women.

Performance status was the second strongest variable, but again the relationship is much stronger among women than among men (.14 compared to .07, respectively). Apparently women's physical performance ability was an important determinant of their organizational activity, but this was less true for men.

Men's organizational activity seems primarily affected by their intelligence and their belief in internal control. Perhaps the more intelligent men engaged in more organizational activity because of their greater capacity for such activity. Similarly a greater belief in internal control implies a more "active-mastery" approach to life, which one might expect to be associated with more organizational activity.

Correlates of Internal Control

We also examined the multiple regressions of internal control (Table 6–15), because it was the third strongest variable related to satisfaction in the total group and was especially strong among women and among those over 60.

The difference between men and women was the primary variable related

Table 6–15. *Multiple regression of strongest* variables related to internal control, by sex.*

Variable	Zero-order correlation	Multiple correlation	Cumulative variance	Beta (slope)
Total Group (N = 502)				
Sex	−.21	.207	.043	−.342
Productive hours	.14	.239	.057	.007
Organizational activity	.08	.263	.069	.023
Moves	−.11	.279	.078	−.101
Sexual enjoyment	.19	.291	.085	.099
Social activity hours	.02	.297	.088	.013
Intelligence	−.04	.305	.093	−.008
Men (N = 261)				
Employment	.15	.145	.021	.414
Organizational activity	.12	.189	.036	.041
Social contacts	−.08	.213	.045	−.003
Confidant	.10	.246	.061	.233
Intelligence	−.06	.267	.071	−.012
Women (N = 241)				
Social contacts	.19	.188	.035	.003
Sexual enjoyment	.18	.262	.069	.168
Self-health rating	.14	.285	.081	.078

* All variables significant at .05 level.

to internal control orientation for the total group: men tended to have more internal control orientation than women. This finding is contrary to most of the previous studies, which indicate that there are no consistent sex differences (Hersch and Scheibe, 1967; Hamsher, 1968; Jessor et al., 1968; Strickland, 1965; Lichtenstein and Kentzen, 1967). Only Rotter (1966) found a significant difference with males having more internal control orientation among a sample of college students. However, these studies have been limited to young persons, ethnic groups, and severely restricted populations of adults that had been selected in order to test other hypotheses. Ours appears to be the first finding of a significant sex difference in orientation toward internal control among adults ($p < .001$). The mean difference between men and women on these first person items is small (.43), but it is twice as large if one uses the entire 11 items in the scale (mean difference .85, $p < .001$). This difference seems to fit with the traditional assumptions in our society that men have a more "active-mastery" approach to life and women have a more "passive-dependent" approach. Perhaps this difference has disappeared among the younger generation along with the growth of women's liberation and trends toward greater equality between the sexes.

Productive hours is the second strongest variable related to internal control for the total group and organizational activity is the third variable. There is probably two-way causality in these associations: persons who are more productive and active may have had experiences that tend to make them believe more in their ability to control their life, and those who believe more in their internal control may tend to become more active and productive.

The number of moves is the fourth variable in the total group and has a significant negative relationship to internal control. Perhaps some of these frequent moves have been involuntary and such moves may diminish beliefs in internal control.

The amount of sexual enjoyment is the fifth variable significantly related to internal control for the total group: apparently persons with greater sexual enjoyment tend to believe they are in more control of their lives. The significant positive relationship for the total group of number hours spent in social activity fits in with the above interpretation of the general association of activity with belief in internal control.

It is puzzling that the last significant variable, intelligence, is negatively related to internal control orientation. This seems to be contrary to the other associations of internal control with activity, productivity, and income. We suspect that, although the relationship is barely significant, it is so low that it has no substantive importance.

Among men, employment is the strongest variable, which fits with the expected importance of employment in men's lives and the general association of activity with internal control. The fact that the second strongest variable among men is organizational activity, indicates that work is not the only sphere of activity strongly related to internal control among men.

There is an unexpected negative relationship between the total number of social contacts and internal control among men. This seems strange because most forms of activity are positively associated with internal control, and among women the number of social contacts has a strong positive relationship to internal control. Perhaps the men high on internal control are so busy with their employment and organizational activities that they do not have much time left for a large number of wider social contacts.

Finally, having a confidant contributes somewhat to a belief in internal control among men, while better health contributes to a belief in internal control among the women.

Summary

A multiple regression analysis of 18 variables thought to affect life satisfaction, in a sample of 502 community residents aged 45–69, resulted in the following principal findings.

1. Self-rated health was by far the strongest variable related to life satisfaction and it alone accounts for two-thirds or more of the explained variance in all groups analyzed. This seems to confirm the old adage, "Your health is the most important thing."

2. The second most important variable was organizational activity, which suggests that involvement in social organizations is the type of activity that most contributes to life satisfaction among the middle-aged.

3. Belief in internal control was the third strongest variable, which suggests a two-way effect: persons believing that they control their lives may engage in life styles that provide more satisfaction and persons who have more satisfying experiences may develop a stronger belief that they control their lives.

4. Having a confidant, performance status, employment, and social activity are significantly associated with satisfaction among men, but not among women. This suggests that men's life satisfaction is more dependent on a variety of active roles.

5. Income and education were more strongly related to satisfaction among the younger middle-aged and among those with below average incomes.

6. Several variables thought to be related to life satisfaction actually show little or no relationship to it: age, sex, total social contacts, career anchorage, marital status, and intelligence.

7. The main determinant of self-rated health was objective performance status as rated by the physician.

8. The main correlates of organizational activity among men were intelligence and internal control orientation, but among women *lack* of employment and high physical performance status were the main correlates.

9. The main overall correlates of internal control orientation were sex

(men believed more in internal control), productive hours, and organizational activity.

There were some puzzling relationships that call for further research, but the main finding is clear enough: life satisfaction in middle-age is most strongly related to perceived health and secondly to involvement in social organizations. Although we lack experimental or longitudinal evidence, this finding suggests the hopeful hypothesis that health improvement and increased organizational activity tends to increase life satisfaction among the middle-aged.

References

Atkinson, J., and Feather, N. (Eds.). *A Theory of achievement motivation.* New York: Wiley, 1966.

Berkman, P. Life stress and psychological well being. *Journal of Health and Social Behavior,* 12:35–45, 1971.

Blalock, H., *Causal inferences in nonexperimental research.* Chapel Hill: University of North Carolina Press, 1964.

Bradburn, N., and Caplovitz, D. *Reports on happiness.* Chicago: Aldine, 1965.

Cantril, H. *The pattern of human concern.* New Brunswick, N.J.: Rutgers University Press, 1965.

Erikson, E. Identity and the life cycle. *Psychological Issues I,* (whole issue), 1959.

Gurin, G., Veroff, J., and Field, S. *Americans view their mental health.* New York: Basic Books, 1960.

Gurin, P., Gurin, G., Lao, R., and Beatty, M. Internal-external control in the motivational dynamics of Negro youth. *Journal of Social Issues,* 25:29–53, 1969.

Hamsher, J., Getler, J. D., and Rotter, J. B. Interpersonal trust, internal-external control, and the Warren Commission Report. *Journal of Personality and Social Psychology,* 9:210–215.

Havighurst, R., and Albrecht, R. *Older people.* New York: Longmans, Green and Company, 1953.

Havighurst, R. Successful aging. In R. Williams (Ed.), *Processes of aging.* New York: Atherton Press, 1963, 1:299–320.

Hersch, P., and Scheibe, K. Reliability and validity of internal-external control of reinforcement as a personality dimension. *Journal of Consulting Psychology,* 31:609–613, 1967.

Jessor, R., Graves, T., Hanson, R., and Jessor, S. *Society, personality, and deviant behavior.* New York: Holt, Rinehart and Winston, 1968.

Kutner, B., et al. *Five hundred over sixty.* New York: Russell Sage Foundation, 1956.

Labovitz, S. Some observations on measurement and statistics. *Social Forces,* 46:151–159.

Lichtenstein, E., and Keutzer, C. Further normative and correlational data on the I-E Scale. *Psychological Reports,* 21:1014–1016, 1967.

Lowenthal, M., and Haven, C. Interaction and adaptation: Intimacy as a critical variable. *American Sociological Review,* 33:20–30, 1968.

Maddox, G., and Eisdorfer, C. Some correlates of activity and morale among the elderly. *Social Forces,* 40:254–260, 1962.

Maddox, G. Persistence of life style among the elderly. *Proceedings of the 7th International Congress of Gerontology,* pp. 309–311. Reprinted in E. Palmore (Ed.), *Normal aging.* Durham, N.C.: Duke University Press, 1970.

Maddox, G. Self-Assessment of Health Status. *Journal of Chronic Diseases,* 17:449–460. Reprinted in Palmore (Ed.), *Normal aging.* 1970.

McClelland, D., Atkinson, J., Clark, B., and Lowell, E. *The achievement motive.* New York: Appleton-Century Crofts, 1953.

Neugarten, B. Personality and the aging process. In R. Williams (Ed.), *Processes of aging.* New York: Atherton Press, 1963, 1:321–334.

Palmore, E. The effects of aging on activities and attitudes. *Gerontologist,* 8:259–263. Reprinted in Palmore (Ed.), *Normal aging.* 1970.

Riley, M., and Foner, A. *Aging and society.* New York: Russell Sage, 1968, vol. 1, chap. 15.

Rotter, J. Generalized expectancies for internal vs. external control of reinforcement. *Psychological Monographs,* 80 (whole No. 609), 1966.

Seeman, M. On the meaning of alienation. *American Sociological Review,* 24:782–791, 1959.

Sells, S. (Ed.). *The definition and measurement of mental health.* PHS publication number 1873. Washington, D.C.: U.S. Government Printing Office, 1969.

Soddy, K. *Men in middle life.* London: Tavistock, 1967.

Strickland, B. The prediction of social action from a dimension of I-E Control. *Journal of Social Psychology,* 66:353–358, 1965.

Streib, G. Morale of the retired. *Social Problems,* 3:270–276, 1956.

Suchman, E., Phillips, B., and Streib, G. An analysis of the validity of health questionnaires. *Social Forces,* 36:223–232, 1958.

Tausky, C., and Dubin, R. Career anchorages: Managerial mobility motivations. *American Sociological Review,* 30:725–735, 1965.

Tobin, S., and Neugarten, B. Life satisfaction and social interaction in the aging. *Journal of Gerontology,* 16:344–346, 1961.

Wechsler, D. *Manual for the Wechsler Adult Intelligence Scale.* New York: The Psychological Corp., 1955.

White, R. Motivation reconsidered: The concept of competence. *Psychological Review,* 66:297–333, 1959.

Metaphors as Test of Personal Philosophy of Aging   *Kurt W. Back*

Aging can be looked at from several points of view. It can be defined as physiological deterioration, as status change, as an accumulation of experience, or as entrance into a discriminated-against minority. Each of these definitions has some use for specific purposes, but none of them is unique to aging; each definition makes aging equivalent to some other social process. There is one feature, however, which is unique to human aging. The human being has a definite notion of the normal life span and also, to a certain degree, has some picture of the course of human life. Aging means, to a great extent, coming to the end of one's life span and also entering into a period which is the last period of human life, both of which conditions have a definite meaning for individuals. We may call this the personal-philosophy aspect of aging.

Like other aspects of personal philosophy, these facts seem obvious, and just because they are assumed and form the background of experience, it is hard for people to put their philosophy into words. Large-scale studies of

Reprinted by permission from *Sociological Focus,* 5:1:1–8, 1971. The author thanks Mrs. Joanna Morris for invaluable assistance in the analysis of the data.

aging people seldom take measures of this aspect of aging into account, but use other measures which are more easily obtainable. Thus it is questionable how closely people really look at the course of their lives, how explicit the personal philosophy is, and it is difficult to get people to express ideas by which we can look at people's ideas about the course and the approaching end of their lives.

The difficulty in devising measures of this kind lies in the fact that some answers are so obvious. If you ask people whether they are going to die, they say yes, and also agree that their life span is limited. In the same way, everybody accepts the fact that time passes, and that stages of life are different. Somewhat more subtle measures have to be used to see how aware people are of these facts during the normal course of their activities. It can be shown, for instance, that individuals are quite able to illustrate the course of their lives pictorially, and draw graphs corresponding to their lives (Back and Bourque, 1970; Bourque and Back, 1969). These life graphs are even quite consistent, showing a climax of life for most people between the ages of 40 and 50, and after that a gradual decline. In this paper we shall investigate the usefulness of a different technique, namely that of the use of metaphors for the words *time* and *death*.

This technique was developed by Knapp and Garbutt (1958; Knapp, 1960) and has been used mainly for the purpose of developing a measure of achievement motive. They also used mainly young subjects, such as college students. In studying the course of life, the subjects were on opposite ends to the aging people, people at the stage where the decline of the life graph might be felt most strongly. In this paper we shall investigate the applicability of this technique to relating a course of life, starting with age 45, a time which is usually considered to be the climax of life (Bourque and Back, 1969), and going to 70.

Method

The data were collected as part of an ongoing panel study of a cross-section of the 45–70 population in Durham, North Carolina. . . . The present data are based on the first wave of study in which 502 interviews were collected. . . .

As the metaphors for age and death, twenty-five statements were taken from Knapp's previous study. In his two papers, Knapp used two different techniques for measuring the suitability of the metaphor. In the research for his first paper (Knapp and Garbutt, 1958), he asked the subject to sort the twenty-five statements into five piles, ranging from most suitability for the concept to least. In that study, however, he used only the concept of time. In a second study (Knapp, 1960), he used six concepts and had the subjects rate the statements for suitability simply on a scale from one to seven. In this study we used the first technique. The reason was mainly that in a population with varying education, there was a danger that there would be insufficient variability between concepts unless a forced distribution was obtained. The drawback is, however, that we cannot compare the means of the statements with the means which Knapp had found in his metaphor study on the young subjects.

Results

Table 6–16 shows the pattern of differences of the different metaphors by sex and age. The first striking effect which we see is that sex is much more important than age in the respondent's judgment of the metaphors. Only one time image and four death metaphors show a monotonic difference by age, although, in addition, two time images and one death metaphor show a

Table 6–16. *Two-way analyses of variance age* × *sex for 25 time images and 25 death images.*

Time image	Age and/or sex group favoring image	Death image	Age and/or sex group favoring image
A large revolving wheel	M*	An infinite ocean	<50**
A whirlwind	F*	A grinning butcher	M*
A road leading over a hill	M*	A glass of bitter wine	
Budding leaves		Silent birds	<50*
An old man with a cane	M*	A trumpet	
A bird in flight	F*	A hothouse full of lilies	
Weaving cloth rapidly	F**	A chilling frost	
A rope unwinding		A compassionate mother	
A speeding train		A gentle veiled lady	F*
A quiet, motionless ocean	<50*	A misty abyss	<50**
A burning candle		An understanding doctor	F*
A stairway leading upward		A falling curtain	F**
A dashing waterfall		A cracked bell	
A jet in flight		A hangsman with bloody hands	M*
Wind-driven sand	M*	The end of a song	<50 and 50–59*; F*
An old woman spinning	M*	A leafless tree	
Drifting clouds		A shadowed doorway	
Marching feet		Windswept leaves	
A vast expanse of sky		A dreamless sleep	
The Rock of Gibraltar		A broken thread	50–59**
A fleeing thief		A toppled house of cards	
The all-swallowing monster		A satanic wrestler[b]	
A tedious song	50–59*	A bursting rocket	
A string of beads		A crumbling tower	M**
A galloping horseman	50–59*	A dark lake	

* Group liked the image more than the others at *p* .05.
** *p* .01.
[b] Interaction between sex and age significant at *p* .05. Older women and younger men liked it best; other interaction is not significant.

curvilinear significant relationship. If we look at the metaphors, however, a consistent picture emerges. Younger people see time more like a quiet ocean and death more like an infinite ocean, a silent bird, a misty abyss, and the end of a song. All of these metaphors seem to have in common a static quality although probably also a somewhat subdued emotional tone. Conversely, we can see that the older people reject these images and therefore might see time as a more rushing kind of event. We cannot say whether this is particularly positive or negative. As we have said, there are more sex differences than age differences for both kinds of images. Women see time like a whirlwind, a bird in flight, a rapidly weaving cloth, and death like a gently-veiled lady, an understanding doctor, a falling curtain, and the end of a song. Men see time like a large revolving wheel, a road leading over the hill, an old man with a cane, wind-driven sand, and an old woman spinning. They see death like a grinning butcher, a hangman with bloody hands, and a crumbling tower. We might say women see time as being active, and men see it more as a diffused event. But if we see inside the end of time, namely death, women are much more accepting of death than men. This would correspond to a picture of women as being more realistic than men, accepting events as they come, accepting the passing of time and impending death, while men reject the picture of time passing and look at death in a very negative way.

We can obtain additional patterning of the metaphors by factor analysis. The fifty questions were factored by centroid methods and rotated for the best structure. Knapp (1960) had factored his data too, and extracted one principal factor which is quite consistent with achieving motivation. In our study, however, we found a number of factors and none of those factors went across concepts; that is, no other factor had metaphors from both death and time. They are shown in Table 6–17 with questions which are part of the factors and tentative names for the description of the factors.

Factor one includes six metaphors for death, all of which see death in a favorable light. It was called the harlequin factor for reasons which will appear below. The second factor came from the time perspectives and had mainly activity or lack of facility as its leading indicators. We can identify this factor with the need-for-achieving measures which Knapp has found in his studies. The third factor, again, is concerned with death. It seems to be a dimension ranging from personalizing death to giving it an impersonal and natural image. The fourth factor has six time metaphors, all of which are concerned with speed and slowness. We can call this the speed factor, actually similar to the needs-achievement factor, although it came out separately. The fifth, again a time factor, has four items distinguishing active and passive. We can count these last two factors as really elaborations of factor two, the needs-achievement factor. The sixth factor, again consisting of death metaphors, has four items which look at death as a desert landscape or at least as an unpleasant one.

The six factors referrred to are especially interesting, giving the leading

Table 6–17. *Factor structure of time and death images (each factor is composed of either time or death images exclusively).*

Factor	Factor loading of variable	Variable
I Harlequin (death)	.57	a trumpet
	.71	a compassionate mother
	.48	a gentle veiled lady
	.72	an understanding doctor
	−.47	a crumbling tower
	−.45	a dark lake
II Need achievement (time)	−.63	a quiet, motionless ocean
	−.62	a vast expanse of sky
	.54	a fleeing thief
	.41	a galloping horseman
III Death as personal attack against impersonal nature (death)	−.45	an infinite ocean
	.55	a grinning butcher
	−.42	silent birds
	.65	a hangsman with bloody hands
	−.50	a dreamless sleep
	.53	a satanic wrestler
IV Speed (time)	−.47	a road leading over a hill
	.54	a speeding train
	−.58	a stairway leading upward
	.56	a jet in flight
	−.40	a tedious song
	−.59	a string of beads
V Active-passive (time)	−.49	a whirlwind
	.72	an old man with a cane
	.56	a burning candle
	−.49	a dashing waterfall
VI Desolate nature (death)	−.46	a chilling frost
	−.42	a cracked bell
	−.44	windswept leaves
	−.44	a bursting rocket

ideas on the two concepts of death and time. The first factor we have called the harlequin factor, as it corresponds to the harlequin complex as described by McClelland (1963). McClelland described this complex as the desire of some women to see death as a demon lover who conquers and gently brings death. The identification of lover and death is typical of this complex. McClelland uses two lines of evidence, one from literature and one from clinical experience. The literary evidence starts with the character of harlequin in the Italian *Commedia dell 'Arte* which is a combination of the figures of death and a lover. Other literary examples are the stories of Agatha Christie, such as "The Mysterious Mr. Quinn," which shows, first, death as a detective solving murders and then gradually as a gentle murderer. Clinical evidence shows similar fantasies arising out of case studies of women. The metaphors included in the first factor show the characteristics of the harlequin figure. Death is seen as a trumpet, a compassionate mother, a gently-veiled lady, and an understanding doctor, while the desolate metaphors, crumbling tower and dark lake, are rejected in this factor. Following McClelland's theory, we might consider a high score on this factor as acceptance of the harlequin complex.

The second factor is close to the one which Knapp has identified, namely the needs-achievement factor. It consists of time images, endorsing positively a fleeing thief, and galloping horsemen, and rejecting the opposite, quiet ocean and vast expanse of sky. In effect, the two other factors which have time measures are very similar. We have called them speed and activity, and it might be better to see the three of them as really representing one kind of factor, showing time as active, fast, and speeding along against the more static conception of time. In one of his studies, Knapp (Knapp and Garbutt, 1958) has called a similar class of time images the "dynamic-hasty cluster." We find, therefore, an agreement with Knapp on the existence of factors of this kind.

We can now analyze the six factors according to sex and age. Only one of the factors has a consistent age difference. This is the needs-achievement factor. Here, in general, the older groups look at time as more dynamic. This analysis was done on five time periods, and the highest one was the middle group between 55 and 60, followed by the two older and afterwards by the two younger groups. We might say that the youngest group, who is really at the peak of life between 45 and 55, has no fear yet of time passing by. The group where it becomes crucial, then, the crisis group between 55 and 60, sees time speed fastest and the older groups also accept it. Four of the other factors show sex differences. The harlequin factor and the other two time factors, speed and activity, show higher scores among women, and looking at death as a personal opponent shows a higher score among men. These patterns correspond to what we have seen in individual questions. Men see death more as an opponent; women are more accepting of it, and at the same time are more realistic, more accepting of the passage of time.

Conclusion

Despite the difficulty of getting mass data on mainly philosophical concepts such as the meaning of life, death, and time, the measure we used gave meaningful results on a group of people with varied educations. We may say that the implicit philosophy of life can be measured by different techniques with most population groups. The measure which we have been using can be administered to a group with various ranges in education, giving consistent and important data. The main finding in this study relates more to sex than to age. Women are more accepting of death and are more aware of the passage of time, especially in the later years of life. This is also true of older people in general as compared to those in the middle years.

It may be tempting to speculate that the difference between men and women is related to the ideas of cultural historians who associate women with the more agricultural, natural way of life, and men with industrial, urban life.

Expansion of the implications of a study of this kind must await further field study with larger populations and further analysis of data derived from this test.

For the present, we shall stay with a poetic experience, like Bernard Shaw's hero Tanner in *Man and Superman*, who realizes at the end that men talk and fight the Life Force, but women vanquish because they *are* the Life Force.

References

Back, K. W., and Bourque, L. B. Life graphs: Aging and cohort effect. *Journal of Gerontology*, 25:249–255, 1970.

Bourque, L. B., and Back, K. W. The Middle years seen through the life graph. *Sociological Symposium*, No. 3 (fall), 1969.

Knapp, R. H. A study of the metaphor. *Journal of Projective Techniques*, 24:389–395, 1960.

Knapp, R. H., and Gurbutt, J. T. Time imagery and the achievement motive. *Journal of Personality*, 26:426–434, 1958.

McClelland, D. C., The Harlequin Complex. In White, R. W. (Ed)., *The study of lives.* New York: Atherton, 1963.

Transition to Aging and the Self-Image   *Kurt W. Back*

Research on aging has shown important contrasts between objective social and behavioral changes and the individual's reaction to them. Faculties and abilities as well as social rewards and objective social conditions decline rather consistently during the later years of the life cycle. On the other hand, subjective satisfaction and morale not only do not decrease correspondingly but seem to improve during old age (Riley and Foner, 1968; Back and Gergen, 1966). It is plausible to explain this apparent contradiction by the fact that morale is a personal comparison of self-worth with a realization of loss of socially important roles. While the loss itself may be traumatic, the new status may be acceptable later; for the aged, even social losses might be welcome adaptations to reduced capacity. It might be conjectured that physical capacity and energy decline steadily from early middle age on, while *psychological extent*, the size of the psychological life space, is maintained until a relatively sudden decline sets in at a comparatively late date. Thus, in early middle age we would find conformity between age and ability. During onset of old age,

Reprinted by permission from *Aging and Human Development,* 2:296–304, 1971. The author thanks Mrs. Joanna Morris for invaluable assistance in analysis of the data.

psychological extent would remain higher than actual life situation. But as psychological life space declines, the two would be rejoined again, and a high level of satisfaction is attained again (Back and Gergen, 1968).

Theoretical advance in this field must await measurement techniques that capture the personal meaning of the self-concept. We are seeking a measure not of morale in the general sense, but of evaluation of the self, the discrepancy of the self-image one holds to the way one feels he is seen by others, and the different features of the self-image which may become important. The present paper deals with the evaluation of two possible measures of self-image: one an adaptation of the semantic differential, and the other an adaptation of Kuhn's Who-Are-You test (Kuhn and McPartland, 1954). These measures had been used previously to show not only the dimensions of the self-image but also the discrepancy between ideal, real, and actual self-image and self-presentation (Brehm and Back, 1968; Back and Paramesh, 1969).

The utility of these measures can be determined by their sensitivity to adaptation to aging of varying population groups, especially those with different problems during the aging process. Among the crises which can occur during the later parts of the life cycle, some appear in almost every life. One is the loss of occupational role through voluntary or forced retirement; another, the loss of family role through the leaving home of grown children—the "empty nest" stage of the family sociologist. It can be suggested that the first crisis is of particular importance to men, while the second is of greater importance to women. A valuable use of the measures of self which we are trying to develop is therefore to assess the relative impact of chronological age, retirement, and leaving of children on men and women.

Method

The data to be reported here were collected as part of a panel study on adaptation and aging of persons 45–70 being conducted at the Duke Center for the Study of Aging and Human Development. The present data are based on the first wave of study in which 502 interviews were collected.

The questions used in this paper were part of the social history section of the study. Social history gave age, sex, working status, and family situation, including separation from children. The measures of self-orientation were of two kinds: one was a semantic differential and the other the Who-Are-You test. The semantic differential consisted of a list of seven bipolar scales, each scored from one to seven, each of which rated three concepts. The concepts were "what I really am"; "what I would like to be"; and "how I appear to others." The seven scales were, "useful, busy, effective, free to do things, respected, looking to the future, and satisfied with life." The first three (busy, effective, and useful) can be characterized as involvement, the last three (respected, looking to the future, and satisfied with life) as evaluation.

Several different measures of the three concepts could be obtained from the twenty-one scales. One measure, the direct rating, could be used on each of the concepts, evaluation of self, ideal self, and self-presentation, along the seven dimensions. Second, on each of the dimensions, differences could be shown between members of each pair of the three concepts. Thus, for instance, we could determine whether the person felt he was more or less busy than he would like to be. Third, the overall difference between members of each pair of the three concepts could be computed. This was done by the difference formula suggested by Osgood, Tannenbaum, and Suci (1957), which is the square root of the sums of the squared differences of all the seven scales. It can be visualized as a simple geometrical distance in a dimensional space. We shall be concerned here with the difference between the "real self" and "how I appear to others," the reality-appearance difference.

The Who-Are-You test is simply an open-ended rating of the self: "If someone were to ask you, 'Who are you?' what would you say?" The respondent himself can fill in all the dimensions which he likes and which seem to be important. The answers were scored in three main categories: (*a*) answers referring to *personal background,* family situation, ancestry, ethnic or religious identification, i.e., ascribed characteristics; (*b*) *personal characteristics* such as character, ambition, occupation; and (*c*) *personal values* such as beliefs, opinions, and attitudes. These three categories represent Reisman's classifications into other directed, inner directed, and traditionally oriented character structure (Reisman, Denny, and Glazer, 1950; Back and Paramesh, 1969). Each respondent gave three answers to the question, so that when the answers were combined, each of the three variables (personal background, personal characteristics, and personal values) had a possible range from zero to three. If a person gave three personal background items, he would be given a score of three on this variable and zero on the other two. If he listed two personal characteristics and one value, he would be scored two on characteristics and one on value. Here again, we can use the scores for each question as a basis of self-determination of the relevant variables of the self.

We have thus two ways of measuring the self-concept: (*a*) a qualitative self-anchored way, which lets the respondent choose the variables which he finds critical; (*b*) a measure based on a predetermined set of scales, which makes mathematical transformations possible.

Results

Real Self versus Apparent Self

Let us look at one of the crises of the self-image occurring in aging—the contrast between what a person really feels about himself and the image that he presents to others. This is expressed by the difference between the semantic differential measures of the two concepts, the real self and the apparent self. An analysis of the distance measure between the two concepts, classified by sex and five-year age categories, shows significant differences by age, especially among men, although not in a monotonically increasing fashion. For women, the largest divergence between self and appearance of self occurs in the two oldest groups (60 to 64 and 65 and over), but the next is in the youngest group (45 to 49), followed by the other two groups (50 to 54 and 55 to 59). Among men, the sequence is almost regular, increasing with age, the only exception being a large difference in the 50 to 54 group. This sequence would indicate that the discrepancy is not due to an intrinsic effect of aging but to events in the life cycle which change the position of a person in the world.

There are two ways to learn more about the meaning of this changing reality-appearance contrast. One is by investigating the components and qualities which make up the self-image; the other is by comparing the reactions to

Table 6–18. *Distance between apparent and real self (semantic differential) by sex and age.*

	Under 50	50–54	55–59	60–64	65 and over
Male	2.38	2.88	2.46	3.02	3.25
Female	2.64	2.59	2.49	2.69	2.92

Sex: $F(1,489) = 1.09$ NS
Age: $F(4,489) = 3.32; p < .05$
Sex $\times$ Age: $F(4,489) = .94$ NS

the different crises of the later years. First, let us examine the semantic differential itself to determine which scales contribute most to the reality-appearance difference. Dividing the scales into three groups, involvement (busy, useful, and effective), evaluation (looks to future, satisfied, and respected), and freedom to do things (Guptill, 1969), only the involvement factor distinguished significantly between age groups, but this was affected by the sex of the respondent; the differences of the men were almost in the same order as the total difference; among women the youngest group (45 to 49) had the greatest difference, then the oldest, and then the intermediate groups. Overall, the interaction between sex and age was statistically significant.

Going beyond the semantic differential itself, we can find some clues to the meaning of the reality-appearance difference in the answers to the Who-Are-You question. The strongest difference is revealed in the personal background directed answers. When asked who they are, women, in general, gave more answers relating to personal background, but this *declines* with age; men give fewer answers regarding personal background and their scores remain constant over the years; thus there is a great difference between the sexes in the youngest age group but none in the oldest group. Among women, therefore, personal background characteristics, which include family relations, become of diminishing importance with age.

Children Leaving Home

Because of the sex differences in the influence of age on the reality-appearance discrepancy, we shall investigate the particular crises which may affect the sexes differently using the semantic differential. Let us examine first the departure from home of the children. Controlling for this variable we find age differences only in men. In other words, the age difference in the discrepancy of the real self and appearance to others is due mainly to the departure of the children among women, but not among men.

The influence of age on the reality-appearance difference among women is thus partially accounted for by the fact that older women have fewer children living at home. Child separation, however, does not affect age changes in the interpretation of the meaning of the self. In response to the Who-Are-You question, the shift among women from personal background to achieved traits becomes stronger if controlled for child separation. Among men there is little change in the Who-Are You question, while among women there is a sharp decline of personal background items by age and an increase in value items with age in each group, classified according to child separation.

Retirement

By contrast, work and retirement affect both sexes in the same manner. Controlling for work status, we find no more differences according to age, but definite differences by sex and work status: men and nonworkers claim the bigger difference between appearance and reality of the self-image. Looking at the Who-Are-You question we can see traits that may account for these differences. Among the retirees, women mention significantly more personal background data and more individual characteristics. Among the workers there is no difference in amount of personal background data, but women mention more individual characteristics.

In order to assess the relative importance of separation from work and child, we have to control simultaneously for work and family status. Because there are too few male nonworkers in the younger ages, we cannot control for both in the whole age range. Instead we can measure the influence of child separation in the working respondents in this group: for men the reality-appearance discrepancy increases with age, and for women it declines; further, for men the discrepancy increases with child separation, and for women it declines. There are no significant differences according to the Who-Are-You question.

Table 6–19. *Difference of three scale clusters between apparent and real self by sex and age.*

	Involvement		Evaluation		Freedom	
	Male	Female	Male	Female	Male	Female
Under 50	.11	.19	.30	−.01	−.09	−.16
50–54	.28	.02	.12	.11	.19	−.43
55–59	.25	.26	.33	.22	.32	−.04
60–64	.36	.10	.35	.15	−.11	−.04
65 and over	.09	.32	.32	.35	.32	−.24
Sex $F(1,492)$	.39 NS		3.82; $p < .10$		4.77; $p < .05$	
Age $F(4,492)$	.42 NS		1.73 NS		.55 NS	
Sex × Age $F(4,492)$	2.25; $p < .10$		1.08 NS		.89 NS	

Table 6–20. *Who-Are-You Score by age and sex.*

	Personal background		Personal characteristics		Values	
	Male	Female	Male	Female	Male	Female
Under 50	.43	1.35	1.09	1.00	1.00	.23
50–54	.53	.98	1.16	1.27	.86	.61
55–59	.57	.81	1.02	1.00	.73	.71
60–64	.38	.67	1.40	1.20	.78	.70
65 and over	.39	.41	1.27	1.13	.85	.94
Sex $F(1,492)$	24.82; $p < .01$		.56 NS		6.67; $p < .05$	
Age $F(4,492)$	5.00; $p < .01$		1.55 NS		1.29 NS	
Sex × Age $F(4,492)$	3.81; $p < .01$		.37 NS		3.60; $p < .01$	

Table 6–21. *Distance between apparent and real self by sex, age and children's residence (parents only).*

	Male		Female	
	Children not at home	Children at home	Children not at home	Children at home
Under 50	1.92	2.43	2.83	2.64
50–54	2.45	3.21	2.40	2.67
55–59	2.33	2.37	2.29	2.43
60–64	2.95	3.33	2.66	2.18
65 and over	3.30	3.54	2.96	2.57

Sex $F(1,402) = 1.97$. NS
Age $F(4,402) = 2.68$; $p < .05$
Child residence $F(1,402) = .64$. NS
Sex × Age $F(4,402) = 2.20$; $p < .10$
Other interactions not significant.

Table 6–22. *Who-Are-You Score by age, sex and children's residence* (*parents only*).

	Male		Female	
	Children not at home	Children at home	Children not at home	Children at home
Personal background				
Under 50	.38	.46	1.13	1.63
50–54	.50	.60	1.10	1.11
55–59	.53	.75	.81	.73
60–64	.35	.63	.75	1.29
65 and over	.43	.45	.51	0.00

Sex $F(1,404) = 14.88; p < .01$
Age $F(4,404) = 3.41; p < .01$
Child residence $F(1,404) = 1.26$ NS
Sex $\times$ Age $F(4,404) = 3.61; p < .01$
Other interactions not significant.

	Male		Female	
Personal characteristics				
Under 50	1.00	1.08	1.50	.68
50–54	1.36	1.08	1.10	1.32
55–59	1.11	1.06	.88	1.36
60–64	1.32	1.25	1.21	.57
65 and over	1.28	1.36	1.13	.80

No significant F ratios

	Male		Female	
Values				
Under 50	1.23	.92	.13	.21
50–54	.93	.72	.70	.37
55–59	.74	.94	.75	.73
60–64	.91	.38	.71	.86
65 and over	.85	.73	.85	2.00

Sex $F(1,404) = 1.04$ NS
Age $F(4,404) = 2.71; p < .05$
Child residence $F(1,404) = 0.00$ NS
Sex $\times$ Age $F(4,404) = 6.05; p < .01$
Sex $\times$ Child $F(1,404) = 3.84; p \sim .05$
Other interactions not significant.

Table 6–23. *Distance between apparent and real self by age, sex and work status.*

	Male		Female	
	Working	Not working	Working	Not working
Under 60	2.55	2.71	2.62	2.45
60–65	2.91	3.14	2.49	2.69
Over 65	3.23	3.56	1.92	3.29

Sex $F(1,487) = 7.00\ p < .01$
Age $F(2,487) = 2.07$; NS
Work $F(1,487) = 4.51; p < .05$
Age $\times$ Work $F(2,487) = 2.35; p < .10$
Other interactions not significant.

Table 6–24. *Who-Are-You Score by age, sex, and work status.*

	Male		Female	
	Working	Not working	Working	Not working
Personal background				
Under 60	.54	2.00	.88	1.20
60–65	.36	.20	.59	.67
Over 65	.59	.30	.42	.40

Sex $F(1,490) = 11.63; p < .01$
Age $F(2,490) = 1.91$ NS
Work $F(1,490) = .92$ NS
Sex $\times$ Age $F(2,490) = 4.92; p < .01$
Sex $\times$ Work $F(1,490) = 4.74; p < .05$
Other interactions not significant.

	Male		Female	
	Working	Not working	Working	Not working
Personal characteristics				
Under 60	1.07	1.57	1.26	.84
60–65	1.41	1.60	1.47	.97
Over 65	1.07	1.30	1.33	1.06

Sex $F(1,490) = 2.33$ NS
Age $F(2,490) = .95$ NS
Work $F(1,490) = .13$ NS
Sex $\times$ Work $F(1,490) = 8.33; p < .01$
Other interactions not significant.

	Male		Female	
	Working	Not working	Working	Not working
Values				
Under 60	.82	.71	.56	.50
60–65	.82	.70	.76	.93
Over 65	1.03	.79	.92	.90

No significant F ratios

Table 6–25. *Distance between apparent and real self by age, sex, and children's residence (working only, parents only).*

	Male		Female	
	Children not at home	Children at home	Children not at home	Children at home
Under 50	1.92	2.43	3.24	2.62
50–54	2.45	3.21	2.29	2.49
55–59	2.30	2.37	2.62	2.61
60–64	3.03	3.16	2.13	1.38
65 and over	2.77	4.41	1.94	1.71

Sex $F(1,265) = 6.76; p < .01$
Age $F(4,265) = .26$ NS
Child residence $F(1,265) = .78$ NS
Sex $\times$ Age $F(4,265) = 5.99; p < .01$
Sex $\times$ Child $F(1,265) = 5.43; p < .05$
Other interactions not significant.

Discussion

The data presented here have shown the values and limitations of the two measures which we have employed in studying the changes in self-concept brought on by old age. The most consistent result has been the sex differences in the answers to the Who-Are-You question. Women are more likely to answer in terms of personal background, such as family relations and demographic characteristics, but this emphasis declines after the fifties such that in the last age groups, 60 to 64 and 65 and over, there is no difference between the sexes in this regard. Correspondingly, personally achieved positions and characteristics, as well as personal values, become more important for women with age. This development remains constant even if controlled for varying experiences, such as retirement and child separation during aging.

Thus, neither retirement nor separation from children affects the content of the self-image as much as the aging process alone. However, the discrepancy between reality and appearance of the self is influenced by these factors. Both crises are important; but separation from children accounts only for the effect on women, while retirement or nonworking affects both sexes. In general, men have a greater problem with the discrepancy between who they feel they are and what they imagine other people think about them. This is also true with nonworking members of both sexes.

During the aging process, women tend to shift self-image from their relationship to others, the social characteristics, to their own abilities and feelings; the separation from children can be viewed in this way. Freed from family obligations, they may feel that they can now much more easily be accepted for what they are. Men, on the other hand, are involved in the work role more personally, and difficulties with this role through aging may make life even more difficult for them. Separation from children may, therefore, aggravate this discrepancy, making them more dependent on the work role in which they have difficulty in presenting the right image. Hence the increase in self-image discrepancy in working men separated from children, while for women the discrepancy decreases with age and separation from children.

Measures of the self-image that can be administered in a relatively simple manner to a large sample can show some of the more subtle features of the management of crises incumbent on the aged.

References

Back, K. W., and Gergen, K. J., Personal orientation and morale of the aging. In J. McKinney and I. Simpson (Eds.), *Social aspects of aging.* Durham, N.C.: Duke University Press, 1966.

Back, K. W., and Gergen, K. J. The self through the latter span of life. In C. Gordon and K. J. Gergen (Eds.), *The self in social interaction.* New York: Wiley, 1968.

Back, K. W., and Paramesh, C. R. Self-image, information exchange and social character. *International Journal of Psychology,* 4:109–117, 1969.

Brehm, M. L., and Back, K. W. Self-image and attitude toward drugs. *Journal of Personality*, 35: 299–314, 1968.

Guptill, C. S., A measure of age identification. *Gerontologist*, 9 (summer):96–102, 1969.

Kuhn, M. H., and McPartland, T. S. An empirical investigation of self-attitudes. *American Sociological Review*, 19:68–76, 1954.

Osgood, C., Suci, G., and Tannenbaum, P. *The measurement of meaning.* Urbana: University of Illinois Press, 1957.

Riesman, D., Denny, R., and Glazer, N. *The lonely crowd.* New Haven: Yale University Press, 1950.

Riley, M. W., and Foner, A. *Aging and society,* vol. 1: *An inventory of research findings.* New York: Russell Sage Foundation, 1968.

Perception of Self and the Study of Whole Lives   *Kurt W. Back and Joanna D. Morris*

In biographical or longitudinal studies of human life we are faced with two different principles. One is the continuity of a person in the course of his life; the fact that we can discern something, call it personality or character, as a consistent predictor of a person's actions. The other is change in a person, which derives partly from maturation and aging and partly from certain events which happen in the course of his life. In attempting to integrate these two ways of looking at people, we are led to look for some mediating mechanism which is both constant and flexible. The mechanism should explain how life events affect people in general but should also take into account the fact that they happen to unique personalities who are able then to integrate them into the general course of their lives.

Finding objective measures of this mediating process is a difficult task. One possible approach is phenomenological; it assumes that people, themselves, have some picture of the consistency of their personalities or of their own selves. We attempt here to present some measures of this kind and to evaluate them according to their sensitivity to changes in the life courses of the persons concerned. While it is likely that there are differences between individuals in the definiteness of their pictures of themselves, we shall assume that everybody has at least some vague idea of his own self, even if he cannot express it very well. Individuals visualize or verbalize themselves in different ways, and therefore different measures might be appropriate to different people, and it might be hard to find any measure which is equally relevant to everyone.

In the present study we tried out several ways of assessing a self-image of this kind. Some of them have been described already in my two previous papers in this volume. We were able to assess changes on these measures in a reinterview two years after the initial interview and to relate them to certain relevant events in the persons' lives. We were able to compare the effects of general development and aging with those of specific events in occupational and family life.

Method

The data were collected from a sample of middle-aged and older people in Durham, North Carolina. The composition of the sample and the method of data collection are described elsewhere in this volume. Since the study was conducted as a panel, data are available from two interviews taken two years apart. We will here be concerned mainly with changes of two kinds: changes in the respondents' background characteristics, especially work participation, and changes in relationships with their children. These are significant events in the aging process which had happened to the respondents during the two years. Differences in scores on the self-image measures can then be taken as changes in relevant aspects of the self-image. Of course it is possible that some of the changes are simply a consequence of unreliability in the re-interview. The unreliability portion of the change can be considered, however, to be a random kind of occurrence; systematic relationships are unlikely to be due to simple interviewing error.

Life Conditions

Seven variables were assessed. They were change in labor force status (working or nonworking), change in job level, change in spouse's labor force status, change in spouse's job level, change in income, change in whether any children were living at home, and change in number of children living at home. Thus five variables were related to work activity and two to relationships with children in the family.

Self-Image

Fourteen variables were used as measures of self-image. They were derived from four different questionnaires. The first questionnaire used the semantic differential technique and comprised seven scales describing each of three concepts. The seven scales were grouped together to form three measures. The first, consisting of three scales, was called involvement; the second, also consisting of three scales, was called optimism; and the third, consisting of only one scale, was called freedom (Back, pp. 206–216 in this volume, and Back and Guptill, 1966). The three concepts were "What I really am," "What I would like to be," and "How I appear to others." For purposes of the present study the involvement, optimism, and freedom scores for "What I really am" were used. In addition, the Euclidean distance between all pairs of the three concepts, using all seven dimensions, was computed. This yielded three distance scores (Really am—Like, Really am—Appear, and Like—Appear). Thus six measures were derived from the semantic differential.

The second set of questions used items from Rotter's I-E Scale (Jessor, 1968). It yielded one measure: the score of internal versus external locus of control.

The third set of questions was the Knapp Time Death Metaphors which was discussed in a previous paper (Back, pp. 201–207 in this volume, and Knapp, 1960). The responses of the panel on the first interview had been factor-analyzed. This time, using the combined data from both interviews, new factor analyses were done which yielded a slightly different factor structure. The last two factors of the previous analysis ("active-passive" and "desolate nature"), which were based on very few items, were discarded, and three of the other four factors were somewhat changed. In the "harlequin" factor the item "a dark lake," which had the lowest loading, was eliminated and "a hothouse full of lilies" was added. This, the most important factor, indicated a positive attitude toward death—the "demon lover" myth. The "need achievement" factor stayed the same. In the "death as personal attack against impersonal nature" factor, two items with the lowest loadings, "silent birds" and "an infinite ocean," were eliminated and "the end of a song" was added. In the fourth factor, "speed," three items ("a speeding train," "a jet in flight," and "a tedious song") were eliminated. The meaning of the factors was not substantially changed by the substitutions. Scores on these four factors constituted four more measures of self-image.

The final three measures were taken from the life graph (Back and Bourque, 1970; Bourque and Back, 1969). This technique consists of presenting the subject with a two-dimensional grid and telling him that the horizontal line corresponds to his life (assuming that he will reach 80 years). The line is marked off at 10-year intervals. The subject is asked to draw a line representing his life, showing the ups and downs. No further definition is given, in order to allow the subject to give his own definition of what is important in producing the ups and downs. In interpreting the graph, one can look at the general shape of the line or at its relative height above baseline for different age ranges. Three measures were taken in the present study. The first was based on the general shape of the graph and consisted of the standard deviation of the height of the graph at 15 five-year intervals between 10 and 80. This shows the amount of variability or flatness of the subject's view of his whole life. The second was the subjective estimation of the peak of one's life: the age at which the line was highest. The third was the relative height of the older ages (from 60 to 80), standardized for average height and standard deviation.

Results

Two preliminary analyses were performed before assessing the effect of different life events on the self-image. The first question was "Is there any underlying dimension of the self-image which would tap the measures used to different degrees?" Therefore, factor analyses were performed on the 14 measures for the first wave, the second wave, and the change scores from the first to the second wave. All three analyses gave the same result, namely that there was no factor which went across measures. Each factor extracted represented only measures taken from the same instrument, such as the Semantic Differential, Life Graph, or Knapp Metaphors. Thus it seems that each of the measures taps a different kind of aspect of looking at the self, which may be related to different ways people have of verbalizing or visualizing themselves.

A second preliminary check was made to see whether there was a consistent change in the 14 self-image measures due simply to age. There were no consistent changes between the first and second wave data, reflecting pure age change, and those that occurred were insignificant. In fact, the critical ratios of mean change to standard deviation of change were all much less than 1.

Since few of the seven possible demographic changes occurred in the relatively short time of two years, it will be better to compare the respondents who experienced any changes at all with those who did not experience any changes. Thus summary measures can be constructed by counting the numbers of changes in background items from the first to the second interview. All changes mentioned are statistically significant at the five percent level or better.

Among the types of measures of self-image we used, the semantic differential measures proved to be the most sensitive. Of those, the involvement index is the most important measure. When sex is controlled, involvement decreases with changed status in men, but the opposite occurs in women. Thus changes tend to raise the involvement level in women. The life graph becomes flatter (decreased standard deviation) when negative changes occur (i.e., loss of job, lowering of job status) but becomes less flat with positive change or no change. If we consider any change at all (positive as well as negative), the score on the harlequin factor increases with change. If we distinguish positive and negative change, we find that age is an important discriminating variable. For all the respondents 60 and older the harlequin score increased with changes for the better, while younger respondents' scores increased with changes for the worse.

When life events are looked at individually, the measures discussed above are again relevant. Involvement as well as optimism ratings decreased or showed little change with lowering of one's own or spouse's job status and optimism showed little change with loss of income. Both involvement and optimism increased substantially, however, with no change or positive change in these life events. Lowered job status was also associated with a flatter life graph, higher score on the harlequin factor, and more external locus of control on the I-E scale. An increase in job status was associated with a relatively higher life graph in the older age range. Another measure, the discrepancy between real and apparent self, seems to be less consistent. This discrepancy increases for men who acquire a job, but decreases for women who do so, and also increases with improvement in the spouse's job status and decreases with an increase in number of children in the home. It is hard to see, therefore, whether this discrepancy is a positive or negative indicator of the self-image. Finally, changes in the two measures associated with the respondent's children do not seem to relate to the self-image variables as much as do changes in the job-status measures.

Discussion

The tentative results presented here confirm other research and also give some indications of the ways in which life events become important in molding and interacting with the self-image (pp. 207–216 in this volume). Change in one's own or spouse's job status becomes an important factor in changing self-image while relationship to one's children does not. We can speculate that changes in the family life cycle have already been anticipated and thus do not affect the long-range view held of one's self. Although one can also expect changes in job status with aging, they apparently still affect the person when they actually arrive, especially if one's image in the eyes of the world is pretty much dependent on one's job title. One might easily feel that the difference between what one is and what one appears does change when one's job title changes.

It is also striking how little these changes are dependent on age. General changes with age were not found, and controlling for age did not help much in understanding the relationships of the other measures. The only place where age was important was in the harlequin factor of the Knapp Metaphors. This factor, which indicates an acceptance of death and implies a positive evaluation of it, mirrors changes in life events differently depending on how old the respondent is.

On the other hand, sex differences were important in the change in self-image. Males acted according to the expectation that changes associated with aging would be disturbing. Female respondents, however, seem to be sometimes even stimulated by these events and their changes in self-image frequently go in the opposite direction to those of men. These differential changes correspond to sex differences in the measures in general, women showing more increase in score on the Harlequin factor (see pp. 205–206) and on the optimism scale of the semantic differential. Women seem to be better adapted than men to changes in the rhythm of life.

Finally, it is surprising how well the semantic differential is able to reflect life changes. It is, for this purpose, probably a better instrument than most of the other measures. It is the most direct measure, because the person is really asked how he evaluates himself. It seems here that the direct question is the most fruitful one, especially for a large group of people. The other more indirect measures of self-image may capture different facets of the personality and might be better for intensive individual studies, but the direct question "What do you feel about yourself?" is most easily answered by most people.

References

Back, K. W. Transition to aging and the self-image. In this volume, pp. 207–216.

Back, K. W. Metaphors as tests of personal philosophy of aging. In this volume, pp. 201–207.

Back, K. W. and Bourque, L. B. Life graphs: Aging and cohort effect. *Journal of Gerontology*, 25:249–255, 1970.

Back, K. W. and Guptill, C. S. Retirement and self ratings. In Simpson, I. H., and McKinney, J. C. (Eds.), *Social aspects of aging.* Durham, N.C.: Duke University Press, 1966, chap. 7.

Bourque, L. B. and Back, K. W. The middle years seen through the life graph. *Sociological Symposium*, No. 3, 1969.

Jessor, R. *et al., Society, personality and deviant behavior.* New York: Holt, Rinehart & Winston, 1968.

Knapp, R. H. A study of the metaphor. *Journal of Projective Techniques*, 24:389–395, 1960.

Achievement and the Self-concept in Middle Age   *Linda M. Breytspraak*

Among sociologists (especially the symbolic interactionists) the self-concept is believed to develop in a fundamentally social context—that is, it is integrally tied to—and emerges out of—one's various roles in the social world. One's social roles are important, for they provide one with a set of significant others whose real and perceived evaluations of one's self are taken quite seriously.

Ralph Turner (1968) and Erik Erikson (1959) both add to this common sociological understanding of the self-concept by their suggestions that the self-concept is not totally manipulated by the reactions of other social actors. Turner concludes that there is also a more stable component of the self-concept which is based on the feelings one has about his capabilities and potential for desired accomplishments. Erikson states a similar position in his argument that the identity (which is one's own variant on the way others master experience) is formed not only by the sum of one's identifications with others, but also by the ego which is a "central organizing agency" that edits these identifications.

In line with these views of the self-concept, it is argued, for analytic purposes, that we can talk about both a *cognitive* and *affective* dimension to the self-concept—that is, we have perceptions of where we stand in our social worlds in relation to where we wish to be (cognitive dimension), yet we also have varying degrees of positive or negative self-feelings about our standing (affective dimension). These feelings may very well be tied to our sense of capability for future achievement and evaluations of past achievements.

Buhler (1968), Frenkel-Brunswick (1968), Neugarten (1968), Butler (1968), and Erikson (1959) have all observed that most individuals undergo a period of serious self-examination, self-assessment, and life review in the middle and later years. Erikson's formulation of the eighth and final life crisis of ego integrity versus despair is one of the more articulate statements of this view. It is at this stage that the person comes to grips with whether he can accept the appropriateness and meaningfulness of his life.

It appears quite understandable that a person comes to such a point of review and assessment of achievements in late middle age. According to Kuhlen (1968), motivational changes usually occur during these years. Strong career and achievement drives may drop off as the society frustrates the individual by no longer rewarding such drives. Neugarten (1968, 1972) comments that we each seem to have a sense of "social time clocks" operating in various areas of our lives, and we also have a sense of our own timing in family and occupational events as "early," "late," or "on time." Hence, social expectations about age-appropriate behavior can act as prods or brakes on motivations. The research of Atkinson (1957) is also suggestive of the idea that motivation to work and achieve decreases when a person becomes satiated with success. He demonstrated experimentally that motivation to achieve is strongest when the uncertainty regarding the outcome is greatest (i.e., probability of success or failure = .50). Hence, a person's motivation to achieve may decline as the probability of success approaches 1.00.

In spite of the widely accepted position that there are motivational changes along with serious self-assessment of one's accomplishments throughout the lifetime, there appears to be little published research in gerontology looking directly to the interconnections of the various facets of achievement and the self-concept. This research was begun in an effort to explore some of these dimensions in middle- and older-aged people. The central question under investigation was whether differences in cognitive and affective dimensions of the self-concept could be partially accounted for by differences in orientation toward achievement, in the extent of previous achievements, and in possibilities for yet achieving (assuming that many people will not have yet undergone the shift in motivation of which Kuhlen and Neugarten speak).

Methodology

Sample

The sample under study was composed of 502 white men and women between the ages of 45 and 71 who were considered representative of the "middle mass" of middle- and older-aged persons in Durham, North Carolina. Subjects were a random sample of policy holders with a major insurance underwriter with industrial and governmental, as well as individual coverage. The study is ultimately to be longitudinal in nature; however, this particular analysis is cross-sectional in that it focuses on subjects only at the time of first interview.

Measurement of Self-Concept

A dual measure of self-concept was utilized in line with the view that the self-concept can be viewed as having both a cognitive and an affective component. The cognitive component was measured by a semantic differential score (Osgood et al., 1957). Subjects were presented with seven bipolar adjective scales and asked to rate themselves from one to seven on each scale with reference to the concepts of "What I really am" and "What I would like to be."[1] The overall semantic differential score is computed by the difference formula suggested by Osgood which is the square root of the sums of the squared differences of all seven scales with reference to each concept. (This will be referred to as the "actual-ideal discrepancy.")[2]

---

1. Busy-inactive; useless—useful; effective-ineffective; respected—not respected; satisfied with life—unsatisfied with life; look to the future—look to the past; free to do things—not free to do things.
2. Intercorrelation analyses of the seven adjective pairs in each scale indicated that there were higher correlations among the scales "busy," "useful," and "effective" (summarized as the activity factor) and among the scales "respected," "satisfied with life," and "look to the future" (summarized as the optimism factor). One remaining scale, "free to do things," did not correlate highly with other scales, and is labeled as the autonomy factor. These are the same factors found in most applications of the semantic differential technique (Osgood and Suci, 1955).

The affective component of the self-concept was measured by a shortened form of Bradburn and Caplovitz's (1965; 1969) Affect Balance Scale (ABS). This scale taps the general balance of positive and negative feelings one has about the way his life is going. The items are as follows:

How often during the last week did you feel—

1. On top of the world?
2. Very lonely or remote from other people?
3. Particularly excited or interested in something?
4. Depressed or very unhappy?
5. Pleased about having accomplished something?
6. Bored?
7. Proud because someone complimented you on something?
8. So restless you couldn't sit long in a chair?

Responses were coded 0, 1, or 2 according to whether the person indicated he had these feelings "not at all," "once," or "several times." Although these items do not cover every dimension of affect, Bradburn and Caplovitz found

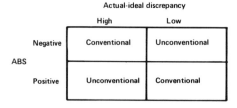

Figure 6–1. *Four self-concept types.*

them to be representative of one's total affective picture. Scores are calculated by taking the total of the positive affect items (nos. 1, 3, 5, and 7) and subtracting from it the total of the negative items (nos. 2, 4, 6, and 8). Scores can (and do) range between -8 and $+8$.

The logic of using both the Semantic Differential and the Affect Balance Scale in describing the self-concept is reinforced by Ruth Wiley's (1961) observation that high or low actual-ideal discrepancies may take on different meanings to people in different life situations. For instance, a high discrepancy might be more disturbing when the person feels he has few resources and capabilities for achieving what he aspires to achieve than it would be if he does have these resources—or if he feels that he already has considerable accomplishments. The Affect Balance Scale should provide a corrective by also giving a picture of one's general level of affect or "happiness." Hence, four self-concept types emerge for analytical purposes (see Figure 6–1).

Two of these could be considered the conventional or expected relationship between discrepancy and affect (i.e., high discrepancy with negative affect balance, and low discrepancy with positive affect balance). The remaining two types appear to be less obviously interpretable (i.e., high discrepancy with positive affect, or low discrepancy with negative affect). The subjects were typed according to whether their discrepancy score was above or below the median and their ABS score was balanced on the negative or positive side.

Mode of Analysis

The technique for analysis was a stepwise multiple discriminant function analysis that allows for the combination of multiple variables into a linear function that will best discriminate between a priori groups. The major advantage of this technique is that a number of variables can be considered simultaneously and their covariances taken into account (Anderson, 1966; Overall and Klett, 1972). Whereas a certain predictor variable might not appear significant in a univariate analysis, it might become significant when considered together with other predictors and covariances are taken into account. Conversely, variables that are significant by themselves in distinguishing between groups may become insignificant when other variables are considered simultaneously.

The Predictor Variables

In the case of the analysis reported here, the a priori groups were the four self-concept types, and the predictors were fifteen variables relating to achievement. (In the analysis of males and females together, sex was included as a sixteenth variable.) The achievement variables were of several types. First, there were those that could be considered indicative of one's overall position and success: education in years, income, occupation, and occupational mobility from first to last occupation. Occupation was coded using Duncan's socioeconomic index for occupations. An *occupational mobility* score was computed by subtracting Duncan's coded score on the first occupation from the score on the most recent occupation.

Second, there were those which give various kinds of indication of one's desires to achieve and strive: Rosen's (1959) achievement value scale and the Tausky and Dubin (1965) career-orientation anchorage scale. The achievement value score is derived from seven statements with which subjects must agree or disagree. A score of seven describes those who value achievement the most strongly.

The career-orientation anchorage scale was originally composed of six pairs of statements where the subject agreed with one alternative. The scale was reduced to four parts of items in this study since two of the pairs proved to be redundant in this sample. A score of four indicates that career anchorage is directed toward future accomplishments, and a score of zero represents anchorage at the beginning of a career (i.e., the person prefers to look at how far he has come over how far he has yet to go).

Third, there were those variables which have to do with one's potential for yet doing what must be done to meet life's goals: self-perception of health, age, several types of activity involvement, internal-external locus of control (Rotter, 1966), and feelings about time scarcity. To determine *self-perception of health* the self-anchoring ladder technique was utilized (Cantril, 1965). Subjects were asked to imagine that the top of the ladder represents perfect health and the bottom represents the most serious illness. Then they were asked where on the ladder their health is at the present time. Scores ranged from a low of zero to a high of nine.

Four measures of activity were utilized: (*a*) Productive activity refers to the number of hours in a week spent at a job, volunteer work, and home maintenance activities. Scores originally ranged from 0 to 87, but were transformed into deciles. (*b*) Organizational activity is the number of meetings (religious, club, union, or association) attended per month (range is 0 to 18). (*c*) Social contacts are the number of times per month one has contacts with close relatives, friends, neighbors, a confidant, or contacts with others through religious services, club, union, or association meetings (range is 0 to 120, but these were transformed into deciles). (*d*) Social activity is the number of hours per week spent at sports or hobbies, watching sports events in person, attending church or other meetings, doing volunteer work, visiting or telephoning friends and relatives, eating out, and entertaining (range is 0 to 63).

Internal-external locus of control was a score ranging from zero to eleven. Subjects were asked to agree with one or the other of eleven pairs of statements where one statement reflected a sense of internal control and the other a sense of external control. The higher the score the more external the locus of control.

Two questions pertaining to time scarcity were asked. One question used a week and the other life as the referent for one's feeling that he had more than enough, enough, or less than enough time to accomplish what he wished to do in that period of time. A score of three corresponded to having less than enough time, and a score of one to having more than enough.

The analyses reported here were performed on 296 of the 501 subjects. Those who fell in the middle ranges of both the discrepancy and ABS scores were deleted, as they would have served to blur the significance of the discriminating variables.

Results

Of the sixteen predictor variables the most significant discriminators for males and females together are (1) education, (2) health, (3) internal-external locus of control, (4) achievement value, and (5) occupational mobility.

Table 6–26. *Multiple discriminant function analyses for 296 males and females.*[a]

Variable entered	*F* at entry	Approximate *F*	Percent correctly grouped
Education	9.06**	9.06	25.0
Health	5.67**	7.34	35.8
Internal-external control	4.11**	6.28	37.9
Achievement value	2.45*	5.33	38.9
Occupational mobility	2.17*	4.71	40.0
Social contacts	1.39	4.16	37.9
Occupation	1.24	3.75	40.2
Time scarcity (week)	1.46	3.46	41.6
Income	.91	3.18	40.9
Social activity	.89	2.95	39.5
Time scarcity (life)	.89	2.76	41.6
Sex	.29	2.55	42.9
Organizational activity	.30	2.37	43.9
Age	.26	2.21	43.9
Productive activity	.39	2.08	42.9
Career anchorage	.10	1.96	43.9

[a] The variables are listed in the order in which they appeared in the stepwise discriminant function. "*F* at entry" refers to the *F* value for the variable at its entry into the function. "Approximate *F*" tests the equality of the group means for each variable.

** Significant at $< .01$ level.
* Significant at $< .10$ level.

The sixteen predictor variables together lead to 44 percent of the subjects being correctly placed in their groups (compared to 25 percent by chance). Looking at the patterning of these variables for each of the four self-concept types, the following characterization of each group emerges:

Table 6–27. *Mean values of first six variables entered in discriminant function analysis, by self-concept type (males and females).*

Variable	High discrepancy negative ABS	Low discrepancy positive ABS	High discrepancy positive ABS	Low discrepancy negative ABS
Education	12.00	11.73	12.78	8.25
Health	6.38	7.11	6.59	5.91
Internal-external control	5.11	3.90	4.26	4.17
Achievement value	4.68	4.46	4.96	3.46
Occupational mobility	8.17	4.60	4.04	5.33
Social contacts	3.94	4.57	4.60	4.00
	(N = 53)	(N = 127)	(N = 92)	(N = 24)

Conventional types. The subjects having a *high discrepancy* and *negative ABS* are relatively oriented toward achievement, have a higher than average education, and have experienced the most occupational mobility of any group. Yet health is perceived to be lower than two of the other groups, and these subjects perceived themselves as the most externally controlled of any group. Social contacts are also low. Hence, the subjects in this group have high aspirations and accomplishments, but they perceive themselves as having certain kinds of blockages to further desired attainments.

The other conventional pattern is the group with *low discrepancy* and *positive affect.* The individuals making up this group seem to have been able to meet the goals they have set for themselves. Educational attainments and achievement values are not as great as in the first two groups, but these individuals are well equipped with the resources to achieve what they wish to—excellent health, the second largest number of social contacts of any group, and a feeling of internal control.

Unconventional types. The unconventional types present an especially interesting picture. Those who experience a *high discrepancy* with a *positive ABS* score value achievement the most of any of the groups, suggesting that they have set high goals for themselves. Occupational mobility achieved, however, is comparatively low, perhaps suggesting a reason for the higher discrepancy between actual and ideal self. Yet the subjects in this group also seem to have more resources for doing well in the social environment—the highest education of any group, relatively high self-perception of health, and a high level of social contacts. They fall in the middle ranges of the internal-external control dimension. In essence, these persons seem not yet to be in the position that they would ideally like to be, but affect remains positive because chances for success at their goals still look good.

The individuals who experience both *a low discrepancy* and *negative affect* seem to be in an almost anomic state. Their aspirations seem to be extremely low, and they also have relatively fewer resources than any other group. Achievement values are the lowest of any group, although this may be related to the fact that education is also very low (M = 8.25 years). Health is the lowest and social contact the second lowest of any group. Also the income factor did not appear significant in the overall discriminant function analysis, but did seem to differentiate this group from the other three ($5,500 compared to incomes in the $9,000 range in the others). In essence, this group seems to have very few aspirations and also little in the way of resources for living comfortably. Strangely enough, these subjects are more internal in their sense of control—perhaps suggesting that self-blame is a factor in the low Affect Balance Score.

When females and males are analyzed separately, the order of entry into the discrimination is different. Education is the most important predictor for males, yet it has little significance for females. Health is the most important for females, yet it takes fourth position for males. The discriminators for

Table 6–28. *Multiple discriminant function analyses for 141 males.*

Variable entered	*F* at entry	Approximate *F*	Percent correctly grouped
Education	5.38***	5.38	32.6
Internal-external control	2.84**	4.07	29.1
Occupational mobility	2.95**	3.71	34.0
Health	2.43*	3.41	43.3
Time scarcity (life)	2.95**	3.34	50.4
Age	2.40*	3.21	48.2
Achievement value	1.96	3.04	53.2
Income	1.86	2.91	58.2
Social contacts	1.18	2.72	55.3
Social activity	1.15	2.56	54.7
Career anchorage	1.00	2.42	56.0
Occupation	.71	2.27	53.9
Time scarcity (week)	.36	2.11	52.5
Productive activity	.26	1.97	52.5
Organizational activity	.12	1.83	51.8

*** Significant at < .01 level.
** Significant at < .05 level.
* Significant at < .10 level.

males, taken together, represent more tangible measures of success-education, occupational mobility, and income, along with the perceptual variables of locus of control, health, and achievement value. Age is also important, whereas it has no significance for females. For females, after health, achieve-

Table 6–29. *Multiple discriminant function analyses for 154 females.*

Variable entered	*F* at entry	Approximate *F*	Percent correctly grouped
Health	5.65***	5.65	29.2
Achievement value	3.03***	4.31	34.4
Social activity	1.39	3.32	35.7
Time scarcity (week)	1.25	2.80	37.0
Productive activity	1.25	2.49	39.6
Social contacts	1.18	2.27	40.3
Career anchorage	1.13	2.11	41.6
Income	1.20	2.00	39.6
Internal-external control	1.04	1.89	46.8
Occupation	.76	1.78	44.2
Occupational mobility	.61	1.67	42.9
Organizational activity	.67	1.58	44.8
Education	.48	1.49	43.5
Age	.34	1.40	43.5
Time scarcity (life)	.10	1.30	44.8

*** Significant at < .01 level.
** Significant at < .05 level.
* Significant at < .10 level.

ment value is most important, followed by several activity variables. This may suggest that female resources can be viewed more in terms of health and opportunities for activity.

When males are analyzed separately and all fifteen predictor variables are considered, 51.8 percent of the males are correctly discriminated into their a priori self-concept type. However, the last seven variables appear to suppress correct discrimination, as 58.2 percent of the subjects are correctly discriminated at the time the eighth variable (income) is entered into the analysis. When females are analyzed separately, there is no gain in the percent correctly grouped (45).

Conclusions

To summarize, the implication of these findings seems to be the following: variables measuring achievement, orientation to achievement, and resources relating to possibilities for future achievement do seem to discriminate subjects into four self-concept types substantially better than would occur by chance. When males are analyzed separately the percent correctly discriminated is even greater. The most significant discriminating variables seem to form a pattern in relation to each self-concept type. Those with a high discrepancy and negative affect pattern yield a picture of persons with high aspirations, but few resources to attain them, while those with a low discrepancy and positive affect have only moderate aspirations and are well-equipped with resources to fulfill them. Those who have a high discrepancy and positive affect have high unmet aspirations, but also indicate important resources present for meeting goals, while those with a low discrepancy and negative affect have few goals and few resources.

Even though about half the subjects are left incorrectly placed by this analysis, the potential importance of looking at dimensions of achievement in relation to the self-concept is indicated. It is suggested that these factors might be taken into consideration in dealing with some of the inconsistencies and unexplained cases encountered in the controversy between the activity and disengagement theories of aging.

References

Anderson, H. E. Regression, discriminant analysis, and a standard notation for basic statistics. In R. B. Cattell (Ed.), *Handbook of multivariate experimental psychology*, Chicago: Rand McNally, 1966.

Atkinson, John W. Motivational determinants of risk-taking behavior, *Psychological Review*, 64 (November 1957):359–372.

Bradburn, Norman M. *The structure of psychological well-being*. Chicago: Aldine, 1969.

Bradburn, Norman M., and Caplovitz, David. *Reports on happiness.* Chicago: Aldine, 1965.

Buhler, Charlotte, and Massarik, Fred. *The Course of human life: A study of goals in the humanistic perspective.* New York: Springer, 1968.

Butler, Robert N. The life review: An interpretation of reminiscence in the aged. In Bernice Neugarten (Ed.), *Middle age and aging.* Chicago: University of Chicago Press, 1968, 486–496.

Cantril, Hadley. *The pattern of human concerns.* New Brunswick, N.J.: Rutgers University Press, 1965.

Erikson, Erik. *Identity and the life cycle: Selected papers,* published in *Psychological Issues* 1, (1959).

Frenkel-Brunswick, Else. Adjustments and reorientation in the course of the life span. In Neugarten (Ed.), *Middle age and aging.* 1968, pp. 77–84.

Kuhlen, Raymond G. Developmental changes in motivation during the adult years. In Neugarten (Ed.), *Middle age and aging.* 1968, pp. 115–136.

Neugarten, Bernice L. Adult personality: Toward a psychology of the life cycle. In Neugarten (Ed.), *Middle age and aging.* 1968, pp. 137–147.

Neugarten, Bernice. Personality and the aging process. *The Gerontologist,* 12:9–15, 1972.

Osgood, Charles E., and Suci, George J. Factor analysis of meaning, *Journal of Experimental Psychology,* 50:325–338, 1955.

Osgood, Charles E., Suci, George J., and Tannenbaum, Percy H. *The measurement of meaning.* Urbana: University of Illinois Press, 1957.

Overall, John E., and Klett, C. James. *Applied multivariate analysis.* New York: McGraw-Hill, 1972, chap. 10.

Reiss, Albert J., Duncan, Otis D., Hatt, Paul K., and North, Cecil C. *Occupations and social status.* New York: The Free Press, 1961.

Rotter, Julian B. Generalized expectancies for internal versus external control of reinforcement. *Psychological Monographs,* 80, 1966.

Rosen, Bernard. Race, ethnicity, and the achievement syndrome. *American Sociological Review,* 24:47–60, 1959.

Turner, Ralph H. The self-conception in social interaction. In Chad Gordon and Kenneth J. Gergen (Eds.), *The self in social interaction.* New York: Wiley, 1968, pp. 93–106.

Chapter 7. Leisure and Sexual Behavior

While leisure time generally increases with age, sexual activity generally decreases. This chapter contains three reports which deal with factors associated with these two opposite changes. The report on leisure finds that those in the Adaptation Study were more work oriented than leisure oriented, and the men in the 66–71 year age category seem to experience the most difficulty with unwanted leisure. Women, on the other hand, seem to experience more difficulty between the ages of 46–55 when they complain most of having too little leisure time.

The study of sexual behavior in middle life found that while there was an overall pattern of decline in interest and activity with advancing age, sex still continued to play an important role in the lives of most of the men and the majority of the women. The third article reports that sexual activity and interest among men is influenced mainly by past sexual experience, age, health factors, and social class; whereas women are more influenced by marital status, in addition to age and past enjoyment of sexual activity. The authors suggest that much of the decline in sexual interest among aging women is not physiologically based but is rather a defense against their lack of opportunity for sexual fulfillment.

The Use of Leisure Time in Middle Life   *Eric Pfeiffer and Glenn C. Davis*

Historically the use of leisure time has been the subject of scientific and philosophical discourse only at certain times and under special circumstances. Thus in the ancient world the use of one's free time was a matter of concern only to those who had free time and plenty of it; then only in times of peace or relative peace, that is, times in which wars were fought, but fought far from the hearth of the leisured. Then the question regarding leisure was somewhat as follows: How should a man of intellect and vision apply his time and effort toward his own and his fellow man's improvement, elevation, and ennoblement?

More recently, particularly in the twentieth century, an entirely new concern with regard to leisure time has become evident. Technological, economic, social, and political events have conspired to create unwanted leisure. Individuals previously unaccustomed to the luxury of free time have had free time

Reprinted by permission from the *Gerontologist,* 11:3:187–195, 1971.

thrust upon them. No longer was leisure regarded only as an opportunity for the elite, but also a potential problem, even a catastrophe, for the nonelite. A case in point was the widespread unemployment during the depression of the 1920s and the 1930s, particularly severe in the United States. Another is the current dilemma of the ever-increasing number of *aged* but still able individuals involuntarily retired from their work.

It is not our intention in this paper to systematically and critically review the considerable body of literature on leisure. The earlier studies referred to in this paper are cited only to give an indication of general directions taken by previous investigators. Any detailed discussion of their research methods and strategies of analysis is beyond the scope of the present communication, although the desirability of undertaking such a task is acknowledged.

It is of interest, then, to point out that each of the events cited above (the Great Depression, and the more recent expansion of the number of elderly) gave rise to a wave of scientific as well as popular studies of the uses and abuses of free time. Thus the studies of Lundberg, Komarovsky, and McInerny (1934) as well as those of Lynd and Lynd (1929, 1937) pioneered a systematic approach to leisure behavior. In their study of Westchester County, Lundberg et al. were the first to use time logs which detailed actual daily activities. These scientific studies contrast sharply with the popular literature of that time. The latter authors (Aiken, 1931; Cutten, 1926, 1933) saw leisure as a potential danger to the society, threatening to undermine the work ethic and thereby the entire fabric of the society.

In the 1950s and 1960s gerontologists concerned themselves with the problems created by the empty postretirement years. Michelon (1954) and Bell (1967) sought out the elderly in nursing homes and in trailer parks and studied social involvement in those communities. Clarke (1956) and White (1955) attempted to find determinants of leisure behavior in social class or occupational prestige. Kaplan (1960) studied the relationship between the value placed on leisure and job roles and job satisfaction. Kleemeier's (1961) edited volume provided a good summary of research on leisure in aging populations up to that time, and Meyersohn (1969) has recently published an important bibliography of the sociological literature on leisure up to 1965. DeGrazia (1964), Huizinga (1950), Larrabee and Meyersohn (1958), and Martin (1967) have published valuable treatises on leisure geared more to the general reader than to the research investigator.

The single most important force in the field of social gerontology and leisure in the last two decades has been Havighurst. In a series of studies (Havighurst 1954, 1957, 1961; Havighurst and DeVries, 1969) he and his associates focused attention not only on how people occupied their unobligated time but also on social and personality determinants of leisure behavior. Havighurst's 1957 study is of particular relevance to our own because it specifically dealt with leisure activities in middle life. Havighurst analyzed interviews with 124 women and 110 men aged 40 to 70 regarding the question of the subjects' two most favored leisure activities. He classified his subjects' activities into 11 content categories (e.g., participation in sports) and also rated each activity along 19 significance scales (e.g., enjoyment versus time-killer). He then examined the relationship between content categories and significance variables and between each of these and several important social and personality variables including sex, age, social class, personal adjustment, and social mobility. His most important conclusions were that even though content of leisure activity was most closely related to sex and social class, the significance of the activity to the individual was most closely related to personality factors. He also pointed out that differing leisure activities might have the same personal significance and that therefore an analysis of both type of leisure activity and meaningfulness of that activity was indicated.

Recently the Gerontological Society (1969) issued a report on research and development goals in social gerontology in which leisure was given prominent attention. The report suggests that research is needed on "representative samples of persons from middle age through extreme old age" in regard to their over-all life styles and with special reference to "the accommodation of free time within a life style;" research is needed on how people currently use their vacation; on how they mix work and recreation; and on how they make the transition from work to leisure.

The present study, although not directly influenced by the above report, lies within the outlines of the kind of research suggested by that report. In regard to leisure activities we were not so much concerned with questions such as "What should people do?" or "What should people not do?" but rather "What is it you actually do with your free time?" And while we are particularly interested in how the aged allocate their time, we are convinced that the behavior of old age cannot be understood without also examining its antecedents in middle age.

Subjects and Methods

Subjects for this study are 261 men and 241 women, aged 46 to 71 at the time of their examination.

Of the men, 98 percent were married, 1 percent was widowed, and 1 percent had never married. By contrast, only 71 percent of the women were married and living with their spouses, 18 percent were widowed, 5 percent had never married, and 6 percent were separated or divorced. Of the men, 81 percent were either employed or engaged in business, while only 49 percent of the women were employed (Table 7–1).

The data on leisure behavior were gathered by a trained interviewer as part of the social history. The interview dealt with three categories of leisure behavior: (a) a diarylike assessment of how time is typically spent by the

Table 7-1. *"Do you have a job or business at the present time?"* (*paid employment*).

Men (N = 261)	No (%)	Yes (%)
46–71	19	81
46–50	5	95
51–55	5	95
56–60	5	95
61–65	19	81
66–71	53	47
Women (N = 241)		
46–71	51	49
46–50	30	70
51–55	29	71
55–60	38	62
61–65	64	36
66–71	80	20

subject, (*b*) an assessment of vacation behavior, (*c*) attitudes toward and satisfactions derived from leisure activities.

All the results in the present communication are cross-sectional only. As such they do not indicate how individuals change over time. They only indicate how groups of persons of a given chronological age function in comparsion with groups of persons of a different age. However, the study is so designed that longitudinal data will become available eventually. Longitudinal as well as cross-sequential analyses, as described by Schaie and Strother (1968), can then be carried out.

Results

As indicated, the first series of questions sought to establish how much time subjects spent in a variety of activities during a typical week. Activities for which time estimates were obtained included work (including travel to work), subsistence time (eating, personal care), and a variety of free-time or recreational activities.

Total Amount of Time Accounted For

This diary-like accounting of time usage permitted an analysis of the total number of hours accounted for in a given week. There are 168 hours in a week. Assuming an average of 8 hours of sleep per day, there remain 112 waking hours to be accounted for. Subjects on average were able to account for 96 hours per week, leaving only 16 hours per week, or roughly 2 hours per day, unaccounted for. The number of hours accounted for per week varied widely between individuals, ranging from a low of 48 to a high of 151 hours

(SD = 19 hours). Perhaps not surprisingly, individuals who were employed generally were able to account for a larger number of hours than nonworking subjects (100 hours for employed men and women, but only 82 hours for non-employed men and 92 hours for nonemployed women).

Table 7–2 presents the mean number of hours spent per week by men and women on a variety of activities. Several of these deserve special comment. Work, including work-related travel, accounts for the largest single number of hours, 36.8 hours per week for men and 34.5 hours per week for women. This finding, while obviously expected, is the first piece of evidence toward a thesis which will be developed throughout this paper, that ours is a largely work oriented, not a leisure oriented, culture.

Table 7–2. *Mean hours spent/week.*

Activity	Men	Women
Eating	9.8	9.8
Personal care	7.7	8.4
Working	36.8	34.5
TV	11.6	13.2
Reading	8.3	9.0
Sport hobby	3.9	3.4
Sport in person	0.6	0.3
Church and meetings	2.3	2.9
Volunteer work	0.7	1.1
Socializing	4.8	7.2
Activity around house	5.7	3.6
Other (specified)	0.7	0.6
Just sitting around	3.3	2.6

The next largest amount of time is given over to watching TV and listening to the radio. It was the impression of our interviewers that TV rather than radio accounted for the vast majority of this time. Men spent an average of 11.6 hours, women 13.2 hours per week so engaged. Among women the amount of time devoted to TV and radio was significantly greater in the older age groups ($p < 0.001$); among men it was the same in all the age groups studied.

The amount of time spent in reading books and magazines was also considerable, amounting to 8.3 hours per week for men and 9.0 hours per week for women. Time spent reading was significantly greater ($p < 0.01$) in the older age groups.

Active participation in hobbies or sports accounted for only a small number of hours per week, 3.9 in men and 3.4 in women. Interestingly, 44 percent of the men and 52 percent of the women did not spend any time engaged in a hobby or sport. Similarly, personal attendance at sports events was not common; 68 percent of the men and 85 percent of the women did not attend at all. Among those who did attend, the time spent was about 2 hours per week, roughly the duration of most spectator sports events.

Data on church attendance in old age have been reviewed by Palmore (1969). One persistent idea in the literature has been religiosity increases with advancing age; another has been that patterns of religious attendance, once firmly established, remain relatively stable throughout life. Unfortunately our question regarding church attendance also included attendance at "other meetings," such as union meetings, etc. It was, however, the impression of our interviewers that the subjects gave responses primarily in terms of church attendance. In our panel average attendance was slightly lower among men than women (2.3 versus 2.9 hours per week) but attendance was not age-related.

A number of social planners in gerontology have suggested that volunteer work or volunteer service might be one of the major activities for the elderly after retirement. Our data would seem to indicate that this view should be advanced only with caution. Among the age group studied, volunteer work accounted for only a tiny fraction of their activities; 64 percent of men and 66 percent of women said they engaged in no volunteer work whatever. The rest spent between 1 and 2 hours a week engaged in volunteer work. This finding makes it seem unlikely that volunteer work could be made attractive for more than just a small portion of older subjects no longer engaged in remunerative work. We have quite another opinion in regard to paid service activities for those no longer regularly employed.

One of the major ways in which men and women differed from each other was in the amount of time spent socializing. This amounted to 4.8 hours per week for men but 7.2 hours per week for women. Age was not a factor in the amount of socializing done by men, but was age-related in women, more socializing being done by the older age groups ($p < 0.05$). Average amounts of time spent on yard care, gardening, and other activities around the house, including mending and sewing for women, is also indicated in Table 7–2. Age was not a significant factor in these activities.

Subjects were also given the opportunity to indicate other, nonlisted activities. Only 16 percent of men and 13 percent of the women listed any activities under this category, indicating that most of the activities were covered in the listed categories. Activities most prominently mentioned here were hunting, fishing, hiking, or other outdoor recreation.

Only a small proportion of subjects, 34 percent of men and 29 percent of women, admitted that they ever spent any time "just sitting around, doing nothing." This finding is the second piece of evidence in our developing thesis of a work orientation rather than a leisure orientation in our society.

Vacations

A second segment of our study of leisure behavior dealt with vacations. The most striking finding in regard to vacations was the relatively small amount of variation which existed in regard to vacation taking. Vacations seem to be a highly institutionalized, almost a mandatory, type of leisure behavior. Only

15 percent of men and 20 percent of women said they had not taken a formal vacation during the last year. The majority of subjects had taken vacations from 1 week's to 4 weeks' duration, with an average amount of 2.8 weeks per person, a figure identical for both men and women. Eighty-nine percent of the men and 94 percent of the women indicated they had traveled for pleasure during their vacations; the remaining few percentages were distributed between "taking it easy around the house" and "just working around the house." Not a single subject mentioned having spent time either in self-improvement activities or in volunteer activities during their vacation.

Amounts of money spent during vacation varied from less than $50 to more than $2,000, with the modal amount lying between $200–$500. Subjects were asked whether the money spent on their vacations was money well spent; 98 percent of the men and 99 percent of the women said it was. In summary, vacations are a relatively institutionalized form of leisure behavior. One is expected to and does take a trip. A certain amount of money is spent and it is expected that one regard the money spent as distinctly well applied.

Satisfactions Derived from Leisure Activities

The last segment of our study deals with the satisfactions derived from participation in leisure activities. This topic was approached in several different ways. The relevant findings in regard to these are presented in Table 7–3.

Subjects were asked whether they had too much, too little, or enough free time (Table 7–3), 71 percent of the men and 65 percent of the women said

Table 7–3. *"Are you satisfied with the amount of free time you have now, or do you feel you have too much free time or too little free time?"*

Men (N = 261) Age (%)	Satisfied	Too much free time (%)	Too little free time (%)
46–71	71	6	23
46–50	72	0	28
51–55	63	2	34
56–60	74	3	23
61–65	78	4	19
66–71	68	16	15
Women (N = 241)			
46–71	65	7	28
46–50	58	7	37
51–55	49	7	44
56–60	72	4	24
61–65	66	9	26
66–71	75	8	17

they were satisfied with the amount of free time they currently had available; 6 percent of the men and 7 percent of the women said they had too much free time; 23 percent of the men and 28 percent of the women complained that they had too little free time. Men in the 66 to 71 age group had the highest percentage, 16 percent, complaining of too much free time. Women in the 46 to 50 and in the 51 to 55 age categories had the highest percentage of subjects complaining of too little free time. These findings suggest that men tend to experience the years from 66 to 71 as particularly difficult psychologically while women tend to experience years from 46 to 55 as particularly difficult (see Discussion below).

Subjects were also asked whether their work or their leisure activities were more satisfying to them (Table 7–4). More than half indicated that

Table 7–4. *"What is more satisfying to you, your work or leisure activities?"*

Men (N = 215) Age	Both (%)	Work (%)	Leisure (%)
46–71	35	52	13
46–50	39	44	17
51–55	31	62	8
56–60	35	53	10
61–65	44	37	20
66–71	23	68	10
Women (N = 134)			
46–71	28	55	16
46–50	22	50	28
51–55	33	57	10
56–60	32	56	12
61–65	22	57	22
66–71	33	60	7

they derived greater satisfaction from their work than from their leisure activities (52 percent of men and 55 percent of women). The next largest proportion indicated that they derived equal satisfaction from both their work and their leisure; 35 percent of the men and 28 percent of the women. Only 13 percent of the men and 16 percent of the women indicated that they derived their greatest satisfaction from leisure activities. The data in Table 7–4 and also in Table 7–6 are confined to subjects who were employed at the time of the examination. To the degree that only a proportion of the subjects was working (see Table 7–1) the data in these two tables are not entirely representative of the over-all panel. However, we would cite these findings as further evidence of a work orientation.

Subjects were also asked: "When was the last time you really had fun?" Most subjects found this an intriguing question. The findings are presented in Table 7–5. Two-thirds of the men and two-thirds of the women said they had fun either within the last day or within the last week. But 16 percent of

Table 7–5. *"When was the last time you really had fun?"*

Age	Last Day (%)	Last Week (%)	Last Month (%)	"Months" or "Years" (%)	Don't Know (%)
Men (N = 261)					
46–71	42	25	12	16	8
46–50	40	30	14	16	0
51–55	34	29	10	15	12
56–60	56	20	7	15	3
61–65	33	24	17	22	4
66–71	43	22	13	13	10
Women (N = 241)					
46–71	30	34	16	16	5
46–50	26	33	26	14	2
51–55	29	32	17	20	2
56–60	36	34	16	12	2
61–65	34	28	9	21	9
66–71	25	40	15	13	7

men and 16 percent of women answered that it had been "months" or even "years" since they last had fun. These findings were not age-related. However, among men employment status was important; 77 percent of working men as against over 56 percent of nonworking men said they had had fun within the last week. This difference was significant at the .05 level. Employment status did not affect the response to this question among women.

Subjects were also asked: "If you did not actually have to work for a living, would you still work?"—90 percent of the men and 82 percent of the women said "Yes" (Table 7–6). Among men in the 66 to 71 age group, 97 percent said they would still work. This is the group containing the largest

Table 7–6. *"If you did not actually have to work for a living, would you still work?"*

Age	Yes (%)	No (%)
Men (N = 213)		
46–71	90	10
46–50	85	15
51–55	97	3
56–60	86	14
61–65	89	11
66–71	97	3
Women (N = 125)		
46–71	82	18
46–50	68	29
51–55	86	14
56–60	91	9
61–65	79	21
66–71	86	14

percentage of men no longer employed (compare Table 7-1). These findings are comparable to those of Morse and Weiss (1955) who found between 61 and 90 percent of men aged 21 to 65 plus would still work even if they had enough money (as from an inheritance).

The final question in this series sought a definition of leisure activity from the subjects themselves; 45 percent of the men and 37 percent of the women chose "anything that is relaxing" as their definition; 32 percent of the men and 33 percent of the women chose "anything that is fun," with less than 10 percent each choosing "anything you don't have to do," "free time," and "other" definitions. Among "others" the combination of "anything that is fun *and* relaxing" was the definition most commonly chosen.

From this it is clear that our subjects had rather pragmatic and down-to-earth definitions of leisure, definitions far removed from the lofty or "Arcadian" concept of leisure held by the aristocrats of the ancient world.

Discussion and Conclusions

The results of this study force upon us the conclusion that ours is a work oriented, not a leisure oriented, culture; at least in the age groups covered by this study. This conclusion is based on finding that the majority of our subjects would still work even if they did not have to; that they derived greater satisfaction from their work than from their leisure activities; that only a small percentage felt that they did not have enough free time; and that subjects who were employed or engaged in business had experienced fun more recently than nonworking subjects.

This conclusion has important public policy implications. Individuals now in their middle age will arrive in old age essentially unprepared for the meaningful utilization of large amounts of free time. In order to avoid serious degrees of dissatisfaction in old age our society must provide either more training for leisure in middle age, or more opportunity for continued employment in old age. Or, we must create a more even distribution of both work and leisure over the life-span. This idea has been discussed from an economic point of view by Kreps (1969). She points to some European countries in which a greater portion of life-time leisure is allocated to the working years than is the case in the United States. This is generally done in the form of a shorter work week and/or longer vacations.

Perhaps a combination of these two approaches, education for leisure and flexible retirement policies, might work best in the United States. One possible way of accomplishing this would be to increase vacation time after age 50 or 55 by 2 weeks each succeeding year. Part-time or part-year work might then be continued past the so-called retirement age to the extent an individual wished or was able to work. In the process, individuals might gradually learn to use increasing amounts of free time meaningfully and enjoyably.

It must be admitted that what has been said here in regard to the relationship between work and leisure applies primarily to men in our society, since men still function as the primary breadwinner in American families. However, the percentage of women employed outside the home is increasing, and some of the observed differences may be erased in time.

A few other differences between men and women in regard to leisure behavior deserve comment. Between the ages of 46 and 55 the percentage of women complaining of too little (free) time reaches a peak. This may be related to the fact that women who work outside the home (the percentage of women gainfully employed also reached a peak at this time—see Table 7–1) are still expected to work inside the home as well. Having a job does not relieve them of having to cook and keep house. That this seems to be a difficult period for women generally is apparent from other sources: reproductive capacity ends; children grow up and move away; depression and suicide among women reach their highest peak in this age group (Busse and Pfeiffer, 1969).

Men, on the other hand, at least in the age groups covered by this study, seem to experience their most difficult time in the 66- to 71-years category. In this group the percentage of men complaining of too much free time reaches a peak, at the same time the percentage of men still gainfully employed drops sharply. This is also the time of life in which, again according to unrelated studies (Busse and Pfeiffer, 1969), the rates of suicide and of depression are highest among men.

In our discussion we have come a long way from considering the delights of spending one's free time as one sees fit to the self-willed deaths of despairing men. Many other factors, other than the style of leisure-time usage, enter into the nature of adaptation to old age, and the last few remarks may seem to be overdrawn. However, Eisdorfer in his 1969 Kleemeier Lecture (1970) admonishes us to build bridges between research findings and clinical phenomena. Future research may well discard any such connection. However, the attempt to link up diverse events occuring at the same stage of the life cycle seems worth making.

References

Aiken, R. A laborer's leisure. *North American Review*, 232:268–273, 1931.
Bell, T. The relationship between social involvement and feeling among old residents in homes for the aged. *Journal of Gerontology*, 22:17–22, 1967.
Busse, E. W., and Pfeiffer, E. Functional psychiatric disorders in old age. In E. W. Busse and E. Pfeiffer (Eds.), *Behavior and adaptation in late life*. Boston: Little, Brown & Co., 1969.
Clarke, A. C. Leisure and levels of occupational prestige. *American Sociological Review*, 21:301–307, 1956.
Cutten, G. B. *The threat of leisure*. New Haven, Conn.: Yale University Press, 1926.
Cutten, G. B. *The challenge of leisure*. Columbus: American Education Press, 1933.
DeGrazia, S. *Of time, work and leisure*. Garden City, N.Y.: Doubleday, 1964.

Eisdorfer, C. On the issue of relevance in research. *Gerontologist,* 10 (No. 1, Pt. 1): 5–10, 1970.

Gerontological Society Committee on Research and Development Goals in Social Gerontology. Work, leisure, and education: toward the goal of creating flexible life styles. *Gerontology,* 9 (No. 4, Pt. 11): 17–35, 1969.

Havighurst, R. J. Flexibility and the social roles of the retired. *American Journal of Sociology,* 5:309–311, 1954.

Havighurst, R. J. The leisure activities of the middle aged. *American Journal of Sociology,* 63:152–162, 1957.

Havighurst, R. J. The nature and values of meaningful free-time activity. In R. W. Kleemeier (Ed.), *Aging and leisure.* New York: Oxford University Press, 1961.

Havighurst, R. J. and DeVries, A. Life styles and free time activities of retired men. *Human Development,* 12:34–54, 1969.

Huizinga, J. *Homo Ludens.* New York: Roy Publications, 1950.

Kaplan, M. *Leisure in America: A social inquiry.* New York: Wiley & Sons, 1960.

Kleemeier, R. W. (Ed.). *Aging and leisure.* New York: Oxford University Press, 1961.

Kreps, J. M. Economics of retirement. In Busse and Pfeiffer (Eds.), *Behavior and adaptation in late life.* 1969.

Larrabee, E., and Meyersohn, R. *Mass leisure.* Glencoe, Ill.: Free Press, 1958.

Lundberg, G. A., Komarovsky, M., and McInerny, M. A. *Leisure: A surburban study.* New York: Columbia University Press, 1934.

Lynd, R. S., and Lynd, H. M. *Middletown.* New York: Harcourt Brace & Co., 1929.

Lynd, R. S., and Lynd, H. M. *Middletown in transition.* New York: Harcourt Brace & Co., 1937.

Martin, P. *Leisure and mental health.* Washington: American Psychiatric Assn., 1967.

Meyersohn, R. The sociology of leisure in the United States: Introduction and bibliography, 1945–1965. *Journal of Leisure Research,* 1:53–68, 1969.

Michelon, L. C. The new leisure class. *American Journal of Sociology,* 59:371–378, 1954.

Morse, N. C., and Weiss, R. S. The function and meaning of work and the job. *American Sociological Review,* 20:191–198, 1955.

Palmore, E. Sociological aspects of aging. In Busse and Pfeiffer (Eds.), *Behavior and adaptation in late life.* 1969.

Schaie, K. W., and Strother, C. R. A cross-sequential study of age changes in cognitive behavior. *Psychological Bulletin,* 70:671–680, 1968.

White, R. C. Social class differences in the uses of leisure. *American Journal of Sociology,* 61:145–150, 1955.

Sexual Behavior in Middle Life *Eric Pfeiffer, Adriaan Verwoerdt, and Glenn C. Davis*

We have previously reported data on sexual behavior in old age (Pfeiffer et al., 1968; Pfeiffer et al., 1969; Verwoerdt et al., 1969; Verwoerdt et al., 1969; Pfeiffer, 1969). In these studies, 271 subjects aged 60 to 94 were initially interviewed, and the survivors were interviewed repeatedly at two-

Reprinted by permission from the *American Journal of Psychiatry,* 128:10:1262–1267, 1972. Copyright 1972, the American Psychiatric Association.

to three-year intervals for at least ten years. Cross-sectional as well as longitudinal analyses were carried out.

To date the most important findings have been the following: (1) elderly men in the sample differed markedly from elderly women in reported sexual behavior; (2) the intensity, presence, or absence of sexual interest and activity among elderly women was primarily a reflection of the availability of a socially sanctioned, sexually capable partner; (3) with advancing age, patterns of declining sexual activity and interest were common, but patterns of stable, as well as of increasing, sexual activity also occurred; and (4) when both husband and wife were available for study, a high level of congruence between the reports of the two partners was observed, suggesting that sexual behavior was being reliably reported.

The past studies, however, not only answered some questions but also raised a number of new ones. What were the antecedents of sexual behavior in old age? Did male-female differences in reported sexual behavior exist in middle age as well? At what age was a decline in sexual function noted most commonly, and was this age the same for men and for women? Were there factors in middle age that could account for the striking differences between men and women in regard to sexual behavior in old age? The present study was undertaken in an attempt to answer some of these questions. . . .

Subjects

Of the 261 men, 257 were married (98 percent). Two were widowed (1 percent) and two had never married (1 percent). By contrast, 170 of the 241 women were married (71 percent). Forty-four were widowed (18 percent), 13 had never married (5 percent), and 14 were separated or divorced (6 percent).

Method

The data on sexual behavior were gathered as part of a self-administered medical history questionnaire. The questions were similar to those used in the earlier studies. However, this information had previously been gathered during a face-to-face structured interview. This method yielded only incomplete data due to embarrassment about the questions on the part of either the subjects or the interviewers. The data were especially sparse on the current sexual behavior of women who had never married or who were widowed, separated, or divorced. It was hoped that use of the more impersonal paper-and-pencil technique would decrease this embarrassment and thereby increase the yield of data. This was in fact so.

Data were generally far more complete on widowed, separated, and divorced women; however, the 13 women who had never married still provided virtually no data on either current or earlier sexual interest and/or activity. Responses to questions on sexual behavior were given by 250–256 of the 261 men in the sample and by 219–229 of the 241 women.

Table 7–7. *Age-sex cohorts.*

Age group	Men	Women
46–50	43	43
51–55	41	41
56–60	61	50
61–65	54	47
66–71	62	60
Total	261	241

The areas of sexual behavior covered in the study were as follows (possible choices are indicated in parentheses):

1. Enjoyment of sexual relations in younger years (none, mild, moderate, strong).

2. Enjoyment of sexual relations at the present time (none, mild, moderate, strong).

3. Sexual feelings in younger years (absent, weak, moderate, strong).

4. Sexual feelings at the present time (absent, weak, moderate, strong).

5. Frequency of sexual relations in younger years (never, once a month, once a week, two to three times a week, more than three times a week).

6. Frequency of sexual relations at the present time (never, once a month, once a week, two to three times a week, more than three times a week).

7. Awareness of any decline in sexual interest or activity (yes, no); if yes, at what age was it first noted (five-year age groupings).

8. If sexual relations have stopped, when were they stopped? (still continuing, less than a year ago, one to two years ago, two to five years ago, six to ten years ago, 11–20 years ago, more than 20 years ago).

9. Reason for stopping sexual relations (not stopped, death of spouse, illness of self, illness of spouse, self lost interest, spouse lost interest, self no longer able to perform sexually, spouse not able to perform sexually, separated or divorced from spouse).

All the results reported in this paper are cross-sectional only. Thus they do not indicate how individuals change over time. They only indicate how groups of persons of a given chronological age function in comparison with groups of persons of a different age. However, the study is so designed that longitudinal data will eventually become available. Longitudinal as well as cross-sequential analyses, as described by Schaie and Strother (Schaie et al., 1968), can then be carried out.

Results

A great deal of interest centers on the current level of sexual interest and activity of men and women at different ages. The basic data in regard to these two variables are presented in Tables 7–8 and 7–9.

Current Level of Sexual Interest

Only six percent of the men in the sample said they no longer had any sexual feelings. On the other hand, strong current sexual interest was indicated by 12 percent. While there is, as Table 7–8 shows, a decline in cur-

Table 7–8. *Current level of sexual interest, in percentages.*

Group	Number	None	Mild	Moderate	Strong
Men					
46–50	43	0	9	63	28
51–55	41	0	19	71	10
56–60	61	5	26	57	12
61–65	54	11	37	48	4
66–71	62	10	32	48	10
Total	261	6	26	56	12
Women					
46–50	43	7	23	61	9
51–55	41	20	24	51	5
56–60	48	31	25	44	0
61–65	43	51	37	12	0
66–71	54	50	26	22	2
Total	229	33	27	37	3

rent interest in each of the age brackets from 45 to 65 years of age, there is actually a small rise in interest in sex in the oldest age category. This suggests that individuals who survive into their late 60s and early 70s may constitute an elite group, their weaker brothers having succumbed at an earlier age (Pfeiffer et al., 1969; Pfeiffer, 1970). We have already pointed out previously that decline is not the only pattern in evidence when sexual behavior is followed longitudinally. Steady or even increased performance has been noted (Pfeiffer et at., 1969; Verwoerdt et al., 1969).

Among the women, a similar pattern of declining interest was shown. However, the percentage of women indicating no sexual interest was higher than that among men in all the age categories; the percentage indicating strong sexual interest was lower than that among men in all the age categories. As with men, the percentage of women indicating moderate or strong sexual interest was higher in the oldest age category than in the next-to-the-oldest category, suggesting again that the oldest group constitutes a group of elite survivors.

Table 7–9. *Current frequency of sexual intercourse, in percentages.*

Group	Number	None	Once a month	Once a week	2–3 times a week	More than 3 times a week
Men						
46–50	43	0	5	62	26	7
51–55	41	5	29	49	17	0
56–60	61	7	38	44	11	0
61–65	54	20	43	30	7	0
66–71	62	24	48	26	2	0
Total	261	12	34	41	12	1
Women						
46–50	43	14	26	39	21	0
51–55	41	20	41	32	5	2
56–60	48	42	27	25	4	2
61–65	44	61	29	5	5	0
66–71	55	73	16	11	0	0
Total	231	44	27	22	6	1

Overall, however, the data clearly indicate a pattern of decline in sexual interest from the younger to the older age categories for both men and women ($p < .001$).

Current Frequency of Sexual Intercourse

Only 12 percent of the men in the sample said they no longer had any sexual relations. None in the group aged 46–50 but 24 percent in the group aged 66–71 gave this reply, with a stepwise increase in this percentage with increasing age. In the same direction, the higher frequencies of sexual relations (two to three times a week and more than three times a week) were checked less and less frequently by the older age groups. Interestingly, sexual activity showed no increase in the oldest age category compared with the next-to-the-oldest category (see Table 7–9). This widening interest-activity gap, as we have called it, has already been described previously for elderly men (Pfeiffer et al., 1969).

Among the women a similar pattern of declining sexual activity obtained. The frequency of sexual relations was lower for women than for men in all age categories. There was no increase in sexual activity in the oldest age group in comparison with the next-to-the-oldest age group.

For both men and women, the data showed a significant decline in sexual activity with increasing age ($p < .001$).

Awareness of Decline in Sexual Interest and Activity

A question concerning the subjects' own awareness of decline in sexual interest and activity was not included in the previous studies. However, this question suggested itself on the basis of the previous studies. It demands of the subjects a longitudinal assessment of their own sexual behavior. One of us (E. P.) has previously pointed out the superiority of such longitudinal assessments over single-point-in-time assessments (Pfeiffer, 1970). Thus a "change in health status" question was a more powerful predictor of longevity than a "current health status" question.

The results in regard to an awareness of decline are presented in Table 7–10. In the youngest age group, 51 of the men reported no decline in sexual

Table 7–10. *Awareness of decline in sexual interest and activity.*

Group	Men		Women	
	Number	No decline (percent)	Number	No decline (percent)
46–50	43	51	43	42
51–55	41	29	41	22
56–60	61	28	48	21
61–65	54	11	43	12
66–71	61	12	54	4
Total	260	25	229	19

activity or interest up to that time. But this percentage dwindled in stepwise fashion for each succeeding age group. However, even in the oldest group, 12 percent still averred no decline. The sharpest drop in the proportion reporting no awareness of decline occurred between the group aged 46–50 and the 51–55 groups.

Age of Cessation of Sexual Intercourse

Only 36 men but 97 of the women in the sample indicated that they had stopped having sexual relations. They gave a wide scattering of responses as to when they had stopped. This ranged from "within the last year" (eight men and four women) to "more than 20 years ago" (one man and eight women). Not only did a larger proportion of women than of men indicate that they had stopped having sexual relations, but a greater proportion of the women than of the men who had stopped indicated that they had done so more than five years ago (62 out of 97 women, or 64 percent; 12 out of 36 men, or 33 percent). A partial explanation of why more women than men have stopped relations, and why they have done so at an earlier age, becomes apparent when the reasons for stopping are examined for men and women respectively.

Reasons for Stopping Sexual Intercourse

Thirty-five men and 97 women gave reasons why they had ceased to have sexual relations. The results are shown in Table 7–11. These reasons can be grouped according to whether the subject attributes responsibility for cessation to himself (herself) or to his (her) spouse. These groupings are presented in Table 7–12. As can be seen, women overwhelmingly attributed re-

Table 7–11. *Reasons for cessation of sexual relations.*

Reason	Men		Women	
	Number	Percent	Number	Percent
Death of spouse	0	—	35	36
Separation or divorce from spouse	0	—	12	12
Illness of spouse	5	14	19	20
Loss of interest by spouse	3	9	4	4
Spouse unable to perform sexually	2	6	17	18
Illness of self	6	17	2	2
Loss of interest by self	5	14	4	4
Self unable to perform sexually	14	40	4	4
Total	35		97	

sponsibility for stopping to their husbands, while men generally attributed the responsibility to themselves ($p < .001$). This study thus confirms our earlier finding that in a marriage it is generally the man who determines whether sexual relations continue or cease (Pfeiffer et al., 1968). While "death of

Table 7–12. *Responsibility for cessation of sexual relations.*

Responsibility	Men		Women	
	Number	Percent	Number	Percent
All reasons included				
Attributed to spouse	10	29	87	90
Attributed to self	25	71	10	10
Total	35		97	
Loss of spouse excluded				
Attributed to spouse	10	29	40	80
Attributed to self	25	71	10	20
Total	35		50	

spouse" accounts for the largest number of women who attribute responsibility for cessation to their spouse (35 out of 97), the general finding that men blame themselves and women blame their husbands still holds up even after "death of spouse" and "separation from spouse" are removed from the analysis ($p < .001$).

Summary

We have previously reported data on sexual behavior in old age. These findings made it clear that the aging processes were not confined to persons beyond age 65; instead many of the changes observed in old age had their antecedents in middle age. The present study was undertaken to examine some of these antecedents.

Data on sexual behavior were gathered on 261 white men and 241 white women aged 45 to 69. The subjects were chosen randomly from the membership lists of the local medical group insurance plan. They were thus broadly representative of the middle and upper socioeconomic strata of the community.

Dramatic differences between men and women of like age were observed in regard to virtually all indicators of sexual behavior, with the men generally reporting greater interest and activity than the women. While there was an overall pattern of decline in interest and activity with advancing age, it was also clear that sex still continued to play an important role in the lives of the vast majority of the subjects studied. Only 6 percent of the men and 33 percent of the women said they were no longer interested in sex. Only 12 percent of the men and 44 percent of the women said they no longer had sexual relations. Interestingly, the oldest age group indicated higher levels of sexual involvement than did the next-to-the-oldest age group. This suggests that this oldest group actually constituted a group of elite survivors from whose midst less highly advantaged individuals had already been removed.

By age 50, some 49 percent of the men and 58 percent of the women admitted they had noted some decline in their sexual interest and activity. By age 70, 88 percent of the men and 96 percent of the women admitted an awareness of such a decline. The sharpest increase in the percentage of those admitting awareness of a decline occurred between the 45–50 group and the 51–55 group.

Some 14 percent of the men and 40 percent of the women indicated that they had stopped having sexual relations and offered reasons for having done so. The present study confirmed our previous finding that women overwhelmingly attribute responsibility for cessation of sexual relations to their husbands, while men generally hold themselves responsible for cessation.

References

Pfeiffer, E. Sexual behavior in old age. In Busse, E. W., and Pfeiffer, E. (Eds.), *Behavior and adaptation in late life.* Boston: Little, Brown and Co., 1969, pp. 151–162.

Pfeiffer, E. Survival in old age: Physical, psychological and social correlates of longevity. *J. Amer. Geriat. Soc.,* 18:273–285, 1970.

Pfeiffer, E. and Davis, G. C. The use of leisure time in middle life. *The Gerontologist,* 11:187–195, 1971.

Pfeiffer, E., Verwoerdt, A., and Wang, H. S. The natural history of sexual behavior in a biologically advantaged group of aged individuals. *J. Geront.,* 24:193–198, 1969.

Pfeiffer, E., Verwoerdt, A., and Wang, H. S. Sexual behavior in aged men and women. I: observations on 254 community volunteers. *Arch. Gen. Psychiat.,* 19:753–758, 1968.

Schaie, K. W., and Strother, C. R. A cross-sequential study of age changes in cognitive behavior. *Psychol. Bull.*, 70:671–680, 1968.
Verwoerdt, A., Pfeiffer, E., and Wang, H. S. Sexual behavior in senescence. *Geriatrics*, 24:137–154, 1969.
Verwoerdt, A., Pfeiffer, E., and Wang, H. S. Sexual behavior in senescence—changes in sexual activity and interest of aging men and women. *J. Geriat. Psychiat.*, 2:163–180, 1969.

Determinants of Sexual Behavior in Middle and Old Age
Eric Pfeiffer and Glenn C. Davis

Only in the last twenty-five years have investigators focused systematic attention on sexual behavior in old age. In fact, the studies by Kinsey and associates (Kinsey et al., 1948; Kinsey et al., 1953) in the late 1940s and early 1950s established this area of behavior as a legitimate field for scientific inquiry. Masters and Johnson (Masters et al., 1966; Masters et al., 1970) broke new ground with their detailed studies of the physiology of human sexual responses, studies which appropriately included a number of subjects above age 60. More recently, investigators at Duke University, including the senior author, have published their findings regarding sexual behavior in old age. In these latter studies, data on sexual behavior were obtained as part of a larger research strategy seeking to identify the psychologic, social, and physical determinants of adaptation in late life (Newman et al., 1960; Pfeiffer et al., 1968; Pfeiffer et al., 1969; Verwoerdt et al., 1969; Verwoerdt et al., 1969; Pfeiffer, 1969). These studies indicated that sex continued to play an important role in the lives of many elderly persons. Elderly men were found to differ markedly from women of like age in reported sexual behavior. Notably, levels of sexual interest and activity among elderly women principally reflect the availability of a socially sanctioned, sexually capable partner. Although with advancing age there was a tendency for declining sexual activity and interest, longitudinal studies demonstrated that stable patterns as well as patterns of increasing sexual interest and activity also occurred in old age.

These past studies answered some old questions, but they also raised a number of new ones. What are the middle-age antecedents of sexual behavior in old age? Do male-female differences in reported sexual behavior already exist in middle age? At what age is decline in sexual function noted most commonly? Is this age the same for men and for women? Partial answers to these questions are provided in a recent publication growing out of

Reprinted by permission from *Journal of the American Geriatrics Society*, 20:4:151–158, 1972.

this same study (Pfeiffer et al., 1972). The present communication is principally concerned with the following question: What are the multiple determinants of sexual behavior in middle and late life, and for how much of the variance in sexual behavior does each of these factors account?

Materials and Methods

Subjects

The subjects were 502 persons (261 white men and 241 white women) in the 45–69 age group. . . . Of the 261 men, 257 were married (98 percent), 2 were widowed (1 percent) and 2 had never married (1 percent). By contrast, 170 of the 241 women were married (71 percent), 44 were widowed (18 percent), 13 had never married (5 percent), and 14 were separated or divorced (6 percent).

Methods

The data on sexual behavior were gathered as part of a self-administered medical history questionnaire. Areas of sexual behavior covered in the study were as follows (possible choices are indicated in parenthesis):

1) Enjoyment of sex relations in younger years (none, mild, moderate, very much).

2) Enjoyment of sex relations at present time (none, mild, moderate, very much).

3) Sexual feelings in younger years (absent, weak, moderate, strong).

4) Sexual feelings at present time (absent, weak, moderate, strong).

5) Frequency of sex relations in younger years (never, once per month, once a week, up to three times a week, more than three times a week).

6) Frequency of sex relations at present time (never, once per month, once a week, up to three times a week, more than three times a week).

7) Awareness of any decline in sexual interest or activity (yes, no). If yes, at what age first noted? (5-year age brackets).

8) If sex relations stopped, when stopped? (still have, less than year ago, 1–2 years ago, 2–5 years ago, 6–10 years ago, 11–20 years ago, more than 20 years ago).

9) Reason for stopping sex relations (not stopped, death of spouse, illness of self, illness of spouse, self lost interest, spouse lost interest, self no longer able to perform sexually, spouse not able to perform sexually, separation or divorced from spouse).

For purposes of this paper, stepwise multiple regression analysis was the principal tool used. Multiple regression analysis is a method which permits the simultaneous handling of many variables in order to isolate the effect of each factor adjusted for the presence of the remaining factors. This type of analysis permits an estimate of the independent contribution of each factor to the observed variance in the dependent variable—in this case, to the variance in sexual behavior. Three measures of current sexual functioning were used as dependent variables: level of current sexual interest, current frequency of sex relations, and current enjoyment derived from sexual relations (questions 2, 4, and 6 above). A list of the most significant independent variables used, along with the zero order correlated obtained, appears in Table 7–13. Additional variables used, but not included in Table 7–13, were the subjective health rating of the person at various ages (by decades); the expressed concern over the findings of the physical examination; alcohol and

Table 7–13. *Independent variables and zero-order correlations.*

	Present enjoyment	Present interest	Present frequency
Sex	−.40	−.34	−.30
Age	−.34	−.35	−.46
Education	.13	.14	.03
Income	.38	.36	.32
Employed	.30	.30	.26
Social class	.09	.08	.01
Past sexual enjoyment	.52	.45	.34
Past sexual interest	.39	.44	.31
Past sexual frequency	.27	.29	.41
Subjective health rating now	.16	.20	.15
Subjective health rating 5 yrs. ago	.14	.13	.11
Subjective health rating 5 yrs. from now	.12	.18	.13
Objective physical function rating (PFR)	.18	.20	.19
Life satisfaction now	.14	.12	.18
Life satisfaction 5 yrs. ago	.10	.09	.12
Life satisfaction 5 yrs. from now	.12	.14	.15

tobacco use; and the regular use of a variety of medications, including amphetamines, tranquilizers, sleeping pills, appetite suppressants, analgesics, and sex hormones (women only).

Results

From the previous studies we had had indications that a number of major demographic variables—in particular age, sex, marital status (among women), and previous sexual experience—had considerable effect on the degree of sexual interest and activity. In addition, health factors have been suggested as contributing to the variance in sexual behavior in late life (Kinsey et al., 1948; Kinsey et al., 1953; Masters et al., 1966; Masters et al., 1970; Newman et al., 1960; Finkle, 1967; Peberdy, 1967; Post, 1967).

The results of a stepwide multiple regression analysis, using present enjoyment, present sexual interest, and present frequency of intercourse as dependent variables, are presented in Table 7–14. Both men and women

Table 7-14. *Multiple regression analysis re sexual activity for men and women—past sexual experience included.*

Present enjoyment			Present interest			Present frequency		
variable	multiple R	F value	variable	multiple R	F value	variable	multiple R	F value
Past enjoyment	.52	162.63	Past enjoyment	.45	108.40	Age	.45	106.87
Sex	.58	42.42	Age	.52	43.46	Past frequency	.57	78.20
Age	.65	57.89	Sex	.58	40.42	Sex	.63	54.95
Past interest	.66	12.75	Past interest	.61	19.36	Income	.65	12.45
Amphetamines	.66	4.73	Tranquilizers	.62	12.30	PFR	.65	3.91
PFR	.67	4.05	Social class	.63	11.66	Tranquilizers	.65	2.46
			Income	.64	5.36			
			Past frequency	.64	3.83			
			PFR	.65	3.39			
			Antihypertensive Rx	.65	2.49			
45% variance explained			42% variance explained			42% variance explained		

were included in this and in the next analysis in order to be able to use the sex of the subject as an independent variable. From the table it is apparent that the most important factors independently contributing to the variance in sexual behavior in the age range studied are past sexual experiences (positively correlated), age (negatively correlated) and the sex of the individual (maleness was positively correlated). Listed in the table are multiple-*R* values; each increment in the multiple *R* indicates the extent of variation contributed independently by each factor. Additional factors which significantly contribute to the variance in the dependent variables include income (positively correlated), social class (positively correlated), and an objective physical function rating (PFR) (positively correlated). All the factors listed as significantly contributing to the variance in observed sexual behavior together account for 42 to 45 percent of the total variance in sexual behavior.

Since it was apparent that previous sexual experience made a major independent contribution to present sexual behavior, previous sexual experience was eliminated as an independent variable in the next analysis. It was hoped that this procedure would allow a number of other variables to come to the foreground that had previously been overshadowed by the magnitude of the contribution made by previous sexual experiences. The results are presented in Table 7–15. Sex and age continued to be important factors, but the individual's subjective assessment of present health status, past health status, and expectation of future life satisfaction, now became prominent as contributors to the total variance. Without past sexual experience as an independent variable, the total multiple *R* only reached .60, explaining from 32 to 36 percent of the total variance.

In Tables 7–16 and 7–17 are presented the results of multiple regression analyses for men and women separately. Except for the elimination of the sex of the subject, the independent variables used were largely the same as in Table 7–15, with the addition of marital status, menopausal status, and sex hormone usage for women. Some interesting differences between men and women emerged. Among the men a sizable number of factors contributed independently to current sexual functioning: age (negatively), present health status (positively), social class (positively), taking of antihypertensive medication (negatively), present life satisfaction (positively), physical function rating (negatively), and excessive concern over physical examination findings (negatively), among others. Among the women, a much smaller number of factors made significant independent contributions to present sexual functioning. They were principally marital status (intact marriages were positively correlated) and age (negatively correlated). Small contributions were made by the educational level (positively correlated), by being employed (positively correlated), and by being post menopausal (negatively correlated). However, the smaller number of significant variables among the women explained a greater percentage of the total variance in sexual functioning than did the larger number of significant variables among the men (up to 44 percent of

Table 7-15. *Multiple regression analysis re sexual activity for men and women—past sexual experience excluded.*

Sexual enjoyment			Sexual interest			Frequency of intercourse		
variable	multiple R	F value	variable	multiple R	F value	variable	multiple R	F value
Sex	.40	76.50	Income	.36	4.88	Age	.48	100.26
Age	.54	53.99	Sex	.44	46.91	Sex	.56	49.50
Present health	.57	5.10	Age	.52	50.10	Future life satisfaction	.57	8.39
Income	.59	5.17	Present health	.54	3.30	Health, 0–10 yrs.	.58	3.67
Health, 21–30 yrs.	.59	4.25	Tranquilizers	.55	6.48	Income	.59	3.35
Social class	.60	3.31	Health, 10–20 yrs.	.56	5.44			
			Social class	.57	2.60			
36% variance explained			32% variance explained			34% variance explained		

Table 7-16. *Regression analysis re sexual activity—men only—past sexual experience excluded.*

Sexual enjoyment			Sexual interest			Frequency of intercourse		
variable	multiple R	F value	variable	multiple R	F value	variable	multiple R	F value
Age	.33	37.88	Age	.33	35.44	Age	.51	68.00
Present health	.41	8.77	Present health	.46	8.81	Future life satisfaction	.52	5.30
Social class	.43	5.59	Tranquilizers	.48	4.96	PFR	.53	2.36
Antihypertensive Rx	.45	5.61	Social class	.49	5.13			
Present life satisfaction	.47	5.63	Concern re physical exam.	.50	3.62			
Health, 21–30 yrs.	.48	2.64	Health, 11–20 yrs.	.51	3.37			
Sleeping pills	.49	2.76						
Concern re physical exam.	.50	2.55						
25% variance explained			26% variance explained			28% variance explained		

Table 7-17. *Regression analysis re sexual activity—women only—past sexual experience excluded.*

Sexual enjoyment			Sexual interest			Frequency of intercourse		
variable	multiple R	F value	variable	multiple R	F value	variable	multiple R	F value
Marital status	.54	35.37	Marital status	.57	41.64	Marital status	.58	52.60
Age	.61	20.48	Age	.60	3.38	Age	.64	12.40
Education	.62	3.81	Education	.61	3.87	Future life satisfaction	.65	4.26
			Post-menopause	.62	4.09	Post-menopause	.66	3.00
			Employment status	.62	2.76			
38% variance explained			38% variance explained			44% variance explained		

variance explained for women, up to 28 percent of variance explained for men).

The contribution of past sexual experience to present sexual functioning was assessed separately for men and women (Table 7–18). Again, some interesting differences between men and women were observed. Whereas for men all three indicators of early life sexual functioning (past sexual enjoyment, past interest, and past frequency) were highly correlated with present sexual interest and activities, for women past sexual enjoyment was most highly correlated with continued current sexual functioning.

Table 7–18. *Past sexual behavior—multiple regression analysis.*

Males N = 261 Present sexual enjoyment			Females N = 227 Present sexual enjoyment		
	multiple R	*F value*		*multiple R*	*F value*
Past enjoyment	.38	44.54	Past enjoyment	.47	65.14
Present sexual interest			*Present sexual interest*		
Past interest	.32	16.96	Past enjoyment	.43	17.59
Past frequency	.34	5.61	Past interest	.45	3.19
Present frequency of intercourse			*Present frequency of intercourse*		
Past frequency	.39	46.39	Past frequency	.36	18.03
			Past enjoyment	.42	11.65

Discussion

Over two decades ago Kinsey wrote that it was impossible at that time to speculate how much the decline in sexual frequency with age was due to physiologic, psychologic, or social factors (Kinsey et al., 1948). The present study was aimed precisely at that issue, that is, to identify the various determinants of sexual behavior in middle and old age.

A number of investigators (Kinsey et al., 1948; Kinsey et al., 1953; Masters et al., 1966; Masters et al., 1970; Newman et al., 1960; Post, 1967) have suggested that continued sexual activity in older age groups is dependent upon previous sexual behavior and experience. Our analyses support this conclusion. Past experience is an extremely important determinant of present behavior, not only of frequency of intercourse but also of sexual enjoyment and interest. Furthermore, for women, the enjoyment of sexual relations in younger years, rather than frequency or level of sexual interest in younger years, seems to be of particular importance in determining the extent of present sexual interest and frequency of intercourse.

The importance of a socially sanctioned sexually capable partner has been emphasized (Kinsey et al., 1948; Kinsey et al., 1953; Masters et al., 1966; Masters et al., 1970; Newman et al., 1960; Post, 1967; Weinberg, 1969). It is clear from these determinations that the role of marital status for the female is a powerful determining factor in her sexual behavior. This likely reflects both the relative greater attrition of males in our society as well as the difficulty that single or widowed elderly women may encounter due to social disapproval and lack of opportunity.

The importance of physical well-being has been emphasized by other authors (Kinsey et al., 1948; Kinsey et al., 1953; Masters et al., 1966; Masters et al., 1970; Newman et al., 1960; Post, 1967). In the present study this notion was supported primarily among men. Strikingly, subjective assessments of health status are important in determining sexual enjoyment and interest, but an object health rating (PFR) is a significant determinant of present frequency of intercourse among men (Table 7–16). Both objective and subjective health ratings play lesser roles in female sexual behavior (Table 7–17).

Adaptability, a feeling of satisfaction, mental health, and a variety of psychologic variables have been postulated to have important influences on sexual behavior (Masters et al., 1966; Masters et al., 1970; Peberdy, 1967; Denber, 1968). In the present study it was apparent that subjects who expected they would look back on their lives with much satisfaction had higher levels of sexual activity than those who did not.

Conclusions

Keeping in mind the limitations of the present study (the subjects were primarily white, middle and upper-middle-class, nonmetropolitan residents of one of the southeastern states of the United States, age range, 46–71), the extent to which the findings can be generalized to apply to other populations depends upon the similarity of those populations to the sample under study. Nevertheless, a number of conclusions emerge which have important implications for the practitioner, to the extent that his patients' characteristics approximate those of our sample. The practitioner should be aware that sex continues to play an important role in the lives of the majority of middle-aged people, as it does in the lives of many old people. Equally important to realize, however, is the wide range of differences which exist between persons in this general age group. Many diverse factors influence the extent of sexual activity and interest among men in the age range studied; the most important include past sexual experience, age, subjective and objective health factors, and social class. Relatively fewer factors determine the extent of sexual activity and interest among women; they are principally marital status, age, and enjoyment derived from sexual experience in younger years.

The finding of a significant positive correlation of high levels of sexual activity in younger years with greater sexual activity in later years runs counter to the popular myth that extensive early sexual experience will lead to an early demise of such capacity. Rather, the data support another, more scientific notion, that is, the continuity of life style (Busse et al., 1969; Havighurst et al., 1969). Persons to whom sex was of great importance early in life are more likely to continue sexually active late in life. Persons to whom sex was of little importance early in life will be more likely to reach an early terminus to their sexual activity late in life.

In addition, this study reconfirms earlier findings that the extent of an aging woman's sexual activity and interest depends heavily upon the availability to her of a societally sanctioned, sexually capable partner. The average life expectancy of women exceeds that of men by seven years (Brotman, 1971). Women marry men who are on average some four years older than themselves (Newman, et al., 1960). Women may thus expect to experience an average of eleven years of widowhood. Only a very small proportion of widowed women remarry; a much larger percentage of widowed men remarry. With each passing year, women in our society become increasingly supernumerary. Thus, according to the 1970 census figures, at age 65 there are 138.5 women for every 100 men in the United States, and at age 75 this ratio has risen to 156.2 women for every 100 men. It is the authors' interpretation that much of the decline in sexual interest among aging women is not physiologic but is defensive, that is, protective. It may well be adaptive to inhibit sexual strivings when little opportunity for sexual fulfillment exists. With advancing age, fewer and fewer women have a sexual partner available. The remedy would seem to lie in efforts directed at prolonging vigor and extending the life span of men.

References

Brotman, H. B. *Facts and figures on older Americans, number 2. The older population revisited: First results of the 1970 census.* Washington, D.C.: Administration on Aging, U.S. Department of Health, Education, and Welfare, 1971.

Busse, E. W., and Pfeiffer, E. Functional psychiatric disorders in old age, In E. W. Busse and E. Pfeiffer (Eds.), *Behavior and adaptation in late life.* Boston: Little, Brown and Co., 1969, pp. 183–185.

Denber, H. C. Sexual problems in the mature female. *Psychosomatics* 40–43, 1968 (Suppl. 1).

Finkle, A. L. Sex problems in later years. *Med. Times* 95:416–419, 1967.

Havighurst, R. J., and DeVries, A. Life styles and free time activities of retired men. *Human Development,* 12:34–54, 1969.

Kinsey, A. C., Pomeroy, W. B., and Martin, C. R. *Sexual behavior in the human male.* Philadelphia: W. B. Saunders Co., 1948.

Kinsey, A. C., Pomeroy, W. B., Martin, C. R., and Geghard, P. H. *Sexual behavior in the human female.* Philadelphia: W. B. Saunders Co., 1953.

Masters, W. H., and Johnson, V. E. *Human sexual inadequacy.* Boston: Little, Brown, and Co., 1970.

Masters, W. H., and Johnson, V. E. *Human Response*. Boston: Little, Brown and Co., 1966.

Metropolitan Life Insurance Company. *Statistical Bulletin*. August 1967, pp. 8–10, and March 1969, pp. 7–9. (Based on statistics from the National Center for Health Statistics).

Newman, G., and Nicholas, C. R. Sexual activities and attitudes in older persons, *J.A.M.A.* 173:33, 1960.

Peberdy, G. Sex and its problems. X. Sexual adjustment at the climacteric. *Practitioner* 199:564–571, 1967.

Pfeiffer, E. Sexual behavior in old age, In Busse and Pfeiffer (Eds.), *Behavior and adaptation in late life.* 1969.

Pfeiffer, E., and Davis, G. C The use of leisure time in middle life. *Gerontologist*, 11, No. 3:187–195, 1971.

Pfeiffer, E., Verwoerdt, A., and Davis, G. C. Sexual behavior in middle life, pp. 243–251 in this volume.

Pfeiffer, E., Verwoerdt, A., and Wang, H. S. The natural history of sexual behavior in a biologically advantaged group of aged individuals. *J. Gerontol.*, 24:193–198, 1969.

Pfeiffer, E., Verwoerdt, A., and Wang, H. S. Sexual behavior in aged men and women. I. Observations on 254 community volunteers, *Arch. Gen. Psychiat*, 19:753–758, 1968.

Post, F. Sex and its problems. IX. Disorders of sex in the elderly, *Practitioner*, 199: 377–382, 1967.

Verwoerdt, A., Pfeiffer, E., and Wang, H. S. Sexual behavior in senescence—Changes in sexual activity and interest of aging men and women. *J. Geriat. Psychiat.*, 2:163–180, 1969.

Verwoerdt, A., Pfeiffer, E., and Wang, H. S. Sexual behavior in senescence. II. Patterns of sexual activity and interest. *Geriatrics* 24:137–154. 1969.

Weinberg, J. Sexual expression in late life. *Am. J. Psychiat.*, 126:713–716, 1969.

Chapter 8. Longevity

Our last set of reports have to do with longevity and death. Aging should not be equated with dying. On the contrary, much of the evidence from our longitudinal studies indicate that a distinction can be made between normal aging processes which produce little decline over long periods of time versus those terminal changes which indicate the dying process has begun.

The first report finds that brain impairment accounts for a rather small proportion of the variance in longevity, although there is a significant statistical relationship. This finding is related to that in the earlier report that terminal changes in intelligence occur primarily among aged persons with both chronic and acute illnesses.

That long-term survivors are characterized by high intelligence, sound financial status, well maintained health, and intact marriages is the conclusion of the second report. The final report, using multiple regression analysis, finds that the most important factors in longevity are health maintenance (including avoidance of cigarettes), useful and satisfying roles in society, and a positive view of life. These factors together account for one-quarter to almost one-half of the variance in longevity remaining after age, sex, and race have been controlled.

Brain Impairment and Longevity   *H. Shan Wang and Ewald W. Busse*

Brain disorders are very common among elderly persons. They usually result from a primary degenerative disease of the brain, from cerebral vascular disease or from a metabolic disorder that originates outside the brain. The literature is full of reports on the prognosis of brain disorders in the elderly, and most of these reports agree that the mortality rate in these cases is high, regardless of the cause of the brain disorder (Wang and Whanger, 1971). Some brain disorders—for example, those due to a major stroke—are of such nature and severity that they constitute an immediate threat to survival. It is not clear, however, in what way and to what extent brain disorders also affect the life expectancy of individuals who survive the initial stage of a stroke and those who have an insidiously progressive brain disorder such as generalized cerebral arteriosclerosis or senile or presenile dementia.

We would like to thank Dr. Carl Eisdorfer for use of the psychological data collected by his laboratory, and Dr. Walter Obrist for his contribution in collecting the EEG data.

For several reasons, it is difficult to interpret the findings reported in the literature. One problem is that almost all these studies were based on patients confined to neuropsychiatric institutions. It is well known that many elderly persons who have brain disorders are admitted to an institution not because of their brain condition but because of a variety of social, psychological, and physical factors. Another problem is that patients with brain disorders are in general characterized by their advanced age, low socioeconomic background, and poor physical health. Very few studies have carefully controlled these factors by comparing elderly patients who have a brain disorder with those who do not. Without such a comparison, it is impossible to determine whether the high mortality rates are due to the brain disorder per se or to one or more of many other factors that are characteristic of this group of elderly patients. Trier (1966) has shown that institutionalized patients with organic mental disorders were on the average, eight years older than those with psychogenic mental disorders. When these two groups of patients were matched by age, the difference in prognosis, although still significant, was smaller than the difference observed when the ages were not matched.

If brain disorders have a direct effect on longevity, one would expect a linear relationship between longevity and the severity of brain impairment. The paucity of data on this relationship is due largely to the many difficulties encountered in quantifying the severity of brain impairment in vivo. Inability to determine the severity of brain impairment and to diagnose accurately the type of lesion probably accounts for some of the conflicting results obtained in different studies. Out of four studies comparing the longevity of stroke patients with that of persons of comparable age in the general population, two (Adams and Merrett, 1961; Robinson, Cohen, Higano, Meyer, Lukowsky and McLaughlin, 1959) found the mortality higher in the former group, while the other two (Pincock, 1957; Eisenberg, Morrison, Sullivan and Foote, 1964) showed no significant difference between the two groups. Both Roth (1955) and Kidd (1962) reported a higher mortality in patients with senile dementia than in those with cerebral arteriosclerosis; but in the studies carried out by Corsellis (1962) and Epstein (1964) opposite results were obtained.

The present report is based on a longitudinal study of a group of elderly community volunteers at the Duke University Center for the Study of Aging and Human Development. From findings obtained in this study, we have attempted to evaluate the usefulness of different indicators of brain impairment, several of which are quantifiable, in the prediction of longevity.

Subjects and Methods

The subjects were 265 volunteers 60 years of age or older who were maintaining an active life in the community. The mean age of this group initially was 70.9 years (S.D. ± 7.0). All subjects were given thorough examinations by a multidisciplinary team at intervals of about three years; the surviving ones have recently completed their sixth examination.

The condition of the brain was judged on the basis of the EEG findings, the neurological examination, and psychological testing. The methods of EEG recording and analysis are the same as those previously reported (Wang and Busse, 1969). In brief, the electroencephalograms were divided into four categories on the basis of dominant background activities: (1) alpha, (2) low-voltage fast (LVF), (3) diffuse fast (DF), and (4) diffuse slow (DS). The mean occipital dominant frequencies were measured manually. Based on symptoms and signs from the neurological examination, patients were classified as having evidence of a central nervous system disorder (CNS+) or no evidence of such a disorder (CNS−).

From the Wechsler Adult Intelligence Scale, the deterioration quotient was calculated according to the formula given by Wechsler (1958). This quotient indicates the percentage of loss in four "don't hold" subtests (similarities, digit span, digit symbol, and block design) as compared with the four "hold" subtests (vocabulary, information, picture completion, and object assembly). We found that the deterioration quotient was independent of education ($r =$ 0.03).

Two criteria of longevity—the *longevity index* and the *longevity quotient* —were employed (Palmore, 1971). The longevity *index* represents the total number of years from the initial study to death. For living subjects, the index is the number of years from initial examination to the sixth examination plus the expected number of years remaining at the sixth examination based on the actuarial life expectancy table (U.S. Public Health Service, 1966). The longevity *quotient* is the ratio between the longevity index and the actuarial life expectancy at the time of the initial examination. A longevity quotient greater than 1 means that the individual lived longer than expected, and a longevity quotient of less than 1 means that he did not live out his life expectancy.

Results

The mean longevity index for our community subjects is 12.8 years, and the mean longevity quotient, 1.14—respectively 1.6 years and 14 percent greater than would be expected on the basis of the actuarial table. As can be seen in Figure 8–1, the mean longevity index was definitely shorter in subjects who showed electroencephalographic evidence of brain impairment (the "diffuse slow" group) or clinical evidence of a central nervous system disorder (the CNS+ group). These subjects, however, were significantly (about five years) older than those without such abnormalities; therefore the difference in the longevity quotient, though still statistically significant, was much smaller than the difference in the longevity index.

Table 8–1 summarizes the product-moment correlation coefficient be-

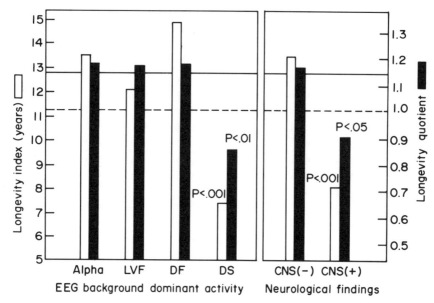

Figure 8–1. *Longevity index and longevity quotient in groups with different EEG background dominant activities and neurological findings. The solid horizontal line indicates the mean of our community subjects; the dotted horizontal line indicates the mean in the general population according to the actuarial life table. The statistical probabilities indicate the significance of the difference between DS and Alpha groups, or between CNS+ and CNS− groups.*

tween longevity indicators and age and brain indicators. As expected, the longevity index is significantly correlated with chronological age, while the longevity quotient is not. The best cerebral correlate of the longevity index was the EEG occipital dominant frequency. The longevity quotient, on the other hand, correlated about as well with the WAIS deterioration quotient and the

Table 8–1. *Correlations of age and brain variables with longevity (product-moment correlation coefficient).*

	Longevity index	Longevity quotient
Age	−.527**	−.035
EEG occipital dominant frequency	.399**	.194*
WAIS deterioration quotient	−.203*	−.198*
Neurological evidence of CNS disorder	−.273**	−.195*
EEG focal disturbance	−.035	−.029

* Significant at the .01 level.
** Significant at the .001 level.

neurological findings as with the EEG occipital dominant frequency. The focal disturbances that appear predominantly over the left anterior temporal area in the EEG showed no correlation with either of the two longevity indicators.

By stepwise multiple regression analysis (Table 8–2), we found that the combination of three brain indicators (EEG frequency, deterioration quotient, and neurological findings) did improve the correlation with both the longevity index and the longevity quotient, the respective correlation coefficients being 0.48 and 0.32. These three brain indicators together, however, account for

Table 8–2. *Stepwise regression analysis of brain variables with longevity index and longevity quotient.*

	Multiple correlations (r)	Cumulative variance (r^2)
Correlation with longevity index		
EEG occipital dominant quotient	.399	15.9
WAIS deterioration quotient	.443	19.6
Neurological evidence of CNS disorder	.482	23.2
Correlation with longevity quotient		
WAIS deterioration quotient	.198	3.9
Neurological evidence of CNS disorder	.288	8.3
EEG occipital dominant frequency	.319	10.2

only 23 percent of the variance in the longevity index and 10 percent of the variance in the longevity quotient.

Discussion

The data from our group of elderly community volunteers indicate that there is a significant statistical relationship between brain impairment and longevity. The more severe the brain impairment (as revealed by electroencephalographic, psychometric, and neurological examination), the shorter the subject's longevity. The correlation between brain impairment and longevity index is better than that between brain impairment and longevity quotient. This is expected because the longevity index and brain impairment are both age-dependent while the longevity quotient is an indicator that has already been adjusted for age.

Alone or together, however, indicators of brain impairment account for only a rather small proportion of the variance in longevity. Analysis of our data indicates that physical functioning, happiness and work satisfaction also play an important role in longevity (Palmore, 1969a, 1969b). From a clinical point of view therefore, we should not use the degree of brain impairment alone, particularly when based on a single examination, to predict the outcome of any elderly person. The common belief that all elderly persons with brain impairment have a poor prognosis is clearly unjustified.

References

Adams, G. F., and Merrett, J. D. Prognosis and survival in the aftermath of hemiplegia. *Brit. Med. J.*, 1:309–314, 1961.

Corsellis, J. A. N. *Mental illness and the aging brain*. London: Oxford University Press, 1962.

Eisenberg, H., Morrison, J. T., Sullivan, P., and Foote, F. M. Cerebrovascular accidents, incidence and survival rates in a defined population, Middlesex County, Connecticut. *J.A.M.A.* 189:883–888, 1964.

Epstein, L., Simon, A., and Mock, R. Clinical neuropathologic correlations in senile and cerebral arteriosclerotic psychoses. In Hansen, P. F. (Ed.), *Old age with a future*. Copenhagen: Munksgaard, 1964, pp. 272–275.

Kidd, C. B. Old people in mental hospital: A study in diagnostic composition and outcome. *Irish J. Med. Sci.* Ser. 6, 434:72–77, 1962.

Palmore, E. Physical, mental, and social factors in predicting longevity. *The Gerontologist*, 9:103–108, 1969a.

Palmore, E. Predicting longevity: A follow-up controlling for age. *The Gerontologist*, 9:247–250, 1969b.

Palmore, E., and Jeffers, F. C. (Eds.). *Prediction of life span: Recent findings*. Lexington, Mass.: D. C. Heath, 1971.

Pincock, J. G.: The natural history of cerebral thrombosis. *Ann. Intern. Med.*, 46:926–930, 1957.

Robinson, R. W., Cohen, W. D., Higano, N., Meyer, R., Lukowsky, G. H., and McLaughlin, R. B. Life-table analysis of survival after cerebral thrombosis—10 year experience. *J.A.M.A.* 169:1149–1152, 1959.

Roth, M. The natural history of mental disorder in old age. *J. Ment. Sci.*, 101:281–301, 1955.

Trier, T. R. Characteristics of mentally ill aged: A comparison of patients with psychogenic disorders and patients with organic brain syndromes. *J. Geront.* 21:354–364, 1966.

Wang, H. S., and Busse, E. W. EEG of healthy old persons, a longitudinal study: I. dominant background activity and occipital rhythm. *J. Geront.* 24:419–426, 1969.

Wang, H. S., and Whanger, A. Brain impairment and longevity. In Palmore and Jeffers (Eds.), *Prediction of life span*. 1971.

Wechsler, D. *The measurement and appraisal of adult intelligence*. Baltimore: Williams & Wilkins, 1958.

U.S. Public Health Service. *State life tables: 1959–1961*. Washington, D.C.: U.S. Government Printing Office, 1966, 2, No. 27–51.

Survival in Old Age   *Eric Pfeiffer*

Purpose of the Study

Goldfarb has found four characteristics associated with mortality among institutionalized elderly persons: (*a*) psychiatrically determined chronic brain syndrome of severe degree; (*b*) high proportion of errors in a brief mental status exam; (*c*) diminished capacity for self-care and mobility; and (*d*) incontinence (1969). Quint and Cody, on the other hand, found that prominent men over 45 listed in *Who's Who* had a mortality which was 30 percent below that of white males of like age in the general population (1968). In a similar vein, statisticians of the Metropolitan Life Insurance Company have reported that death rates from heart disease, one of the major causes of death in old age, was substantially lower among Standard Ordinary policyholders than among Industrial policyholders (1967). Standard Ordinary policyholders are drawn chiefly from urban middle and well-to-do classes engaged in the professions, in business, trade, and clerical occupations. Industrial policyholders are mainly members of wage-earning families in the lower income brackets.

The present study seeks to discover physical, psychological, and social factors which differentiate short-term from long-term survivors among elderly persons *living in the community*. Simultaneously, this study becomes a comparison between elite and nonelite groups of aged individuals. The study is an outgrowth of the larger interdisciplinary research on age-related changes, begun at the Duke University Center for the Study of Aging and Human Development in 1954 and still in progress. An overall description of the larger study is found elsewhere (Palmore, 1970).

Sample and Methods

In a previous longitudinal study which focused on sexual behavior in old age and which utilized a sample of some 260 community volunteers, a subgroup of 39 individuals (20 men and 19 women) was identified who showed the following characteristics: they had given codeable responses to interview questions about their sexual activity and sexual interest, on each of four separate examinations over a period of ten years (Pfeiffer, 1969). When these subjects were studied more closely, it became apparent that they represented a kind of physical, psychological, and social elite, in comparison with the en-

Reprinted by permission from the *Journal of the American Geriatrics Society,* 18:4:273–285, 1970.

tire panel of subjects from which they had been drawn. In addition, these 39 subjects, whose average age was 67 at the start of the study, by virtue of surviving for at least ten more years, also represented a longevous elite. This observation became the starting point for the present study.

In this study we wished to compare this relatively long-lived elite with a group of subjects, drawn from the same panel and matched for age and sex, who represented the opposite extreme with respect to longevity. For this purpose we first selected the 39 subjects (20 men and 19 women) who had been the earliest to die following entry into the study. This procedure caused problems, since the average age at the start of the study in the group thus chosen was significantly greater for both the men and for the women than for the corresponding longevous groups. Since none of the persons in the longevous group had reached age eighty at the time of the start of the study, we therefore chose the 20 men and 19 women below age 80 who were the first to die. Using this procedure, the average age of the longevous males was 68 years and of the short-term surviving males was 71 years, a difference which was no longer statistically significant. However, we still had statistically significant age differences between the two groups of women. In order to include women of more comparable age, we eliminated the two youngest women among the longevous group and the two oldest women in the short-lived group, thus reducing the number of women in each group from 19 to 17. The average age of these two groups was 66 for the longevous women, and 68 for the women with short-term survival, a difference no longer statistically significant.

To assure comparability, only data collected during the first examination were utilized in this study. For while all of the subjects in the longevous groups were studied on four different occasions, the majority of the short-lived subjects were studied only once.

Throughout the study, long-lived women are compared only with short-lived women, and long-lived men with short-lived men. It is well known that sex has a major determining influence on life expectancy as well as on a number of the other factors which were examined. Thus, analyses were carried out on the following groups:

17 long-lived women
17 short-lived women

20 long-lived men
20 short-lived men

The average interval from entry into the study to the time of death was 2.42 years for the short-lived men, 5.5 for the short-lived women. All of the long-lived men and women remained alive for at least 10 years following entry into the study, and all but one of those selected into the long-lived group are still alive at the time of this writing (July 1969).

The tests of significance used in this study were: the t test, when comparisons among means were involved; the Kendall rank correlation coefficient, when ordinal distributions were compared; and the chi-square test, when nominal distributions were compared. In the multiple regression analysis, the *F* test was used to determine significance levels.

Health Factors

Attention is focused first on health factors. To facilitate comparison with results reported in a recent paper by Ryser and Sheldon (1969), data with respect to self-assessment of health status are presented first.

Subjects were asked: "How would you rate your health at the present time?" (Self-Health Rating). Responses were classified into three categories, as follows:

excellent
1. excellent for my age
good

good for my age
2. fair
fair for my age

3. very poor
poor

Results for the four groups are presented in Table 8–3.

Table 8–3. *Self-health rating.*

	Long-lived N	Long-lived %	Short-lived N	Short-lived %	*p*
1.	12	71	7	41	Women
2.	5	29	6	35	<.01
3.	0	0	4	24	
	17	100	17	100	
1.	14	70	5	25	Men
2.	5	25	9	45	<.001
3.	1	5	6	30	
	20	100	20	100	

Subjects were also asked: "How concerned do you feel about your health troubles?" (Self-Health Concern). Responses were classified into three categories, as follows:

1. not concerned
2. moderately concerned
3. very concerned

Results are presented in Table 8–4.

Table 8–4. *Self-health concern.*

| | Long-lived | | Short-lived | | |
	N	%	N	%	p
1.	11	65	9	56	Women
2.	5	29	6	38	NS
3.	1	6	1	6	
	17	100	16	100	
1.	10	54	7	37	Men
2.	6	35	9	47	<.05
3.	1	11	3	16	
	17	100	19	100	

Subjects were also asked: "How many days did you spend in bed last year because of not feeling well?" (Days in Bed). Responses were classified into three categories, as follows:

1. no days in bed
2. a few days in bed
3. 2 to 4 weeks in bed, up to "all the time"

Results are presented in Table 8–5.

Table 8–5. *Days in bed.*

| | Long-lived | | Short-lived | | |
	N	%	N	%	p
1.	8	50	9	54	Women
2.	6	38	4	23	NS
3.	2	12	4	23	
	16	100	17	100	
1.	16	80	10	59	Men
2.	3	15	4	23	<.05
3.	1	5	3	18	
	20	100	17	100	

Subjects were also asked: "How much do your health troubles stand in the way of your doing the things you most want to do?" (Degree of Limitation). Responses were classified into three categories:

1. no limitation
2. some limitation (mild to moderate)
3. a great deal of limitation (severe)

Results are presented in Table 8–6.

Table 8–6. *Degree of limitation.*

	Long-lived N	Long-lived %	Short-lived N	Short-lived %	p
1.	4	33	3	37	Women
2.	7	58	3	37	NS
3.	1	9	2	25	
	12	100	8	100	
1.	7	50	2	14	Men
2.	6	43	8	57	<.001
3.	1	7	4	29	
	14	100	14	100	

As can be seen from these four tables, the majority of long-lived and short-lived women saw themselves in relatively good health, admitting to little or no limitation in their functioning. This finding is in agreement with those of Ryser and Sheldon (1969), and of Shanas and her associates (1968). The Self-Health Rating was the only measure which differentiated the two groups of women.

While the majority of long-lived men also saw themselves in relatively good health, the same was not true for the short-lived men. On three out of the four health measures used, the short-lived men rated their health as significantly poorer than did the long-lived men. Heyman and Jeffers had previously found similar relations of health to survival (1963).

The self-assessments of health status presented thus far are relatively static measures, requiring subjects to rate themselves *only at one point in time.* These measures are not very successful in differentiating short-lived from long-lived women, and are only moderately successful in differentiating similar groups of men. We therefore wondered whether a measure which required the subjects to make a *longitudinal* assessment of their health might be a more sensitive indicator of remaining life expectancy. This was in fact the case. The subjects were asked: "Is your health better or worse now than it was when you were 55 years of age?" (Self Rating of Health Change). The responses were classified as follows:

1. better
2. the same
3. worse

The results of this analysis are presented in Table 8–7. The majority of persons who have only a short number of years left perceive their health as having declined since age 55, while only a few of the long-lived persons do so, a difference which is statistically significant at the .01 level for the women and the .001 level for the men.

Table 8–7. *Self-rating of health change.*

	Long-lived N	Long-lived %	Short-lived N	Short-lived %	*p*
1.	8	47	1	6	Women
2.	3	18	7	41	<.01
3.	6	35	9	53	
	17	100	17	100	
1.	6	30	0	0	Men
2.	9	45	4	20	<.001
3.	5	25	16	80	
	20	100	20	100	

We also had available on each subject an "objective" health measure, the "physical functional rating." This rating was based on the physical examination and on the examining physician's assessment of pathology and disability. Physical functional ratings were classified as follows:

1. no pathology
   pathology; no disability
   disability, mild 0–20%

2. disability, moderate 20–50%
   disability, severe 50–80%
   total 80–100%

The results are presented in Table 8–8. As can be seen, this "objective" measure is not associated with survival in the groups of women and has a relatively low but significant association with survival in the groups of men.

Table 8–8. *Physical function rating.*

	Long-lived N	Long-lived %	Short-lived N	Short-lived %	*p*
1.	10	59	10	59	Women
2.	7	41	7	41	NS
	17	100	17	100	
1.	12	63	8	40	Men
2.	7	37	12	60	<.05
	19	100	20	100	

It is of interest that the various health measures seem to have greater predictive value for the men than for the women. This may be related to the fact that the short-lived men on average were significantly nearer death than were the short-lived women at the time these measures were taken (2.42 versus 5.50 years).

Intelligence Test Scores

Mean intelligence test scores for the long-term survivors were significantly greater than for short-term survivors. This was true for the Verbal, Performance, and Full Scale Weighted Scores of the Wechsler Adult Intelligence Scale (WAIS). This finding is thus in agreement with those of Jarvik and Falek (1963) and of Riegel, Riegel, and Meyer (1967) (Table 8–9).

Table 8–9. *Intelligence test scores.*

Means	Long-lived	Short-lived	t	p
Women				
Verbal	66.58	46.17	2.96	$<.01$
Performance	35.70	24.47	2.65	$<.02$
Full Scale	102.29	70.64	2.95	$<.01$
Men				
Verbal	63.85	48.30	2.58	$<.02$
Performance	31.35	21.26	2.65	$<.02$
Full Scale	95.20	70.42	2.59	$<.02$

Education

The mean number of years of education was greater for the long-term survivors than for the short-term survivors. The difference was statistically significant among the women and approached significance among the men (Table 8–10.)

Table 8–10. *Years of education.*

	Long-lived	Short-lived	t	p
Women	12.23	8.41	2.18	$<.05$
Men	11.65	7.60	1.94	NS

Social Factors

In order to obtain a subjective indication of the subjects' economic situation, they were asked: "How would you describe your present financial position in life?" (Financial Self-Rating). Responses were categories as follows:

1. wealthy
   well-to-do

2. comfortable

3. enough to get along
   can't make ends meet

As can be seen from Table 8–11 there was no significant difference in finan-

Table 8–11. *Financial self-evaluation.*

	Long-lived		Short-lived		
	N	%	N	%	p
1.	1	6	0	0	Women
2.	9	53	10	59	NS
3.	7	41	7	41	
	17	100	17	100	
1.	0	0	0	0	Men
2.	14	70	4	20	<.001
3.	6	30	16	80	
	20	100	20	100	

cial self-assessment between the two groups of women, but there was a very significant difference in financial self-assessment between the two groups of men, with 80 percent of the short-lived men ranking themselves at the lower end of the continuum.

Subjects were also asked: "Are you in a better or a worse position financially now than you were at age 55?" (Financial Self-Evaluation Change). Responses were categorized as follows:

1. better now
2. about the same
3. worse now

Results are presented in Table 8–12. The two groups of women did not differ

Table 8–12. *Financial self-evaluation change.*

	Long-lived		Short-lived		
	N	%	N	%	p
1.	9	53	9	56	Women
2.	1	6	3	19	NS
3.	7	41	4	25	
	17	100	16	100	
1.	9	45	5	25	Men
2.	5	25	3	15	<.01
3.	6	30	12	60	
	20	100	20	100	

from each other in this analysis, but the two groups of men differed significantly, with the short-lived group of men showing significantly greater worsening of their financial status since age 55.

Occupation

As a rough but relatively objective indicator of socioeconomic status, subjects were categorized according to whether their principal occupation (or their husband's principal occupation, in the case of married or formerly married women) had been manual or nonmanual. Significantly fewer long-lived women were found in the manual category. The difference between the groups of men was in the same direction, but barely missed attaining statistical significance (Table 8–13).

Table 8–13. *Occupation.*

| | Long-lived | | Short-lived | | |
	N	%	N	%	*p*
Nonmanual	13	76	5	29	Women
Manual	4	24	12	71	<.01
	17	100	17	100	
Nonmanual	14	70	8	40	Men
Manual	6	30	12	60	NS
	20	100	20	100	

Marital Status

Among the short-lived women the proportion of those not married was significantly greater than in the long-lived group. Among the two groups of men the trend was in the same direction but did not attain statistical significance. The results are presented in Table 8–14.

Table 8–14. *Marital status.*

| | Long-lived | | Short-lived | | |
	N	%	N	%	*p*
Married	12	71	5	29	Women
Nonmarried	5	29	12	71	<.05
	17	100	17	100	
Married	19	95	15	75	Men
Nonmarried	1	5	5	25	NS
	20	100	20	100	

Other Factors

The racial distribution of the two long-lived groups did not differ significantly from that of the short-lived groups. The several groups were also compared, using a series of attitude and activity measurements. Only a few of these measurements were able to differentiate significantly short-term from long-term survivors, and the relatively meager average results are not included in this article.

Longevity Index and Longevity Quotient

Palmore, working with data from the Duke longitudinal study, has recently developed two new concepts which are of interest in connection with the present study: the longevity index and the longevity quotient. The *longevity index* is defined as follows: the number of years from the time of entry into the study to death, for those subjects who have already died; or, the number of years from the point of entry into the study up to the present, plus the expected remaining years, based on current life expectancy tables, for subjects still alive. For the four groups in the present study the means of the longevity indices were as follows:

long-lived women	19.30 years
short-lived women	5.50 years
long-lived men	17.22 years
short-lived men	2.42 years

The *longevity quotient* is defined as follows: the longevity index divided by the number of years the subject was expected to remain alive at the time of entry into the study. Thus, it is a measure of whether a subject lived a longer or a shorter time than would have been actuarially expected at the time of entry into the study. Thus, a longevity quotient of greater than 1.00 is indicative of longer than expected survival, a value of less than 1.00 is indicative of shorter than expected survival. The mean longevity quotients for the four groups were as follows:

long-lived women	1.32
short-lived women	0.44
long-lived men	1.56
short-lived men	0.24

These findings merely confirm that polar groups were indeed chosen in constituting the sample.

Multiple Regression Analysis

Having found a number of variables which significantly differentiated short-term from long-term survivors, we were of course interested in determining which of the variables contributed most to the variance observed and which did so independently. To accomplish this, a multiple stepwise regression analysis was carried out, using the longevity index (defined above) as the dependent variable. The findings are presented in Table 8–15.

Table 8–15. *Multiple stepwise regression analysis of selected variables with longevity index.*

Variable	Zero order corr.	Multiple R	Cumul. var.	Add. var.
Women				
Full Scale Wtd. WAIS Score	0.42	0.42	0.18	0.18
Self-health change	0.40	0.52	0.27	0.09
Marital status	0.39	0.56	0.31	0.04
Physical function rating	−0.31	0.59	0.35	0.04
Financial status change	−0.02	0.60	0.36	0.02
Performance Wtd. WAIS Score	0.41	0.61	0.37	0.01
Self-health rating	0.24	0.61	0.37	0.00
Financial status	0.23	0.62	0.38	0.01
Socioeconomic status	−0.33	0.62	0.38	0.01
Men				
Financial status	0.53	0.53	0.28	0.28
Self-health change	0.51	0.61	0.37	0.09
Physical function rating	−0.46	0.66	0.44	0.07
Financial status change	0.21	0.70	0.49	0.05
Marital status	0.33	0.72	0.52	0.03
Verbal Wtd. WAIS Score	0.34	0.73	0.53	0.01
Socioeconomic status	−0.17	0.76	0.58	0.05
Self-health rating	0.44	0.76	0.58	0.00
Performance Wtd. WAIS Score	0.36	0.76	0.58	0.00

For the women in this study, Full Scale Weighted WAIS Score, perception of health change, marital status, physical functional rating, and change in financial status, in that order, contributed most significantly to the variance in longevity, and together these five factors accounted for 36 percent of the total variance observed.

For the men in the study, the findings were similar though by no means identical. Financial status, perception of health change, physical functional rating, change in financial status, and marital status, in that order, contributed most significantly to the variance in longevity, and together these five factors accounted for 52 percent of the total variance observed.

A number of other factors (Performance Weighted WAIS Score and occupational status for the women, and self-health rating and Verbal and Performance Weighted WAIS Scores for the men) were also significantly correlated with longevity but did not make a significant *independent* contribution to the total variance in longevity.

Conclusions

The present study, utilizing subgroups of a panel of community volunteers, has presented evidence to suggest that group characteristics of long-term survivors differ sharply from those of short-term survivors in old age. It further suggests that there is no single factor which determines longevity but rather a constellation of biological, psychological, and social factors, amounting to what may best be described as *elite status*. Persons with high intelligence, sound financial status, well-maintained health, and intact marriages, may be expected to live significantly longer than their less intelligent and poorer brothers and sisters whose health is also declining and whose marriages are no longer intact. It is lamentable that many of the factors which we have identified as contributing to longevity are not readily subject to individual, social, or political manipulation, with the possible exception of financial factors. It is hoped that investigations in other parts of the country and with differing populations of elderly people may be able to determine whether the hypotheses put forward here apply to elderly persons generally. It would also be interesting to know if these factors are similarly important in influencing survival at other stages of the life cycle.

References

Goldfarb, A. Predicting mortality in the institutionalized aged. *Arch. Gen. Psychiat.*, 21:172–176, 1969.

Heyman, D., and Jeffers, F. Effect of time lapse on consistency of self-health and medical evaluations of elderly persons. *J. of Gerontology*, 18, No. 2:160–164, 1963.

Jarvik, L., and Falek, A. Intellectual stability and survival in the aged. *J. Geront.* 18: 173–176, 1963.

Metropolitan Life Insurance Company. Cardiac mortality and socioeconomic status. *Statistical bulletin*, June 1967.

Palmore, E. Physical, mental, and social factors in predicting longevity. *Gerontologist*, 9:103–108, 1969.

Palmore, E. (Ed.): *Normal aging.* Durham, N.C.: Duke University Press, 1970.

Pfeiffer, E. The natural history of sexual behavior in a biologically advantaged group of aged individuals. *J. Geront.* 24:193–198, 1969.

Quint, J., and Cody, B. Preeminence and mortality: Longevity of prominent men. Paper given before the Annual Meeting of the American Public Health Association, November 13, 1968. A summary was also published in *Statistical bulletin* of the Metropolitan Life Insurance Company, January 1968, pp. 2–5.

Riegel, K., Riegel, R., and Meyer, G. A study of dropout rates in longitudinal research on aging and the prediction of death. *Journal Personality and Social Psychology* 5:342–348, 1967.

Ryser, C., and Sheldon, A. Retirement and health. *J. Amer. Geriat. Soc.* 17:180–190, 1969.

Shanas, E. et al.: *Old people in three industrial societies.* New York: Atherton, 1968, pp. 49–70.

Predicting Longevity: A New Method   *Erdman Palmore*

In earlier articles, we reported that the use of physical, mental, and social examinations can substantially improve the accuracy of longevity predictions compared to actuarial life expectancy predictions, and that the relative importance of these factors varied between different age, sex, and race categories (Palmore, 1969a; Palmore, 1969b; Palmore, 1971; Palmore and Stone, 1973). The present paper reports on a new method of analysis which substantially improves the accuracy of these predictions by maximizing the number of variables and cases that are included.

Methods

The sample on which these predictions are based are the 271 community volunteers, aged 60–94 at the initial examination in the period 1955–1959. The longevity quotient (LQ) is the measure of longevity used in this study. The LQ is the observed number of years survived after initial examination, divided by the actuarially expected number of years to be survived after examination based on the person's age, sex, and race. For those who were still living (about one third of the panel), an estimate was made of how many years they will have lived since initial testing by adding the present number of years survived since initial testing to the expected number of years now remaining according to actuarial tables. Thus, an LQ of 1.0 means that the person lived as long as expected, an LQ greater than 1.0 would mean that he lived more than expected, and an LQ of less than 1.0 would mean that he lived less than expected. For example, if a man lived 15 years after initial examination and had an actuarial expectancy of only 10 years, his LQ would be 1.5. Since the LQ standardizes for the known effects of age, sex, and race, it allows the analysis to concentrate on the relative importance of the physical, mental, and social factors on longevity once the age, sex, and race related life expectancy has been allowed for. Thus, it should be remembered that all of the variance explained in the present multiple regression analysis represents an increase in predictive accuracy over and above the predictive ability of age, sex, and race related life expectancy tables.

Previous analysis indicated that there were about 20 variables measured at the initial examination which had substantial correlations with longevity. The new method of analysis of these 20 predictor variables was to enter them into a stepwise multiple regression procedure which maximizes the number of cases used in each correlation through the use of pair-wise deletion for missing data. The previous method of multiple regression analysis required that each case which had any missing data on any one of the variables be dropped from the entire analysis. This resulted in the necessity of omitting certain variables for which there were frequently missing data, and a substantial reduction in the number of cases that were usable for the other correlations. The new method of analysis resulted in an overall proportion of variance explained which is 59 percent higher than in the earlier method. The proportion of variance explained more than doubled among men in their 60s and women in their 70s.

The significant predictors of longevity that emerged from this analysis will be described in the order in which they appear in Table 1.

Cardiovascular disease was a rating by the examining physician based on his examination, the electrocardiograph, and the medical history. The scores used in this analysis range from O (definite heart disease, severe symptoms) to 9 (no cardiovascular disease).

The *work satisfaction* scale awards 1 point for agreement with each of 3 positive statements (I am happy only when I have definite work to do; I am satisfied with the work I now do; I do better work now than ever before) and for disagreement with each of 3 negative statements (I can no longer do any kind of useful work; I have no work to look forward to; I get badly flustered when I have to hurry with my work).

Cigarette smoking is a scale with the following scores: 0 = Any cigarette smoking within the last year; 1 = Other forms of tobacco used in the last year; 2 = No tobacco use in the last year; and 3 = Never used tobacco. This scale was found to correlate more highly with longevity than alternate scales based on the amount of tobacco currently consumed.

Physical functioning is a score given by the examining physician based on the medical history, the physical examinations, X-rays, electroencephalogram, electrocardiogram, and laboratory studies of the blood and urine. The scores as used in this analysis range from 1 for total disability to 6 for no pathology.

The *happiness rating* is a score given by the social worker for the amount of happiness and contentment, ranging from 0 for unhappy, discontented, worried, to 9 for very happy, great contentment.

The *health self rating* was a 9 point scale based on the subject's evaluation of his own health ranging from 1 for very poor to 8 for excellent.

The *performance IQ* is made up of tests on digit symbols, picture completions, block designs, picture arrangement, and object assembly from the Wechsler Adult Intelligence Scale. The performance intelligence quotient results from dividing the observed score by the expected score for a person of a given age.

Findings and Discussion

Table 8–16 presents the results of the stepwise regression analysis, showing the significant predictors of the LQ (those predictors which increase the

Table 8–16. *Stepwise regression of significant predictors* with longevity quotient by age and sex.*

Predictor	Correlation (*r*)	Slope (beta)	Proportion of total variance (*r* × beta)
Total panel (N = 271)			
Cardiovascular disease	.41	.33	.13
Work satisfaction	.27	.13	.04
Cigarette smoking	.19	.14	.03
Physical function	.32	.15	.05
Happiness rating	.22	.12	.02
Total with 5 predictors	.52		.27
Men aged 60–69 (N = 54)			
Cigarette smoking	.48	.46	.22
Cardiovascular disease	.38	.35	.13
Work satisfaction	.40	.24	.10
Total with 3 predictors	.67		.45
Men aged 70+ (N = 72)			
Cardiovascular disease	.55	.45	.25
Work satisfaction	.32	.25	.08
Health self rating	.47	.22	.10
Total with 3 predictors	.66		.43
Women aged 60–69 (N = 65)			
Cardiovascular disease	.48	.37	.18
Physical function	.45	.33	.15
Total with 2 predictors	.57		.33
Women aged 70+ (N = 68)			
Happiness rating	.38	.29	.11
Socioeconomic status	.16	.25	.04
Performance IQ	.29	.25	.07
Total with 3 predictors	.48		.22

* Only variables which increased the variance accounted for by an amount significant at the .05 level were included in this table.

variance accounted for by an amount significant at the .05 level of significance). The table presents a separate regression analysis for the total panel and for the age-sex subgroups. The first column of the table presents the zero-order correlations, so that one can see how strongly associated each of the predictors are with the LQ when the variable is considered by itself. The second column presents the standardized slope (beta weight) for each predictor, so one can see the relative influence of each predictor on the LQ when all the others are considered simultaneously. The last column presents the proportion of the total variance accounted for by each variable, estimated by multiplying the correlation (*r*) times the slope value (beta). This estimate of variance explained by each variable is not influenced by the order in which the variables were entered into the equation, but considers all the variables simultaneously.

In the total panel, it is clear that the cardiovascular disease rating is by far the strongest predictor of longevity, whether it is considered singularly or in combination with the other significant predictors. The correlation of cardiovascular disease with the LQ is substantially higher than any others and it alone explains about one-half of the amount of variance explainable by all five predictors. This reflects the fact that cardiovascular disease is by far the greatest killer among both men and women in this age group.

More suprising is the fact that a social-psychological variable, work satisfaction, is the second strongest variable to enter the regression equation. The fact that work satisfaction remains as a relatively strong predictor even when the other four variables are taken into account simultaneously, indicates that its association with longevity cannot be explained by some secondary association with cardiovascular disease or other aspects of physical function. This suggests that maintaining a satisfying and meaningful social role may contribute to longevity by providing physical exercise, intellectual stimulation, gratifying and supportive social relationships, and a general motivation to take care of one's self and increase his longevity.

The third variable to enter the regression equation is cigarette smoking. This presumably reflects the well-known relationship between cigarette smoking and cancer as well as cardiovascular diseases. Cigarette smoking became the single strongest predictor of longevity among the men in their 60s, apparently because there was greater cigarette smoking in this age-sex group compared to the older men and the women.

General physical functioning also was a strong predictor of longevity, indicating that diseases and impairments in areas other than cardiovascular have independent and significant effects on longevity.

The final significant predictor of longevity among the total group was the happiness rating made by the social worker. This indicates that one's overall mental attitude may have a significant psychosomatic effect on longevity. For example, there is considerable evidence that high levels of anxiety, depression, or "nervous tension" may have detrimental effects on ulcers and hypertension.

The total multiple correlation using all five significant predictors is .52, meaning that .27 or just over one quarter of the total variance in the LQ can be explained by these five variables. It should be recalled that the longevity quotient measures only the variance remaining after the effects of age, sex, and race are removed. Also, the table shows that the proportion of variance explained among men is almost double the amount explained in the total group, indicating that these predictors are more closely associated with longevity among men than among women. For example, among the men under 70, cigarette smoking and work satisfaction have much higher correlations and explain much more of the variance than in the total group (which includes women).

Among the men over 70, cardiovascular disease has the highest correlation of any single variable in any age-sex group (.55). This presumably reflects the fact that men over 70 are in the age-sex group with the highest rate or mortality for cardiovascular disease. Nevertheless, work satisfaction is still the second strongest variable to enter the regression equation among these older men and seems to indicate the continuing importance of meaningful social roles for the longevity of older men.

Among the women under 70, cardiovascular disease and physical function are the only two significant predictors, and they seem to have about equal strength. Among the women over 70, the happiness rating is the strongest single predictor followed by performance IQ and socioeconomic status. This seems to indicate that among women who survive beyond 70, social-psychological factors are relatively more important as predictors of longevity than the physical health measures.

Summary

A new method of analyzing predictors of longevity among the 271 volunteers aged 60 and over at initial testing showed that cardiovascular disease, work satisfaction, cigarette smoking, physical function, and happiness ratings were the five strongest and significant predictors of longevity when the effects of age, sex, and race are controlled by the use of a longevity quotient. Cigarette smoking was the strongest predictor among the men in their 60s, work satisfaction was a stronger predictor for men than for women, and social-psychological variables seem more important than physical variables among the women in their 70s.

For the total panel, the multiple correlation was .52 indicating that over one quarter of the variance remaining after age, sex, and race are controlled can be accounted for by these predictors. The amount of variance explained increases to almost one half among the men. Compared to the earlier method, this new method of pair-wise case deletion results in substantial increases in variance explained.

While the new method of analysis reported in this paper results in higher correlations, the findings tend to generally support our earlier conclusion that the most important ways to increase longevity are: maintain a useful and satisfying role in society, maintain a positive view of life, maintain good physical functioning, and avoid smoking cigarettes.

References

Palmore, E. B. Physical, mental, and social factors in predicting longevity. *Gerontologist,* 9:103–108, 1969a.
Palmore, E. B. Predicting longevity: A follow-up controlling for age. *Gerontologist,* 9:247–250, 1969b.
Palmore, E. B. The Relative importance of social factors in predicting longevity. In E. B. Palmore and F. Jeffers (eds.), *Predicting life span,* Lexington, Mass.: D. C. Heath Co., 1971, pp. 237–247.
Palmore, E. B. and Stone, V. Predictors of longevity: A follow-up of the aged in Chapel Hill, N.C. *Gerontologist,* 13, No. 1:88–90, 1973.

Chapter 9. Summary

Erdman Palmore

Before summarizing the findings of this volume, it may be worthwhile to spell out some of the standard cautions one should bear in mind when evaluating such data. First, the samples studied are somewhat unrepresentative of the universe from which they were drawn. The older longitudinal study was drawn from a pool of volunteers to approximate the demographic composition of Durham, but they were volunteers nevertheless and therefore differed in various ways from a strict cross-section of Durham. The Adaptation Study was based on a probability sample of members of the local health insurance association, but we were able to get the participation of only half those eligible. While the participants appear similar to nonparticipants in basic characteristics, they undoubtedly differ in some ways (See Appendix A). In general, the two samples appear to underrepresent the poorer, sicker, and less able members of the community. We can only guess how our findings might change if we were able to get more representative samples.

Second, the universe from which the samples were drawn was limited to fairly normal middle-aged and older persons living in the Durham area. We do not know how well our findings might apply to other areas or to less normal persons such as the institutionalized, although some of the reports discuss this through comparison with other studies.

Third, there are usually errors of measurement, coding, and processing that creep into the data despite our best efforts to catch and correct them (See Appendix B). There is also the problem of interpreting some chance fluctuation as significant, or on the other hand, of ignoring an important finding because the numbers were small.

A last caution is the old maxim: "Association does not prove causation." We had no classical experiments in these studies because we wanted to study the aging process in its natural state. On the other hand, it is true that associations which persist with proper controls do provide evidence that a causal relationship may exist.

Propositions

Keeping in mind these cautions, we will summarize the major findings of these reports in the form of 37 propositions about normal aging among persons over 45 living in the community.

A. Physical Aging

1. Aging is related to an overall drop in immunoglobulin concentration as well as to a marked increase in its variability.

2. Asteatosis and scrotal angiomas increase with age, while nevi decline.

3. Asteatosis, scrotal angiomas, and nevi are related to shorter longevity.

4. There is a marked longitudinal decrement in best corrected vision, as well as a marked increase in glaucoma and cornea guttata.

5. There are significant associations between poor vision and several social variables, but not between vision and longevity. Also there is little association between specific conditions and social variables or longevity.

6. Hearing acuity diminishes with increasing age at about the same rate for those 60–69 as for those 70–79.

7. Women have better hearing than men in the higher frequencies, but men have better hearing than women in the normal speech frequencies.

8. Blacks, and particularly black men, have better hearing than whites.

B. Health Care

1. Medicare brought little overall increase in physicians' visits and hospitalizations, but there was some increase among lower income persons, and there was a marked shift to meeting medical expenses with health insurance.

2. Health practices such as exercise, weight control, and avoiding cigarettes contribute to better health and longevity.

3. A substantial majority of aged persons tend to agree with physicians' ratings of their health throughout repeated examinations, although there are more aged who overestimate their health than who underestimate it.

4. Among the aged, vitamin B_{12} levels are not lower in older groups, but are higher after age 90, and higher among blacks.

5. Overweight middle-aged persons tend to have greater cardiovascular disease risk as shown by elevated blood pressure, higher serum triglyceride levels, and EEG evidence of cardiovascular disease.

6. Anxiety before a medical examination tends to decline during and after the examination, with women having greater anxiety than men before the examination by a male physician.

C. Mental Aging

1. Cognitive decline among the aged is usually secondary to some pathologic process such as hypertension.

2. Among the aged who survive ten years beyond initial testing, those initially aged 60–69 have only slight cognitive decline, but those initially aged 70–79 have larger declines.

3. Terminal declines in intelligence occur primarily among those suffering both chronic and acute illness.

4. Decline of intellectual functioning among the aged is related to slow EEG frequencies, low cerebral blood flow, and perhaps to focal abnormalities.

5. EEG occipital frequencies tend to decline with age, but there are substantial variations in different demographic groups.

6. Reaction time increases with age, but percent correct detections are similar throughout the middle years.

D. Mental Illness

1. Brain impairment tends to occur more among those with decompensated heart disease, those with lower socioeconomic status, and those with fewer activities.

2. Mild elevation of blood pressure may help to preserve the brain in some aged persons.

3. Depression and poor health are closely related and tend to reinforce each other.

E. Social Roles and Self Concepts

1. Older drivers have relatively good health, a realistic appreciation of their limitations, and are able to maintain more activities and life satisfaction than ex-drivers.

2. Widowhood produces little or no long-term reduction in activities, attitudes, adjustment, or health.

3. Self-rated health is the most important factor in life satisfaction, but organizational activity, internal control, performance status, and productivity make additional contributions to satisfaction in middle age.

4. Older persons and women tend to view time as moving rapidly and to be more accepting of death than are the middle aged and the men.

5. Discrepancies between the real and apparent self-images tend to increase with age, separation from children affects women more than men, and nonworking affects both sexes but men have more problems with discrepancy than women.

6. Self-image is generally affected more by changes in job status than by changes in relationship to one's children, but men are more disturbed by these changes than are women.

7. Differences in self concepts can largely be accounted for by differences between aspirations and the resources to fulfill aspirations.

F. Leisure and Sexual Behavior

1. Middle aged men are more work oriented than leisure oriented.

2. Men 66–71 experience more difficulty with unwanted leisure than younger men, while 46–55 complain more of having too little leisure time than other women.

3. Although sexual interest and activity are lower in older age groups, sex continues to play an important role in the lives of most men and the majority of women through the seventh decade of life.

4. Male sexual activity and interest are mainly influenced by past sexual

experience, age, health, and social class, whereas women are more influenced by marital status in addition to age and past experience.

G. Longevity
1. Brain impairment accounts for a small but significant amount of the variance in longevity.
2. Long-term survivors, when compared with a matched group of non-survivors, are more intelligent, healthier, have better incomes, and more intact marriages.
3. The most important overall factors in longevity among the aged are health maintenance (especially avoiding cigarettes), maintaining a useful and satisfying role, and a positive view of life.

Themes

When we review these specific findings on normal aging, some general themes emerge which tie together findings from several substantive areas. The summary chapter of the first *Normal Aging* volume pointed out five such themes. The same themes are echoed and extended in this volume:

1. Advantages of longitudinal and interdisciplinary study of aging. The longitudinal method analyzed changes in the same persons over time in dermatology, ophthalmology, hearing, health care after Medicare, physician and self-health ratings, cognitive functioning, EEG frequencies, functioning and adjustment after widowhood, and self-concepts. The various analyses of factors related to longevity also required a longitudinal design. The advantages of interdisciplinary collaboration is evident in the fact that most of these reports involve the joint analysis of variables from two or more areas: biology, physical medicine, psychiatry, psychology, and sociology.

2. Patterns of declining health and physical functioning. This theme is repeated with some variations in the overall declines in immunoglobulin concentrations, skin conditions, vision, hearing, health ratings, and sexual activity. This confirms the expected pattern of normal aging.

3. Exceptions to physical decline. Despite the overall declines as measured by averages or group percentages, substantial minorities show no decline and may even have improvement in various measures of skin conditions, vision, hearing, health ratings, vitamin levels, and sexual activity. Thus, the process of physical aging is not necessarily an irresistible and irreversible force. Health and functioning can and do improve for some older persons just as they do for younger persons.

4. Little or no decline in social and psychological functioning. This theme is in direct contrast to the theme of declining physical functioning. The first volume presented several findings showing little or no decline in activities, attitudes, cautiousness, recall, and general adjustment. This volume reports only small overall declines in intelligence scores (especially among those aged 60–69 and those free of hypertension), reaction times, correct signal detections, and EEG frequencies. It is impressive how many of the normal aged are able to compensate for their growing physical handicaps and maintain fairly stable levels of social and psychological functioning. This evidence tends to refute the disengagement theory that decline and withdrawal are typical, inevitable, and normal.

5. Wide variation in aging patterns. This theme takes two forms: documenting the range of individual differences which group averages obscure, and attempting to account for individual and group differences. The aged usually show more individual variability than the young. This is shown dramatically in the report on immunoglobulin concentrations and is reflected in most other comparisons of the old and young. Thus, even when there are significant mean differences between the old and young, there is usually considerable overlap between the two distributions. This means that many older persons have better functioning and better scores than many younger persons. These reports attempt to account for this individual variation by analyzing differences by sex, race, socioeconomic group, health practices, chronic and acute illness, retirement, children leaving home, etc.

Thus, the complex and difficult enterprise of exploring and charting the territory of aging continues. We believe this enterprise will eventually allow more older people to safely reach "the promised land" of a better and longer life.

Appendix A. Design of the Adaptation Study

Erdman Palmore

Goals

As the number and variety of gerontological studies increased during the sixties, there was a growing awareness that the aging process is not confined to persons over 65. The aging processes were recognized as extending over the entire life span, with special problems of adaptation during middle age and the preretirement years. Potentially stressful events such as death of spouse, serious illness, menopause, children leaving home, and preparation for retirement often occur before the age of 65. The adaptation study was designed to study responses to such events and the aging processes in general during the ages of 45 through 69. More specifically, the study is particularly interested in the factors or mechanisms which contribute to "successful" aging, defined in a variety of ways.

The study was also designed to be interdisciplinary, to be representative of the broad middle and upper socioeconomic levels of our society, and to allow cross-sectional, longitudinal, and cross-sequential types of analysis. It is an interdisciplinary study because of its inclusion of several types of investigators and of variables representative of the physical, psychological, and social aspects of adaptation to aging. The sample is designed to be representative by drawing on a random sample of all members of the major health insurance association residing in the Durham area, stratified into ten age-sex cohorts. The design allows cross-sectional analysis between the ten age-sex cohorts and longitudinal analysis over a period of at least five years, and cross-sequential analysis comparing different age cohorts at different points in time.

Variables

The major variables being investigated are summarized in Figure A–1, "Diagram of Variables for Adaptation Study." As this diagram indicates, there are three main types of independent variables: physical, psychological, and social. These are conceived of as the resources which should be related to how well a person adapts to aging and to stressful events. A person's physical resources include his current mobility and general health, as well as his more specific musculoskeletal functioning, his cardiovascular capacity, and his abil-

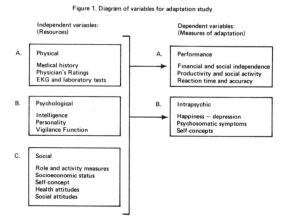

Figure 1. Diagram of variables for adaptation study

Figure A-1. *Diagram of variables for adaptation study.*

ity to see and hear. His psychological resources include his intelligence and his personality characteristics such as his tendency to be outgoing, emotionally stable, assertive, conscientious, imaginative, experimental, self-sufficient, etc. Another psychological resource is the ability to concentrate and respond quickly and accurately under stress conditions (Vigilance Test). Abnormal electroencephalograph recordings indicate possible limitations on a person's mental resources. The person's various social resources are measured by counting the number of different social roles that a person is engaged in; the number of role partners he interacts with; the number and type of social contacts he has per month; the number of hours per week he spends in various activities; his socioeconomic resources such as education, income, neighborhood, and parent status; his concept of who and what kind of a person he is, what kind of person he would like to be; what kind of a life he has had and expects to have; and his knowledge about and attitudes toward community resources. His attitudes toward his own health and his willingness to take the sick role as well as his attitudes toward time, death, achievement, planning, and internal control may also be important resources in adaptation.

There are two main types of adaptation measures: performance and intrapsychic reactions. Whether or not a person is able to perform so as to maintain his financial and social independence is considered an important measure of adaptation. The amount of time spent in productive activities and social activities are other measures of performance. Reaction time and accuracy are a measure of a person's ability to respond to external stimuli. The intrapsychic measures of adaptation are designed to measure whether or not a person is satisfied and happy with his adaptation or whether he has become more depressed with feelings of meaninglessness, powerlessness, normlessness, and isolation. The psychosomatic symptoms are an indirect measure of a person's adaptation and have been found to be related to unhappiness, psycho-neurosis, and other indicators of poor adaptation. Finally, a person's self-concept should be related to how well he has adapted.

During the eight hours of examination and interviews, data on more than 1000 variables are recorded and entered on electronic tape for each person.

Types of Analysis

These various measures can be looked at cross-sectionally by comparing different age groups at one point in time, or longitudinally by comparing individual and group differences over time, particularly after potentially stressful events such as death of spouse, serious illness, menopause, children leaving home, or retirement. The design, which involves five-year age groups who will be retested periodically for at least five years, makes possible various kinds of cross-sequential types of analysis. These analyses can control for cohort differences (generational effects), age changes (developmental effects) and period differences (time effects). The longitudinal design also makes possible the inference of cause and effect relationships through time-lag analysis which examines those changes more likely to follow other changes than visa versa.

Sample

In order to be fairly representative of the broad middle and upper socio-economic levels in Durham, the sample was drawn from the membership list of the major health insurance association in Durham County. This membership list includes the majority of middle- and upper-income-level Durham residents. The list underrepresents the lower class and poverty stricken, but the purpose of this study was to concentrate on the large "middle mass" rather than attempting representative numbers of the poor, the chronically ill, the illiterate or those in physical or mental hospitals. Illiterate persons were excluded because they could not take the written tests. Institutionalized or homebound persons were excluded because they could not come in for the examinations. Blacks were also excluded from this study because they were being studied separately in another project.

A total of 502 persons were interviewed and tested, with the numbers in each age-sex cohort ranging from 45 to 58 (see Table A–1). The purpose of selecting these various quotas of persons in the various age-sex cohorts was to allow approximately 40 persons to be retested in each of the 10 age-sex cohorts at the end of five years, assuming a 10 percent dropout rate and the 1960 North Carolina age-sex specific mortality rates. Thus, there were larger numbers included in the older age groups because these groups have higher

Table A–1. *Numbers in age-sex cohorts, 1968 and 1973.*

Age in 1968	# Tested in 1968–70		Age in 1973	# To be retested in 1974–75*	
	Male	Female		Male	Female
45–49	47	45	50–54	40	40
50–54	49	46	55–59	40	40
55–59	52	47	60–64	40	40
60–64	55	50	65–69	40	40
65–69	58	53	70–74	40	40
Totals	261 +	241 = 502		200 +	200 = 400

* Assuming a 10% dropout rate and 1960 North Carolina mortality rates.

mortality rates. It was decided that 40 was the minimum number of cases in each age-sex cohort group which would allow the desired level of precision for the types of analyses planned.

An initial 2000 names and addresses were randomly drawn from the membership lists to serve as a pool for target numbers to be interviewed and tested. Persons were contacted and scheduled in a random order until enough subjects had been interviewed and tested to fulfill the target number in each age-sex cohort. Persons were first mailed an introductory letter explaining the purpose and procedures of the study and then were contacted by telephone or by visits for those without telephones.

Because the study requires eight hours of examinations and interviews without compensation offered to the subjects (other than a free medical examination and laboratory tests), about half of the persons contacted either refused to participate or did not schedule a day for the examinations before the target number of subjects for that age-sex cohort had been reached (see Table A–2). The remaining persons in the initial pool were either ineligible

Table A–2. *Response rate by age and sex.*

Cohort	Total contacted and eligible	Inter-viewed	Noninter-viewed	% inter-viewed
Males				
45–49	92	47	45	51
50–54	95	49	46	52
55–59	96	52	44	54
60–64	95	55	40	58
65–69	113	58	55	51
Females				
45–49	94	45	49	48
50–54	107	46	61	43
55–59	103	47	56	46
60–64	111	50	61	45
65–69	144	53	91	37
Total	1050	502	548	48

because they lived outside of the Durham area, were in the wrong age bracket, were Negro, illiterate, housebound, etc., or were not contacted before the target number had been reached.

Because about one-half of the persons contacted were not interviewed and tested, an important question is the degree of representativeness of our interviewed subjects compared to the noninterviewed persons. We carried out a special study of noninterviewed persons in order to estimate how representative our sample is. A random sample of 100 noninterviewed persons was drawn and minimum information on their age, sex, education, occupation, marital status, and health was secured by telephone or home visits. We also got tabulations from the health insurance association on the hospital and medical care usage of both the interviewed and noninterviewed persons. This study found no significant differences between those interviewed and those not interviewed, except that those not interviewed tended to have more in the extreme health categories (excellent health, poor health) and less in the middle categories (good health, fair health). Thus, while there probably are some undetected differences between the interviewed and noninterviewed, there does not appear to be any gross demographic or health bias in the sample of those interviewed.

A special problem was encountered in the 65–69 year age group. Persons in this age group who are still members of the health insurance association are a somewhat elite group, because they are insuring themselves against only those health care costs not covered by Medicare. These persons are about one-half of all persons over 65. In order to make our sample in this age category more representative we included thirty-two subjects randomly drawn from persons who had been in the Duke Hospital during 1968–1969. It was thought that hospitalized persons would complement the Blue Cross–Blue Shield sample by more nearly representing those in poorer health. As it turned out, there were only small differences between the Duke Hospital group and the health association group over 65, with the Duke group having somewhat higher income, education, and intelligence scores. Therefore, our sample of persons 65–69 is probably above average and not as representative as the rest of our sample. This age category should be treated with caution in cross-sectional comparisons.

Summary of Sample Design

Five hundred two men and women aged 45–69 were tested from August 1968 through April 1970, and 443 of the survivors were retested by March 1972. The subjects were a random sample stratified by age and sex, of the major health insurance assocation in the Durham area. The numbers in each age-sex cohort were greater in the older ages in order to allow for the greater mortality rate of older persons. The goal is to have approximately 40 persons retested five years after initial testing in each of the 10 age-sex cohorts. A supplementary sample of persons who had been in the Duke Hospital was added to the cohort aged 65–69 in an attempt to make this cohort sample more representative. About one half of the eligible persons contacted were interviewed and tested. A special follow-up study of noninterviewed persons found little difference between those interviewed and those not interviewed. The five-year cohorts are being retested periodically for at least five years in order to allow cross-sectional, longitudinal, and cross-sequential types of analysis.

Appendix B. Data Processing in Longitudinal Studies

Dietolf Ramm and Daniel T. Gianturco

Introduction

Statistical and data handling procedures are an important part of most scientific studies. The Center for the Study of Aging and Human Development has long been a heavy user of computer facilities and the Center's computational staff and equipment are an important part of its core operation. In this paper we will describe the important aspects of these data handling operations with special emphasis on the two ongoing longitudinal studies. Problems in handling large amounts of data over large periods of time are discussed. A brief description of the most heavily used statistical package, TSAR, is also included. The detection and correction of errors in the collection and storage of data are carefully described. We also provide suggestions for future improvement in procedures for these and future studies.

Data Processing Resources of the Center

The Center has available for its use both its own computer, an IBM 1130 system, and Duke University's computational facility. Heavy use is made of both. The computing facility in which the Center's data processing personnel work is centrally located for other Center staff members. This organization provides for efficient use of services, facilitates the exchange of technical information, and provides for training and support of investigators.

Facilities and Staff

The 1130 system (I.B.M., 1968). The basic computer in the center is an IBM 1131, model 2B with 8192 binary words consisting of 16 bits, plus two parity bits. Attached to this are an IBM 1442 card reader-punch and an IBM 1132 printer. A Redcor Analog-to-Digital (A-D) converter is attached to the 1131 via a special Redcor interface.

Additional equipment essential to the operation of the A.D converter has been added, including a Hewlett-Packard FM tape playback unit, a Hewlett-Packard present controller, and a Hewlett-Packard Viso Scope.

To allow the processing of larger psycho-physiological studies and to generally increase efficiency of computer utilization, an IBM 2310 disk drive and a corequisite IBM multiplexer are being leased, as are two IBM 029 key-punches for program and data preparation. An IBM 2741 typewriter terminal for direct access to the Triangle Universities Computation Center is also available.

The 1130 system is used in several different ways. For our Adaptation Study there is programmed conversion and analysis of psychophysiologic data. In this experiment, each longitudinal subject is exposed to a paced continuous performance task ("vigilance task") with a minute by minute assessment of physiologic response (EKG, GSR, respiration, digital plethysmography) as well as measurement of response time and other measures of performance. The data generated consist of ten minutes of waves which have to be analysed in great detail (using the A-D converter) to evaluate the adaptive pattern of the individual. This work currently involves 502 individuals who are seen every two years.

Other activities include analysis of cortical evoked potentials and alerting signals of the EEG, analysis of cerebral blood flow data, and extensive statistical study of immunoglobulins of elderly and middle-aged subjects. The availability of the facility is encouraging the development of new statistical techniques, (e.g., missing data statistics). These latter methods have application over a wide range of research interests.

The staff. The staff of the computational facility includes seven people—three with faculty status. The administrator is a psychiatrist who has had a long time interest in applying computers to medicine. His responsibilities include representing the data processing unit in dealing with the Duke Medical Center administration and insuring that the data processing group is responsive to the needs of the Aging Center. A computer scientist is responsible for maintaining the software and hardware of the computing system. He is also available to consult with staff in dealing with software problems involving the University computer facilities. The Center statistician is vital to planning experiments and collaborating in the analysis of data. This recent addition to the staff has reduced the need to consult with statisticians outside of the Center.

The bulk of the programming is done by two Center programmers. They work with senior investigators to do analysis runs on Center data and see that data are properly stored and updated on the files. A keypunch operator is available to code and punch the longitudinal data, as well as programs for the programming staff. The staff of the Aging Center's computational facility also includes a secretary who, in addition to normal secretarial duties, helps maintain the library of computer reference documents and does card punching for text processing programs.

The university's data processing facilities. In 1965, Duke University joined with the University of North Carolina and North Carolina State University to form a nonprofit corporation called the Triangle Universities Computation Center (TUCC) (Brooks et al., 1969; Williams, 1972). This facility was located centrally to the three schools. The TUCC is used via terminals from the respective campuses.

Presently the TUCC equipment includes an IBM 370–165 (I.B.M., 1972) computer with two million bytes (characters) or memory. For auxiliary memory, eight IBM 3330 disk drives (at 100 million bytes/drive), sixteen IBM 2314 disk drives (at 29 million bytes/drive) and five IBM tape drives are available.

Some of the most important equipment at TUCC is the teleprocessing equipment. This allows users at remote sites to communicate with the computer facility. All communication is by means of telephone lines. The high speed connections to the campus computation centers, such as those at Duke are by means of a "bundle" of phone lines which are leased from the telephone company. Connections for slow terminals such a teletypes and typewriters are available through regular dial-up telephone connections. The Aging Center owns an IBM 2741 typewriter terminal which is used for direct access to TUCC.

The Duke University Computation Center (DUCC) has an IBM 370–135 (Brooks et al., 1969; Williams, 1972) computer. Attached to this are four IBM 2314 disk drives and several tape drives. The computation center has two IBM 1403 line printers which can print up to 1100 lines per minute and three IBM 2501 card readers which read cards at 1000 cards per minute. One of these card readers is in the hall for "self-service" use of the computer.

This campus computation center serves both as a high speed terminal to TUCC and as a local processor for smaller jobs. The Aging Center uses it only as a terminal. A courier picks up work at the Aging Center computer facility three times a day and takes it to the Duke Computation Center to be run. Completed work is returned by the courier service. Two self-service, medium speed terminals to TUCC are also within easy walking distance of the Aging Center, and they are becoming increasingly popular.

History of Data Processing at the Duke Aging Center*

A brief history of the data processing activities related to the longitudinal studies illustrates some of the problems one can expect to encounter. The first longitudinal study started in 1955 and is still continuing, spanning several "generations" of computer hardware and software.

Tabular equipment. The study began before the computer was commonly in use by behavioral scientists ("TSAR User's Manual," 1972). The kind of equipment then available is referred to as "tab" equipment. Data were punched on Hollerith (or IBM) cards with a keypunch, but instead of being fed into a computer, the cards were processed by a collection of special pur-

* The authors are indebted to Professor T. M. Gallie for assistance on the history of computing at Duke University.

pose data processing machines. These included counting sorters, accounting machines (essentially for printing the contents of a sorted or processed deck of cards), reproducing punches (usually used for transferring a subset of the data on the master deck to a working deck), and collators. The final result was usually data analyzed in a contingency table format.

Most of these machines had to be controlled by plug boards on which wires were used to specify the specific action the machine was to take. In a sense these machines were programmed, but in a much more constrained way than one programs the modern digital computer. Another practice common in those days (which caused some problems later on), was the punching of several items of data into one card column. This practice of "multipunching" made extremely efficient use of the cards and was well suited to tab equipment, but made the cards much harder to process with later generations of machines.

The IBM 650. In 1958 Duke acquired an IBM 650 digital computer; it was the first digital computer to come into widespread use, and its success put IBM out in front. The 650 used vacuum tube logic circuits and a 2000 word magnetic drum memory. It was, of course, much slower than modern machines and, due to the tubes, was certainly far less reliable.

This computer was not heavily used in Center research, both due to the reluctance to change to new systems and to the lack of convenient, general purpose statistical programs. Programs to do linear regression were among the first to arouse an interest.

The IBM 7072. In 1961, the University replaced the 650 by an IBM 7070 computer (which was later upgraded to a variation of the 7070—the 7072). This was one of the first transistorized machines and brought with it tremendous gains in speed and reliability. The 7072 used tape drives exclusively for input and output. The cards were actually read by a small IBM 1401 computer and copied to tape. This then could be processed by the 7072. The output tapes from the 7072 were also copied to the printer by the 1401. This "off-line" reading of cards and printing is a technique still used in some systems today. This change of computer systems was responsible for the first reprogramming at Duke. Actually, since the 650 had had only limited use, there were no really big conversion problems. The use of the 7072 brought the first real effort on the part of the computer laboratory staff to urge the users of tab card equipment to use the computer instead. Initial programs for the 7072 were designed to duplicate the functions available with the tab equipment. These programs were used to produce contingency tables and do some other simple statistics.

It soon became clear, however, that much more could be done. The needs of the longitudinal study in particular made a more sophisticated program highly desirable. In response to this need, the TSAR system (tape storage and retrieval) was developed. This was one of the first sophisticated statistical packages ever written for digital computers which was suitable for use by behavioral scientists. It will be described in more detail later. The TSAR system won general acceptance and the present version is still the major program used in analysing the data of the longitudinal studies. All of the longitudinal data were stored on magnetic tapes for analysis by the system. TSAR has provisions for systematically updating such data bases.

TUCC. In 1965 Duke joined with the University of North Carolina and North Carolina State University to form the Triangle Universities Computation Center (the present status of which was described earlier). With this came the use of the IBM 360 series of computers. This also caused a crisis for computing at Duke and for the Aging Center. The TSAR system had become indispensible. While the statistical package was successfully reprogrammed for the 360, the tapes were not compatible and tape conversion programs which were available on the 7072 were not used before that machine was removed. Although the tapes were finally rebuilt successfully, the problems were symptomatic of the times—everybody having trouble with reprogramming and very few people around who understood the new system. (The problems were so great that when IBM brought out its new 370 series of computers to replace the 360 series, the changes were designed to be evolutionary in nature with old programs still useable in the new systems.)

In 1965 the Center began a second longitudinal study (the "Adaptation Study") which included a study of psychophysiological measurements made during a "vigilance task." To process these data, the Center purchased an IBM 1130 with an Analog-to-Digital Converter attached. This facility became the nucleus of the Aging Center's present data processing and statistical equipment, as described previously. The 1130 is also used for preprocessing other data for ultimate storage on the TSAR tapes at TUCC.

Data Handling and Analysis

In this section we will trace the "path" of the longitudinal data from their collection to their analysis.

Data Collection and Storage

Forms. Most data in the study are collected first on forms appropriate to the particular study. Then they are keypunched and verified and finally stored on the tape.

The forms used in the initial collection of data are usually designed by the investigator responsible for the data involved. They are normally mimeographed sheets with questions and space for the answers. Information to aid in the keypunching of the data is also printed on the forms. This usually includes a card number for each sheet of paper and then card-column numbers under each answer space.

Most of the forms are filled out by the person administering the test or questionnaire. Some, however, are filled out by the subject. Special care is taken to keep these forms simple and clear.

Another method of source data collection often considered is the use of machine readable forms. Duke University has a mark sense reader available at a moderate cost. The greatest advantage of automated forms reading would be the bypassing of one transcription step (keypunching) which is potentially a source of errors. This was carefully considered but the following problems ruled out this approach. The cost of printing machine-readable forms is high, easily in excess of $100 per page for set-up alone, plus a relatively high printing cost per page. The high cost of set-up would tend to discourage changes and improvements in questionnaires. The layout of the form is somewhat limited and free text cannot be entered. Numbers require some care in entry and the only easy way to respond is to check true/false or multiple choice boxes. Also, while data are now added to the tapes at frequent intervals as the subjects complete the study, the economics of running small batches of sheets through the scanner would be poor since there is a minimum charge per use.

Coding and punching. The step that follows the actual collection of data on forms is the transfer of these data to Hollerith (or IBM) cards. Often, when studies are made these days, the data must first be coded and transferred to special coding sheets from which keypunchers at some central keypunch pool will punch the data. This extra coding of data and concurrent transcription on another form is a great source of potential error and often this operation is not properly checked. In our longitudinal study, this step is bypassed altogether. Since our data processing group includes a keypunch operator, the keypuncher learns to punch directly from the forms on which the data are collected. Any data which must be converted to some code is done by our own keypunching staff who become familiar with the data. The data are then verified in the normal manner (essentially a repunching of the same cards on a special device—an IBM 059 verifier.) Normally the verification is done by someone other than the person who did the original keypunching. Thus, the coding and interpretation of handwriting, etc., is also verified by another person, not just the correctness of the keying.

Error checking is done also in two other ways. The punched cards are sent through a special program on our IBM 1130 to check that all values are in the correct range. The data are also checked by TSAR programs for internal consistency after they are written on the tape.

Storage of data. Data are actually stored in several ways. At this time, all of the original forms are still available in 10 five-drawer filing cabinets. The cards are also available, although some of them reflect the peculiarities of previous data processing systems. Finally, the data reside on the tapes. For actual research, the tapes contain the information in its most accessible form. The other forms of the data exist for various reasons. The forms contain some information which was collected but was never coded. From time to time, interest in some of these data is shown and more are coded, punched and added to the tapes.

Microfilming these source data has also been considered. The cost, in combination with the increased difficulty in handling the data for keypunching, for example, has ruled out this space saving process. Also, for subjects that are still being actively studied, the data are increased all the time. This means that a subject's file would be partly microfilms, partly paper. However, the sheer space requirements for all of these files may require some type of action soon.

The data are saved on cards, obstensibly to restore the tapes should they be destroyed. However, due to the various formats used on the cards, this would be a rather tedious procedure. Instead, several copies are kept of the tape, so that if one is destroyed, the data can be restored from another. Copies of the data are also kept on disk packs. The format is the same as for tapes.

Security and confidentiality of the data.   Security and confidentiality are two rather different ideas, but since many of the precautions and methods are the same, they are usually discussed together. Confidentiality of the data is maintained by restricting access to staff actually analyzing the data. Source data (which identifies the individual's name) is normally seen only by the persons collecting and coding the data. All filing cabinets and card files are kept locked.

The data on the tapes require some different considerations. First, the names of the subjects are not recorded on the tapes. Second, the data are identifiable on the tapes only with the help of code books. The name of the variable on the tapes is often insufficient to explain the meaning of that item.

A potentially more serious problem is that of security. Data can be destroyed either by accident or through malicious mischief. Precautions have been taken to secure the tapes and the code books. In both cases, security is provided by the maintenance of at least two copies in geographically widely separated locations. Tapes are stored at TUCC and at another location. Periodically, the backup tapes are updated to reflect additions to the data. In practice, this requires at least three sets of tapes, because copying a tape requires that two tapes be at the same location. A copy of the code books is also kept at a remote site.

Data Retrieval and Analysis

The investigator who wants to do a statistical analysis of the longitudinal data must be intimately acquainted with the data. Code books are available to all investigators indicating which variables have been coded and what they are called on the main data tape. Usually the investigators work with the Center programming staff, but some do their own computer runs.

Code books.   The code books are extremely important for accessing the data. They not only give the variable name and location on the cards, but they are also used to record any problems encountered in the data. If certain variables seem to be incorrect, notes are added to the code book explaining the problem. Also names are chosen to be indicative of certain facts about the data. The subjects return periodically for restudy in "waves." In the Adaptation Study, the variables in the first wave start with the letter A; the second with the letter B, etc. Corresponding variables from wave to wave will have the same name except for this prefix. However, changes are sometimes made and the measures are similar, but not the same. This is indicated by a change in the suffix so that the assumption is not made accidentally that these variables can be strictly compared.

TSAR ("*TSAR User's Manual*," 1972). As mentioned, most of the primary analyses of the longitudinal data are done with the TSAR system. There are several ways to use this system, and for small amounts of data, its use can be extremely simple. TSAR has a special utility subprogram called IVAN which is used to put data on tape in the special format which is suited to the main analysis programs. In this format, all variables are given names. A directory is formed at the beginning of the tape file which stores the variable names, and the location in each subject record (identified by a subject number) where that particular record is stored. This means that for a later data analysis, the data are referred to by name, and one does not need to worry about where, or in what particular format, the data are stored. The IVAN program is used also to update the files. As additional data are coded and punched, they can be easily added to the tapes and, if necessary, old variables can be replaced—to correct an error, for example.

After the data are put on "TSAR Tapes," they can be used for any analysis in the TSAR system. For a typical analysis run, TSAR makes it easy to do two kinds of things to the data: transformations and grouping. By means of transformation operations, the variables may have constants added or subtracted, they may be multiplied by a factor, or new variables may be defined which are functions of one or more of the original variables. For example, one often wants to use the logarithm of a variable rather than the original variable in the analysis.

The grouping operations allow one to define groups or subsets of the data. These groups are each given a unique number rather than a name. For example, the most common groupings are by sex and age. With the necessary groups defined, and any necessary transformation made, the particular type of analysis desired is stated—such as analysis of variance, cross sort, regression, etc.

There are also other statistical programs in use such as those included in the Statistical Package for the Social Sciences (SPSS) (Nie et al., 1970) and the U.C.L.A. BIOMED package. Several Multivariate Analysis Variance (MANOVA) programs are also in use at TUCC and on the Aging Center's 1130 system.

Problems and Solutions

Fighting Errors

As in any data processing operation of this magnitude, errors are a constant problem. Despite the verification and checks for range and consistency, a few errors remain. One can hope that these few errors will tend to cancel out or not have significant effects in studies of this size. This is true, however, only for random errors. Errors due to misunderstandings, confusion over the way digits are handwritten by certain people (confusing 1 and 7, 2 and 1, 4 and 9, etc.) can lead to systematic errors. Also, while the number of subjects is substantial, investigators often subdivide the sample into groups so small that an error in just one value can lead to spurious results.

Interactive data collection. Two possibilities for improving error detection have been considered. One is to use interactive source data collection. This means that the data are entered into a computer terminal at the time of collection. Certain errors are checked for immediately, and the technician entering the data (or the subject in some cases) is immediately notified of the error. This may mean that the data can be reentered correctly before the source of the data has disappeared. Although the technology for this type of procedure is now available, it is still expensive. A problem that is even more serious than the cost is that many human engineering problems have yet to be solved. Most programs are much too unforgiving if the user makes a mistake. Often he has to restart the program from the beginning.

Printouts for verification. A less costly effort towards error reduction would involve the use of computerized printouts of the data. Whenever data for a reasonable number of subjects have been coded and punched, the computer would be programmed to print out this data in such a way that the responsible investigator can quickly check through the data for consistency and reasonableness. This may seem easy, but first the program must be written to print out the data in such a way that the investigator can clearly see what measurements were involved and yet make the printout concise enough for quick review. The other trick is to find the right number of subjects to print out for review at any one time. If too many are done in a batch, the investigator will be overwhelmed and put off checking the data indefinitely. If the number of subjects is too small, then it becomes a nuisance and the investigator may save the printouts to look at later. The end result of that is also depressing.

Displaying the results in graphic form would also aid in checking data. In spite of the listed problems, a printout type feedback system will be instituted in the near future.

Interactive Data Access

Another area where much could be done is in the access to the data. Ideally, an investigator would have a terminal in his office from which he could instantaneously access any of the longitudinal data. Complex statistical analyses could be completed in seconds. Even a partial step in the direction of interactive data access and analysis could be a great improvement over the batch processing approach now in use.

One of the most promising possibilities for interactive data analysis is the use of the Time Sharing Option (TSO) (Brooks, et al., 1969; Williams, 1972) if IBM's Operating System for its 360–370 series of computers. It has been in experimental use for several months at TUCC and its full capabilities under multiuser use are not clear yet. Limits on on-line disk space for the data and on-memory space for the analysis programs may doom efforts towards this approach. Also, a suitable interactive statistical program must yet be found or developed.

Other Uses of Computers

Data processing techniques could be used in other areas relating to the longitudinal studies. One example is that of computerized text processing. It would be used to store, update, and print out the forms used in collecting the data. By keeping the forms on the computer, minor changes would not require the retyping of the whole form by a secretary. Only the changes in text would be fed to the text processing system and then the new form would be typed out by the computer system on masters for duplication.

Conclusions

From our experiences at the Duke Center for the Study of Aging and Human Development, we find the following points worthy of special emphasis. The procedures for handling and accessing data should be as machine independent as possible. In long term studies, equipment will change and conversion of programs and procedures can be traumatic.

One needs to identify and use a good statistical package—one that can reasonably be expected to survive changes in hardware, as was the case with Duke's TSAR package. More important than the actual statistical procedures which the package performs, are its ability to handle and transform data.

The avoidance and elimination of errors are important goals. They become especially important in studies that long outlive the tenure of technicians and even investigators involved in collecting data. Security is also a continuing problem since there is so much irretrievable data that could be lost.

To reap the full benefit of the large quantities of data available, two features are necessary. One is easy access to the data. It is hoped that time-sharing systems will improve to bring the data into easy reach of all researchers. The other necessary ingredient is a competent data processing staff. They must be readily accessible for consultation and they must become involved in the "life" of the study. At Duke, most of the data processing staff attend all of the research and administrative meetings. They are actively involved in planning new work. Only in this way can a longitudinal study be a true success.

References

Brooks, F. P., Ferrell, J. K., and Gallie, T. M. Organizational, financial and political aspects of a three university computing center. *Information processing, 1968.* Amsterdam: North Holland Publishing Company, 1969, 2:923.

I.B.M., "*IBM 1130 Bibliography,*" IBM Document GA26–5916, 1968.

I.B.M., "*IBM System/360 and System/370 Bibliography,*" IBM document GA22–6822, 1972.

Nie, N. H., Bent, D. H., and Hull, C. H. *SPSS.* New York: McGraw-Hill, 1970.

TSAR User's Manual. Duke University Computation Center: Durham, N.C., 1972.

Williams, L. H. A Functioning Computer Network for Higher Education in North Carolina. *AFIPS Conference Proceedings,* 41:899, 1972, F.J.C.C.

Index